Worshiping in Season

Worshiping in Season

Ecology and Christ through the Liturgical Year

Joseph E. Bush Jr.

AN ALBAN INSTITUTE BOOK

ROWMAN & LITTLEFIELD
Lanham • Boulder • New York • London

Published by Rowman & Littlefield
An imprint of The Rowman & Littlefield Publishing Group, Inc.
4501 Forbes Boulevard, Suite 200, Lanham, Maryland 20706
www.rowman.com

86–90 Paul Street, London EC2A 4NE, United Kingdom

Copyright © 2021 by The Rowman & Littlefield Publishing Group, Inc.

Unless otherwise noted in the text, all Scripture quotations are from New Revised Standard Version Bible: Catholic Edition, copyright © 1989, 1993 National Council of the Churches of Christ in the United States of America. Used by permission. All rights reserved worldwide.

Scripture quotations marked (RSV) are from Revised Standard Version of the Bible, copyright © 1946, 1952, and 1971 National Council of the Churches of Christ in the United States of America. Used by permission. All rights reserved worldwide.

"Scripture quotations taken from the (NASB®) New American Standard Bible®, Copyright © 1995 by The Lockman Foundation. Used by permission. All rights reserved. www.lockman.org"

Scripture quotations marked (NIV) are taken from the Holy Bible, New International Version®, NIV®. Copyright © 1973, 1978, 1984, 2011 by Biblica, Inc.™ Used by permission of Zondervan. All rights reserved worldwide. www.zondervan.comThe "NIV" and "New International Version" are trademarks registered in the United States Patent and Trademark Office by Biblica, Inc.™

Excerpts from the English translation of *Collection of Masses of the Blessed Virgin Mary* © 1989, 2012, International Commission on English in the Liturgy Corporation. All rights reserved.

All rights reserved. No part of this book may be reproduced in any form or by any electronic or mechanical means, including information storage and retrieval systems, without written permission from the publisher, except by a reviewer who may quote passages in a review.

British Library Cataloguing in Publication Information Available

Library of Congress Cataloging-in-Publication Data
Names: Bush, Joseph Earl, 1956– author.
Title: Worshiping in season : ecology and Christ through the liturgical year / Joseph E. Bush, Jr.
Description: Lanham : Rowman & Littlefield, [2021] | Includes bibliographical references and indExod | Summary: "Worshiping in Season guides ministers through a meaningful framework for ecologically oriented worship. Following the liturgical calendar and maintaining a Christocentric emphasis, Joseph E. Bush Jr. aligns earthly seasons with the liturgy and suggests readings, songs, and other acts of worship to amplify an ecologically informed Christology"—Provided by publisher.
Identifiers: LCCN 2021035437 (print) | LCCN 2021035438 (ebook) | ISBN 9781538121986 (cloth) | ISBN 9781538121993 (pbk) | ISBN 9781538122006 (electronic)
Subjects: LCSH: Public worship. | Church year. | Ecology—Religious aspects—Christianity.
Classification: LCC BV30 .B87 2021 (print) | LCC BV30 (ebook) | DDC 263/.9—dc23
LC record available at https://lccn.loc.gov/2021035437
LC ebook record available at https://lccn.loc.gov/2021035438

Dedicated to the diverse and diversely gifted church of Jesus Christ—
gathered weekly in worship and praise,
and sent daily into God's Spirt-graced creation
to seek social justice and ecological flourishing.

—Pentecost 2021

Contents

Introduction: Celebrating Christ and Creation ... ix

PART I: MORTAL NATURE AND NEW CREATION: LENT/EASTER/ASCENSION/PENTECOST CYCLE ... 1

1. Prelude: Transfiguration ... 3
2. Lenten Beginnings: Ash Wednesday and Temptation in the Wilderness ... 15
3. Entering Jerusalem: Palm Sunday, Jewish Festivals, and Earth's Seasons ... 41
4. Christ's Passion: Maundy Thursday and Good Friday ... 57
5. Easter: Life Resurgent ... 83
6. Easter Season and Christ's Ascension: To Fill All Things ... 103
7. Pentecost: Let Everything that Breathes Praise the LORD ... 125
8. Trinity: The Dance of Life ... 141

PART II: DIVINE NATURE IN FLESH LIKE OURS: ADVENT/CHRISTMAS/EPIPHANY ... 161

9. Interlude: Reign of Christ Sunday ... 163
10. Early Advent: Longing for Wholeness ... 171
11. Late Advent: God's Promised Presence ... 191

12	Turning to the Children: Ecological Threat and Hope in Advent	209
13	Christmas: Birthed and Embodied	227
14	Epiphany: God Manifest on Earth	249

Postlude: Conclusion — 265

Notes — 269

Biblical Citations — 299

Index — 307

About the Author — 319

Introduction

Celebrating Christ and Creation

Every Sunday throughout the year, Christians congregate in the name of Christ to worship our namesake. Every day throughout the year, these same Christians awaken with fellow creatures to a world of God's making. Embodied in this world we see, hear, taste, touch, and smell the bounty of blessings brought by God. But we taste bitterness as well as blessing. We spend our moments seeking security in a world of flux. We not only worry for ourselves, but we also worry for our neighbors—both known and unknown, both near and far—and we worry for the well-being of our fellow creatures and for the earth itself. Increasingly we seek an elusive harmony between ourselves and others, between our species and our planet, between our past and our posterity, between our spirituality and our flesh. How can we connect our worshipful life in Christ with our wonderful/worrisome life in creation?

This book brings our ecological concern and consciousness into consideration of corporate worship during the two great liturgical movements of the ecumenical Christian year—the Advent-Christmas-Epiphany cycle and the Lent-Easter-Pentecost cycle. Both of these cycles revolve around momentous Christic events—Christ's incarnation and Christ's crucifixion and resurrection. How do we view these events and the seasons of worship surrounding these events as ecological beings, as earthlings? How might these Christological dramas pertain to the planet and not only to the people on the planet?

My aim here is to remember the ecological and ecospheric context in which our Christological claims occur—they happen on Earth and with earthly creatures. We are here. So, too, is the gospel of Christ. How might the gospel of Christ be "good news" for the earth? How is Christ's story Earth's story? How is our earthly reality equally real for Christ? How does the earth factor into whatever God might be doing in Christ? How does Christ reveal God's activity in the earth? Moreover, how can we highlight Earth's role in this Christological drama as enacted and remembered in our annual cycles of worship?

This book, hopefully, is in alliance with another approach to incorporating ecological concern into Christian worship. That approach is to designate a particular season as having a theme of creation. The season of creation is a special liturgical season emphasizing creation that has been established with considerable ecumenical contribution. It usually spans five weeks, beginning September 1 on which many Orthodox communities commemorate God's creation of the world as a day of prayer for creation. The season of creation concludes on or near October 4 when the Roman Catholic Church celebrates the feast of Saint Francis. In 2008, the World Council of Churches Central Committee issued a call for such a "'Time for Creation' through prayers and actions."[1] Since then, many Orthodox, Catholic, and Protestant congregations have observed this liturgical season. The seasonal emphasis has encouraged great creativity throughout the Christian churches in developing creation-oriented worship resources and for encouraging creation care.

This is all terrific! But what about the traditional seasons surrounding Christmas and Easter with their Christological focus? Christ and creation are intimately linked. We do not have one without the other. Our worship throughout the year can reflect this—and proclaim this! This book is intended to help Christian congregations explore the relationship between Christ and creation—and between our spiritual life and our creaturely life—through our life of worship, especially during the special seasons focusing on the life of Christ. We have the opportunity to integrate the theme of creation with our understanding of the Christological narrative that is celebrated in the most momentous of our liturgical seasons.

It is my hope that this book will be helpful to worshiping congregations on a regular basis as well as on special occasions. A basic framework for this book is provided by the liturgical year which is used in some form in most congregations of ecumenical denominations. The Christological focus of the liturgical seasons of the Christian year and of congregational worship are assumed and proclaimed throughout this book. The realities of our creaturely existence and our ecological dependence, as well as the challenges to a healthy and sustainable natural world, are also assumed throughout and serve as premises for what follows.

THE CHRISTIAN LITURGICAL YEAR

The Christian year highlights two magnificent dramas that portray God's relationship to God's creatures in Christ. Chronologically, the first of these dramas in the liturgical year is that surrounding Jesus's birth: Advent-Christmas-Epiphany.

The more ancient of these two dramas, though, is that surrounding the death and resurrection of Christ: Lent-Easter-Pentecost. Most Sundays in the Christian year, however, do not fall into these special liturgical seasons. Roman Catholics refer to these Sundays plainly as "ordinary time." Many ecumenical Protestant denominations might refer more cryptically to these Sundays as the "season *after* Epiphany" or the "season *after* Pentecost," but they are not really liturgical seasons in the same way as the two great liturgical dramas involving Christ's birth and the paschal mystery.

For each of these two great dramas, there is a time of preparation (Advent and Lent, respectively) in which expectations build with increasing anticipation and suspense. At the peak of suspense, each respective story climaxes with a great event. This is Jesus's birth in the Christmas narrative. The Easter narrative leads to the momentous events of Holy Week that culminate in the depths of despair on Good Friday and the heights of exultation on Easter Sunday with Christ's resurrection. Then follows a season of celebration and interpretation within each of these dramas. The Christmas season after Christmas Day deepens our reflection on the meaning of incarnation, and it concludes with the feast of Epiphany in which we remember the visit of the magi to the Christ child. The Easter season after Easter Sunday allows for deepening reflection on the meaning of resurrection and new creation. Following the chronology of the Gospel of Luke, the Easter season culminates on Ascension Thursday (or Ascension Sunday) in which we recognize Christ as glorified. The Easter season concludes with the Day of Pentecost in which the Holy Spirit is given to the church for Christ's continued work in the world.

Bounding the great liturgical seasons like bookends are certain days in "ordinary time" that stand as markers for the special seasons. These are the Reign of Christ Sunday before the start of Advent, Baptism of Christ Sunday immediately following the feast of Epiphany, Transfiguration Sunday just preceding Lent, and Trinity Sunday immediately after Pentecost Sunday. I refer to these as "warm-up days" that help us enter into the energy of the special seasons and "cool-down days" that help us to integrate the meaning of the liturgical seasons into our everyday creaturely life.

The seasons of Advent, Christmas, and Epiphany mark our longing for worldly deliverance, Christ's incarnation within creation, and the manifestation of God's glory on Earth. The seasons of Lent and Easter dramatize the passion, death, resurrection, and ascension of Jesus Christ; during this time, we remember that Christ shares our mortal nature, offers victorious life, and claims sovereignty over all creation. Pentecost is the coming of Christ's promised spirit, enlivening creation as well as inspiring the Church. Throughout the Christian drama, creation is centrally involved, not only as the stage on which the play is set but also as the object of Christ's love and the very terrain of salvation history.

Christological emphasis along with ecological concern pervades the chapters of this book. This Christological emphasis corresponds with the Christological emphasis in the special seasons of the ecumenical Christian year and in Christian belief itself. The book is structured according to the seasons of the liturgical year, but the two cycles are presented in reverse order; the Lent-Easter-Pentecost cycle is discussed in the first half of the book, and the second half addresses the Advent-Christmas-Epiphany cycle. In each chapter and for each season of worship, creation and creation's crises are portrayed in their relationship to Christ and to Christ's redeeming love. Earthly life is interpreted Christologically in these pages. Conversely, creation appears as a central paradigm for understanding our salvation in Christ in this age when creation's health and our creaturely well-being can no longer be taken for granted.

STRUCTURE AND ASSUMPTIONS

I am a United Methodist with an ecumenical heart. Each chapter in this book draws from different lines of theological thought and different strands of ecumenical tradition—actually, Judeo-Christian tradition. This is not intended as a work in systematic theology (though I think people interested in systematic theology will find it suggestive), so I attempt neither to reconcile different theological perspectives nor to clarify the differences between them here. A diversity of theological perspectives receive attention in this book because of their apparent affinity with an ecological hermeneutic as applied to the texts and practices of Christian worship in the liturgical year. Each reader is able to make his or her own comparison between these perspectives and to notice how these perspectives may address his or her own theological tradition, ecclesial affinity, and liturgical practice.

Throughout this book, attention is given to both the Roman Catholic Lectionary for the Mass and the Revised Common Lectionary that is used by many ecumenical Protestant denominations. Both lectionaries assume a nearly identical structure for the liturgical year, and they put forward very similar selections of biblical passages to be read on the Sundays of the liturgical seasons. In fact, the Revised Common Lectionary had its genesis with the Roman Catholic Lectionary for the Mass. In addition, Orthodox thought, particularly a theology of divinization, is highlighted in this book, especially in the first chapter on Transfiguration and in the final chapter on Epiphany. Chapter 3 attends in depth to the agricultural seasons associated historically with the Jewish liturgical year, particularly the festivals of Passover and Tabernacles, and their significance for Christian celebration of Palm Sunday.

Occasional reference is made throughout this book to *The Book of Common Prayer* of The Episcopal Church, the *Book of Common Worship* of the Presbyterian Church (USA) and the Cumberland Presbyterian Church, *Evangelical Lutheran Worship* of the Evangelical Lutheran Church in America (ELCA), and *The United Methodist Book of Worship*.[2] My own Wesleyan heritage is probably most noticeable in chapter 4 on Christ's Passion where some of Charles Wesley's hymns find voice. Feminist interpretations of the biblical Sophia tradition are prominent in chapter 7 on Pentecost and in chapter 8 on Trinity Sunday.

This book attends to the lectionaries but does not address every lection advocated by the lectionaries. In addition to omitting some lections from consideration, this book will add to the biblical material considered for reading in the liturgical seasons beyond that provided by the lectionaries. Often, lectionary passages will be expanded here to bring in the wider biblical context in which Earth participates in the story being told. At other times, entirely different scriptural readings might be suggested for guiding worship, such as for Advent in chapter 12 on "turning to the children."

Readers may tack into this book from a number of different angles. The most straightforward way is to begin at the beginning and read the chapters in sequence. Material is presented in such a fashion that the earlier chapters inform the ones to follow. This is one of the reasons, as will become clear, for beginning chapter 1 with Transfiguration rather than Advent. Such sequential order is not necessary, however. Worship leaders can simply turn to whichever chapter is addressing the liturgical season that they are planning. The chapters are named according to these seasons in order to facilitate such intuitive access. When chapters refer to material discussed earlier, reference is usually made to assist the reader in locating that material. It is also possible to use the indices to find areas of the book most directly addressing the reader's particular interest or a particular biblical passage. Some passages are discussed in different chapters, so the scriptural index should prove especially helpful in such instances.

While this book is not intended primarily as a collection of resource materials, resources and suggestions for corporate prayer and worship can be found in each chapter. Moreover, each chapter concludes with examples for liturgical use in worship, which I hope will be helpful. Readers are invited to use or adapt these liturgies for their own use in leading worship. Readers are also invited to pause and prayerfully reflect with these concluding materials for worship, and to allow them to inform one's own prayer. Finally, these concluding acts of worship might be used for worship in the classroom or study group, if this is a book being read in the context of a seminary or in the context of a discipleship group in a congregation. I hope and pray, in reading and in worship you are blessed and that you find yourselves recipients of the means of God's grace. I hope and pray further that, through all our moments of prayer—whether in assembly or in private—God will be worshiped and glorified, God's people inspired and sanctified, and God's creation preserved and blessed.

Part I

MORTAL NATURE AND NEW CREATION

Lent/Easter/Ascension/Pentecost Cycle

Chapter 1

Prelude

Transfiguration

> *All things are said to be transfigured in the transfiguration of Christ in as far as something of each creature was transfigured in Christ. For in His human nature, Christ has something in common with all creatures. With the stone He shares existence; with plants He shares life; with animals, He shares sensation; and with the angels, He shares intelligence. Therefore, all things are said to be transformed in Christ since, by virtue of His humanity, He embraces something of every creature in Himself when He is transfigured.*[1]

Jesuit priest, scientist, and mystic, Pierre Teilhard de Chardin, composed *Hymn of the Universe* as a prayer of Holy Communion, reportedly on the feast of Transfiguration, while he was studying in the Ordos desert. Without bread or wine, he offered the totality of his being along with the consecrated elements of the desert itself and of the whole creation. His Eucharistic vision of Christ's body embraces and enlivens the entire universe, "diffused and active in the depths of matter" and a "power as implacable as the world and as warm as life." The love of Jesus is "hidden in the forces which bring increase to the earth." A person being filled with such love, Teilhard writes, "the earth will lift up, like a mother, in the immensity of her arms, and will enable [that person] to contemplate the face of God.[2] To Christ, the "dazzling center" of all, he prays, "the contours of your body melt away and become enlarged beyond all measure, till the only features I can distinguish in you are those of the face of a world which has burst into flame." Christ and the universe and the worshiper are all transfigured in this vision.[3]

The transfiguration of Christ is the first theme to be explored in this book that brings an ecological hermeneutic to bear on Christian worship during the liturgical seasons surrounding Christmas and Easter. This choice of a beginning might ring with a degree of dissonance to some readers. For one thing, as will be explained, the transfiguration tends to be celebrated on different days for Protestant, Catholic, and Orthodox. The rest of this book will look at occasions for worship during liturgical seasons that are celebrated with a greater degree of commonality ecumenically. More importantly, though, for many readers the story of Jesus's transfiguration seems not only odd but also other-worldly—perhaps a peculiar beginning for a book that takes this world seriously in its ecological relationships as well as in relationship to the divine. As Teilhard's *Hymn of the Universe* reveals, however, and as the quotation from Saint Bonaventure at the outset of this chapter proclaims, Christ's transfiguration conceivably involves the whole world, and this has implications for worship throughout the year.

TRANSFIGURATION AND THE LITURGICAL YEAR

The remembrance and celebration of Christ's transfiguration occurs at different times during the year for different branches of the ecumenical church. Orthodox Christians celebrate the feast of Transfiguration on August 6. Roman Catholics observe this feast on August 6 as well, but also read and preach on the story of transfiguration annually on the second Sunday in Lent. Ecumenical Protestants following the Revised Common Lectionary celebrate Transfiguration Sunday every year on the Sunday before the season of Lent begins, during the "ordinary time" after Epiphany. Many Baptists and other Protestants who do not follow the Revised Common Lectionary might not have any particular time in the year dedicated to reflection on this theme.[4]

Protestants using the Revised Common Lectionary are prodded each year by the Lectionary to attend to the transfiguration of Christ on the Sunday before Lent, but they may not see the logic of prefacing Lent with this story. The story of Christ's transfiguration, though, presages all the events that are about to transpire in the journey to Jerusalem, to Calvary, to the empty tomb, and to Christ's ascension and enthronement throughout creation. Past and promised future are joined together in this moment, as Moses and Elijah attend and as the light of Christ's countenance and clothing shines like a beacon toward the glory yet to come. The story is like a hinge in the composition of the gospels, turning the pages of the life of Christ toward Jerusalem and the events to transpire there. In Jesus's transfiguration, Christ's glory is revealed to Peter, James, and John prior to his death and resurrection.

The transfiguration story as told by the Gospel of Luke makes plain the path to Jerusalem and to the crucifixion and resurrection. Moses and Elijah "appeared in glory," with Jesus, we are told, "and were speaking of his departure which he was about to accomplish at Jerusalem" (Luke 9:31).

Immediately following the transfiguration in Matthew's Gospel, it is stated clearly that "the Son of Man is about to suffer" (Matt 17:12). Also immediately following the transfiguration, both Matthew and Mark have Jesus instruct those with him not to tell others about this vision until, in Mark's version, "after the Son of Man had risen from the dead" (Mark 9:9). Further, the brightness of Christ's transfigured appearance can be seen as revelation of his post-resurrection glory.

Baptist biblical scholar, Douglas Harink, notices that the story of Christ's transfiguration is placed in each of the gospels immediately following Jesus's declaration to those with him that "there are some standing here who will not taste death before they see the Son of Man coming in his kingdom" (Matt 16:28). Harink argues that Christ's transfiguration as seen by those on the mountain with him is that promised glimpse of the glorified Christ coming to reign.[5]

The disciples are invited along this way—to the cross and through the cross to resurrection. The way promises new understanding—of Jesus, of themselves, and of their calling. Worshipers today, as disciples, in hearing this story are invited along the same Lenten and Easter journey of loss and gain, of repentance and revival, of remorse and regeneration, of metanoia and transfiguration. This is the logic for prefacing the seasons of Lent and Easter with a Sunday to focus on transfiguration; it foreshadows and illumines our way ahead. We as worshipers join with the first disciples on this journey with Christ. Further, as we shall see, all creation participates with us in this liturgical journey, even as we travel with the rest of creation toward universal transfiguration. "The world in its entirety forms part of the liturgy of heaven," professes Orthodox theologian, John Chryssavgis, and continues, "the world constitutes a cosmic liturgy."[6]

Moreover, the transfiguration reflects the other Christological themes of the liturgical year celebrated in Advent, Christmas, and Epiphany. These occasions for worship will be the focus of the final chapters of this book and can be anticipated now. They center around Christmas, celebrating God's incarnation in earthly flesh. John Chryssavgis affirms a close relationship between the incarnation and transfiguration in Orthodox theology and iconography with salvific import for the natural world of God's creation. Referring to a theology of *theosis*, or divinization, to be elaborated in the following section, Chryssavgis describes this relationship:

> The two main events for Orthodox iconography are the Incarnation and the Transfiguration. The first reforms what was "originally" deformed through sin and grants to the world the possibility of sanctification. The second realizes the consequences of divinization and grants to the world a foretaste even now of the beauty and light of the last times. We are, in this world, placed at a point of intersection between the present age and the future age, uniting the two as one.[7]

The Christmas season is preceded by the season of Advent that anticipates the coming of Christ and Christ's reign on Earth, and the Christmas season concludes with Epiphany, which recognizes the presence of God made known in Christ and revealed to the world. Epiphany celebrates the manifestation of Christ's glory with the visit of the magi and the baptism of Jesus. In Christ's baptism, the epiphany is announced from the sky to the earth with the same resonance and the same promise as at the transfiguration: "This is my Son, the Beloved" (Matt 3:17).

DIVINIZATION AND TRANSFIGURED CREATION

The connections between Christ's transfiguration and the natural world, however, may not be saliently apparent at first. Matthew, Mark, and Luke all recount the incident. Jesus is on a mountain with Peter, James, and John. His appearance is brightened to a dazzling white light. Moses and Elijah appear and engage in conversation with Jesus. Peter offers to erect three booths. Then a cloud overshadows them and a voice from the cloud declares Jesus to be "my Son, the Beloved" (Matt 17:5, Mark 9:7) or "my Son, my Chosen" (Luke 9:35) and instructs, "listen to him!" After this voice Moses and Elijah vanish, and the disciples are found alone with Jesus. The story is mysterious with the touching of heaven and earth on the mountain, the touching of prophetic past with promised future in the present, and the touching of brilliance and shadow over the person of Jesus. There is little explicitly said here, though, about the natural world of God's creation.

The apparent oddness and other-worldliness of the story is magnified when read with the telling of the event in the context of 2 Peter, which also testifies to this theophany:

> We had been eyewitnesses of his majesty. For he received honor and glory from God the Father when that voice was conveyed to him by the Majestic Glory, saying, "This is my Son, my Beloved, with whom I am well pleased." We ourselves heard this voice come from heaven, while we were with him on the holy mountain. So we have the prophetic message more fully confirmed. You will do well to be attentive to this as to a lamp shining in a dark place, until the day dawns and the morning star rises in your hearts. (2 Pet 1:16b–19)

The book of 2 Peter continues with a warning against false prophets, followed by a list of divine punishments accomplished by God in the past, and an apocalyptic scenario which sounds bizarre to contemporary ears.[8]

For Orthodox Christians, though, the transfiguration of Jesus not only reveals a foretaste of the glory of Christ's post-resurrection life, it presents a picture of creation's participation in that life and glorification. K. M. George attests:

> Transfiguration is the word often used in the Orthodox tradition for preparing the creation for the ultimate experience of glory. Our worship, our prayers, our life that expresses truth and goodness, our efforts to bring justice and peace on earth—all contribute to the process of transfiguration.[9]

Transfiguration, in Orthodox Christianity, has been interpreted as symbolic of earthly transformation and benediction.

Matthew Fox, writing about the centrality of Christ's transfiguration in Eastern Orthodox Christianity, describes the feast of the Transfiguration as "the pivotal point of the liturgical year."[10] In particular, Fox emphasizes the importance of 2 Peter's reference to "glory"—both the revelation of Christ's glory to the disciples and to the naming of God as "Sublime Glory" or "Majestic Glory" (2 Pet 1:17). It is God's own glory revealed in Christ's transfiguration that is being shared with all of creation in its transfiguration. Fox quotes Orthodox theologian Nicolas Berdyaev concerning the theology of *theosis*, or divinization, as key for understanding transfiguration: "The central idea of the Eastern Fathers was that of *theosis*, the divinization of all creatures, the transfiguration of the world."[11]

The words "divinization" and "deification" have become accepted English words for articulating this theology of transfiguration, but they might suggest misleading implications. Divinization or deification should be distinguished from a kind of pantheism that facilely equates creation with God. Stephen Finlan and Vladimir Kharlamov note that some but not all English writers prefer to distinguish between the two words, "divinization (taking on godly qualities) and deification (become a godlike being)," but they reassure that "all Christian authors made such a distinction *conceptually*, whether or not they make it terminologically" and insist that it is "obvious, from the standpoint of Christian theology, that no mortal becomes God."[12] Rather, divinization/deification denotes the understanding that human creatures and even all of creation might share in the glory of the Creator and reflect that glory. This is transformative for creation since it is the very energy of the Creator reflected in the Creator's work. Some writers in an Orthodox mystical tradition refer to the light of God's glory in the transfiguration as the "uncreated light," God's own glory manifested in God's creation, shining through God's Beloved, resplendent throughout creation.[13]

The Greek word that is used to describe this theology of divinization and transfiguration is *theosis*, but there are other related concepts. According to Stephen Finlan and Vladimir Kharlamov, the term *theosis* was coined in the fourth century by Gregory of Nazianzus. Athanasius in the third century, though, used the word *theopoiesis*, a compound word with the verb *poieo* meaning "to make or produce," thus emphasizing divine agency and human receptivity. "*Theopoiesis* connotes the idea of passive deification," explain Finlan and Kharlamov, "the human is acted upon, so God retains primacy and infinity."[14]

While the transfiguration shown in Christ is intended for the entire creation, human beings participate in this transfiguration with a particular role. Worship figures prominently in this role—both in the life of personal devotion and in the worship of the liturgical assembly. In personal devotion and prayer, believers make themselves available to God's transfigurative energy for their closer transformation in God's image that was revealed most fully in Jesus Christ. In the liturgical assembly, our worship as human creatures takes on a representative function. As creatures of God, we represent all of creation in offering praise to God and in making ourselves and the whole creation open to God's transforming grace. Orthodox writers describe humanity as priests for creation.

Metropolitan John (Zizioulas) of Pergamon, writing about this human role as "priest for creation," defines a priest as "the one who takes in his [sic] hands the world to refer it to God, and who, in return, brings God's blessing to what he [sic] refers to God." "Through this act," he continues, "creation is brought into communion with God."[15] Of course, we might affirm all of creation already to be in communion with its Creator, but our priestly role as creatures in God's image gives us the ability to declare with creation praise to God and to proclaim with Christ divine blessing to the world.

Psalm 19 (18) sings:

> The heavens are telling the glory of God;
> and the firmament proclaims his handiwork.
> Day to day pours forth speech,
> and night to night declares knowledge.
> There is no speech, nor are there words;
> their voice is not heard;
> yet their voice goes out through all the earth,
>   and their words to the end of the world. (Ps 19:1–4)

As humans, we are able to add our voice to creation's praise. Writing about the priestly character of the human person, John Chryssavgis quotes Leontius of Cyprus from the seventh century in claiming this cooperation with creation in rendering praise: "It is through me that the heavens declare the glory of God, through me the moon worships God, through me the stars glorify [God], through me the waters and showers of rain, the dew and all creation, venerate God and give [God] glory." Also citing this passage, Bishop Kallistos Ware concludes that we "give to physical objects a voice which in themselves they lack."[16]

This priestly role within creation is palpable in the celebration of the Eucharist. In the context of sacramental worship, we not only praise God for creation and with creation, we lift creation to God for God to bless. According to John Zizioulas, "All ancient liturgies, especially in the East, involve a sanctification of matter and time." In his essay "Priest of Creation," Zizioulas emphasizes the importance of "*Anaphora*," of "lifting up" the gifts of bread and wine. "Liturgiologists today tend to stress this forgotten detail, which can be of particular significance for a theology of creation," he writes and continues, "For it attaches at least equal centrality—if not more—to [hu]man's act as the priest of creation as it does to God's act of sending down the Holy Spirit to transform."[17] Creation as a whole can be understood to be represented in the material elements of bread and wine which are lifted up.

"The Eucharistic bread always symbolizes the universe, the whole created order,"[18] K. M. George attests and explains:

> Bread and wine symbolize the whole material creation, the same creation assumed by Christ. . . . In this Eucharistic offering God's creation is lifted up in its totality to the presence of God. We receive back the Body and Blood of Christ. Again we offer ourselves and the creation. Again we receive back the gift of God. This is the "Eucharistic cycle." The creation is continually transfigured through this offering-receiving."[19]

As creatures ourselves, we too represent the rest of creation in this act of worship. Not only the celebrant who is physically lifting bread and cup, I would add, but also every worshiper present, male and female, created in the image of God, who lifts himself or herself forward to receive the sacrament and who lifts the consecrated elements to his or her lips, is serving as a priest in lifting creation for God's transfiguration.

Koinōnia is translated variously as "fellowship," "communion," and "participation." Paul's words in 1 Corinthians 10:16, "The bread which we break, is it not a *koinōnia* in the body of Christ?" can be translated with each of these three words. Communion is participation is our fellowship in Christ. The cognate word *koinōnoi* is used in 2 Peter 1:4 just prior to recounting Christ's transfiguration in saying that we, too, "may become *participants* of the divine nature."[20] There is a mutuality of identification and participation between ourselves and creation, between ourselves and Jesus Christ, and between Jesus Christ and Godhead. This mutuality of identification and participation can be seen as operative in our priestly act of representing creation to God through Christ—whether at the Table or in our daily bread.

Key here is Christ's identification with us in mortal life and death through *kenosis* or "emptying," assuming creaturely flesh with us in the incarnation and experiencing death with us in crucifixion. K. M. George defines *kenosis* as "God's self-emptying for the salvation of the world," and he draws implications for creation's transfiguration. "God shares the human condition in all its depth and breadth," K. M. George affirms and then declares, "Christ assumed human nature in order to transfigure it 'from glory to glory.'"[21] Moreover, all nature and not just "human" nature participates in this offering and this transfiguration. George explains:

> Christ's self-offering on the cross was also the descent to the deepest layers of the human reality. In his offering the whole created order was offered to the Father. According to the Orthodox tradition in every Eucharistic celebration we participate in the self-offering of Christ by offering ourselves and the whole creation to God.[22]

Whereas *kenosis* as emptying names the process by which God in Christ is able to participate with us in human nature and within the natural world, *theosis* names that process by which we and our world can become transfigured with Christ toward the divine.

Speaking about a human being as a kind of "microcosm," Stanley S. Harakas writes about this link between humanity and creation in this movement toward (or away from) God:

> The material created reality is deeply involved with us. Should we move in the direction of deification of our nature in progress towards God, we will somehow carry the created material world with us. Should we move in the opposite direction, the created world will suffer with us as well.[23]

As mentioned earlier, there is a mutuality of participation between ourselves and creation, between ourselves and Jesus Christ, and between Jesus Christ and Godhead. Orthodox theologies of *kenosis* (emptying) and *theosis* (divinization) help to describe the dynamics of this relationship. Christ's transfiguration illustrates both the complexity of this relationship and its transfigurative potential for humanity and creation. The church's worship brings us into liminal space with Christ where transfiguration is possible. As we discern not only our souls but also the whole universe participating with us in the life of Christ, Christ's own transfiguration becomes less an anomalous oddity and more a paradigmatic promise.

This chapter began by acknowledging two counterintuitive aspects of attending to Christ's transfiguration at the outset of this book. One aspect is the ecumenical variation with regard to the time for commemorating it liturgically. The other has to do with the implications for earthly reality of this imagery, which at first might seem other-worldly. In response, we have engaged a reading of the transfiguration that celebrates the participation of earthly existence in Christ's transfiguration.

TRANSFIGURED WORLD IN WORSHIP

This chapter began with the spiritual vision of transfigured creation by Pierre Teilhard de Chardin while he was surrounded by the natural sights and sounds of the Ordos desert. It concludes now with another spiritual vision of transfigured creation. Metropolitan Tryphon was a Russian Orthodox prelate who served during the years of the persecution of the church in Russia. Eventually becoming blind, his vision continues to illumine for us God's glory throughout creation. An "akathist" is a form of a hymn penned in dedication. Metropolitan Tryphon's hymn is titled "An Akathist in Praise of God's Creation," or sometimes simply, "Glory to God for Everything." An excerpt is given here, edited only slightly to be read as a litany. The full text is twelve times as long and can be found on a number of websites.[24] Following this litany of praise, there are two new verses inspired by this akathist for the hymn, "O for a Thousand Tongues to Sing." This chapter then concludes with a eucharistic prayer for transfiguration.

IN PRAISE OF GOD'S CREATION

Metropolitan Tryphon (Turkestanov)

One: How glorious you are in the triumph of spring, when every creature awakes to new life and joyfully sings your praises with a thousand tongues: you are the source of life, the conqueror of death. By the light of the moon nightingales sing: the plains and the woods put on their wedding garment, white as snow. All the earth is your promised bride awaiting her bridegroom who does not know decay. If the grass of the field is clothed like this, how gloriously shall we be transfigured in the coming age of the resurrection, how radiant our bodies, how resplendent our souls!

Many: **Glory to you,**

One: bringing from the darkness of the earth an endless variety of colors, tastes and scents,

Many: **Glory to you**

One: for the warmth and tenderness of the world of nature,

Many: **Glory to you**

One: for surrounding us with thousands of your works,

Many: **Glory to you**

One:	for the depth of your wisdom: the whole world is a living sign of it,
Many:	**Glory to you:**
One:	on my knees, I kiss the traces of your unseen hand,
Many:	**Glory to you**
One:	for setting before us the dazzling light of eternal life,
Many:	**Glory to you**
One:	for the hope of the unutterable, imperishable beauty of immortality,
Many:	**Glory to you,**
One:	O God, from age to age!

HYMN:[25] Verses for "O for a Thousand Tongues"

> O for a thousand tongues to sing, a thousand creatures' praise!
> Your glory shows in all the works your unseen hand has traced.
>
> O for your wisdom now made known in all life's tenderness,
> in warmth of light, in colors shown, in nature's tastes and scents.

EUCHARISTIC PRAYER FOR TRANSFIGURATION[26]

(*Sursum Corda*)

. . .It is right and a matter of justice to give you thanks and praise,
Almighty God.

Dwelling in light unapproachable, you emblaze the sky with heavenly bodies. You brighten the whole earth and spark iridescence in the sea. Out of the darkness you created light, and the light continues to enliven us. From your light and energy, all plants and animals receive their life.

When our life was nearly extinguished by the flood, you rescued your creatures along with Noah, and you lit a spectrum of light in the sky as a sign of peace for the earth and a promise of life for all animals.

Through the ages, you have called us to walk in the light, and you have sent prophets to illumine the way. When you freed your people from slavery in Egypt, you accompanied them in a fiery pillar. And when you gave them your words through Moses, you made his face to shine with the luminance of your own glory.

When the people forsook your covenant and went after other gods, you responded to Elijah's prayer with your own fire to ignite his offering and then with rains to water the earth, letting it be known and shown that you alone are God.

We therefore praise you with voices in heaven and on earth throughout creation: (*Sanctus*)

In the fullness of time, you sent Jesus, your Beloved, to be the light of the world. We beheld Christ's glory, glory as of your only Begotten. Before being lifted on the cross, rising, and ascending to reign, we saw Jesus transfigured before us on the mountain with Moses and Elijah, dazzling with your radiance, and presenting the promise of transfiguration for us and for your creation. With the heavenly voice, we proclaim Jesus your Beloved.

> **Christ crucified, the sun was dimmed over the land.**
> **Christ risen, the tomb held a sight of dazzling light.**
> **Christ ascended, we look for the fullness of your glory on Earth.**

When the time had come for Christ to be glorified, at supper with the disciples, Jesus took bread, and gave thanks to you, broke the bread, and gave it to them saying: "Take, eat; this is my body which is given for you. Do this in remembrance of me."

In the same way also the cup, after supper, saying, "This cup is the new covenant in my blood. Do this, as often as you drink it, in remembrance of me."

Christ, after dying and rising from the dead, was revealed on the road to Emmaus in the breaking of bread, and on the road to Damascus in blinding light. Having ascended, Christ continues to be revealed, enlivening all creation and enlightening the eyes of faith.

And so, in remembrance of these your generative acts, we present ourselves with these earthly elements, in praise and thanksgiving, in union with Christ's offering for us.

Pour out your Holy Spirit upon us and upon these your creatures of bread and wine. As we receive them, make us to be partakers of Christ's body and blood, and nurture us to grow into Christ's likeness. Grant that we may be for the world the body of Christ and that we may bear witness to your sanctifying presence on Earth. By your Spirit make us one with you, one with each other, and one in ministry to all the world, seeking the healing and restoration of creation, until finally we feast in a new city eternally lit by your own radiant glory, where the Lamb is the light.

(*Agnus Dei*)

Chapter 2

Lenten Beginnings

Ash Wednesday and Temptation in the Wilderness

Wendell Berry's essay "A Native Hill" leads the readers on an intimate tour of a place of personal importance to him, appreciating the landscape and its sweep of social and natural history, and embracing fine details of its particular living ecology. He concludes the essay with this reflective meditation that touches on his own life and mortality in deep connection with this place:

> I have been walking in the woods, and have lain down on the ground to rest. It is the middle of October and around me, all through the woods, the leaves are quietly sifting down. The newly fallen leaves make a dry comfortable bed, and I lie easy, coming to rest within myself as I seem to do now a days [*sic*] only when I am in the woods.
>
> And now a leaf, spiraling down in wild flight, lands on my shirt front at about the third button below the collar. At first I am bemused and mystified by the coincidence—that the leaf should have been so hung, weighted and shaped, so ready to fall, so nudged loose and slanted by the breeze, as to fall where I, by the same delicacy of circumstance, happened to be lying. The event, among all its ramifying causes and considerations, and finally its mysteries, begins to take on the magnitude of history. Portent begins to dwell in it.
>
> And suddenly I apprehend in it the dark proposal of the ground. Under the fallen leaf my breastbone burns with imminent decay. Other leaves fall. My body begins its long shudder into humus. I feel my substance escape me, carried into the mold by beetles and worms. Days, winds, seasons pass over me as I sink under the leaves. For a time only sight is left to me, a passive awareness of the sky overhead, birds crossing, the mazed inter-reaching of the treetops, the leaves falling—and then that too sinks away. It is acceptable to me, and I am at peace.
>
> When I move to go it is as though I rise up out of the world.[1]

INTRODUCING LENT

Early Lent is marked by two themes: mortality and repentance—both of which are related to Earth. These are graphically illustrated on Ash Wednesday with the application of ashes. Earthly and mortal nature is acknowledged with the images of dust and ashes, often with the words from Genesis 3:19, "Remember that you are dust and to dust you shall return." In many worship services, this mortal nature is affirmed with words of assurance from Psalm 103:14 that God is merciful because God "knows our frame" and "remembers that we are dust."

The forty days of Lent continue with the themes of repentance and resisting temptation, with creation participating in the journey. Christ's temptation is remembered on the first Sunday of Lent. The Synoptic Gospels portray Jesus entering and residing in Earth's wilderness for forty days and, as Mark 1:12 has it, "was with the wild beasts." Our forty days of Lent parallels the time of Jesus's sojourn in the wilderness. Our repentance during Lent is here interpreted as linked not only with Christ but also with the earth. The "Invitation to Lent" in *Evangelical Lutheran Worship* makes clear this connection with creation as well as with Christ in calling us to repentance:

> We begin this holy season by acknowledging our need for repentance and for God's mercy. We are created to experience joy in communion with God, to love one another, and to live in harmony with creation. But our sinful rebellion separates us from God, our neighbors, and creation, so that we do not enjoy the life our creator intended.[2]

We are called both to enjoy our life in creation and to turn toward care for creation.

Lent is a directional journey as we travel with Christ. It leads to Christ's death and resurrection and to our celebrations of Holy Week and Easter, the most profound moments in the Christian year. As we are baptized into Christ's death and resurrection (Rom 6:3–6), many churches encourage the historical practice of baptizing at the time of Easter. Historically, Lent initially developed as a season of instruction and preparation for those who were to be baptized on Easter.[3] It became a time of repentance and preparation for all Christians, as we recall and affirm our baptisms and our sharing in the death and life of Christ. Because of this baptismal journey, water as well as dust and desert become symbolic of our life of faith during the penitential season of Lent.

In the lectionary readings, the image of water is especially plentiful for the first Sunday of Lent in year B. The covenant with Noah and other creatures after the flood in Genesis 9 is provided as the first reading in both the Roman

Catholic Lectionary and the Revised Common Lectionary on this day. These lectionaries also give a reading from Genesis on the first Sunday of Lent in year A; they provide for the reading of the eating of forbidden fruit in Genesis 3 preceded by selected verses from Genesis 2, telling some of the story of creation in the Garden of Eden. Although these lections are read in separate years, there is a confluence of themes from Genesis given to us for the beginning of Lent: creation from dust, tilling and keeping the Garden, and covenanting after the flood with all creatures. This chapter will conclude by looking at the creation stories in Genesis more fully to uncover an irony in their telling, especially evident in notions of dominion that might now inform our Lent and our repentance.

The forty-day duration of Lent preceding Easter was determined by the Council of Niace in 325 CE, and this period of preparation has continued in both Eastern and Western churches. But the period is reckoned differently by these ecclesial traditions. In the Eastern churches, the forty days includes Sundays. In the West, Sundays are excluded from the forty days of fasting, thus extending Lent to forty-six actual days. The Eastern churches conclude Lent a week earlier than Easter, though, on the day before Palm Sunday. Both Eastern and Western churches place Easter after Passover and on the first Sunday after the first full moon after the Spring Equinox, but they follow different calendars—the Julian and the Gregorian—in making this calculation. Thus, the beginning of Lent always differs between the Western and Eastern churches, with Ash Wednesday beginning Lent in the West and "Clean Monday" beginning Lent in the East. This chapter assumes the structure of Lent as observed by Roman Catholics and by Protestants following the Revised Common Lectionary. The use of ashes is a particularly Western tradition, dating at least from the eleventh century[4] but is only recently being adopted by many Protestant congregations. Marking the beginning of Lent, ashes mark our bodies, reminding us to mind our mortal living and mortal ending.

REMEMBERING THAT WE ARE DUST

Dust and ashes symbolize both our mortal nature and repentance from sin, but these are not the same. Sin is always a reason for regret and a cause for repentance, but our mortal nature can be a cause for celebration. As Wendell Berry's reflection at the start of this chapter illustrates, both life and death can occasion a response of awe. His meditation leads us into an embrace of our own lives' composition and decomposition in the earth. Less poetically put, we recognize that the ecological cycle of life includes all our elements and energies in an ongoing sharing with the rest of organic existence. Jesus

Christ's body, too, received and returned these same earthly elements to the organic environment we all share.

We are wondrously created to be physical and sensate. Our bodily life is literally sensational—a cause for gratitude and celebration! Biblically, we might be reminded of Psalm 139:13–15 in praise to God for our amazing, earthy bodies:

> For it was you who formed my inward parts;
> > you knit me together in my mother's womb,
> I praise you, for I am fearfully and wonderfully made.
> > Wonderful are your works;
> that I know very well.
> > My frame was not hidden from you,
> when I was being made in secret,
> > intricately woven in the depths of the earth.

That our earthly existence is temporary makes it even more precious—not a cause for repentance. Though sin and death are linked theologically, as will be explained later, there is a distinction between our mortal nature, which we can claim and affirm, and our sinfulness from which we should repent. This distinction can be inferred in a prayer penned by Thomas Cranmer for Ash Wednesday in the 1549 *Book of Common Prayer* and that continues to recur in contemporary services. Addressing our Creator, we pray, "Almighty and everlasting God, you hate nothing you have made and forgive the sins of all who are penitent."[5]

A theme of repentance can be heard in the Bible concurrent with an affirmation of the overall goodness of creation and created existence. Psalm 104, for instance, concludes by excoriating sinners in the final verse only after thirty-four verses of exuberant praise from throughout creation. Also, most notably, Job repents "in dust and ashes" (Job 42:6b) as the final words spoken by Job to God in the book of Job. But Job's response of repentance follows after four chapters of poetry in which God addresses Job in an epiphany out of a whirlwind. In verse after verse, creation's marvels are affirmed and God's own creativity claimed: the foundations of the earth, the dawn of the day, the springs of the sea, the storehouses of snow, the waterskins of rain, the stars of the sky, the gates of death, and animals of life—lions, goats, deer, donkeys, oxen, horses, ostriches, ravens, hawks, and eagles. These all are recounted as parts of God's own creativity and playfulness. And even where there are few animals and no humans, God will water the grass:

> To bring rain on a land where no one lives,
> > on the desert, which is empty of human life,
> to satisfy the waste and desolate land,
> > and to make the ground put forth grass. (Job 38:25–27)

Job is humbled by this epiphany and repents in dust and ashes. Yet his repentance follows after these verses where God is cheering about the animals and habitats that God has created throughout the earth. Bodily life is not disparaged in these verses, and bodily death is not denied. When Job repents, it is not from being created or embodied, but it is from having "uttered what I did not understand, things too wonderful for me, which I did not know" (Job 42:3). The text sounds harsh, though, as Job's repentance is prefaced with a line often translated, "therefore I despise myself and repent in dust and ashes" (Job 42:6). However, the verb for "despise," *em'as*, has no grammatical object in the Hebrew sentence. There is no "myself." It is not at all clear from the text that Job is engaged in self-loathing. He may be deeply regretting his words spoken in complaint earlier.[6] Such a reading would fit this context in which all embodied life provokes not abhorrence but wonderment.

The act of repentance, of turning toward God, is not only consistent with but also inspired by a marveling at the wonders of creation. Moreover, in Paul's writing, the call to turn toward God is premised by proclamation of God's regenerative activity through Christ in "new creation," "reconciling the world" to Godself. Both the Roman Catholic Lectionary for the Mass and the Revised Common Lectionary urge that 2 Corinthians 5:20 and verses following be read on Ash Wednesday: "We entreat you on behalf of Christ, be reconciled to God." The verses immediately preceding this reading, however, make plain the wider context—indeed the cosmic context—of God's reconciling work in Christ to which we are called:

> So if anyone is in Christ, there is a new creation: everything old has passed away; see, everything has become new! All this is from God, who reconciled us to himself through Christ, and has given us the ministry of reconciliation; that is, in Christ God was reconciling the world to himself. (2 Cor 5:17–19a)

Discussing this passage, David G. Horrell, Cherryl Hunt, and Christopher Southgate suggest, "This cosmic focus on universal reconciliation opens up possibilities for an ecologically relevant reading of Paul's theology," and they explain, "Pauline theology is focused on the world-transforming act of God in Christ, an act with cosmic dimensions and implications."[7] Indeed, the summons to us to be reconciled is a call to turn toward that work of reconciliation being accomplished by Christ toward the whole world, toward God's creation, and toward new creation.

Pope Francis, in the papal encyclical *Laudato Si'*, voices a call for repentance that requires reconciliation with creation: "We come to realize that a healthy relationship with creation is one dimension of overall personal conversion, which entails the recognition of our errors, sins, faults and failures, and leads to heartfelt repentance and desire to change." He quotes the

Australian Catholic bishops emphasizing "the importance of such conversion for achieving reconciliation with creation." The Pope continues: "To achieve such reconciliation, we must examine our lives and acknowledge the ways in which we have harmed God's creation through our actions and our failure to act. We need to experience a conversion, or change of heart."[8] The papal encyclical begins with a strong call to such repentance for planetary health and is worth quoting at length. Pope Francis cites Patriarch Bartholomew:

> 8. Patriarch Bartholomew has spoken in particular of the need for each of us to repent of the ways we have harmed the planet, for "inasmuch as we all generate small ecological damage", we are called to acknowledge "our contribution, smaller or greater, to the disfigurement and destruction of creation". He has repeatedly stated this firmly and persuasively, challenging us to acknowledge our sins against creation: "For human beings . . . to destroy the biological diversity of God's creation; for human beings to degrade the integrity of the earth by causing changes in its climate, by stripping the earth of its natural forests or destroying its wetlands; for human beings to contaminate the earth's waters, its land, its air, and its life—these are sins". For "to commit a crime against the natural world is a sin against ourselves and a sin against God".
>
> 9. At the same time, Bartholomew has drawn attention to the ethical and spiritual roots of environmental problems, which require that we look for solutions not only in technology but in a change of humanity; otherwise we would be dealing merely with symptoms. He asks us to replace consumption with sacrifice, greed with generosity, wastefulness with a spirit of sharing, an asceticism which "entails learning to give, and not simply to give up. It is a way of loving, of moving gradually away from what I want to what God's world needs. It is liberation from fear, greed and compulsion". As Christians, we are also called "to accept the world as a sacrament of communion, as a way of sharing with God and our neighbours on a global scale. It is our humble conviction that the divine and the human meet in the slightest detail in the seamless garment of God's creation, in the last speck of dust of our planet".[9]

God meets us on this planet, in each speck of dust, and urges us to turn toward both the Creator and the creation.

The words spoken with application of ashes on Ash Wednesday, "Remember that you are dust and to dust you shall return," are from Genesis 3:19 and have been said for centuries at such services.[10] They are the concluding line of the poem pronounced by God to Adam and Eve and the serpent, following the eating of the forbidden fruit. It is harsh. The snake is condemned to crawl on its belly, the woman is burdened with pain in childbirth, and the ground is cursed on account of the man. The curse of the ground has to do with the difficulty in procuring food from it:

> Cursed is the ground because of you;
> in toil you shall eat of it all the days of your life;
> thorns and thistles it shall bring forth for you;
> and you shall eat the plants of the field.
> By the sweat of your face you shall eat bread
> until you return to the ground, for out of it you were taken;
> you are dust, and to dust you shall return. (Gen 3:17b–19)

No longer does the earth yield its fruit easily. Procuring food from the land becomes laborious, onerous.

The story's ending seems cruel to all involved, hard on the land, and particularly egregious toward the woman and womankind. Adam's attempt to blame Eve is reprehensible, and her penalty seems inordinate. Adding to the bane toward women through the ages is men's continued vilification of women as "temptress" rather than owning their own responsibility for their own sin. Preaching on this passage can easily compound the problem by repeating blame toward Eve and stereotyping women. Curiously, the next verse after "to dust you shall return" declares high regard for Eve: She is named "Eve, because she was the mother of all living" (Gen 3:20b). This is a laudable way to remember and to describe her, as our mother—not just as humanity's ancestral mother but as the mother of all living, all life. How do we regard the rest of living creation knowing that we share a mother?

The sin in the garden of which both Adam and Eve partake can be interpreted variously, such as disobedience or hubris. The sin, though, is not about bodies, about naked bodies, or gendered bodies, or bodies from dust. Even after the unfolding of events in Genesis 3, the ground still feeds us, but our bodies must co-labor with it. And the dust still defines us. We do not need to repent from being grounded in the earth. Indeed, we cannot change or repent from our very nature as flesh and blood, as enlivened beings of earth and water—a nature shared with all of animate existence, a nature which Christ assumes with us as well.

This opening prayer for Ash Wednesday from *Evangelical Lutheran Worship* recalls our creation from dust enlivened by God's breath:[11]

> Gracious God, out of your love and mercy you breathed into dust the breath of life, creating us to serve you and our neighbors. Call forth our prayers and acts of kindness, and strengthen us to face our mortality with confidence in the mercy of your Son, Jesus Christ, our Savior and Lord, who lives and reigns with you and the Holy Spirit, one God, now and forever. Amen.

Benjamin Stewart appreciatively notes that this prayer is not penitential, and that it "takes a compassionate view of human bodies." He notes further, though, that the prayer omits the biblical purpose given for our creation from dust. Citing Genesis 2:15, he reminds us that the human made from dust was put in the garden to "till and keep it" or, as Stewart likes to translate, to "serve and protect" it. He proposes amending the prayer that it might reflect this human purposefulness to care for the garden of the earth. The prayer would then read, "Out of your love and mercy you breathed into dust the breath of life, creating us to serve and protect the garden of your earth."[12]

This verse, Genesis 2:15, is part of the suggested reading for the first Sunday in Lent in year A in the Revised Common Lectionary. Both the Ecumenical Common Lectionary and the Roman Catholic Lectionary provide readings from the second and third chapters of Genesis as the first lection for the first Sunday of Lent in year A. They both include Genesis 3:1–7, but they choose slightly different verses from Genesis 2 to be read. The reading suggested by the Ecumenical Common Lectionary starts with this verse, Genesis 2:15, "The LORD God took the man and put him in the garden of Eden to till it and keep it." The Roman Catholic Lectionary for the Mass, though, begins earlier with verses 7 through 9 of chapter 2. These verses occur immediately after verse 6 when God causes a stream of water to "rise from the earth, and water the whole face of the ground." The story continues:

> Then the LORD God formed man from the dust of the ground and breathed into his nostrils the breath of life; and the man became a living being. And the LORD God planted a garden in Eden, in the east; and there he put the man whom he had formed. Out of the ground the Lord God made to grow every tree that is pleasant to the sight and good for food. (Gen 2:7–9a)

The same ground that produces plants composes the human body. God's own breath enlivens this dust of the ground. There is a pun that speaks a truth of human nature: the man (*ha'adam*) from ground (*adamah*). There is a similar pun with Eve's name which in Hebrew (*Chava*) begins with the same letter as the word for life (*chai*) and sounds much like the word for a living being (*chaya*). Between these first two human beings is represented all earthly life and living earth. This is what we remember when we recall that we ourselves are dust and return to dust.

God, too, remembers that we are dust. Psalm 103:8–14, in which this memory is voiced, is suggested to be read or sung on Ash Wednesday in the Episcopal *Book of Common Prayer* and in *Evangelical Lutheran Worship*. God's knowledge that we are dust, according to the psalm, is a cause for compassion rather than criticism, for mercy rather than judgment. The psalm declares:

> The LORD is merciful and gracious,
>   slow to anger and abounding in steadfast love.

> He will not always accuse,
>   nor will he keep his anger forever.
> He does not deal with us according to our sins,
>   nor repay us according to our iniquities.
> For as the heavens are high above the earth,
>   so great is his steadfast love toward those who fear him;
> as far as the east is from the west,
>   so far he removes our transgressions from us.
> As a father has compassion for his children,
>   so the LORD has compassion for those who fear him.
> For he knows how we were made;
>   he remembers that we are dust. (Ps 103:8–14)

The selected reading for the day ends here, but the psalm itself continues:

> As for mortals, their days are like grass;
>   they flourish like a flower of the field;
> for the wind passes over it, and it is gone,
>   and its place knows it no more.
> But the steadfast love of the LORD is from everlasting to everlasting. (vss. 15–17a)

The Evangelical Lutheran *Worship Guidebook for Lent and the Three Days* suggests that verses from this psalm might be used as words of assurance following confession or the imposition of ashes.

A Fijian Methodist theologian, Ame Tugaue, wrote his thesis on a Fijian understanding of what it means to be "dust of the earth," or *kuvu ni qele*. Dust, according to Tugaue, is both insignificant and important; when dry it is easily blown away, but when wet it produces crops and the ground of existence. He notes that Fijians use a grammatical form when describing the soil (*qele*) which indicates that it is "food"—something internal and not external to the human person.[13] We are not just dust, then, but soil—earth and water. Significantly in Genesis 2, God caused the ground to be watered prior to fashioning bodies or growing plants.

Moreover, at a microscopic level, we know that the soil teams with life. Ginny Stibolt and Sue Reed name some of the numerous residents of the soil's microscopic community:

> One gram (about 1/5 teaspoon) of healthy soil could contain one hundred million bacteria, one million actinomycetes, and one hundred thousand fungi, whose filaments, if strung together, would measure about 16 feet in length. This same gram of soil could also contain hundreds of nematodes living on the damp surfaces of the soil particles and maybe a few insect eggs or larvae and some earthworm cocoons.[14]

Stibolt and Reed emphasize the importance of maintaining healthy soil for growing healthy gardens.

The image of "watered garden" is invoked in one of the readings given by the Revised Common Lectionary for Ash Wednesday, Isaiah 58:1–12. This passage from Isaiah is well known for its call for justice and liberation:

> Is not this the fast that I choose:
>   to loose the bonds of injustice,
>   to undo the thongs of the yoke,
> to let the oppressed go free,
>   and to break every yoke?
> Is it not to share your bread with the hungry,
>   and bring the homeless poor into your house;
> when you see the naked, to cover them,
>   and not to hide yourself from your own kin? (Isa 58:6–7)

The passage begins by criticizing the people for serving their own interests when they fast and "lie in sackcloth and ashes" without working for justice in the community:

> Look, you serve your own interest on your fast day,
>   and oppress all your workers.
> Look, you fast only to quarrel and to fight
>   and to strike with a wicked fist. (Isa 58:3b–4a)

And the passage concludes with the promise of well-being like a "watered garden" if the people strive for justice:

> If you remove the yoke from among you,
>   the pointing of the finger, the speaking of evil,
> if you offer your food to the hungry
>   and satisfy the needs of the afflicted,
> then your light shall rise in the darkness
>   and your gloom be like the noonday.
> The LORD will guide you continually,
>   and satisfy your needs in parched places,
>   and make your bones strong;
> and you shall be like a watered garden,
>   like a spring of water,
>   whose waters never fail. (Isa 58: 9b–11)

This is a matter of care for those in need—the afflicted, the hungry, those without shelter or clothing. At least as importantly, it is a matter of seeking structural justice—economic justice so that workers are not oppressed and political justice so that quarrelling gives way to community. The watered garden, a well-watered earth, is given as the image of promise for that new community.

Finding inspiration in this passage, Benjamin Stewart titles a book *Watered Garden: Christian Worship and Earth's Ecology*. At the outset of the book, he expresses the hope that "by the power of God the Christian worshiping community and the whole wounded earth may come to flourish with renewed abundant life." Moreover, he finds this hope active in our worship on Ash Wednesday:

> One such promise may resound in our places of worship each year on Ash Wednesday, when we are newly reminded of our mortality, shown the ruins caused by our destructive sin, and told to remember, in words and with ashes, our often-forgotten basic identity as creatures made of dust, of the earth.[15]

He then quotes this passage from Isaiah 58 but continues for another verse, linking the picture of the watered garden with habitable streets:

> And you shall be like a watered garden,
>   like a spring of water,
>   whose waters never fail.
> Your ancient ruins shall be rebuilt;
>   you shall raise up the foundations of many generations;
> you shall be called the repairer of the breach,
>   the restorer of streets to live in. (Isa 58:11b–12)

Water and earth, gardens and streets, plants and people—there is a picture of ecological wholeness in this vision.

Stewart finds the "watered garden" a fertile image for Christian worship throughout the year, but he returns again to Ash Wednesday and Lent:

> We begin Lent on Ash Wednesday, being reminded that we in our bodies are made of earth, and to earth we shall return. St. Augustine said that our bodies are "the earth we carry." For a while, this earth rises up, speaks, walks, and sings. To this earth, Lent adds *water*, the waters of late winter and spring rains, the water of baptism. When earth is nourished with living water, when our bodies are bathed in the living water of Christ, the living earth (of the ground, of ourselves) grows and bears fruit.[16]

Liturgically, Ash Wednesday launches us on a Lenten journey that concludes in many churches with baptismal waters on Easter, waters of renewal and of rebirth. We see how Earth walks with us, walks in us, on this journey.

FIRST SUNDAY IN LENT

The very next stop in this Lenten journey, four days after Ash Wednesday, is the first Sunday of Lent. The Lectionaries' Gospel readings for this Sunday all begin with Jesus facing temptation in the wilderness following his own baptism in the waters of Jordan. The Old Testament lection for year A is the selection of verses from the second and third chapters of Genesis which we have already begun to discuss. In year B, the Old Testament lesson is from the ninth chapter of Genesis pertaining to God's covenant with Noah and with every living creature to preserve life on Earth. In year C, the Old Testament lesson is from Deuteronomy 26 pertaining to the offering of first fruits from the land.

All three of these readings from the Old Testament present vivid pictures of people's relationship with the natural world that can enrich Sunday worship. They all carry implications for ecological ethics, and they all pertain at some level to eating and to people procuring sustenance on the land. Chapter 26 in Deuteronomy is about giving thanks to God for the land's agricultural produce and giving thanks to God for liberation from oppression. One is enjoined to bring the first fruits of the harvest before the priest. The presenter is told to rehearse the story of the people's journey through slavery to freedom, beginning with "A wandering Aramean was my ancestor," and concluding:

> The LORD brought us out of Egypt with a mighty hand and an outstretched arm, with a terrifying display of power, and with signs and wonders, and he brought us to this place and gave us this land, a land flowing with milk and honey. So now I bring the first of the fruit of the ground that you, O LORD, have given me. (Deut 26:8–10a)

Political freedom, economic well-being, and nature's flourishing are all celebrated together as provided by God. The passage concludes with eating and sharing—not just between the presenter and priest but including aliens and strangers on the land as well: "Then you, together with the Levites and the aliens who reside among you, shall celebrate with all the bounty that the LORD your God has given to you and to your house" (Deut 26:11). The land's productivity given by God to one house is given to be shared with all the land's residents. Social caring and well-being, religious observance and practice, and nature's productivity and provision are all pictured together.

God's Covenant with All Flesh

The story of Noah and God's covenant with all flesh, a portion of which is read in year B on the first Sunday in Lent, has been of perennial inspiration for an ethics of care toward animals. Bernard Anderson, for instance, referred to the Noahic covenant as "God's universal, ecological covenant" and described it as "the hope for the human and nonhuman creation."[17] Here is theological affirmation of the inclusion of all species in God's covenantal faithfulness. The covenant with Noah is a covenant with all flesh, with all living animals, and indeed with the earth itself. The rainbow in the sky is pretty like the bow of a ribbon, but it is also like a warrior turning to peace and setting aside the weapon of bow and arrow.

> I have set my bow in the clouds, and it shall be a sign of the covenant between me and the earth. When I bring clouds over the earth, and the bow is seen in the clouds, I will remember my covenant that is between me and you and every living creature of all flesh; and the waters shall never again become a flood to destroy all flesh. (Gen 9:13–15)

It is a covenant to preserve life that is made with every animate species.

The Epistle lesson for the first Sunday in Lent for year B, 1 Peter 3:18–22, recalls this story of Noah and interprets it as symbolic of salvation in Christ, the waters carrying the ark prefiguring our baptism. There is a universal dimension of the story in this New Testament rendering as well. Animals are not mentioned here, but the earthly dead and the heavenly denizens are all brought into subjection by the proclamation of salvation through Christ's dying and rising. The animals should not be forgotten though.

There is a tragic irony for the animals, however, in the story, as told in Genesis. While God covenants to preserve the life of all species of animals, humans are now given permission to consume them as food. This was previously not the case. This part of the story of Noah is a continuation of the P or Priestly narrative in Genesis that begins with the first account of creation in seven days in Genesis 1. In that account, human beings and the other animals inhabiting the land were all created on the sixth day. The humans, the other land animals, and the birds of the air were all given plants for food:

> God said, "See, I have given you every plant yielding seed that is upon the face of all the earth, and every tree with seed in its fruit; you shall have them for food. And to every beast of the earth, and to every bird of the air, and to everything that creeps on the earth, everything that has the breath of life, I have given every green plant for food." And it was so. (Gen 1:29–30)

Now, in Genesis 9, much of the language from Genesis 1 is repeated, reminiscent of the creation account and giving a sense of new creation, of creation restored, but with a significant difference for the relationship between people and our fellow animate creatures. The lectionary reading begins at Genesis 9:8, but preceding this verse we read:

God blessed Noah and his sons, and said to them, "Be fruitful and multiply, and fill the earth. The fear and dread of you shall rest on every animal of the earth, and on every bird of the air, on everything that creeps on the ground, and on all the fish of the sea; into your hand they are delivered. Every moving thing that lives shall be food for you; and just as I gave you the green plants, I give you everything. Only, you shall not eat flesh with its life, that is, its blood. (Gen 9:1–4)

The life is in the blood, so there is still given provision for reverently respecting the life of the animals, but the consequences nevertheless are dire for them at the hands of humanity. Then, following this passage, God covenants with all these creatures to preserve them "for all future generations" (Gen 9:12).

The story of Noah in Genesis 6–9 combines elements from both the P narrative, which begins Genesis 1 with the story of creation in seven days, and the J narrative which provides the story of Adam and Even in the Garden of Eden.[18] The final redaction of Genesis with these two traditions reveals deep ironies in the ways that humanity is portrayed in relation to the rest of creation and to animals in particular. Odil Hannes Steck explicates this relationship in terms of the potential for conflict and the realization of conflict between humans and animals. In the first story of creation, according to Steck, God creates habitats on the first three days of creation and then creates inhabitants for them on the second three days of creation. The habitats created are the heavens, the seas, and the earth or land. (Plants are included as part of the habitat on earth on the third day.) The inhabitants created on the next three days are the lights in the sky, fish in the sea, birds of the air, animals on the land, and people. In this P narrative, the potential for conflict is already established on the sixth day of creation when all inhabitants of the land are created—both humans and other animate creatures, and all given the same vegetarian food to eat. This potential for violent conflict is later realized after the flood in the story of Noah when the human survivors are allowed to eat the other survivors.[19]

The potential for conflict on the sixth day of creation is apparent not only in the crowded land and the potential competition for food between humans and animals but in the articulation of blessing given by God toward the creatures in Genesis 1. On the fifth day of creation, God blesses the fish of the sea and the birds of the air with fertility: "God blessed them, saying, "Be fruitful and multiply and fill the waters in the seas, and let birds multiply on the earth" (Gen 1:22). However, on the sixth day, God creates the land animals without invoking this blessing. Rather, God pronounces this blessing of fertility on humanity after creating humans in God's image, and God places the animals—inhabitants of the air and sea as well as the land—under humanity's dominion: God blessed them, and God said to them, "Be fruitful and multiply, and fill the earth and subdue it; and have dominion over the fish of the sea and over the birds of the air and over every living thing that moves upon earth" (Gen 1:28). Instead of receiving their own blessing, the land animals are placed under human dominion.

Dominion, though, has been overstated. The theological doctrine is often termed in Latin, *dominium terrae*, which is a misnomer. It means literally dominion over the land or over the earth, but in Genesis 1 dominion is given to humans expressly over the inhabitants of the land—not the land itself and not the whole wide earth but over "every living thing that moves upon earth." It would likely refer more specifically to animal husbandry, which is an important aspect of economic life involving human interaction with animals over centuries and across cultures. Where the idea of dominion occurs again in the Bible, in Psalm 8, there is perhaps a hyperbolic acclamation that God has put "all things" under humanity's feet, but then those things actually named in the psalm are the living things that move:

> You have given them dominion over the works of your hand;
> > you have put all things under their feet,
> > all sheep and oxen,
> > > and also the beasts of the field,
> > the birds of the air, and the fish of the sea,
> > > whatever passes along the paths of the seas. (Ps 8:6–8)

Dominion simply is not *carte blanche* permission—let alone command—for humans to do whatever they want with the rest of creation. It refers to ruling over animals. Even with regard to dominion over the animals in Genesis 1, though, this is limited. Killing and eating them is not included in humanity's dominion. Still, it would seem to be a raw deal for the animals.

Finally, after the flood, the surviving land animals are given the same blessing of fertility that had been earlier bestowed on humanity, birds, and fish, "that they may abound on the earth, and be fruitful and multiply on the earth" (Gen 8:17). Earlier there had been potential for conflict between humans and animals with both inhabiting the land and depending on plants, with the provision of human dominion perhaps regulating this incipient conflict. Now it escalates into actual violence. Significantly, while the language of being fruitful and multiplying is repeated toward the human survivors of the flood, the language of dominion is not. Instead, "dominion" is replaced by "fear and dread" (Gen 9:2), as quoted earlier. Dominion had given way to consumption. Still, the life understood to be in the animals' blood had to be respected. The tragic irony here is that God's preservation of all life on Earth, and God's promise to continually preserve all life on Earth, is given this compromising provision toward human proclivity to eat meat.

To Rule and Subdue or to Till and Keep

Although dominion would seem to refer to humanity's antediluvian relationship with animals in particular rather than with the whole earth, the P narrative's language that does pertain specifically to humanity's relationship with the earth or with the land is even harsher. In Genesis 1, God blessed them, and God said to them, "Be fruitful and multiply, and fill the earth and subdue it" (Gen 1:28a). While "dominion" comes from a word meaning "to rule," *radah*, and can have a benign as well as an oppressive meaning, the word for "subdue," *kabash*, is always harsh and refers to violent subjugation. While the relationship with animals is described as "dominion," which might refer more benignly to a caring and considerate animal husbandry, the relationship with the land is cuttingly termed "subdue." To subdue the earth probably refers to the plow, an instrument that cuts into the soil in attempt to coerce produce from it. The two main means of wresting livelihood from the land in ancient Palestine—pastorally with flocks or agriculturally with crops—both seem to be invoked here with language of dominion of animals and subduing of land.[20]

That agriculture might be pictured here as violent activity is surprising to many people. Post-industrial peoples, especially people psychologically distanced from their agricultural roots, often imagine agriculture nostalgically, even romantically, as a more ecologically peaceful way of life. It is more difficult, perhaps, to see cultivation as an activity that is intrusive on Mother Earth's integrity. Yet tilling the soil seems to be pictured here in Genesis 1 as problematic activity requiring justification. That requisite justification is given in the context of blessing, but the result is an ironic dissonance which contrasts the blessing of food with the burden of subduing the soil in order to obtain it.

There is a similar ironic reversal in the J account of Adam and Eve in the Garden of Eden. After God made the first human from the "dust of the ground" (Gen 2:7) and breathed into him life, "the LORD God took the man and put him in the garden of Eden to till it and keep it" (Gen 2:15). Many have noticed that this language of tilling and keeping sounds much more benevolent toward the earth than the P narrative's language about ruling and subduing. This is so whether the phrase of tilling and keeping is interpreted as environmental stewardship or with a more egalitarian emphasis, such as Benjamin Stewart's reference to humanity's first vocation of serving and protecting the garden of the earth. Norman Habel similarly sees the phrase as indicative of human kinship with and service for the earth.[21] But this J story of creation that begins benignly in the Garden, as we have seen, concludes with a curse.

Both of these stories of creation dramatize an ironic ambivalence in humanity's relationship with the earth. The relationship is portrayed as problematic—at once both productive and painful. When the two stories are placed next to each other, as they are in the composition of Genesis, the effect is one of double irony. Each is a mirror reflection of the other. One story uses harsh language to describe a relationship in the context of blessing, and the other story using kind language to describe a relationship that concludes in curse. They portray the ambivalence that describes humanity's relationship with the earth and with fellow creatures—as both blessing and burden. These stories are not law codes. They do not really prescribe or mandate. Rather than imperatives, they are indicatives—poetically indicative of the complex relationship we have as humans with the rest of God's creation.[22]

Also, especially with regard to the original blessing of fertility and food—of the continuance of life and what is needed for life—it should be emphasized that this is blessing and not command. It is not that people are individually mandated to have children, but rather that the entire human family is blessed with progeny. Perhaps right "dominion" is a matter of ensuring that all people—both present and future—and indeed all animate species—have access to God's original blessing of life and the necessities of life. In this, blessing is a promise for a future with the flourishing of life on Earth.

With regard to the curse that occurs in the J narrative in Genesis 3, the lectionaries have us read this passage from Genesis 3 on the first Sunday of Lent in year A in conjunction with Paul's words in Romans 5:12–19 as the Epistle lesson. Paul contrasts Adam's transgression with Christ's righteousness, associating the reign of death with Adam and "life for all" (Rom 5:18) with Christ. Justification and new life in Christ are presented in universal perspective, as more than compensating for any universality of sin and death. Leander Keck refers to this as a soteriological "law of parsimony,"[23] that the saving solution must be equal to the need for salvation. It follows that if there is a universal Fall, then there must also be a universal restoration. Interpreting this fifth chapter of Romans and anticipating the eighth chapter of Romans, A. J. M. Wedderburn writes:

> The certainty of grace and the salvation (5:9–10) and reconciliation with God (5:11) that this grace has brought leads Paul on to a further conclusion, that the obedience of this one human being, Christ, has more than counteracted the baneful effects of the disobedience of our common human ancestor, Adam. This is, in its turn, a further ground for confidence in redemption from that futility to which creation was subjected according to 8:20–21, in all probability an allusion to the curse of Gen 3:14–19 that followed upon Adam's disobedience.[24]

Turning to the Gospel readings for the first Sunday in Lent, which pertain to the temptation of Jesus in the wilderness, some scholars have also interpreted this temptation in the wilderness as intimating the reversal of the curse occasioned by Adam. Sharon H. Ringe suggests that Luke's use of the title Son of God for both Jesus and Adam suggests this reversal:

> On one level, Jesus' being tested by the devil is yet another chapter in the story of the Son of God. Adam, the first son of God, failed his test by the devil (Gen 3:1–19), and thereby set all humankind at odds with God's purposes. This Son of God [Jesus], however, by passing the devil's tests, sets in motion a whole new era in God's relationship with all of humankind.[25]

Perhaps not just humankind but all of creation, animals as well as humans, might be included in this cosmic reversal beginning in the wilderness. Susan R. Garrett notes that many readers have interpreted Mark's version of the temptation in the wilderness in this manner—as Christ reclaiming the creation from curse; in the Gospel of Mark, Jesus is said to be with the "wild beasts" in the wilderness[26] (Mark 1:12–15).

From Waters to Desert

Each of the Synoptic Gospels recalls Christ's temptation in the wilderness following his baptism, and each of these three versions of Christ's temptation is offered by the lectionaries as the Gospel lesson for the three respective years of the annual cycle. All three indicate that Jesus was tempted in the desert for forty days, which duration coincides liturgically with the forty days of Lent. Matthew and Luke provide details about specific temptations, which is lacking in Mark. But Mark alone adds the phrase, "And he was with the wild beasts" (Mark 1:13). Garrett writes that for some ancient readers as well as modern interpreters of this passage, "the notice about the wild beasts would have recalled the story of Adam in the Garden of Eden."[27] "In Romans 5," she adds, "which probably predates Mark, Paul had written about Jesus as 'the last Adam,' who by his obedience reversed the effects of the first Adam's transgression."[28]

A most influential scholar positing this interpretation is Joachim Jeremias; citing both Mark 1 and Romans 5, he writes:

> The account of the temptation in Mark (1:13) shows how Jesus as the new man . . . overcame the temptation which overthrew the first man. Jesus, like Adam, is tempted by Satan. Again, as Adam was once honoured by the beasts in Paradise according to the Midrash, so Christ is with the wild beasts after overcoming temptation. He thus ushers in the paradisial state of the last days when there will be peace between man and beast. (Isa 11:6–8; 65:25)[29]

Commenting on Jeremias, Ernest Best adds: "A variant of this view sees in the presence of the wild beasts the sign of victory; as in the Messianic times harmony was expected to be recreated between [hu]man and the world of nature (Isa 11:6–9; 65:25), so this is seen to take place in the presence of the Messiah."[30] The passages cited from Isaiah picture wild and domestic animals at peace with each other—the wolf and the lamb together. This is not really a portrayal of healthy ecological relationships, but it is a vision of creatures at ease and creation at peace. That visionary hope for creaturely well-being can be seen as inaugurated in the wilderness concurrent with the inauguration of Jesus's messianic ministry.

Another interpretation of the presence of wild beasts in Mark 1:13 suggests not a peaceful community of creatures in the wilderness but rather a dangerous and threatening environment as part of the testing of Jesus. This interpretation sometimes refers to Psalm 91:13, which portrays lions and snakes inimically but assures divine protection for those who trust in God.[31] Susan R. Garrett notes these differences of interpretation of the beasts but affirms a similarity between them. "These various possible readings of Mark's testing account reinforce one another," she concludes, "each views Jesus as the faithful and righteous servant of God, who obeys or trusts God and so is protected from harm."[32] It should be added, too, that fierce or docile, it is significant that Jesus begins his ministry and that Mark begins his Gospel with the presence of these animals.

Psalm 91, which is one of the psalms urged by the lectionaries for the first Sunday in Lent, is quoted in Matthew and Luke's version of Jesus's temptation but not in Mark's. The reference in Matthew and Luke (Matt 4:6; Luke 4:10–11) is to Psalm 91:11–12, which the devil voices as temptation:

> For he will command his angels concerning you
>   to guard you in all your ways.
> On their hands they will bear you up,
>   so that you will not dash your foot against a stone. (Ps 91:11–12)

But Jesus responds in deeper resonance with the psalm's message of reliant trust in God alone for deliverance.

Matthew and Luke do not mention the wild beasts that are in Mark, but they do enumerate three particular temptations that are not in Mark's account, though the order of these three differs between Matthew and Luke. The three are to turn stone(s) into bread, to receive power and authority over all nations, and to throw himself off the pinnacle of the temple to let angels bear him up. Sharon Ringe finds these three temptations to typify three different popular expectations hoped for the messiah that might have precluded Jesus's messianic journey to the cross. She writes:

> In each of the tests, the devil proposes to Jesus that he take on one of the forms expected for God's coming Anointed One. Perhaps the awaited one would be

anointed as a prophet like Moses, who could lead the people in their wilderness—feeding them, caring for them, and preparing them to enter God's promised dwelling place. Perhaps the coming one would be a political leader, a royal messiah, who could bring the people to freedom from the rule of their enemies and then establish a reign of justice, peace, and plenty. Or the one in whom hope was lodged might come as a righteous, pure, and worthy priest, who would "live in the shelter of the Most High" and "abide in the shadow of the Almighty" in such a way that he and the whole people with him would see God's salvation. (Ps 91:1, 16)[33]

Each of these messianic roles can be seen as exercising authority within different spheres of power. The political temptation is to exercise authority over the nations, but there is also an economic temptation and a religious temptation. The religious temptation is to take charge of God's angels from the pinnacle of the temple, and the economic temptation is to generate productivity from the earth in the form of bread from rocks.

The animals from Mark's account do not factor into Matthew and Luke's telling of the temptations, but what if they did? One way of reading the temptation stories, as we have seen, is to see them as addressing the problem of the curse of the land dating from Adam's sin in the second creation story in Genesis. The reversal of that curse would be good news for all creatures! But we have read that second creation story—beginning with tilling and keeping, and concluding with curse—as entailing a double irony in conjunction with the first creation story—voicing harsh language of subduing and exercising dominion in the context of blessing all living creatures with sustenance and continuance. If we now read Mathew and Luke's version of Jesus's temptations as pertaining to exercising usurped power over human realms, heavenly realms, and over Earth itself, what might Christ's resistance to these temptations mean for our own exercise of dominion as Christ's disciples? Are there forms of power that we too should forebear? Conversely, are there forms of power that we should share or claim? What are the repercussions of our power or our renunciation of power for our fellow creatures?

Eventually, as Lent journeys to Easter and Ascension, we do find this same Jesus heralded as vested with authority over all of Heaven and Earth—Earth's creatures and Earth's nations. But with Earth's well-being in mind, what might Jesus's renunciation of power in the wilderness at the outset of his ministry mean for our own exercise or renunciation of power as we journey with him through life as well as through Lent?

A Service of Ashes

Opening Prayer[34]

> Gracious God, out of your love and mercy you breathed into dust the breath of life, creating us to serve and protect the garden of your earth. Call forth our prayers and acts of kindness, and strengthen us to face our mortality with confidence in the mercy of your Son, Jesus Christ, our Savior and Lord, who lives and reigns with you and the Holy Spirit, one God, now and forever.

Prayer of Confession such as the Litany of Sorrow from the United Nations' Environmental Sabbath program with the refrain, "We have forgotten who we are":[35]

> We have forgotten who we are
> We have alienated ourselves from the unfolding of the cosmos
> We have become estranged from the movements of the earth
> We have turned our backs on the cycles of life.
>
> **We have forgotten who we are.**
>
> We have sought only our own security
> We have exploited simply for our own ends
> We have distorted our knowledge
> We have abused our power.
>
> **We have forgotten who we are.**
>
> Now the land is barren
> And the waters are poisoned
> And the air is polluted.
>
> **We have forgotten who we are.**
>
> Now the forests are dying
> And the creatures are disappearing
> And the humans are despairing.
>
> **We have forgotten who we are.**
>
> We ask forgiveness
> We ask for the gift of remembering
> We ask for the strength to change.

Assurance of Grace (Ps 103:13–14)

> As parents care for their children, so do you, O LORD, care for those who fear you. For you yourself know whereof we are made; you remember that we are but dust.[36]

Responsive Psalm (Ps 104: 1, 10–18, 20–26; response verses 29–30)

Voice 1:

> Bless the LORD, O my soul.
> > O LORD my God, you are very great.
> You are clothed with honor and majesty. . .
> You make springs gush forth in the valleys;
> > they flow between the hills,
> Giving drink to every wild animal;
> > the wild asses quench their thirst.

Voice 2:

> *When you hide your face, they are dismayed;*
> *when you take away their breath, they die*
> *and return to their dust.*

Response:

> **When you send forth your spirit, they are created;**
> **and you renew the face of the ground.**

Voice 1:

> By the streams the birds of the air have their habitation;
> > they sing among the branches.
> From your lofty abode you water the mountains;
> > the earth is satisfied with the fruit of your work.

Voice 2:

> *When you hide your face, they are dismayed;*
> *when you take away their breath, they die*
> *and return to their dust.*

Response:

> **When you send forth your spirit, they are created;**
> **and you renew the face of the ground.**

Voice 1:

> You cause the grass to grow for the cattle,
>> and plants for people to use,
> to bring forth food from the earth,
>> and wine to gladden the human heart,
> oil to make the face shine,
>> and bread to strengthen the human heart.

Voice 2:

> *When you hide your face, they are dismayed;*
> *when you take away their breath, they die*
> *and return to their dust.*

Response:

When you send forth your spirit, they are created;
and you renew the face of the ground.

Voice 1:

> The trees of the LORD are watered abundantly,
>> the cedars of Lebanon that he planted.
> In them the birds build their nests;
>> the stork has its home in the fir trees.

Voice 2:

> *When you hide your face, they are dismayed;*
> *when you take away their breath, they die*
> *and return to their dust.*

Response:

When you send forth your spirit, they are created;
and you renew the face of the ground.

Voice 1;

> The high mountains are for the wild goats;
>> the rocks are a refuge for the coneys. . . .
> You make darkness, and it is night,
> when all the animals of the forest come creeping out.

Voice 2:

> *When you hide your face, they are dismayed;*
> *when you take away their breath, they die*
> *and return to their dust.*

Response:

**When you send forth your spirit, they are created;
and you renew the face of the ground.**

Voice 1:

The young lions roar for their prey,
   seeking their food from God.
When the sun rises, they withdraw
   and lie down in their dens.

Voice 2:

*When you hide your face, they are dismayed;
when you take away their breath, they die
and return to their dust.*

Response:

**When you send forth your spirit, they are created;
and you renew the face of the ground.**

Voice 1:

People go out to their work
   and to their labor until the evening.
O LORD, how manifold are your works!
   In wisdom you have made them all;
   the earth is full of your creatures.

Voice 2:

*When you hide your face, they are dismayed;
when you take away their breath, they die
and return to their dust.*

Response:

**When you send forth your spirit, they are created;
and you renew the face of the ground.**

Voice 1:

Yonder is the sea, great and wide,
   creeping things innumerable are there,
   living things both small and great.

There go the ships,
    and Leviathan that you formed to sport in it.

Voice 2:

When you hide your face, they are dismayed;
when you take away their breath, they die
and return to their dust.

Response:

When you send forth your spirit, they are created;
and you renew the face of the ground.

Prayer at the Ashes

Creator of Heaven and Earth, whose breath enlivens even the very soil:
We, like Job, in awe of your wondrous creation,
    turn to you with dust and ashes.
Receive us with these signs of our mortality and penitence.
Lead us through this season of Lent to Christ's cross and resurrection,
    that we might gain
        renewed reliance on your grace in every mortal moment, and
        deepened faith so as to embrace eternity with your renewed creation;
through Jesus Christ our Savior. Amen.

Words at the Imposition of Ashes:

Remember that you are dust, and to dust you shall return.

Chapter 3

Entering Jerusalem

Palm Sunday, Jewish Festivals, and Earth's Seasons

HOLY WEEK AND EASTER: POWERFUL TIMES

The crucifixion and resurrection of Jesus Christ are the climax of the Gospel story, the core of the Christian faith, and the center of the Christian liturgical year. Holy Week begins with Christ's entry to Jerusalem as reenacted on Palm/Passion Sunday, and liturgies on that day may move worshipers through the entire story of the passion culminating penultimately in Christ's death. Maundy Thursday commemorates Christ's last meal with the disciples and draws us into communion with him and with them. Good Friday marks Christ's death. Throughout these events, Earth participates. The natural world is included in the unfolding of this story and in the very salvation that is proclaimed and claimed. Though often hidden by the human pathos surrounding these events and our liturgical expression of them, the participation of the natural world in this story is palpable and is highlighted in the pages that follow. It begins with Christ's entry on an unbroken colt[1] and reaches a crescendo with Earth's quaking and rocks breaking in acclamation at Christ's crucifixion. Holy Week then moves into Easter; life interrupts death, and the earth erupts with new life, an empty tomb, a risen Christ.

The epistle reading for Palm/Passion Sunday in both the Roman Catholic Lectionary for the Mass and the Revised Common Lectionary sets the theme and the tone for the events to follow. Philippians 2:6–11 is an ancient Christological hymn placed into the context of this letter from Paul to the Philippians—Christ, though in the form of God, self-emptying, being found in human form and becoming humble and "obedient to the point of death—even death on a cross" (Phil 2:8). Abruptly this ancient hymn continues from death to exultation, "Therefore God also highly exalted him and gave him the name that is above every name, so that at the name of Jesus every knee should bend, in heaven and on earth and under the earth, and every tongue should confess that Jesus Christ is Lord" (Phil 2:9–11a). Here we have in a few short lines the jolting drama taking place: equality with God, taking human form, suffering death on the cross, and being exulted. Earth and earthly realities are invoked in this drama—all entities whether on, below, or above the earth now revere this exalted Christ who had shared intimately with us in earthly life and earthly mortality.

Two themes pertaining to Christ's relationship to Earth resound in this hymn and echo throughout Holy Week and Easter. The first is Christ's total identification with mortal life and death. The second is the acclamation of Christ's rightful reign throughout all creation and new creation—paid homage by all beings whether on the earth or surrounding the earth. While the hymn in Philippians places these themes in chronological order with exaltation following crucifixion, as have many creedal formulations since, the biblical witness as a whole does not always make this sequential separation. Indeed, the establishment of Christ's reign within creation and over any contending powers throughout creation is emphatically affirmed to have occurred on the cross as well as in the resurrection and ascension.

In whatever ways these powers might be impacting the natural world and human societies, their defeat as declared in the crucifixion, resurrection and ascension would have repercussions for both society and the natural world. The nature of these powers will be examined further in the next chapter with the discussion of Christ's crucifixion on Good Friday. There it will be seen that at the very moment when inimical powers seem so forceful in colluding to crucify Christ, they are defeated on that same cross. This is important proclamation for Palm/Passion Sunday, though, as well as for Good Friday. Palm/Passion Sunday begins Holy Week with a dual theme and with two liturgical moments. The beginning of Palm Sunday usually involves remembrance and reenactment of Christ's entry into Jerusalem with the waving of palm branches and shouts of Hosanna. The service of worship, then, usually moves from this joyous beginning to contemplate the crucifixion and the events surrounding Christ's passion. The present chapter focuses in detail on the branches and Hosannas marking Jesus's entry into Jerusalem. The next chapter deepens the reflection about Christ's passion, with attention moving to Maundy Thursday and Good Friday.

Worship leaders preparing to concentrate on events of the passion on Palm/Passion Sunday, though, are urged to move to the next chapter for such pointed consideration. There, discussion about Maundy Thursday will focus on the last supper and the unity of that meal with every other iteration of the Eucharist among believers since that time. The whole earth can be seen to be represented in the elements of Earth broken and sanctified in this meal. Also the whole earth can be seen to be present in the Body of Christ crucified and glorified. Discussion about Good Friday in the next chapter will return to the themes already introduced here—to Christ's total identification with life and death on Earth and to the question of the powers and their defeat. It will be seen that the natural world both discloses the potency of these powers and responds to their ultimate subjugation by Christ.

Although worship on Palm/Passion Sunday moves quickly from reenactment of Christ's entry to remembrance of Christ's passion, this chapter stays focused on Christ's entry into Jerusalem and the symbolism of the branches and the cries of "Hosanna." It will be noticed that these resonate with Jewish liturgies for the feast of Booths or Tabernacles (*Sukkot*) as well as the liturgy for Passover. Both Jewish festivals of Tabernacles and Passover are associated with agricultural seasons and with celebrations of nature's fecundity as well as remembrance of the people's liberation from bondage. This chapter can be seen as a kind of excursus into these symbolic links between the Jewish liturgical calendar and Christian cries of Hosanna. This excursus takes us into earthly agricultural terrain with prayers for rain and the land's productivity.[2]

HOSANNAS: PALM SUNDAY, SANCTUS, AND SUKKOT

As Jesus enters Jerusalem, the crowd greets him with branches and exclaims, quoting from verses 25 and 26 of Psalm 118, "Hosanna!" and "Blessed is the one who comes in the name of the Lord!" All four Gospels describe Christ's entry in this manner with a quotation from Psalm 118; Luke's Gospel alone omits the word "hosanna" but continues with the rest of the quotation (Matt 21:9, Mark 11:9, Luke 19:38, John 12:13). On Palm Sunday, at the beginning of morning worship, we join that crowd by reenacting that moment. We distribute branches, typically palms, and we shout "Hosanna!" "Hosanna" is a word that is defined by layers of meaning informed by layers of practice. Literally it means "save us!" and is initially voiced in the twenty-fifth verse of Psalm 118 as a petition, "Save us, we beseech you."

There are three broad areas of liturgical practice intoning "hosanna" that will be traced here. One is its use in Jewish worship as part of the Hallel collection of Psalms and especially at the conclusion of Sukkot, the annual feast of Tabernacles or the festival of Booths. The second is in annual Christian celebrations of Palm Sunday. The third is the regular reference to "hosanna" by many Christians in recitation of the *Sanctus* and *Benedictus qui venit*, particularly during the celebration of Holy Communion. These are our chants of "Holy, holy, holy . . ." and "Blessed is the one who comes in the name of the Lord. Hosanna in the highest!"

Of these three liturgical practices, the Jewish festival of Sukkot has the most overt ecological connections to the natural world and natural processes.

These ecological connections historically involve both a celebration of harvest for the produce of the land during the past year and prayers for rain in the season ahead. How might this ecological dimension of Sukkot contribute to a green understanding of the Christian liturgical practices taking place on Palm Sunday and in our Communion recitation of "Blessed is the one that comes in the name of the Lord?" How might we understand the ecological roots of these Christian practices with Sukkot tones of hosanna ringing in our Hebrew background?

This question, though, entails two challenges. The first is the challenge of conceptualizing the historical relationship between two different but related religious traditions. The second challenge is the imperative of affording respect in interreligious relationship. Historically, there are only tenuous connections between Sukkot and Jesus's entry into Jerusalem; importantly, all four gospels place this event at the time of Passover rather than Sukkot. The connection is primarily suggestive and rhetorical based on word association with "hosanna." John's Gospel alone, however, does mention the festival of Tabernacles just prior to the story of Jesus's entry into Jerusalem. John's Gospel further is the only one that specifies that the branches waved were palms. The waving of palm branches (*lulav*) is a key part of Sukkot celebration. Before attending further to Jewish Sukkot celebration and to Christian Palm Sunday celebration, however, we need first to attend to the importance for Christians to respect the integrity of Jewish tradition and worship when exploring the influence of Jewish roots on Christian thought and practice.

After reflecting on the need for Christians to respect the integrity of Jewish liturgical tradition, we will highlight some ecological dimensions of Sukkot celebration. We will then examine John's account of Jesus's entry into Jerusalem as it informs Christian Palm Sunday celebrations, and we will speculate about the relevance of earthy Sukkot symbolism for Christian annual observance of Palm Sunday. This chapter's concluding section will turn to the more frequent acclamation of "Hosanna" in the *Sanctus* and *Benedictus que venit* during Holy Communion. Recited together, they combine a reading from Psalm 118:25–26 with the call to Isaiah in Isaiah 6:3, and it will be seen that a cry of "Hosanna" is linked with the "whole earth" being full of God's glory.

Appropriation and Supersession

In her book *Preaching without Contempt,* Marilyn Salmon laments the enduring influence of supersessionist assumptions in Christian preaching and worship. She defines supersessionism as "the belief that Christianity replaced Judaism as heir of the promises of God to Israel," and she notes that this is "the conventional account of the history and theology of Christian origins."[3] She regrets especially the persistence of supersessionism among liberal Christians who value respectful relationship between Jews and Christians, who value the Hebrew roots of Christian thought and practice, and who do not view themselves as antisemitic. Nevertheless, she argues that there is an enduring tendency to define Christianity over against Judaism and to caricature Judaism in the process. She notes even the difficulty of naming the Scriptures pertaining to Jesus in relation to the Hebrew Bible. Naming them as Old and New Testaments infers such a displacement of one by the other; naming them as Hebrew Bible and Christian Testament suggests that the Hebrew Bible is not also Christian Scripture. While this may be at the level of assumption rather than doctrine, she argues, the problem persists in Christian consciousness.

Supersessionist assumptions often reveal themselves in Christian preaching which rhetorically contrasts Jesus's teachings against the teaching of the Pharisees, without recognizing the inherently Jewish nature of both. This becomes especially problematic, she notices, when preaching from the Gospel of John. John most explicitly names *Ioudaioi* (Judeans—usually translated as the "Jews") in the unfolding of the narrative about Jesus, suggesting an antagonist distinction between all Jews and Jesus and his followers. Against this globalizing interpretation, Salmon develops a more nuanced understanding of John's use of *Ioudaioi* to indicate a particular class of individuals in Judea. She interprets John in such a way as to affirm the Jewish identity of Jesus and of the Johannine community of Jews who would have been the context for the writing of this Gospel. Nevertheless, the problem of interpretation and proclamation persists, especially, she emphasizes, with regard to the passion narrative and to the remembrance of the story of the passion during the time of Holy Week.

This presents a dual challenge for Christian liturgy. We can err in either of two directions. One direction would be the crass appropriation of Jewish symbols for Christian worship without honoring their sacred use for Jews themselves. This kind of appropriation occurs, for instance, in some Christian liturgies for a Passover Seder or in the use at different times in some Christian communities of blowing a *shofar* (ram's horn). Insensitive cultural appropriation can amount to cultural theft. We can err in another direction, though, by ignoring Jewish influences within Christian worship—whether historical or continuing—and thus acknowledging neither the historical connection between them nor the potential for new meaning to emerge through the ongoing relationship between living, worshiping communities of faith.

Green Sukkot, Green Pesach, and Green Shavuot

Agricultural seasons underlie all three pilgrimage festivals or feasts associated with temple worship during ancient times and which continue to be celebrated in Jewish homes and synagogues today. These are *Sukkot* (feast of Tabernacles or Booths), *Pesach* (feast of Passover) and *Shavuot* (feast of Weeks or Pentecost). All three have their origins in Scripture, and all three are associated with agricultural seasons as well as with historical events in the life of the Hebrew people. Abraham P. Bloch writes: "A blend of agricultural and historical themes is common to all the pilgrimage festivals. On Passover the historical element is dominant and the agricultural is incidental. On Shavuot it is the reverse. On Sukkot both aspects are equally prominent."[4]

All three may have their origin in agricultural celebration to which was wedded the commemoration of historical events of religious significance.[5] Bloch observes that the three pilgrimage festivals are commanded twice in the book of Exodus, in chapter 23 and then again in chapter 34 after the incident involving the golden calf. The restatement in chapter 34 emphasizes the demand for covenantal faithfulness, "Behold I make a covenant" (Exod 34:10).[6]

Pesach

Passover is called the feast of unleavened bread in Exodus 23:15 and the festival of the paschal lamb in Exodus 34:25. Both names refer to historical events surrounding the exodus from Egypt and the liberation of the Hebrew people from slavery, but Bloch notes that the feast of unleavened bread commemorates events following the exodus, while the festival of the paschal lamb commemorates events leading up to the exodus. Passover, in either case, is coincident with Spring (Exod 23:15; 34:18; Deut 16:1), and the seasonal and agricultural dimension is symbolized in the offering and waving of the first fruits of the barley harvest (Omer or sheaves) on the second day of Passover (Lev 23:10–11).[7]

Shavuot

The symbolic waving of the Omer on the second day of Passover marks the beginning of a countdown to Shavuot (feast of Weeks or Pentecost), the counting of Omer for seven weeks throughout the traditional barley harvest until the festival of Weeks. In Deuteronomy 16:9, the seven-week countdown begins "from the time the sickle is first put to the standing grain." Shavuot is a harvest festival symbolized by the offering and waving of two loaves of bread (Lev 23:15–17), and the harvest festival for "first of all the fruit of the ground" (Deut 26:2). Shavuot also has two names, Shavuot or the feast of Weeks (Exod 34:22) and the festival of the Harvest (Exod 23:16). While the agricultural dimension is salient in Shavuot, the feast also commemorates God's deliverance of the people from slavery in Egypt to bring them to a "land flowing with milk and honey" (Deut 16:12; 26:8–9).[8] "Honey" (*devash*),

Bloch points out, "has two definitions, the honey of bees and the sap or juice of dates." He interprets the phrase "milk and honey" to refer to agricultural fecundity, "a land rich in meat (cattle), dairy, produce of the soil, and fruit."[9]

Sukkot

Sukkot, as with the other two pilgrimage festivals, also has two names: Sukkot or the festival of Tabernacles (or Booths) (Lev 23:34) and the festival of the Ingathering (Exod 23:16). Bloch explains, "The names identify two distinct holidays which coincide to form a single duo-faceted festival." While Tabernacles "commemorates God's protection in the post-exodus period," the festival of Ingathering is clearly a "harvest thanksgiving festival." Deuteronomy combines them: "You shall keep the festival of booths for seven days, when you have gathered in the produce from your threshing floor and your wine press." The festival occurs in the Fall when grapes and other fruits are harvested and wine is made.

Unique to Sukkot are the building and dwelling in booths (sukkah) and the assembly and waving of branches from three species of trees along with the fruit from a fourth. Both practices are described in Leviticus:

> On the first day you shall take the fruit of majestic trees [*hadar* in Hebrew, *etrog* in Aramaic], branches of palm trees [*lulav*], boughs of leafy trees [*hadassim*], and willows of the brook [*aravot*]; and you shall rejoice before the LORD your God for seven days. You shall keep it as a festival to the LORD seven days in the year; you shall keep it in the seventh month as a statute forever throughout your generations. You shall live in booths for seven days; all that are citizens in Israel shall live in booths, so that your generations may know that I made the people of Israel live in booths when I brought them out of the land of Egypt: I am the LORD your God. (Lev 23:40–43)

Although three species of trees are included, the entire set has come to be called by the name of the date palm, *lulav*. Willows and myrtle comprise the other two, and the citron is considered to be the fruit of majestic trees—four species in all.

While the symbolism of these four species is not made specific in Scripture, Bloch asserts that the text from Leviticus cited earlier "gives the unmistakable impression that the motif of the *lulav* ritual is a thanksgiving for the bounteous harvest."[10] He acknowledges that it is surprising that the four species are "hardly likely to be found in the harvest which the average farmer removes from the fields" but still sees them as "selected samples of the harvest, which one must hold in his hand and rejoice before the Lord" (Lev 23:40).[11] Citing the description of a fecund promised land in Deuteronomy 8:7–8, Bloch finds all three species of trees named in that description and concludes that "the *lulav* ritual is a thanksgiving rite which reflects God's fulfillment of his promise of a 'good land.'"[12]

Sukkot also marked the beginning of the rainy season, and the four species of plants came to be associated with water and prayer for rain. Sukkot was thus an occasion not only to offer thanks for the productivity of the past agricultural year, but it also offered an occasion of prayerful hope for rain and continued productivity in the year ahead. Arthur Schaffer notes that there are two distinct seasons in this part of the world. Rain falls from September or October to April and soaks the soil. "*Sukkot*," he observes, "marks the major climatic changes of the year which delimits the end of one agricultural cycle and the anticipated beginning of the next." Daily prayers for rain begin at the conclusion of Sukkot and continue until the beginning of Passover in the Spring, since hard rain after that point can damage crops. "In many respects," writes Schaffer, "water is the dominant theme of the 'Festival of the Harvest,'" and he finds water to be symbolized in all four species of plants.[13]

"In truth," Schaffer continues, "the four species uniquely and specifically represent water, in a manner that bears uncontestable evidence to our ancestors' intimate familiarity with the native flora and ecology of Israel." The willow grows by or even in water in the river valleys. The palm grows by oases amid the desert. The myrtle grows in "riverine thickets" in the hills and mountainous regions. The citron grows in areas under cultivation. Schaffer speculates that these ecological relationships became less obvious to Jewish people after the diaspora into other lands, as did the apparently obvious symbolism of these plants with water.[14] Nevertheless, in the second century CE, Rabbi Eliezer saw these plants as symbolic of the importance of water for the whole world: "Seeing that these four species [*lulav, etrog, hadas, aravah*] are intended only for intercession for water, therefore as these cannot [grow] without water, so the world cannot exist without water" (*Taanit* 2b).[15]

In addition to the waving of the *lulav*, other liturgical aspects of Sukkot point to the importance of water and prayer for water. Every morning during Sukkot, libations of water are made at the altar, symbolizing prayer for rain.[16] Also every morning during Sukkot willow branches (the plant most obviously associated with water) are placed on the altar.[17] Moreover, willows are featured on the final day of Sukkot in a ritual titled "beating the aravot." In this ritual, willow branches are distributed to members of the congregation who beat them on the ground until they are defoliated. "The significance of the beating of aravot," Bloch writes, "may be best understood if it is viewed in the context of a ritual intercession for water." It may be that this is a gesture of prayer for watered ground. Bloch, however, finds symbolism in the willow's ritual destruction. Since willows are notorious for consuming water, Bloch suggests, the defoliation of the willow is "a symbolic gesture of water preservation as one was about to pray for rain."[18] Daily prayer for rain, as mentioned earlier, commences at the conclusion of Sukkot and concludes in the Spring with Passover.

The final day of Sukkot, on which the willows are ritually defoliated, is called *Hoshana Rabba* (many hosannas) due to the multiple prayers of "*hosha na*" recited during the morning service.[19] The prayer of *hosha na*, or hosanna, is from Psalm 118:25: "Save us, please . . ."[20] This verse and Psalm 118 are part of a collection of Psalms (Ps 113–118) called the Hallel, which are read during all the pilgrimage festivals as well as on other Jewish holidays. Throughout Sukkot and especially on *Hoshana Rabba*, however, there is an extensive litany of prayers with the congregational response of "*hosha na*." The *lulav* (palm fronds together with branches of the other two species of trees) and *etrog* (citron) feature prominently throughout the service. Worshipers holding *lulav* and *etrog* wave them in six directions: four compass points, heavenward, and downward. They process around the synagogue along with the Torah scroll, shaking the *lulav* and chanting *hosha na* in response to each petition. The service concludes with the defoliation of the willow branches.

Throughout Sukkot, concluding with *Hoshana Rabba*, the earthy context of worship is palpable. The new prayer book for conservative synagogues introduces the *Hoshanot* for Sukkot as follows:

> While on the High Holy Days we have moved inward, reflecting on our lives, contemplating past behavior as well as new directions, on Sukkot we are thrust back into our physical reality. Entering the *sukkah*—no longer protected by our home's four walls—we are aware of our physical vulnerability. Waving the *lulav* and *etrog* toward the four winds and heaven and earth reminds us of our spatial existence, the world around us—our dependence on the air we breathe, the harvest that sustains us, and the ground we stand on. In these ways, Sukkot is the most physical of holidays and so we should not be surprised that what we pray for as the holiday comes to its conclusion is our physical sustenance.[21]

While every day of Sukkot is marked by a procession with *lulav* and the chanting of *hosha na*, on *Hoshana Rabba* as the final day of Sukkot, there are seven circuits of procession. This prayer book gives the themes for the prayers during each of these circuits as follows: (1) For Your Sake, (2) The temple in Jerusalem, (3) The People Israel, (4) God the Deliverer of a Good Harvest, (5) Nature, (6) A Prayer for the Harvest, and (7) Fire. Here is the English translation for the petitions for the circuit of Nature; after each phrase chanted by the leader, the congregation responds, "*hosha na*."

> *Hosha na*, please save both humans and animals • flesh, soul, and spirit • tissue, bone, and skin • that form shapes, images, and figures • save the human whose glory is fleeting • so like animals • but beautiful, handsome, and upright • renew the face of the earth • the trees that breathe • olive groves and fields of grain •

grape arbors and fruit orchards • planted on the famed land • with dew yielding fragrant bounty • and rain sustaining life • may plants grow tall • and come joyously into their own • let flowers burst forth • emerging in fullness • let cold rain stream down • pouring rain fill the canals • exalting the earth • suspended in the ether. *Hosha na, please save us!*[22]

Palm Sunday and the Gospel of John

There is obvious similarity between the *Hoshanot* (prayers of hosanna) procession with *lulav* during the Jewish festival of Sukkot and the practice of Christians to celebrate Palm Sunday with palms, procession, and praises of hosanna. These Christian celebrations on the Sunday before Easter reenact Jesus's entry into Jerusalem as told in the Gospels. As mentioned earlier, all four of the Gospels depict Jesus entering Jerusalem as the crowd welcomes him with quotes from Psalm 118. All but Luke have the crowd gathering tree branches and shouting "hosanna" from the twenty-fifth verse of Psalm 118 followed by the twenty-sixth verse. Luke omits the branches and the hosannas but does include the twenty-sixth verse: "Blessed is the King who comes in the name of the Lord." In Mark and Matthew, the crowd places the branches on the road. The Gospel of John alone, however, specifies branches of "palm trees" and presumably has the crowd holding the palm branches—not saying anything about spreading them on the road. However, all four gospels place this event at the time of Passover—not Tabernacles.

In fact, only John mentions the feast of Tabernacles. John is unique among the Gospels both with regard to a greater attentiveness to Jewish celebrations held at the temple in Jerusalem and with regard to repeated appearances of Jesus in Jerusalem. Mark and Matthew place Jesus in Jerusalem only at the conclusion of their Gospels as he faces the events surrounding his crucifixion around the time of Passover. Luke adds to this, near the beginning of the Gospel in chapter 2, two appearances of Jesus in Jerusalem: the first following his circumcision and the second for Passover when he was twelve years old. John, however, repeatedly places Jesus in Jerusalem. While the other Gospels present the pericope of Jesus cleansing the temple as part of the final days, John presents this story early (John 2:13–25) at a prior occasion of Passover. In John 5:1, Jesus visits Jerusalem again for an unnamed festival. In chapter 7 of John, Jesus goes to the temple in Jerusalem for the feast of Tabernacles. Jesus returns to Jerusalem again in John 10:22–39 for the festival of the Dedication (Hanukkah) in the winter. Finally, Jesus enters Jerusalem ahead of Passover in chapter 12 (verses 12–19), in the manner celebrated with palms and hosannas, and stays there through his crucifixion.

The historical event that is pivotal in providing the context for writing the Gospel of John, as for all the Gospels, would be the destruction of the temple in 70 CE. The Gospel was being written at a time when the temple no longer existed, and the temple ceremonies no longer performed—at least not in the temple. The entire Jewish community, including the Johannine Jewish community, faced the challenge of finding continuity of religious expression, of religious identity, and of religious fidelity when the central symbol of that religious life and faith, the temple, had been decimated. Part of the rabbinical response to this problem was to shift performance of certain rites and ceremonies to the home and the synagogue.[23] Such was the case with much of the ceremony surrounding Sukkot that has been discussed earlier. The Gospel of John's portrayal of Jesus might also be seen as written after the destruction of the temple in order to inform faithful response within the Johannine Jewish community in the face of this historic challenge.

The literary and theological strategy deployed in John to address the challenge of maintaining religious fidelity, given the temple's destruction in 70 CE, might be seen as follows. By placing Jesus frequently in Jerusalem and at the temple, John identifies Jesus with Jerusalem and with the temple and temple ceremonies. The Gospel of John then spiritualizes that relationship, ironically transforming defeat into victory—both the defeat of crucifixion and—by this symbolic identity between the two—the devastated temple.

Here is a synopsis of the sequence of events in the unfolding of the plot. "My hour has not yet come," (John 2:4) says Jesus at the wedding in Cana immediately prior to his first Passover visit to Jerusalem when, in John's Gospel, he cleanses the temple of the money changers and speaks cryptically about the "temple of his body" (John 2:21). In chapter 7, following Jesus teaching in the temple at Sukkot, there is an attempt to arrest him that comes to naught because "his hour had not yet come" (John 7:30). On the final day of Sukkot which would have been *Hoshana Rabba*, on "the great day," according to John, Jesus declares: "Let anyone who is thirsty come to me, and let the one who believes in me drink. As the Scripture has said, 'Out of the believer's heart shall flow rivers of living water'" (John 7:37–38). Water, it will be recalled, is a central theme of Sukkot.

Finally at Passover, immediately following his entry into Jerusalem with the palm branches and the hosannas, Jesus declares to his disciples, "The hour has come for the Son of Man to be glorified" (John 12:23). He further ponders, "What should I say—'Father, save me from this hour? No, it is for this reason that I have come to this hour'" (John 12:27). Just before the festival of Passover, "Jesus knew that his hour had come to depart from this world and go to the Father" (John 13:1). And at the conclusion of the farewell discourse, Jesus prays: "Father, the hour has come; glorify your Son so that the Son may glorify you" (John 17:1). Then at last from the cross, "It is finished" (John 19:30).

Pivotal in this story is the entry into Jerusalem. It is the turning point from "my hour is not yet" to "his hour had come." "Hosanna" marks that pivotal point. The entry into Jerusalem occurs in John's telling of the story between the two festivals: Sukkot and Passover. Chronological time here is giving way to liturgical time in the rhetorical structure. It's as if sacred time is collapsing into this moment and the events that follow. Tabernacles and Passover are both present in this ride into Jerusalem. "Hosanna" itself resounds with ambiguity as both the plea for salvation and the acclamation of victory. Even so, when "it is finished" on the cross, it is both ending and fulfillment, both life's conclusion and glorification.

Applying an ecological hermeneutical lens to our worship, then, the question that arises is this: if Christian celebrations of Palm Sunday resound with echoes of Sukkot, how can the sounds of Sukkot associated with Earth's productivity be amplified within these occasions of Christian worship? Christians already wave palm branches and shout hosanna. How might these actions also recall the growth of plants, the provision of food, the sending of rains? How might Palm Sunday recover something of the prayers for a watered earth's productivity that has historically characterized Sukkot?

Of course it is possible simply to borrow prayers, such as the *Hoshanot* for the circuit of Nature and integrate them into Palm Sunday processions. We do similar borrowing all the time, hopefully with attribution. But the borrowing becomes more complex when it is from the official prayer book of another religion. Respectful interreligious relationships would suggest that we consult with rabbis or cantors from the other religious organization about appropriate use.

There is wide latitude among many Christian denominations and congregations in the ways that Palm Sunday can be celebrated. Respectful integration of Sukkot prayers into the liturgy with palms seems distinctly possible and desirable. Great care needs to be taken, however, when moving from an opening Palm Sunday procession that might include Jewish prayers to the remainder of the liturgy pertaining to Christ's passion. Such transitions are already awkward in many congregations—sometimes intentionally abrupt in order to emphasize the shift of mood in the crowd from one of welcome to one of crucifixion. Simply reading the passion narrative without further homiletic interpretation, as is often done, can reinforce popular assumptions that vilify the Jews and that further a supersessionist rendering of the story. A more generous and nuanced understanding of the relationship between Jewish communities in the first century needs to be provided within the time for proclamation on Palm/Passion Sunday and throughout Lent and Holy Week. Implications for respectful relations between our contemporary religious communities also need to be made explicit.

Palm/Passion Sunday is liturgically crowded, however, limiting the opportunity to preach and thus problematizing liturgical expression. Without making meaning explicit, symbols carry implicit meaning. These assumed and implicit meanings can remain most powerful in participants' minds even when alternative frameworks of interpretation are explicitly provided. This is a perennial point to hermeneutics: listeners bring their own meaning to words, gestures, and symbols. The preacher and the liturgist never have complete control over the messages conveyed to others in their words and actions. Indeed, the more powerful and multivalent the symbols involved, the more difficult it is to narrow their received meaning with the precision intended by the speaker.

Another opportunity for introducing Sukkot imagery to a Christian congregation and providing homiletic interpretation would be Sukkot itself. Sukkot occurs in the Fall during liturgically ordinary time for Christians, allowing for more focused concentration on Sukkot itself. A local rabbi or cantor could be invited to come to the congregation with symbols of Sukkot and help lead in congregational prayer. The invitation might be very much welcomed. In Deuteronomy 16:14, people are enjoined to include everyone resident in the community in observance of the festival: "Rejoice during your festival, you and your sons and your daughters, your male and female slaves, as well as the Levites, the strangers, the orphans, and the widows resident in your towns." Having experienced something of Sukkot during Sukkot, Christians might then be better predisposed to hear and appreciate Sukkot symbolism in the palms waved and hosannas sung on Palm Sunday later in the Spring—including Sukkot symbolism grounded in the earth.

A more cryptic point of connection between Christian worship and Sukkot is the frequent use of the *Sanctus* and *Benedictus qui venit* in many congregations during the Communion liturgy. The *Benedictus qui venit* is originally from Psalm 118:26, "Blessed is the one who comes in the name of the LORD." This verse follows immediately after verse 25 which voices the prayer of "Hosanna . . ." The version used by most Christian congregations, though, is actually Matthew's citation of this psalm in Matthew's version of Jesus's entry into Jerusalem and concludes, "Hosanna in the highest!" The *Benedictus qui venit* is thus directly linked to the welcoming of Jesus into Jerusalem as celebrated on Palm Sunday.

The *Sanctus* is originally from Isaiah 6:3, "Holy, holy, holy . . ." It is also a repeated refrain in Jewish worship, including worship during Sukkot, "*Kadosh, kadosh, kadosh*." Jewish worship, however, stays with a literal reading of Isaiah 6:3 proclaiming, "The whole earth is full of [God's] glory." Christian liturgies amend this with certain variations to the verse from Isaiah, including the introduction of heaven, "Heaven and earth are full of your glory." Personally, I have a preference for the Jewish and original version. I would prefer to keep it earthy. In Christian use of the *Sanctus*, the *Sanctus* is often introduced by Cherubim and Seraphim and the whole company of heaven. It is important that we situate ourselves and our Communion within the wider fellowship of saints. But with so many indicators pointing heavenward, it is easy to lose sight of the ground beneath our feet. The whole earth is full of God's glory.

Waving toward the ground as well as toward the sky, toward all four compass points, the whole earth is full of God's glory. With fruit of majestic trees, branches of palm trees, boughs of leafy trees, and willows of the brook, the whole earth is full of God's glory. Having provided us already with food and water, and hoping to continue to provide in years ahead food and water, the whole earth is full of God's glory.

The Gospel of Luke is the only Gospel providing neither hosannas nor leafy branches when Jesus enters Jerusalem. But Luke alone has rocks: "If these were silent, the very stones would cry out" (Luke 19:40). Indeed the stones do cry out; the waters cry out; the plants cry out; the earth cries out. Hosanna! The whole earth is full of God's glory.

A SERVICE OF PALMS

Call to Worship: Psalm 118: [19–20] 24–27 (This psalm can be read or sung responsively,[24] or it can be read or sung as a litany with interjected responses of "Hosanna!" or with verse 25 read as a response: "Save us, we beseech you, O LORD!")

Collect (based on Phil 2:5–11):

> Christ our Sovereign, honored this day as centuries ago with festal branches:
> receive us with you in your entry to Jerusalem and on your journey to the cross,
> that witnessing both your humility in death and your exaltation in glory,
> our acclamation this day might be joined with every tongue confessing and
> every knee bending "in heaven and on earth and under the earth" that you
> indeed are Sovereign; to the glory of God. Amen.

Distribution of the palms to worshipers (may occur here or following the thanksgiving over the palms below or earlier as people gather).

Thanksgiving over the Palms:

Blessed are you, O Lord our God, Ruler of the Universe!

When you created the earth, you planted it and watered it, making this a habitable place.

You made animals and humanity out of the same elements of soil from which plants grow.

Season after season, through innumerable years, you continue to send rains to water the earth, bringing productivity to wilderness and to pasture and to cultivated fields. By your provision we are fed, and by your grace we are nurtured in body and spirit.

When your people were oppressed in Egypt, you liberated them with signs of your power throughout creation. You sustained them in the wilderness, giving them food to eat and water to drink, and led them to a land flowing with milk and honey. You commanded annual observances commemorating your gracious acts. You told them: "Take the fruit of majestic trees, branches of palm trees, boughs of leafy trees, and willows of the brook; and you shall rejoice before the LORD your God."[25] Each year your acts of salvation are celebrated, as we do now on this day, chanting "Hosanna" with those who have come before:

> **Hosanna! "Save us we beseech you, O LORD!**
> **O LORD, we beseech you, give us success!**[26]

When tyrants invaded to colonize and oppress, "hosanna" has continued to be your people's prayer, that you would send a liberator to establish your own reign of justice among us. We remember how Jesus was welcomed to Jerusalem with such a hope on the lips and in the hearts of the people. With them, we welcome him this day, waving branches and chanting:

> **Hosanna! "Save us we beseech you, O LORD!**
> **O LORD, we beseech you, give us success!**
> **Blessed is the one who comes in the name of the LORD.**[27]

Bless our worship this day as we process with prayer and praise, with palms and psalms. Bless the branches we wave, that these plants might place us with Christ as his parade proceeds toward his passion. Hosanna!

> **Hosanna! Blessed is the one who comes in the name of the LORD.**[28]

Distribution of the palms if this has not already occurred

Gospel lesson: John 12:12–16 (or Synoptic parallels)

Procession with songs of Hosanna!

Chapter 4

Christ's Passion

Maundy Thursday and Good Friday

> Then take the towel, and break the bread,
> and humble us and call us friends.
> Suffer and serve till all are fed
> and show how grandly love intends
> to work till all creation sings,
> to fill all worlds, to crown all things.[1]
>
> —Brian Wren

On Ash Wednesday the season of Lent begins with an acknowledgment of our creaturely mortality as human beings. On Palm Sunday, we are drawn with Jesus into Jerusalem and into the depths of his communion with us—in life, in death, in creation, in eternity. Throughout Holy Week there is a contending of powers—culminating in the events of Good Friday and then the astonishing turn of events on Easter Sunday. On Maundy Thursday our communion with Christ is enacted with bread and wine and remembered as Christ's body and blood. With the conclusion of the Lenten season, Good Friday shows how profound is this communion, indeed, and how deeply Christ shares mortal nature with us and with creation. With us and with all creaturely life, Christ dies. The identification is complete.

The Revised Common Lectionary follows the Roman Catholic Lectionary in rotating through the three Synoptic versions of Christ's passion for each of the three years of the lectionary for Palm/Passion Sunday, and both lectionaries provide the passion story from John for the Gospel reading on Good Friday every year. Worship leaders in congregations with greater freedom in their use of the lectionary, though, can choose to read from any of the four Gospels in any given year on either Palm/Passion Sunday or Good Friday. The reflections in this chapter are based on the story of Christ's crucifixion as presented to us in all four Gospels which do differ from each other. Also, reflections here turn to various passages from the Epistles pertaining to the cross of Christ, regardless of whether or not these passages occur in the lectionaries specifically for either Palm/Passion Sunday or Good Friday.

MAUNDY THURSDAY AND COMMUNION: THESE THY CREATURES

Gathering on Maundy Thursday, we participate in a meal. Earthly elements are gathered with us: bread and wine in the meal itself and water in the washing of feet. "The cup of blessing which we bless," writes Saint Paul, "is it not a participation in the blood of Christ? The bread which we break" Paul continues, "is it not a participation in the body of Christ?" (1 Cor 10:16 RSV). The word "participation" is one English translation of *koinōnia* , which is also translated as "fellowship" or as "communion." Our fellowship, our communion, is one of participation with one another in the body of Christ and our participation with one another as the body of Christ. The bread and wine are identified with this participation; in fact, they are identified as this participation. Our participation, our communion, our fellowship is with one another, with Christ our head, and with the elements of Earth. These earthly elements which continually sustain us in body now participate with us in this meal pertaining to our very salvation. Our salvation incorporates these elements present in the meal.

"What a holy depth of meaning lies waiting for our understanding," Joseph Sittler exclaims, "in that moment portrayed on the last evening of Christ's life" when Jesus blessed and shared bread and wine. "Here in one huge symbol are God and [hu]man and nature together," Sittler continues, "Bread and wine, the common earthy stuff of our life when we have it, and of death when we've lost it" are held at the last supper in the hands of the one we now confess to be both human and divine, facing his own death in the hours ahead.[2]

We have begun to affirm two particular aspects of this depth of meaning. Informed by Orthodox theology of *theosis*, we have seen creation's transfiguration prefigured in the lifting and blessing of the communion elements as well as in humans' priestly representation of creation through participation in the Eucharist. Also, informed by a respect for the Jewish liturgical year and the agricultural cycles historically concurrent with major Jewish feasts, we have attended to the symbolism of food. "Hosanna" sounds a prayer for Earth's productivity that seems to echo in the Christian liturgy of bread and cup.

It can be seen that these two themes point our attention in different directions chronologically—both to the past and to the future. In speculating about connections between Christian liturgy and Jewish liturgy, and the link between Jewish worship historically and agriculture, our attention is drawn to the past and to all of salvation history as remembered and recalled in the liturgies for Pesach and Sukkot. We might ask: How does the land itself and the promise of milk and honey, of vine and fig tree, factor into this remembering and retelling? In other words, how is creation history related to salvation history in our memory and in our liturgy?

Conversely, though, our attention to transfiguration looks toward creation's promise; it is directed toward creation's future and indeed toward eschatology. When Saint Paul quotes Jesus as having said, "do this in remembrance of me" (1 Cor 11:24–25), this can be fathomed as a very broad and very deep memory, recalling the whole history of salvation and at the same time anticipating the future of renewed creation. Past and future are focused on this moment when Jesus breaks bread and passes the cup. Past and future are focused again on each moment when we eat and drink this meal with Christ and invoke this memory in our fellowship. In many ways, the "last supper" can be seen to be the "first supper," the first of many for the followers of Jesus and inaugurating hope for creation.

This section looks further at the participation of the world of nature in this meal and the implications this meal holds for nature's benediction. The previous chapter examined some of the possible connections the Eucharist might hold with salvation history, Jewish liturgy, and agriculture. We turn now in this section toward the soteriological promises for creation anticipated in our celebrations of the Eucharist. In doing so, we return to the Orthodox practice of lifting up the elements, and we will find parallel actions and meanings in other traditions of the ecumenical church.

At the outset of our Lenten journey, when viewing the transfiguration, we appreciated an Orthodox perspective that recognizes the participation of all creation in the earthly elements of the communion meal. This participation prefigures creation's transfiguration along with these elements and promises the material world's regeneration and transformation in new creation. As our salvation as human creatures is effected by Christ and enacted at this supper, creation's transfiguration is enacted as well. From this perspective, we can view all of creation being present in the bread and wine and being sanctified with the bread and the wine. As humans, we are able to serve as priests for creation in this sacrament—bringing the earth with us to be blessed and sanctified. As flesh and blood, we represent creaturely reality for spiritual blessing and, as the image of God, we represent the Creator's love for our fellow creatures. Christology is at the center of this hope. Christ as the perfect image of God draws all humanity and creation with us toward a greater likeness in a process of *theosis*, termed variously as deification, divinization, or sanctification. The link between ourselves and Christ as our savior is established in the incarnation and continues in the resurrection.

Patriarch Bartholomew, known as the Green Patriarch, declares:

> In the bread and wine of the Eucharist, as priests standing before the altar of the world, we offer the creation back to the Creator in the context of a mutual relation to [the Creator] and to each other. Indeed, in our liturgical life, we realize by anticipation the final state of the cosmos in the kingdom of heaven. We celebrate the beauty of creation and consecrate the life of the world, returning it to God with thanks. We share the world in joy as a living mystical communion with the Divine. Thus we offer the fullness of creation at the Eucharist, and receive it back as a blessing, as the living presence of God.[3]

All of creation and all of creation's history are included in eucharistic offering and consecration—from creation's primordial beginnings to creation's eschatological fulfillment. From this sacramental perspective, eschatology is not denigrating of the world but rather affirming and fulfilling of it and of earthly life. John Chryssavgis defines eschatology not just as "last-ness" of things but of the "'lastingness' of things."[4]

There is a similar theological identity between the elements and the whole of creation in the Western church. Geoffrey Wainwright has noted among Roman Catholic theologians this idea "to bring the consecration of the Eucharistic bread and wine into relation with the notion of a transfigured creation."[5] The recent papal encyclical by Pope Francis, *Laudato Si'*, brings to fruition Roman Catholic social teaching, linking the call for social justice with need for ecological care. In it, Pope Francis speaks of creation's transfiguration and divinization as represented in the Eucharist:

> It is in the Eucharist that all that has been created finds its greatest exaltation. . . . In the Eucharist, fullness is already achieved; it is the living centre of the universe, the overflowing core of love and inexhaustible life. Joined to the incarnate Son, present in the Eucharist, the whole cosmos gives thanks to God. Indeed the Eucharist is itself an act of cosmic love: "Yes, cosmic! . . ." The Eucharist joins heaven and earth; it embraces and penetrates all creation. The world which came forth from God's hands returns to [God] in blessed and undivided adoration; in the bread of the Eucharist, "creation is projected towards divinization, towards the holy wedding feast, towards unification with the Creator . . ." Thus, the Eucharist is also a source of light and motivation for our concerns for the environment, directing us to be stewards of creation.[6]

Pope Francis also cites Patriarch Bartholomew regarding the "world as a sacrament of communion" where "the divine and the human meet in the slightest detail in the seamless garment of God's creation, in the last speck of dust of our planet."[7]

Anglican and Methodist liturgical traditions also show elements of a connection between creation, communion, and eschatology. Our creaturely fellowship with the communion elements of bread and wine is already noticeable in the old words of the Anglican *Book of Common Prayer* found in the editions from the sixteenth and seventeenth centuries which refer to the bread and wine as "creatures." The prayer of invocation in the 1552 edition reads: "Grant that we, receiving these thy creatures of bread and wine, according to thy son our saviour Jesus Christ's holy institution, in remembrance of his death and passion, may be partakers of his most blessed body and blood."[8] This language continued into the 1662 edition, which remained the official *Book of Common Prayer* through the most of the millennium. It was this exact language that John Wesley chose for the American Methodists when he provided them with an order for the celebration of the Lord's Supper in 1784.[9] The language from this order of worship has been repeated in the prayer books and services of Methodist denominations through the years and continues to be used by some, notably the African Methodist Episcopal Church and the African Methodist Episcopal Zion Church.[10]

Most recent versions of both Methodist and Episcopalian eucharistic prayers, though, have abandoned this reference to the bread and wine as "creatures," often substituting instead reference to them as "gifts of bread and wine." The language of "gifts" for naming the communion elements is deeply historical. Ostensibly, though, the move away from the word "creatures" was made because of popular perceptions of "creatures" as referring to animals. But theologically all entities within creation are God's creatures. The language of "gifts," on the other hand, implies to many minds possession rather than mutual relationship or dependence on God's generativity. Interestingly, the original *Book of Common Prayer*, Thomas Cranmer's Prayer Book of 1549, contained both: "Hear us (O merciful father) we beseech thee: and with thy holy spirit and word vouchsafe to bless and sanctify these thy gifts, and creatures of bread and wine, that they may be unto us the body and blood of thy most dearly beloved son Jesus Christ."[11] The language of "creatures," while perhaps sounding arcane, reinforces a sense of commonality between partakers and that of which we partake—fellow creatures within creation being transformed by God's grace into new creation.

Creation and new creation are both present and intermingled in the sacrament, as are heaven and earth. Indeed, also comingled are spirit and flesh, symbol and symbolized, and past and future.

On Maundy Thursday, remembering and reliving the last supper, time points back toward previous historic manifestations of God's salvation, notably the exodus as commemorated during the Passover. It also points forward to the future in the fullness of blessing. "I tell you," Jesus says to the disciples at that last supper, "I will never again drink of this fruit of the vine until that day when I drink it new with you in my Father's kingdom" (Matt 26:29). Not only does the meal and the soteriological symbolism of the meal point backward and forward through time; the meal and its symbolism extend out broadly to incorporate every meal. "Do this, as often as you drink it, in remembrance of me," Paul quotes Jesus in 1 Corinthians and explains, "For as often as you eat this bread and drink the cup, you proclaim the Lord's death until he comes" (1 Cor 11:25b–26).

The connection between Holy Communion and earthly beatitude can also be affirmed in Wesleyan theology. John Wesley encouraged frequent communion among Methodists and communed frequently himself. For John Wesley, the material elements were important to the rite; he was critical of more spiritualist practices that eschewed bodily ingestion of bread and wine.[12] Also for John Wesley, action was important; he was critical of Communion services that extended verbal exposition extensively into the meal itself.[13]

The Lord's Supper, the promise of heaven, and earthly existence are eloquently connected in a collection of 166 eucharistic hymns written and published by John and Charles Wesley, which include twenty-three hymns in a section titled "The Sacrament a Pledge of Heaven." J. Ernest Rattenbury interprets these hymns as demonstrating "realized eschatology."[14] This realized eschatology can be seen to extend in two directions at once. Most literally, it extends toward heaven and heavenly salvation as we share in a foretaste of heavenly banquet and blessing. This is poetically described as "earnest" or "pledge" of heaven. Horizontally, though, as the whole earth awaits transformation and regeneration, creation and new creation are present in the communion meal. Hymn 101 from this collection assures:

> The light of life eternal darts
>   Into our souls a dazzling ray,
> A drop of heaven o'erflows our hearts,
>   And deluges the house of clay.
>
> Sure pledge of ecstasies unknown
>   shall this Divine communion be;
> The ray shall rise into a sun,
>   The drop shall swell into a sea.[15]

The earthly eschatological direction does not displace the heavenly direction, as the Wesleys' theology was framed within metaphysical dualism. Rather, they affirm that we receive heavenly benediction even now in the experience of earthly salvation. Hymn 116 from this collection intones:

> We need not now go up to Heaven
>   To bring the long-sought Saviour down,
> Thou art to All already given:
>   Thou dost ev'n Now thy Banquet crown.[16]

In recent years, Methodist theologians have recovered this more earthly dimension and given it greater emphasis with ecological interpretation and ramifications. So, for instance, Hoyt Hickman, in his introductory guide for United Methodist worship, writes: "Joyous celebration of the whole range of God's mighty acts contrasts with the overwhelming preoccupation with Jesus' death that gave previous communion texts their funereal tone. We celebrate the joy of God's creation."[17] Quoting the words of the prayer at Communion that "'we may be for the world the body of Christ' and 'one in ministry to all the world,'" Hickman reminds that "the term 'the world' includes not only human beings but an ecological concern for the whole world."[18]

Laurence Hull Stookey interprets the Eucharist with reference to five themes: creation, covenant, Christ at the center, church, and the coming Kingdom. Concerning the theme of creation in the Eucharist, Stookey writes:

> Creation is intended to reveal God's love to all created things. The Eucharistic meal is about sharing—sharing both with all people (particularly those who are not permitted to see divine goodness because greed has kept God's bounty from them) and with the whole created order.[19]

He notes further that "human responsibility in relation to creation" is represented in the bread and wine, which are products of human labor with the natural gifts of creation. He enjoins:

> Thus what we eat and drink at the Table of the Lord suggests cooperation between Creator and creature as we are called responsibly to tend, prepare, and share with one another. Needless to say, the bread and wine at the Lord's Table also imply the need to care for the environment, even if this demands self-sacrifice.[20]

Regarding the relationship between heaven and earth in the sacrament of Holy Communion, Stookey eschews escapist understandings of heaven in favor of an interpretation that connects past and future with the present. The Eucharist points to a redemptive hope for creation requiring human activity and made possible by divine activity on Earth. The idea of heaven does not preclude but rather inspires this human response of hope and action on Earth. Stookey writes: "Established and sustained by Christ, who has inaugurated the new creation and the new covenant, the church proclaims the fulfillment of God's purpose. That fulfillment often goes under the shorthand term *heaven*."[21] And he continues:

> The Eucharist is the feast of the whole church as it participates in and yet awaits the perfect reign of God. And what we expect to become, we seek to be now. The future of God is not some escapist notion that allows us to make peace with

unrighteousness on earth; instead it is the divine tug that motivates the reform of the present state of things.[22]

The eschatological theme of the Eucharist incorporates our participation with the entire communion of saints—with both our predecessors in the faith and with the final future consummation—and it unites our hope for Earth with our heavenly promise. Stookey further explains:

> To this Great Feast, guests will come from north and south and east and west to sit at table. We who now share the Eucharist are joined in unity with those who preceded us, even as we struggle to open our earthly tables to all of God's people, even as we seek to make the present creation conform to the image of the new heaven and the new earth envisioned in the Revelation. . . . The Eucharist provides strength for the journey and consolation when cares overtake us.[23]

The official United Methodist statement on Holy Communion, approved at the 2004 General Conference, makes reference to this eschatological direction of the Eucharist toward a new earth with implications for holy living on this earth:

> Celebrations of Holy Communion are, therefore, a foretaste of the realm of God, when God's future breaks into our present world. Here the church enacts the words of Jesus, "Then people will come from east and west, north and south, and will eat in the kingdom of God." (Luke 13:29)

The implications are that the church might model for the world genuine community of mutual love, that we might work for liberation of the oppressed and the renewal of the social order, and that we might care for the earth. These are related: "Receiving the bread and wine as products of divine creation reminds us of our duties of stewardship of the natural environment in a time when destruction and pollution imperil the earth, and unjust distribution of the planet's resources destroys the hopes and lives of millions."[24]

The last supper with Christ's disciples is explicitly recalled and reenacted in the words of institution at Holy Communion "that the Lord Jesus on the night when he was betrayed took a loaf of bread" (1 Cor 11:23b). Maundy Thursday and the memory of that particular Passover, therefore, are always present when we commune. But the United Methodist statement reminds that the sacrament is not referred to as the last supper but as the Lord's Supper. It encompasses every meal with Christ—from the wedding party in Cana to the wedding banquet in New Jerusalem. Christ broke bread with us on the night before being crucified and was also revealed to us in the breaking of bread after rising from death. It includes as well a sense of participating with Christ and the disciples and generations before them in the Passover and in the exodus. Moreover, our memory extends beyond the meal itself to all of God's generative and saving action throughout history, even before the exodus—establishing the very universe, bringing forth a living earth, covenanting with all life as well as with Abraham and Moses. And this history—and proleptically our "memory" of it—extends ahead to God's generative establishment of new creation for all time where God's justice reigns. All of this is present to us whenever we celebrate Communion and hear those words spoken by Jesus at the last supper still echoing.

Contemporary prayers of Great Thanksgiving in many denominations recover this wealth of images, making explicit our thanks to God for all that God has done and is continuing to do throughout creation, even as the liturgy eventually focuses on the words spoken to the disciples in the upper room, now being spoken to us. Some of the most beautiful eucharistic prayers incorporating images of God's love manifest in creation are found in the liturgies of the ELCA and the Episcopal Church. Eucharistic Prayer C in *The Book of Common Prayer*, for instance, glorifies God for creating the magnificence of the universe and the fragility of Earth:

> God of all power, Ruler of the Universe, you are worthy of glory and praise.
> *Glory to you for ever and ever.*
>
> At your command all things came to be: the vast expanse of interstellar space,
> galaxies, suns, the planets in their courses, and this fragile earth, our island home.
> *By your will they were created and have their being.*

For Maundy Thursday, the ELCA *Worship Guidebook for Lent and the Three Days* recommends using "Thanksgiving at the Table IV" from *Evangelical Lutheran Worship*, as it "proclaims our movement through Israelite history into our Christian present, and is particularly appropriate."[25] This prayer also invokes images of creation at its beginning and conclusion, thus framing both the story of the exodus and the remembrance of the last supper. It begins:

> Blessed are you,
> O God of the universe.
> Your mercy is everlasting
> and your faithfulness endures
> from age to age.
>
> Praise to you for creating
> the heavens and the earth.
> Praise to you for saving earth
> from the waters of the flood.

It concludes:

> . . . with the earth and all its creatures,
> with sun and moon and stars,
> we praise you, O God,
> blessed and holy Trinity,
> now and forever.
> Amen.[26]

This prayer places us within creation at the outset and concludes by voicing our thanksgiving as united with the praise of other creatures.

Other prayers of Thanksgiving at the Table in *Evangelical Lutheran Worship* are also rich with images of God's creative activity throughout the natural world. Thanksgiving at the Table VII addresses Holy God with adoration:

> You formed the earth from chaos;
> you encircled the globe with air;
> you created fire
> for warmth and light;
> you nourish the lands with water.
>
> You molded us in your image,
> and with mercy higher than the mountains,
> with grace deeper than the seas,
> you blessed the Israelites
> and cherished them as your own.[27]

Thanksgiving at the Table IX begins by uniting our praise in cosmic proportion with the whole universe and microscopically with cellular life:

> The universe declares your praise:
> beyond the stars;
> beneath the sea;
> within each cell;
> with every breath.[28]

In the rich poetry of these prayers of Thanksgiving, we convey creaturely praise that places us at once on Earth and in eternity—as we hear again, "this is my body."

GOOD FRIDAY: POWERS CONTENDING

Christ's humility and mortality and Christ's exaltation and sovereignty are proclaimed at once in Philippians 2:6–11, an ancient hymn given as the

Epistle lesson by the lectionaries to launch our observance of Holy Week on Palm/Passion Sunday. In the introduction to Holy Week in the previous chapter, we noticed that this proclamation from Philippians about Christ includes the earth—Christ taking on human flesh, living an earthly life, suffering mortal death, and rising in order to supremely reign over all "names" whether in, under, or above the earth. There is a similar confession of faith in Colossians. Christ is presented in Colossians as the "firstborn of all creation" and as being active in creating and sustaining all things. Colossians reads:

> He is the image of the invisible God, the firstborn of all creation; for in him all things in heaven and on earth were created, things visible and invisible, whether thrones or dominions or rulers or powers—all things have been created through him and for him. He himself is before all things, and in him all things hold together. He is the head of the body, the church; he is the beginning, the firstborn from the dead, so that he might come to have first place in everything. For in him all the fullness of God was pleased to dwell, and through him God was pleased to reconcile to himself all things, whether on earth or in heaven, by making peace through the blood of his cross. (Col 1:15–20)

This entire passage is about Christ, but it begins in primordial creation and concludes by referencing the cross. Colossians further states that God nailed the record against us to Christ's cross and at the same time "disarmed the rulers and authorities and made a public example of them, triumphing over them in it," that is in this same cross of Christ.

Both the passage from Philippians and these verses from Colossians are remarkable in their Christological scope—spanning creation's beginning and fulfillment. These passages are also remarkable in the ways that rule and authority are pictured. Heaven and earth are both invoked. Philippians proclaims the name of Jesus to be above every name and that "every knee should bend, in heaven and on earth and under the earth." Colossians names all thrones (*thronoi*), dominions (*kuriotētes*), rulers (*archai*), and powers (*exousias*)—whether in heaven or on earth, having been created through Christ and for Christ—and proclaims Christ as "head of every rule (*archēs*) and authority (*exousias*)" (Col 1:16; 2:10b), having disarmed all of them on the cross (Col 2:15). The span of creation, the picture of Christ, and the scope of authority all become focused on the cross. Powers are contending in these passages and on this cross. Since the mid-twentieth century, much of the theological debate about the biblical references to principalities and powers has focused on two questions: one concerning the nature of these powers and the second concerning the relationship of these powers to the sovereignty of God.[29] Concerning their nature, to what degree do we understand these powers to be spiritual or even supernatural forces, on the one hand, or as this-worldly historical forces, on the other hand, manifested in social, political, and economic structures? Further, how might these spiritual and historical conceptions of the powers be related? Moreover, importantly, how are these powers, which seem inimical to God's purposes, understood to be related to God's creation and to God's sovereign power in creation and in redemption?

On Good Friday, we see inimical spiritual forces at work within human systems colluding in crucifying Christ: religious authority, political empire, cultural force of the populace, and economic interests too, if we interpret the overturning of the moneylenders' tables at the temple as a provocative challenge to economic interests. With Christ's death, they seem very realistically to have prevailed, but our witness and our proclamation is that Christ reigns victorious over them—yes in the resurrection—but even on the cross; in the midst of ignominy and despair, we find and declare victory. Our confession of Christ victorious, however, raises yet another question: Why must we still contend with these vanquished powers, and when will the victory won on the cross be our uncontested historical reality? When will peace and justice and ecological flourishing fully prevail?

Paul seems to have historical human structures in mind when he refers to "rulers of this age (*archontōn tou aiōnos toutou*)" having crucified Christ. Paul speaks of God's wisdom that is "not of the rulers of this age . . . which God declared before the ages for our glory" (1 Cor 2:6–7) and continues: "None of the rulers of this age understood this; for if they had, they would not have crucified the Lord of glory" (1 Cor 2:8). While these "rulers" appear to be worldly and temporal forces, they are presented by Paul in antagonistic relationship to the Spirit, wisdom, and power of God, and to the mind of Christ now imparted to us (1 Cor 2:1–16). This antagonism between the rulers of this age and the wisdom of God becomes focused on the cross of Christ. Paul begins this whole section in 1 Corinthians, claiming, "I decided to know nothing among you except Jesus Christ, and him crucified" (1 Cor 2:2b). Near the end of this letter to Corinth, though, Paul speaks of the ultimate destruction of "every ruler" under the reign of the crucified and risen Christ:

> Then comes the end, when he hands over the kingdom to God the Father, after he has destroyed every ruler (*archēn*) and every authority (*exousian*) and power (*dunamin*). For he must reign until he has put all his enemies under his feet. The last enemy to be destroyed is death. For "God has put all things in subjection under his feet." (1 Cor 15:24–27a, quoting Ps 8:6)

Here these sound like spiritual forces, enemies of Christ, still to be vanquished during the risen Christ's reign. In the meantime, they are placed in subjection under him. They include death.

The contemporary discussion concerning the degree to which these principalities and powers are to be understood as social structures or as spiritual entities, though, is perhaps anachronistic in two ways. First, ancients tended to link particular deities with the authority of nations and their earthly rulers, and they associated the power of such patron deities with the success of conquerors. The two are conceptually aligned—the authority of earthly principalities and the panoply of powers perceived to be empowering them. Second, it also seems anachronistic in this conversation to miss the natural world and forces of nature. The forces of nature were seen as compliant to these powers, and natural events were interpreted in conjunction with divine favor or disfavor—whether natural disasters or the productivity of lands and fields. To a large degree in the ancient world, force was force and power was power—whether natural events, political fortune/misfortune, or the assumed involvement for good or ill of spiritual powers. Post-enlightenment thinking distinguishes between these, that is between social structures, natural processes, and religious phenomena, and we investigate them separately according to particular academic disciplines. Hence the biblical language about principalities and powers strikes us as ambiguous and confusing, referencing alternately, or even at once, both mysterious spiritual energies and concrete political power.

The forces of nature, however are often ignored in this conversation, since natural processes are now interpreted as following natural laws irrespective of human whim, public policy, or enchanted beings. Yet we see today to our dismay how natural processes do in fact respond to social trends, public policies, and economic forces. Climate change and resultant storms and floods, destruction of habitat and resultant extinction of species, a hole in atmospheric ozone caused by chemical pollution now causing cancer to those living beneath, the proliferation of environmental contaminants previously unknown in nature resulting in harm for plants and animals as well as people—all these natural distortions are responses to human structures that are political, economic, social, and even religious. Under these influences, nature is seen as both sadly vulnerable to social structures and as vehemently forceful in its response.

G. B. Caird

Among those interpreting biblical references to the principalities and powers in the mid-twentieth century, G. B. Caird described a tight interconnection between the forces of nature, political power, and religious authority in his explication of these powers. His understanding of them takes him to the cross. With regard to the forces of nature, Caird argues:

> Israel never had conception of natural law operating independently of the personal agency of God. Indeed the Old Testament knows of no distinction between natural and miraculous events: all events are equally supernatural. The one word *niphla'oth* ("wondrous works" or "marvels") is used frequently to describe any works of God in creation or providence which have excited the abiding admiration of [God's] worshipping people. Nature, then, is stable: but its stability depends upon the trustworthiness of God.[30]

Yet within the biblical canon, Caird finds that "there were always some recalcitrant elements which refused to be brought within the scope of the divine sovereignty."[31] He notes a persistence of objects of Canaanite worship which required continuing attention by either prohibition (e.g., Deut 18:10–14; 32:17) or regulation. An example of the latter is the use of two goats on the Day of Atonement—one sacrificed as a sin offering to the LORD, and the other "presented alive before the LORD to make atonement over it, that it may be sent away into the wilderness to Azazel" (Lev 16:10). Moreover, Caird notes the prophecies in Isaiah (13:20–22; 34:13–15) against Babylon and Edom in which their desolation is described as becoming inhabited by a consortium of demons and wild animals.

Caird's explication begins with the world of the Hebrew Scriptures, with the conflictual and neighborly relations between the Hebrew people and the nations they encountered, and with the theological challenge presented to them of understanding the supremacy of their God amid the gods confessed by those nations. Caird names three cognitive strategies employed for understanding God in relation to the gods of the nations. One was to confess extreme monotheism; the other gods were considered nonexistent. All real power belonged to the one true God—whether expressed in political events or natural occurrences and whether for the Hebrew people's fortune or their chastisement. Another strategy was syncretism, for the God of the Hebrew people to take on the roles attributed to the gods of their neighbors. A third strategy was to conceptualize a hierarchical relationship distinguishing between God and subordinate beings. According to Caird, this third strategy of subordination was common and perennial. It carried forward into the world of the New Testament and is reflected in the language of principalities and powers.

Any power these subordinates had was sourced in and designated by God to be used for God's purposes within creation and among peoples. Indeed these subordinates were conceptualized as having been created by God to serve these purposes—to establish just order in society, or right religious practice, or nature's flourishing and productivity. They become counterproductive, however, idolatrous and even demonic, when trusted and relied on to the exclusion of their Creator and the Creator's purposes. Caird writes:

Like the angelic guardians of the pagan state and the angelic guardians of the Torah, the powers of nature are created beings who can still fulfil [sic] something of the purpose for which they were created, in spite of having undergone a corruption which has frustrated the full realization of that purpose and has turned them into enemies of God. For the sake of clarity we have analysed the concept of principalities and powers into these three elements, but we must remember that such distinctions were less obvious in antiquity than they are to us.[32]

The three interwoven elements to which Caird refers are the spiritual forces at work in the areas of political power, religious authority, and nature's dynamics. He interprets these powers as divinely appointed for governance, fidelity, and sustenance. But when trusted and relied upon to the neglect of their Creator, they become counterproductive, destructive, and even demonic.

The hold of these powers over human life is thus due to humanity's sin, and our vulnerability to them is commensurate with our vulnerability to death. Christ's victory over them, to interpret Caird, is affected through: (1) the revelation of Christ's sovereign glory, (2) the identification of Christ with our creaturely existence, and (3) Christ's obedience even unto death on the cross. In the revelation of Christ's sovereign glory, the powers are unmasked, as "usurpers of the divine majesty and impostors in the claims which they made upon [our] allegiance."[33] Christ's identification with sinful and mortal humanity leads to his crucifixion, but being without sin, Christ's death was liberating, absolving any grip the powers might have held on him. Caird explains this as both Christ's victory and ours:

Sin separates [us] from God, and death is the final separation, the final defeat. But for [Christ] who knew no sin, death had exactly the opposite effect. As long as [Jesus] was in the flesh [Christ] was subject to temptation, and the possibility remained [to] do the works of the flesh, and so allow sin to reign in [Christ's] mortal body; but with the death of the flesh that possibility no longer existed. Thus in putting Christ to death the powers were not asserting their control over [Christ], they were losing the only chance of control they ever had, "For he that is dead is freed from sin" (Rom 6:7).

The Cross, then, was a personal victory for Christ which carried [Christ] beyond the dominion of the powers; by liberating [Christ] from the body of flesh it enabled [Christ] also to "disarm the principalities and authorities" (Col 2:15), to take from them the only weapon they could ever use against [Christ]. But the Cross was also a corporate victory. By identifying [with humans] in their sinfulness and humiliation Christ had made it possible for [us] to be identified with [Christ] in [Christ's] righteousness and triumph.

By "unwavering obedience to God," Caird affirms, Christ was able to neutralize the powers and "absorb all that the powers could do." Caird quotes the passage from Philippians with which this section began (Phil 2:7–11) and confirms that "in the last analysis it is to the obedience of Jesus that the powers in heaven, along with all other creatures, must bow the knee."[34] All creatures, whether in heaven or earth, participate in this exultation made possible by this crucifixion.

Between the victory established in Christ's crucifixion and resurrection and the final consummation of that victory in Christ's return, however, we continue to struggle under these ersatz powers and their devastating influence. They "represent organized evil, embedded in the structure of society or woven into the fabric of the universe."[35] While the cross ensures the victory, our hope for freedom from them is effectively possible by faithful response: by being awakened through the revelation of Christ's glory, by living into Christ's identification with us so as to share in Christ's exalted freedom, and by striving for obedience to Christ over any other conflicting or lesser loyalties. In Caird's words:

> The powers of evil have been defeated by the obedience of Christ; they are constantly being defeated whenever Christians face them in the panoply of God; but the final triumph comes only when divine love has absorbed the whole momentum of evil, drawn out its last sting, neutralized its full effects.[36]

The world of nature is included in this cosmic drama. Caird writes, "The solidarity of [humanity] with the rest of creation is so close that in some way or other nature must bear the consequences of [our] sin."[37]

Caird notes that the relationship between creation and human sin is not simply a matter of the Fall. He cites biblical passages where natural disaster is prophesied as the consequence of human sin (Jer 4:23–26) or where beatitude in nature is prophesied as the result of forgiveness and reconciliation (Isa 11:6–9). At the same time, Caird affirms that "God is interested in creation for its own sake," and he cites Job:

> The book of Job, for example, ends with a magnificent protest against any narrowly anthropocentric and utilitarian conception of the universe. The ox may know its owner and the ass its master's crib, but what of the wild ass which scorns the shouts of the driver and the wild ox which has never bowed its neck to the yoke? What of the ostrich, the eagle, the crocodile, the hippopotamus?[38]

Caird suggests that the rest of "creation is too intimately related to [humanity] to be the mere backcloth to [our] spiritual drama."[39] This intimate relation between humanity and the rest of earthly creation means that the natural world is not just the environment for humanity's spiritual journey but is itself dynamically involved in the struggle with evil.

The modern mind, accustomed to theories of evolution, finds it a little hard to lay at [humanity's] door all the evils of . . . creation. We do not need Scripture to tell us that [humans'] ignorance and greed may turn a paradise into a dust bowl; but this does not seem to provide an all-sufficient explanation of cosmic evil.[40]

We increasingly see, though, a confluence of forces creating "dust bowls"—ignorance and greed institutionalized as rudderless economics, religious authorities eviscerated by their own scandals unable to provide trustworthy moral direction, political influence in service of the wealthiest to the detriment of the poor and the world in which we all live. A confluence of factors contribute to the realities of evil in creation, and creation responds with both vulnerability and force. All of creation along with humans and human organizations is in need of freedom from this evil—a freedom already won, yet a freedom promised to be consolidated, and a freedom needing to be claimed.

Caird's concluding paragraph—and the concluding paragraph of this section—summarizes his perspective of humanity's dilemma in relation to these powers and the relation of these powers to the primacy of Christ's cross. Our hope and our salvation is in the cross. Our dilemma is that we live under these conditions:

Under divinely appointed authorities—the powers of state, the powers of legal religion, the powers of nature—which through sin have become demonic agencies. To expect that evil will be defeated by any of these powers, by the action of state, by the self-discipline of the conscience, or by the processes of nature, is to ask that Satan cast out Satan. The powers can be robbed of their tyrannical influence and brought into their proper subjection to God only in the Cross. The final victory, then, is the parousia of [Christ] who once was crucified; and that means that when God pronounces [the] last word in the drama of this world's redemption, [God] will vindicate the way of the Cross.[41]

The Gospels and Christ's Passion

Power is at play in the passion stories of the Gospels. Power and powerlessness are presented in dynamic tension in the unfolding of these stories, but each of the Gospels displays this power and this tension differently. One of the ways in which they differ is in the portrayal of Earth's participation in the passion and death of Christ and the ways in which the natural world reflects, reveals, or responds to this power.

Maybe the most striking is the account in Matthew which marks the moment of Christ's death with the earth itself moving and vehemently making witness. "The earth shook, and the rocks were split," Matthew makes known and moreover declares, "The tombs also were opened, and many bodies of the saints who had fallen asleep were raised" (Matt 27: 51b–52). It is as if the impregnable potency of Christ's life, now released in death, must reverberate through the earth and even revive the dead who rise in witness. Only Matthew provides this story of earthquake,[42] but it coincides in Matthew's Gospel with the tearing of the curtain in the temple which occurs in all three Synoptic Gospels (Matt 27:51a; Mark 15:38; Luke 23:45b). It results in the confession of the centurion, which also occurs in all three Synoptic Gospels in some form, but Matthew expands the centurion's response to include others and presents it as explicitly in response to the earth's moving testimony: "When the centurion and those who were with him, keeping watch over Jesus, saw the earthquake and what took place, they were filled with awe, and said, 'Truly this was the Son of God!'" (Matt 27:54 Revised Standard Version [RSV]).

For the hours prior to Christ's death, all three Synoptic Gospels indicate that the whole earth or all the land was darkened as Christ hung on the cross (Matt 27:45; Mark 15:33; Luke 23:44). Matthew uses the phrase, *pasan tēn gēn*, the same words used by the Septuagint in Isaiah when declaring the "whole earth" is full of God's glory (Isa 6:3). Mark and Luke use the phrase, *olēn tēn gēn*, which also means all the land or the whole earth. Earth's light dimming coalesces with Christ's life dimming. Luke's Gospel alone clarifies that the darkness was due to a dimming of the sun's light over the land, apparently a solar eclipse (Luke 23:45); both the sun and the earth, both the sky and the land, can be seen as intertwined with Christ's dying.

Uniquely also, Luke accompanies Christ on the road to crucifixion Friday morning with a chorus of women lamenting. "A great number of the people followed," Luke reports, "among them were women who were beating their breasts and wailing for him" (Luke 23:27). Jesus responds with puzzling and troubling words:

> Daughters of Jerusalem, do not weep for me, but weep for yourselves and for your children. For the days are surely coming when they will say, "Blessed are the barren, and the wombs that never bore, and the breasts that never nursed." Then they will begin to say to the mountains, "Fall on us": and to the hills, "Cover us." For if they do this when the wood is green, what will happen when it is dry? (Luke 23:28–31)

Here Earth is involved or at least invoked in lamentation. Jesus's response sounds distressingly harsh, but this is not a rebuke. Rather it expresses a kind of solidarity in suffering between the pending crucifixion, these women of Jerusalem, and the land. It is an expansion of the mourning in that moment toward the future and the devastation that will follow in the near years ahead.

While the crucifixion occurred prior to the destruction of the temple in 70 CE in the Jewish-Roman war, the Gospel of Luke was written after this devastating event. For Luke's first audience in the aftermath of that war, Jerusalem's sorrow would be salient. It is foretold here in the telling, and remembered in the reading, as Christ's cross is carried.

Many commentators find allusion in this passage to the weeping and morning prophesied in Zechariah 12:10–14, although Zechariah is not explicitly quoted here as it is in John's Gospel (John 19:37).[43]

> And I will pour out a spirit of compassion and supplication on the house of David and the inhabitants of Jerusalem, so that, when they look on the one whom they have pierced, they shall mourn for him, as one mourns for an only child, and weep bitterly over him, as one weeps over a firstborn. (Zech 12:10)

Zechariah continues by specifying, "The land (*haaretz*, LXX *hē gē*) shall mourn, each family by itself" (Zech 12:12). The families of David, Nathan, Levi, and Shimei are named as mourners, and within each family Zechariah explicitly adds "and their wives by themselves." The land mourns and the women give voice.

The plea in Luke that the mountains and hills "fall on us" and "cover us" echoes words directly from Hosea 10:8[44] and anticipates a scene in Revelation 6:12–17. In Hosea, though, the earth (thorns and thistles as well as mountains and hills) is pictured as destroying altars to idols in judgment against Israel's idolatry. The passage in Revelation is also judgmental, but the plea to the mountains and rocks "to fall on us and hide us" is a plea voiced by "the kings of the earth and the magnates and the generals and the rich and the powerful, and everyone, slave and free" for protection from judgment for having persecuted the saints.

The situation in Luke 23, however, seems quite different from the situations addressed in these other biblical passages. The women wailing and following Jesus are not engaged in idol worship or persecution of the saints. Indeed, they would appear to be saints themselves—following Jesus and bewailing the crucifixion. Luke, unlike the other gospels, indicates that a multitude, presumably still including these women, remained with Jesus throughout the day until he died, and that they then "returned home beating their breasts" (Luke 23:35, 48); they are not pictured as persecuting him. The Zechariah passage provides the closest context to Luke, in that the mourning in Zechariah is in response to an outpouring of "a spirit of compassion and supplication on the house of David and the inhabitants of Jerusalem" (Zech 12:10). If this is referring to remorse for sin, however, again there is something of a misalignment with these women in Luke who do not seem to be sinning. Perhaps they are bewailing other people's sins that have led most proximately to this crucifixion—the sins of those wielding political power or religious authority or the cries of the mob earlier to crucify. These Judean women, though, are lamenting this injustice and bewailing the suffering and death to which it is leading.

Anne F. Elvey provides an "ecological feminist reading of the Gospel of Luke" in her book by that name, the subtitle being "A Gestational Paradigm." She brings an embodied interpretation to the lament of these women and Jesus's response to them, finding the danger of impending death to be linked between the bodies of these women, the body of Jesus about to be crucified, and the land and its inhabitants to be torn apart by war in the years following. Key to her interpretation is a comparison of passages throughout Luke in which women and women's bodies are described in conjunction with moments in the narrative about Jesus.

> Lukan theology is complex and plural, and while it is possible to read there a God who grieves over Jerusalem with the Lukan Jesus, it is impossible to avoid reading there a danger to bodies—beginning with the body of the Lukan Jesus—that the divine necessity implies. The danger to bodies, which the text poses, echoes in the curse on maternal bodies accompanying the narrative of the destruction of Jerusalem (21:20–24; cf. 23:28–31). But infused with the assurance of the divine necessity, the narrative unfolds along a way toward a tragedy, which comes to be remembered otherwise—as more than tragic. In this remembering, the text constructs its *other* and stores not only death, but also an ambiguous relationship to the maternal and toward earth.[45]

Jesus's words to the wailing women on the road to the crucifixion is not actually a curse but rather ironic beatitude, "Blessed are the barren, and the wombs that never bore, and the breasts that never nursed" (Luke 23:29). Elvey compares these words with the lament spoken in Luke 21:23 (cf. Matt 24:19; Mark 13:17), "Woe to those who are pregnant and to those who are nursing infants in those days! For there will be great distress on the earth." While these words recur in the apocalyptic discourse for all three Gospels, Luke alone explicitly names Jerusalem as the locus for warfare prompting this lament: "When you see Jerusalem surrounded by armies, then know that its desolation has come near" (Luke 21:20).[46]

Elvey contrasts both of these sayings (Luke 21:20 and Luke 23:29) with the blessing spoken by an unnamed woman to Jesus about his mother earlier in another passage unique to Luke: "A woman in the crowd raised her voice and said to him, 'Blessed is the womb that bore you and the breasts that nursed you!'" (Luke 11:27). To which Jesus responds, "Blessed rather are those who hear the word of God and obey it!" (Luke 11:28). Women's reproductive bodies figure into a rhetorical chiasmus here that reverses the expected relationship between bane and blessing and life and death. This rhetorical inversion in Luke occurs against the background of the land's pending suffering, while focusing in on the foreground of Christ's looming crucifixion.[47]

There is a keeping and a gestation of life both in women's bodies and in the body of the earth. Jesus born of Mary is the fruit of her womb and a child of the earth. As he walks toward crucifixion and bodily death, the women walking with him embody the impending suffering and death—both for Jesus and for those who would inhabit this land in the years soon following. At least their bodies signify this suffering and death in a tragic chiasmus. Gestating life, they now are also symbolically gestating the foreboding suffering and death.

In his response to them, Jesus is not dismissing their grief or negating their lament. Rather he is indicating the degree to which this injustice and this death further extends throughout the land and to future generations. Jerusalem is the central focus, but the reverberations extend outward.

And on the other side of Christ's crucifixion, the proclamation of salvation will also extend outward from Jerusalem to all the world. Luke's Gospel concludes, with the resurrected Jesus saying to those gathered just prior to ascending, "that repentance and forgiveness of sins is to be proclaimed in [the Messiah's] name to all nations, beginning from Jerusalem" (Luke 24:47b). The book of Acts will continue this story, following that proclamation as it expands from Jerusalem throughout the known world.

Today, nonetheless, traveling around the world and across the millennia, our ears continue to hear echoes of these women's lament. Suffering and death unite us in sorrow and grief. The woundedness of the earth itself is united with the suffering of all Earth's inhabitants. Through violence or careless disregard, the reverberations of civilization have resulted in the extinction of species and the marginalization of peoples.

Personally, I have heard this lament most literally, most sonically, in the voices of Maori women when my spouse and I were welcomed to Aotearoa New Zealand. Maori are the first peoples populating this land and refer to themselves as *tangata whenua*, the "people of the land." Aotearoa is the traditional Maori name for New Zealand and means "Land of the Long White Cloud." When visiting a Maori community, it is customary for the visitors to present themselves to be welcomed by the people of the land. The welcome extends to both the living and the dead. The welcome ceremony begins with women representing the land and calling to the visitors, extending welcome to them and to their ancestors and loved ones who are now deceased. An example of such a welcoming chant is translated: "Welcome to the representatives of our many dead, welcome!"[48] The chant's intonation is respectful and mournful. Even without understanding the language, the chanting itself moved us to tears upon first hearing it. We were being invited into mourning with the land and the people of the land. In response, the visitors then greet their hosts—both the living and the dead—and honor the meeting house and grounds where the living and the dead are gathering.

In Christian liturgical ceremony, there is also an entering into community with the living and the dead across the ages. We often name this the fellowship of the saints when we gather around the table for Eucharist, perhaps just prior to reciting the *Sanctus*. We believe ourselves to be incorporated into a community of saints, gathered from throughout the ages, including both the martyred before us, and extending into the eschaton and new creation. The body of Christ includes both the dead and the living. During the liturgical year, perhaps we name this inclusive fellowship most explicitly on All Saints Day. Good Friday focuses attention on Christ's death in particular. But Christ in dying is at once sharing with us in earthly mortality even as Christ is sharing with us in earthly existence. In death as well as in life, Christ's incarnation is earthy and communal. The chant of the women on the road to crucifixion unites us with them and with Christ on that road. It unites us with Christ's suffering in the events of that Friday and with Earth's suffering in the years that follow.

OCCASIONS OF WORSHIP ON MAUNDY THURSDAY AND GOOD FRIDAY

Worship services on Maundy Thursday usually recount and reenact events at the last supper, especially partaking of the meal of the Lord's Supper and perhaps participating in a foot washing. Worship on Good Friday follows a meditative and prayerful pattern. There may be opportunities for meditations on the stages of the cross and liturgical moments for veneration of the cross. Liturgies on Good Friday often include a number of petitions or short bidding prayers for the church and the world, interspersed with silence. The ELCA includes among these a prayer for God's creation:

> Almighty and eternal God
> you are the creator of a magnificent universe.
> Hold all the worlds in the arms of your care
> and bring all things to fulfillment in you.
> We ask this through Christ our Lord.
> Amen.[49]

Also included is a prayer for the Jewish people:

> Almighty and eternal God,
> long ago you gave your promise to Abraham and your teaching to Moses.
> Hear our prayers that the people you called and elected as your own
> may receive the fulfillment of the covenant's promises.
> we ask this through Christ our Lord.
> Amen.[50]

This is a Christian prayer for the Jewish people. It is particularly important at this time in the Christian year that our liturgies not reinforce the antisemitic vilification of God's chosen people that has been so often—and so horrifyingly—prevalent.

Another Lutheran emendation in this regard is to the traditional Solemn Reproaches. These tell the story of salvation history beginning with the exodus and culminating in the cross, asking, "What more could I have done for you?" To nuance these so as to explicitly address the church directly and not to vilify the Jewish people, each of eleven stanzas of reproach begin, "O my people, O my church" and one in particular asks pointedly toward Christians:

> What more could I have done for you? Answer me. I grafted you into my people Israel, but you made them scapegoats [*sic*] for your own guilt, and you have prepared a cross for your Savior. Holy God, holy and mighty, holy and immortal, have mercy on us.[51]

The Presbyterian Church (USA) and The United Methodists, following the Inter-Lutheran Commission on Worship have likewise amended the Reproaches to explicitly address the church.[52] Even with these changes, though, United Methodists have been advised, "For those situations where the Reproaches may give the impression of anti-Jewish convictions, they should not be used," and for this very reason I myself never use them. However, for those liturgists who do use them, care should be made to minimize anti-Jewish connotations. Ecologically minded liturgists, moreover, might want to amend them further so as to begin with wondrous creation rather than with the exodus and to integrate more of a creation theme throughout while still concluding with Christ's cross.

A service of "seven last words" has been popular in many places, often held for the duration of three hours that Jesus hung on the cross, that is from noon to 3:00 pm. The timing allows people to come and go during this time as they may be available during their lunch hour. These services often are ecumenical in nature, including preachers and perhaps musicians from different congregations. This is also an opportunity for people to sing some of the old favorites of hymns that claim and proclaim Christ's passion and death on the cross for our salvation. The seven last words, or sayings, uttered by Jesus are taken from the narratives of all four Gospels.

Another practice of worship at this time is a service of *Tenebrae*, Latin for "darkness." The darkness refers to the sequential extinguishing of candles at a nighttime service and then exiting the service in darkness at its conclusion, though the Latin word coincidentally also carries a connotation associated with death. The service dates from the twelfth century and evolved from the regular services of matins and lauds in the very early morning hours before dawn, as these hours of worship were practiced during Holy Week.[53] A service of *Tenebrae* can occur appropriately on Maundy Thursday to conclude an evening service, or it can be conducted either very early on Good Friday or later after sunset; it is also appropriate for Holy Saturday either early in the morning or in the evening prior to the start of an Easter vigil. It consists basically of a set of readings or reflections interspersed with the extinguishing of a candle. Traditionally fifteen candles were used, but today the number may vary. Also traditionally, readings were from the Psalms and Lamentations (which is still profoundly appropriate, especially Lamentations), but today the readings might all be taken from the passion narrative, particularly if the entire passion story was not read on Palm/Passion Sunday or otherwise during Holy Week. The Suffering Servant passages from Isaiah are also appropriate. Toward the conclusion of the service, the very last candle is relit after having been extinguished, not only symbolic of the promise of resurrection but also providing light for people to exit the service in darkness and silence. Alternatively, this last candle is simply hidden and then reemerges to provide that final light and promise.[54]

The United Methodist Church has segmented each of the Synoptic Gospels as readings for a *Tenebrae* for each of the three years covered by the lectionary,[55] and the United Methodist *Book of Worship* has scripted a translation of John for a *Tenebrae*. This translation by James H. Charlesworth "accurately translates John 18:1–19:42, with special sensitivity to Jews, Judaism, Jesus' Jewishness, and the Jewish origins of Christianity."[56] Elsewhere, they also provided a paraphrased script of the passion for a *Tenebrae* that is an amalgamation between the Gospels and which is intended to be respectful of Jews and Judaism.[57]

The following suggested readings for a *Tenebrae* are those passages discussed earlier in this chapter which portray Earth's participation in Christ's passion. These are offered without explanation here, but preachers are urged to provide such interpretation during time for a sermon. Instead of following the entire passion story through the telling by one of the Gospels, this *Tenebrae* provides an amalgam of passages or a collage of events from three Gospels, much like a "seven last words" service, and much like Christmas stories are often told. This collage of images has disadvantages, though, as well as advantages, and some worship leaders might prefer to follow a single Gospel narrative through every detail of the telling.

This particular *Tenebrae* as a whole and the individual moments of reflection are brief, allowing this service to function as a response to the Word at the conclusion of a longer service, or allowing it to be further augmented with collects, hymns, and psalms or other Old Testament readings along with the Gospel readings for each of the reflective moments. This *Tenebrae* assumes eight moments of reflection and seven candles. These may be read entirely as provided here, or they may be inserted or substituted individually into other moments of other liturgies for *Tenebrae*.

I prefer the Revised Standard Version [RSV] to the New Revised Standard Version [NRSV] for some of these Gospel readings, such as John 17:2 where the RSV translates *pasēs sarkos* very literally and expansively as power or authority over "all flesh" rather than more narrowly as "all people" as in the NRSV. Also (admittedly more a preference of style than text criticism), the RSV follows those textual variants that conclude Luke 22:19 abruptly with "this is my body" without further interpretation, allowing the listener to hear these evocative words spoken simply within multiple frames of possible meaning.

Tenebrae

Begin the service during dark hours with the room lit only by seven candles, the seventh of which is the Christ candle.

1. Reading: Luke 22:14–19 The Last Supper
extinguish first candle
silent reflection

2. John 17:1–5 Jesus Praying
extinguish second candle
silent reflection

3. Luke 22:39–48 Betrayal
extinguish third candle
silent reflection

4. Luke 22:54–23:1 Jesus's Arrest and Peter's Denial
extinguish fourth candle
silent reflection

5. John 18:37–38a Jesus before Pilate. . . "What is truth?"
extinguish fifth candle
silent reflection

6. Luke 23:24–31 Women Mourning
extinguish sixth candle
silent reflection

7. Matthew 27:45–54 Jesus Dies and Earth Quakes
After verse 50 or at the conclusion of the reading, there should be a LOUD NOISE symbolic of the Jesus's death and the Earth quaking. At the conclusion of the reading, the seventh candle should be either hid or extinguished, followed by silent reflection.

8. Matthew 27:55–66 Interment
return or re-light the seventh candle
silent reflection
depart quietly in the dim light

Chapter 5

Easter

Life Resurgent

> Rejoice now, all heavenly powers!
> Sing, choirs of angels!
> Exult, all creation around God's throne!
> Jesus Christ is risen!
> Celebrate the divine mysteries with exultation;
> and for so great a victory,
> sound the trumpet of salvation.
> Rejoice, O earth, in shining splendor,
> radiant in the brightness of your king!
> Christ has conquered! Glory fills you![1]

EASTER VIGIL

On Easter, light is ignited from within darkness. Both darkness and light hold enlivening blessing for us. It was so on the first Easter morning, beginning in the darkness of an empty tomb and a stone rolled away before the light of day. Women arrived at dawn to find messengers in illumined clothing voicing bewildering words. Christ is risen.

Since the early centuries of Christian worship, Easter has been celebrated with a great service of worship around the time of the Jewish Passover, beginning Saturday night and continuing into Sunday morning. Since biblical times (Acts 20:7, 11; Rev 1:10), it appears to have been a common practice for Christians to gather for worship weekly on Sunday, which is the day of Christ's resurrection.[2] The annual celebration of the Christian Passover, or Pasch, became generally held on Sunday as well. Worship at Pasch embraced the whole story of Christ's passion, crucifixion, resurrection, ascension, the sending of the Holy Spirit, and the expectation of Christ's return. As a

Christian evolution of the Passover observance, it emphasized the Passover meal shared between Christ and the disciples, and the Eucharist was celebrated as a continuing participation in Christ's Passover.[3]

The Easter vigil traces its roots to this early practice of the church in worship. For many congregations, this is the first service of Easter, held on Saturday night or before dawn on Sunday morning. Traditionally, there are four movements through the vigil: igniting of light, proclaiming of word, water and baptism, and bread and cup.[4] All four movements embrace creation in the light of Christ's resurrection. The *Exsultet*, or Easter Proclamation, a hymn dating from at least the fourth century,[5] sounds out early in the service. The opening lines quoted at the beginning of this chapter address the whole earth as well as those gathered, "Rejoice, O earth, in shining splendor . . . Glory fills you!"[6]

Easter Vigil: Service of Light

The Easter vigil begins with the service of light, and the *Exsultet* is chanted during this first part of the vigil. At the very outset of the hymn quoted earlier, the heavenly powers, such as those discussed in the preceding chapter on Good Friday, are addressed and called to rejoice. Next, all creation is addressed and called to exult. The hymn continues, proclaiming, "Christ has conquered!" In conquering death, all powers—whether heavenly or earthly—are brought into harmonious homage before Christ.

Toward the end of this version of the hymn, moreover, heaven and earth are wedded and the bees join in:

> Therefore, in this night of grace,
> receive, O God, our praise and thanksgiving
> for the light of the resurrection
> of our Lord Jesus Christ,
> reflected in the burning of this candle.
> We sing the glories of this pillar of fire,
> the brightness of which is not diminished
> even when its light is divided and borrowed.
> For it is fed by the melting wax
> which the bees, your servants,
> have made for the substance of this candle.
> This is the night **[This is the night]**
> in which heaven and earth are joined—
> Things human and things divine.[7]

The reference to bees in the candle prayer dates back to the fourth century.[8] Here in the *Exsultet*, bees are credited with creating the wax for the candle, and they are called God's servants. Earlier versions of this prayer also drew an analogy between the mysterious nature of bees' reproduction and the miraculous nature of Mary giving birth to Jesus.[9] Inspiration for the early reference to bees in the candle prayer is credited to the influence of the Roman poet Virgil, whose *Georgics* and *Bucolics* were widely read in early centuries and which are verdant with natural images and effusive in praise of nature. Here is an excerpt from his fourth Georgic ode on the bees:

> And let green cassias and far-scented thymes,
> And savory with its heavy-laden breath
> Bloom round about, and violet-beds hard by
> Sip sweetness from the fertilizing springs.
> For the hive's self, or stitched of hollow bark,
> Or from tough osier woven, let the doors
> Be strait of entrance; for stiff winter's cold
> Congeals the honey, and heat resolves and thaws,
> To bees alike disastrous; not for naught
> So haste they to cement the tiny pores
> That pierce their walls, and fill the crevices
> With pollen from the flowers, and glean and keep
> To this same end the glue, that binds more fast
> Than bird-lime or the pitch from Ida's pines.
>
> Some say that unto bees a share is given
> Of the Divine Intelligence, and to drink
> Pure draughts of ether; for God permeates all-
> Earth, and wide ocean, and the vault of heaven-
> From whom flocks, herds, men, beasts of every kind,
> Draw each at birth the fine essential flame;
> Yea, and that all things hence to Him return,
> Brought back by dissolution, nor can death
> Find place: but, each into his starry rank,
> Alive they soar, and mount the heights of heaven.[10]

From blossoms to honeycomb, from earth's crevices to the heights of heaven, from poetry to our prayer, the bees are there.

The bees belong. Symbols of resurrection at Easter include flowers that require pollination as well as other pollinators, notably butterflies. Seldom do we connect these symbols cognitively, though, recognizing the necessary life-sustaining link between flowering plants and the insects that pollinate them. Yet terrestrial life depends on this relationship. Especially today, this relationship is vital. In the past decade, approximately a third of domestic beehives have suffered demise, and wild pollinators have suffered serious decline, leading to the prospect of a "pollination crisis."[11] Toward the end of that decade, the most widely used herbicide was added, along with exposure to pesticides and the decline of flowers, to the list of possible causes for the increase of death among bees and other pollinators.[12] The bees, givers of life as well as wax and honey, are themselves in need of resurrection. The paschal candle burns for them as well.

The idea of the decline of flowers may seem surprising when surrounded by Easter lilies and Spring blossoms. But not all flowers are equal. Different species of pollinators prefer different species of plants. Exotic plants imported from foreign ecosystems are often of little interest to native butterflies and bees. Even cultivars of native plants, intentionally bred to express particular traits of interest to humans, may be of less interest to important insects. Development of areas where wildflowers grow further reduces the diversity of plant life and consequently the diversity of animals dependent on the plants. This becomes particularly important during the Spring when breeding birds require young insect life to successfully reproduce. Can our symbols of life at Easter actually be more conducive to life? Perhaps congregations can encourage decoration with live native plants that can then be transplanted into neighborhood yards or church grounds. The Easter celebration of life would then be more fully inclusive of life and promoting of life.

Fittingly, then, after the bees have done their work and the wax of the paschal candle has been lit, the *Exsultet* concludes, offering the candle's light to God even as Christ gives light to all creation:

> Accept our evening sacrifice,
> the offering of this candle in your honor.
> May it shine continually to drive away all darkness.
> May Christ, the Morning Star who knows no setting,
> find it ever burning—
> he who gives his light to all creation,
> and who lives and reigns for ever and ever. Amen.[13]

The *Exsultet* concludes the first movement of the vigil, the service of light, which begins with the igniting of fire itself and the lighting of the paschal candle.

It is recommended, where possible, that the whole service actually begin outdoors as a bonfire is lit. Being outdoors, we are situated within an actual ecosystem rather than in a built environment, and our worship is thus contextualized within creation. The lighting of a new fire in the Spring has cultural roots that remind us of our life together in community and our dependence on fire as natural energy for the protection of community and the sustenance of life. Moreover, in the context of the vigil, this fire symbolically links us with the first light of creation and the enlivening energy throughout creation. The ELCA *Worship Guidebook* even suggests lighting this fire with flint, "symbolizing God's creation of light and life out of the void."[14] It is fitting that when the paschal candle is lit, representing Christ's resurrection and victory over the powers of death, it is lit from the flames illustrating the universe's beginning and ongoing energy. New creation is sparked from primordial creation.

Easter Vigil: Service of Word

The vigil continues with the service of Word, which also demonstrates the link between creation and resurrection. There is a sequence of readings given from the Old Testament, followed by Romans 6:3–11 as the Epistle lesson, and concluding with the story of the empty tomb from one of the Gospels. The creation story at the beginning of Genesis (Gen 1:1–2:2[4a]) is recommended as the first reading by both the Roman Catholic Lectionary and the Revised Common Lectionary:

> In the beginning when God created the heavens and the earth, the earth was a formless void and darkness covered the face of the deep, while a wind from God swept over the face of the waters. Then God said, "Let there be light." (Gen 1:1–3a)

And creation continues with all of the heavens and all of the waters and all of the land and all of the plants and all of the animals. The service of Word thus begins with the void and concludes with the empty tomb. It begins with the creation of light and concludes with the light of Christ. It begins with the breath of God bringing about embodied life, and it concludes with Christ's resurrection in both body and spirit. It begins with waters divided at earth's beginning, and it concludes by opening the waters of our baptism into Christ's death and resurrection.

The waters of the Reed Sea are also divided, as we remember the exodus of our Hebrew ancestors from slavery in Egypt. The story of this exodus and the parting of the Reed Sea waters is found in Exodus 14 which is given as a non-optional reading for the vigil in the rubrics of the Roman Catholic, Episcopalian, Evangelical Lutheran, and United Methodist services.[15] The recollection of the original exodus reminds us of the connection between our religious observance as Christians on this night and the Passover observance from which it evolved. Indeed the entire rehearsal of events from Hebrew Scriptures, including the exodus, is reminiscent of Passover Haggadah. Not only is the Passover thus conceptually connected with Easter as the Christian Pasch, the divided waters of creation frame both stories of salvation history so as to be seen as creation's story as well.

Other suggested Old Testament readings for the vigil also weave themes of creation with the stories of salvation. The Revised Common Lectionary recommends verses from Genesis 7–9 which recount the story of Noah and the animals being saved from the waters of the flood. Some of this story was also read earlier on the first Sunday of Lent in year B and was discussed earlier in the chapter on early Lent in association with the creation stories in Genesis. Now, as Easter dawns, it is easy to hear this narrative of Noah as a story of death and resurrection for creation, comparative to the death and resurrection of Christ. Indeed, the deep which God divided and ordered at the beginning of creation is here allowed to resurge and retake the earth and its inhabitants: "The fountains of the great deep burst forth, and the windows of the heavens were opened" (Gen 7:11b). While the animals and Noah's family are ultimately saved, it is as if they are entombed within the ark:

> They and every wild animal of every kind, and all domestic animals of every kind, and every creeping thing that creeps on the earth, and every bird of every kind—every bird, every winged creature. They went into the ark with Noah, two and two of all flesh in which there was the breath of life. And those that entered, male and female of all flesh, went in as God had commanded him; and the LORD shut him in. (Gen 7:14–16)

Eventually, as on the very first day of creation, God again caused a wind to blow, and the flood subsided; the watery heavens were restrained, and the earth again appeared (8:11–13). As the animals emerged from the ark, God again blessed them to "be fruitful and multiply" and covenanted with all flesh to never again allow the flood to destroy the earth (8:17–9:17). There is a parallel movement from chaos to creation and from death to life in each of these stories: creation of the heavens and the earth, salvation of all flesh from the flood, and Christ's resurrection from the dead.

Curiously, the verses that are omitted from Genesis 7–9 in the lectionary's recommendation for this reading are the verses that most explicitly name the animals' experience of death as contrasted with their preservation of life. Omitted, for instance, are verses 7:18–24 where, in the midst of the flood, God "blots out" all terrestrial and avian life that was not safely in the ark, and "all flesh died that moved on the earth" (7:21a). Omitted, too, are verses 8:19–22 where Noah sacrifices from among the clean animals that were rescued. Also omitted are verses 9:1–7, where the humans who were heretofore vegetarian are now permitted to eat animal flesh, with the foreboding words, "The fear of you and the dread of you shall rest on every animal." The contrast between death and life in these chapters of Genesis would be more salient if some of these omitted verses were to be included in the reading, and the comparison with death and resurrection in the Easter story would also then be more vivid. Worship leaders with discretion in choosing lections might attend deliberately to the selection of verses read from this story in order to highlight the contrast between death and life while still emphasizing God's covenant with all flesh to protect life.

The Roman Catholic Lectionary does not suggest the reading from Genesis pertaining to the flood but does recommend Isaiah 54:5–14, which invokes the memory of Noah. God addresses the Hebrew people during their captivity in Babylon:

> This is like the days of Noah to me:
>   Just as I swore that the waters of Noah
>   would never again go over the earth,
> so I have sworn that I will not be angry with you
>   and will not rebuke you.
> For the mountains may depart
>   and the hills be removed,
> but my steadfast love shall not depart from you,
>   and my covenant of peace shall not be removed.
> says the LORD, who has compassion on you. (Isa 54:9–10)

The chief metaphor in this passage as a whole is a spousal relationship between God and God's people. God is named as "your Redeemer," "your Maker," and "the God of the whole earth" (Isa 54:5). There is a breadth of focus on God as creator of the whole world and on God's universal covenant through Noah, and this focus then zooms in on God's steadfast love for a particular people awaiting their historical redemption.

The Roman Catholic Lectionary also recommends a reading from the deuterocanonical book of Baruch (Bar 3:9–15, 3:32–4:4). This is also offered as an option in the Revised Common Lectionary, along with a reading from Proverbs as an alternative (Prov 8:1–8, 19–21; 9:4b–6). Both of these passages give voice to God's Wisdom, portrayed as a woman, active throughout creation. The passage from Baruch begins, "Hear the commandments of life, O Israel; give ear and learn wisdom!" (Bar 3:9) and asks: "Who has found her place? And who has entered her storehouses?" (Bar 3:15). Elusive Wisdom is nonetheless ever present to God in fashioning creation. The passage continues:

> Who has gone up into heaven, and taken her, and brought her down from the clouds? Who has gone over the sea, and found her, and will buy her for pure gold? No one knows the way to her, or is concerned about the path to her. But the one who knows all things knows her, he found her by his understanding. The one who prepared the earth for all time filled it with four-footed creatures; the one who sends forth the light, and it goes; he called it again, and it obeyed him trembling; the stars shone in their watches, and were glad; he called them, and they said, "Here we are!" They shone with gladness for him who made them. (Bar 3:29–34)

Here Wisdom is presented as with God in all of God's acts of creation.

Proverbs 8 is even more direct in attributing agency to Wisdom, portrayed as a woman, generatively active throughout creation. The passage begins with Wisdom herself speaking: "Does not wisdom call, and does not understanding raise her voice? . . . she cries out: 'To you, O people, I call, and my cry is to all that live'" (Prov 8:1, 3b–4). The passage concludes with an invitation: "Come, eat of my bread and drink of the wine I have mixed. Lay aside immaturity, and live, and walk in the way of insight." Anachronistically symbolic for listeners at the Easter vigil, her invitation to eat bread and drink wine and to live intimates participation in the communion meal that will conclude the vigil in celebration of new life. Unfortunately, though, the most explicit verses regarding her agency in creation, Proverbs 8: 22–31, are omitted in the lectionary's recommendation. They read:

> The LORD created me at the beginning of his work, the first of his acts of long ago. Ages ago I was set up, at the first, before the beginning of the earth. When there were no depths I was brought forth, when there were no springs abounding with water. Before the mountains had been shaped, before the hills, I was brought forth—when he had not yet made earth and fields, or the world's first bits of soil. When he established the heavens, I was there, when he drew a circle on the face of the deep, when he made firm the skies above, when he established the fountains of the deep, when he assigned to the sea its limit, so that the waters might not transgress his command, when he marked out the foundations of the earth, then I was beside him, like a master worker; and I was daily his delight, rejoicing before him always, rejoicing in his inhabited world and delighting in the human race. (Prov 8:22–31)

The Ecumenical Common Lectionary places these verses as the First Reading for Trinity Sunday, the first Sunday following the day of Pentecost and the conclusion of the Easter season. They will be discussed later in the chapter addressing worship on Trinity Sunday. For the Easter vigil, though, worship leaders with discretion in choosing readings might consider including some of or all of these verses which so clearly indicate that Wisdom who calls us now to live is also Wisdom who has called all life into being.

The ELCA begins the service of Word for the vigil by reading the first creation story in Genesis and concludes with Daniel 3 as the final reading (Dan 3:1–29) and as the canticle in response (Dan 3:57–87). Actually, the canticle in response is the deuterocanonical addition to Daniel, known in Latin by the first three words, *Benedicite, omnia opera*, "Bless the Lord, all you works," or in English simply titled as the "Song of the Three."[16] It is the song of praise by Shadrach, Meshach, and Abednego from the fiery furnace. This hymn as a whole contains some of the richest creation imagery in the Bible, but does not occur anywhere in the Revised Common Lectionary. It is used in worship as a canticle by The Roman Catholic Church, The Episcopal Church, and the ELCA. By concluding the service of Word with this canticle, according to Philip H. Pfatteicher, "The Lutheran rite thus emphasizes the redemption of the cosmos and the role of nature in the praise of God."[17] The hymn chants for more than thirty verses, calling on "all you works of the Lord" to laud and bless their Creator: heavens, angels, waters above, powers, sun and moon, stars, rain and dew, winds, fire and heat, winter cold and summer heat, dews and falling snow, ice and cold, frosts and snows, nights and days, light and darkness, lightning and clouds. "Let the earth bless the Lord," the Song continues (vs. 74a): mountains and hills, "all that grows in the ground" (3:76), springs, seas and rivers, whales and all that swim, birds of the air, wild animals and cattle, and all people on earth. The hymn is in the form of a litany with the verses beginning with "Bless the Lord" and/or concluding with the injunction, "sing to him and highly exalt him forever." The entire hymn or select verses can be chanted or sung as a litany with either one of these phrases as a congregational response.

All of these readings from the Old Testament present God's generative activity promoting life throughout creation. Being read prior to the readings from the New Testament, they provide cosmic context for peering into an empty tomb, for hearing the message of resurrection, and for participating sacramentally in Christ's death and resurrection. Creation opens to new creation. The breath of life now breathes into resurrection. The blessing of all flesh now embodies new life. Earth yields an empty tomb. The waters hold us in baptism.

Our baptism into Christ's death and resurrection is proclaimed by Paul in the Epistle lesson for the vigil:

> Do you not know that all of us who have been baptized into Christ Jesus were baptized into his death? Therefore we have been buried with him by baptism into death, so that, just as Christ was raised from the dead by the glory of the Father, so we too might walk in newness of life.
>
> For if we have been united with him in a death like his, we will certainly be united with him in a resurrection like his. We know that our old self was crucified with him so that the body of sin might be destroyed, and we might no longer be enslaved to sin. For whoever has died is freed from sin. But if we have died with Christ, we believe that we will also live with him. We know that Christ, being raised from the dead, will never die again; death no longer has dominion over him. The death he died, he died to sin, once for all; but the life he lives, he lives to God. So you also must consider yourselves dead to sin and alive to God in Christ Jesus. (Rom 6:3–11)

Explicitly proclaimed is our identity with Christ in both death and resurrection through baptism. We hear these words at the vigil within the context of both creation and exodus as proclaimed through the series of preceding readings. There is moral teaching in Paul's words, but the moral teaching is presented ontologically as a matter of our identity with Christ in death and life. The moral import is that we live out this identity with Christ in Christ's death and resurrection and in the risen Christ's freedom from sin and death. There is a cosmic import to our life in Christ which undergirds the moral. Importantly, Paul announces this cosmic dimension as Christ's freedom from the "dominion" of death. Paul continues in the next few verses to exhort us similarly not to "let sin exercise dominion" in our mortal bodies (Rom 6:12), and to promise: ". . . sin will have no dominion over you, since you are not under law but under grace" (Rom 6:14). We have already discussed Christ's victory over the principalities and powers above in the preceding chapter on Good Friday. We noticed in that context that the defeat of the powers has liberative implications for all of creation. Christ's resurrection now emphatically asserts this freedom won on the cross. We share in this freedom, this grace, sacramentally and even ontologically by virtue of our baptism into Christ's death and resurrection, and we are exhorted to claim this gracious freedom in our embodied living as mortal and moral creatures.

The Gospel reading for the Easter vigil is the story of the empty tomb from any one of the Gospels. The most stark telling of this story, and probably the oldest version of it, is Mark's, which originally seems to end at verse 16:8: "So they went out and fled from the tomb, for terror and amazement had seized them; and they said nothing to anyone, for they were afraid." The women are Mary Magdalene, Mary the mother of James, and Salome; these are our witnesses. In Luke's Gospel, Mary Magdalene, Joanna, and Mary the mother of James come to the tomb and are told, "Remember how he told you while he was still in Galilee, that the Son of man must be handed over to sinners, and be crucified, and on the third day rise again," and they go and tell that which they have seen and heard "to the eleven and to the rest" (Luke 24:6–7, 9b). In Matthew, Mary Magdalene and "the other Mary" go to the tomb. "And suddenly," Matthew tells us, "there was a great earthquake" (Matt 28:2). As occurred at the crucifixion so too again at the resurrection, Matthew has the earth quake in testimony to that which is occurring. In the Gospel of John, Mary Magdalene alone goes to the tomb "while it was still dark" (John 20:1). Seeing the stone rolled away, she ran to tell Peter and the other disciple whom Jesus loved, both of whom came and witnessed the tomb empty except for the linen wrappings. The two disciples then returned home, but Mary remained at the tomb and alone encountered Jesus. Presuming him to be the gardener, she eventually recognized him when he called her by name.

The empty tomb is mysterious. So is the role of the earth at this moment. Is the earth passive in receiving this corpse and then in relinquishing it—a mere receptacle? Or is the earth agentic or active in some way? If so, is the earth's activity nefarious, attempting to hold the dead? Or is it redemptive, birthing resurrection from its depths? Or is it active in a nonjudgmental and regular way, simply allowing the processes of nature under normal circumstances to recycle the material elements of life? The women in Mark's Gospel responded with fear to the tomb and to the messenger. Yet there is something awesomely redemptive, restorative, and regenerative at work in this earth.

The service of Word at the Easter vigil is replete with readings from Scripture. The cumulative effect of these readings is an interweaving of themes of creation, exodus, and resurrection. Worship leaders have considerable discretion concerning the number of lections that might be read. Many congregations, though, do not observe a vigil in this manner and instead celebrate the first service of Easter as a sunrise service on Sunday morning. These services can be of a more informal nature, sometimes held outdoors. Often these sunrise services are succinct with very few readings from Scripture in addition to the core Gospel reading about the empty tomb. Worship leaders are encouraged, though, to glean from the more expansive service of the vigil to enrich worship at these sunrise services. Particular readings can be selected that help to open deeper meaning of the open tomb. The following is an example. It is an excerpt of a sermon by a minister of the African Methodist Episcopal Church. Rev Camille D. Johnson reads from the creation story in Genesis 1 and the empty tomb from Matthew 28. Her witness provides fitting conclusion for this section on proclamation of the Word on the first service of Easter:

> It is in the book of Genesis that we find understanding of our God's intention for the earth; it was not just to be inhabited by humans, but God created the earth for all so that all might know the beauty of its wondrous form. Genesis 1 tells us God hovered over the face of the waters, commanded light to shine out of darkness, and established Day and Night. God brought forth living creatures of every kind, and created the heavens and the seas.
>
> ... we look to Matthew's Gospel where we find an empty tomb carved out of the very earth which our God created. The scripture declares:
>
> After the Sabbath, as the first day of the week was dawning, Mary Magdalene and the other Mary went to see the tomb. And suddenly there was a great earthquake; for an angel of the Lord, descending from heaven, came and rolled back the stone and sat on it. His appearance was like lightning and his clothing white as snow.
>
> It was Sunday morning before dawn, and Mary Magdalene and the other Mary went to the tomb. As they were arriving, there was a great earthquake, and an angel descended from heaven, rolled back the stone from the mouth of

the tomb, and sat on it. The guards were so mesmerized by his glowing appearance they fainted; they could not believe. So often we see the beauty of God's earth—the stars at night, the rain as it falls—and we miss seeing the beauty of the blessing it brings right before our very eyes. But the angel reassured them. There was no need to fear, for the One they sought had risen as promised. "Come see the place where the Lord lay."

The stone had been rolled away, *not to let the Lord out, but to let the two Marys in!*

That's the message of this Easter Sunday; the stone was rolled away so that you might enter into the place and see the beauty and power of Christ's resurrection. The angel deputized the women to go quickly and announce the news to the disciples. The Lord is alive! Jesus lives and they would meet him again in Galilee. I declare today that we too should go and tell our Savior lives. As they were on their way, the scripture declares, they met Jesus, fell at his feet and worshiped Him.

May each of us have our Galilee experience every day, as we remember the earth shaking and the stone rolling so that you and I could enter in! May we have our Galilee experience every time we look and see the trees at attention in praise. May we have our Galilee experience every time the dew of rain hits our faces to remind us of Christ's gentle kiss. As we look around this Easter, may we remember God created the heavens and the earth so that the very earth might be where our savior dwelt and walked. The earth would be the place where a tomb would be carved out of a mountain that He had created and within which He would lay. But early on Sunday morning Christ would rise up with all power in hand, and because He lives, we too can live with the victory that is Christ Jesus.

Service of Water and Service of Table

The Easter vigil still, as in early centuries, culminates in baptismal celebration. Even if baptisms are not actually being conducted on the occasion of a particular Easter service, it is still possible to celebrate the symbolism of baptism, the remembrance of our baptism, and the renewal of our baptismal life in Christ. Water is the central symbol in baptism. Water unites our baptism with every baptism, and baptism unites us with Christ in death and resurrected life.

Water also unites the resurrected Christ and our resurrected life in Christ with all life on this blue planet. Water is necessary for life. This is the reason space exploration searches for water—as an indication of the very possibility of life. We are aqueous beings; human bodies are comprised mostly of water, around 60 percent. Moreover water is continually recycled through all of our bodies. The same atoms of hydrogen and oxygen constituting the water of our bodies are the same as those of primordial bodies. We are made of the same elements that watered ancient soils and that sprouted ancient plants, water that provided drink for all animate life preceding us and water that was then released by them to cycle through the ages and through our own bodies. We are water, and water is life.

In the symbolism of our faith, water also represents death and the absence of creation. It was a watery void out of which God created the heavens and the earth. It was the watery flood that overtook the earth and life on earth in the telling of Noah's tale. The watery chaos continues to contend with creation at least symbolically throughout Scripture. But in Christ, we confess, we come to living water. Thirst is quenched, life restored. Both dimensions of water's symbolism are salient at baptism, especially on Easter morning—death and life—life on Earth and life in Christ, life in our time and life unbounded.

"The renewal of individuals in the waters of baptism is seen in the vigil as part of the same divine activity that creates and renews God's ancient people and the entire creation," explains the ELCA's *Worship Guidebook for Lent and the Three Days*, and continues: "The Easter Vigil takes the stories of creation, renewal, rebirth and resurrection, and at the font, pours them over the baptismal candidates, immersing them in water and the word."[18] The *Guidebook* quotes Samuel Torvend: "We gather with our catechumens at the four rivers of paradise, on the waters of the flood, at the edge of the Red Sea, on the banks of the Jordan, and at this font in order to be immersed in the river, the flood, the sea of God's infinite life."[19] Water is typically present in most prayers of thanksgiving over the waters of the font, but the *Worship Guidebook* recommends particularly for the Easter vigil the "Thanksgiving at the Font V" in *Evangelical Lutheran Worship*. Addressing God as "river of life" and "everlasting wellspring," it pours forth praise:

> Glory to you for oceans and lakes,
> for rivers and streams.
> Honor to you for cloud and rain, for dew and snow.
> Your waters are below us, around us, above us:
> our life is born in you.
> You are the fountain of resurrection.
> Praise to you for your saving waters. . .

The prayer continues by naming the saving waters in biblical stories, such as, Noah and the animals rescued, Hagar's well, exodus through the parted waters, drinking water from a rock in the wilderness, Naaman washed clean, and the Samaritan woman meeting Jesus at the well. The prayer offers a word of epiclesis to bless both the assembly and the creation, "Breathe your Spirit into all who are gathered here and into all creation" and concludes petitioning, "Satisfy all our thirst with your living water."[20]

Baptism flows into Holy Communion. The ELCA *Worship Guidebook for Lent and the Three Days* suggests using Thanksgiving at the Table number IV, VII, or IX from *Evangelical Lutheran Worship* for Easter Sunday.[21] All three incorporate creation imagery with Easter proclamation. Thanksgiving at the Table IV begins with praise to "God of the Universe" for "creating the heavens and the earth" and "for saving the earth from the waters of the flood." It continues with praise for God's acts of salvation throughout biblical history and concludes, "with the earth and all its creatures, with sun and moon and stars, we praise you, O God, blessed and holy Trinity, now and forever."[22] Thanksgiving at the Table VII celebrates: "You formed the earth from chaos; you encircled the globe with air; you created fire for warmth and light; you nourished the lands with water."[23] Thanksgiving at the Table IX encompasses the breadth of the galaxies, the depth of the oceans, and the microscopic glory of each living cell: "The universe declares your praise; beyond the stars; beneath the sea; within each cell; with every breath. We praise you O God."[24]

Every meal is represented here at the Lord's Table, and every creature is represented here at this meal. My personal experience of three different occasions of Communion meals on Easter stand out in my memory, and each of these meals has morphed for me into a broader vista of fellowship in Christ and a deeper relationship with Christ and with creation. One such meal occurred more than thirty years ago worshiping at Union Village United Methodist Church in New Jersey. In passing the peace prior to Communion, my spouse and I shook hands with a couple just moving to New Jersey and visiting for the first time. We communed at Eucharist together, and afterward my spouse and I invited them to join us for lunch at our small apartment— "Nothing special, I said; we were just going to have pancakes." They joined us for this modest Easter meal, in the simplicity of celebration and the celebration of simplicity, continuing our holy communion from the previous hour and extending it beyond that apartment into the decades that followed, a celebration opening to perennial friendship and fellowship.

Another momentous Easter meal for me was outside of Lautoka on the island of Viti Levu in Fiji. I was the invited preacher for Easter services. We baptized twelve adults into the life of Christ that Easter morning, and we celebrated with them in their first partaking of Holy Communion. Following the service, the entire congregation moved outside to the shore where we ate breakfast of fish caught freshly from the surrounding waters. It was as if we were with Jesus resurrected as recounted in John, by the Sea of Tiberias, saying "Come, and have breakfast." In fact, in faith, we were, we are.

Another Easter Eucharist was at Luther Place Memorial Church in Washington, DC. It had been a challenging Lent, encountering realities of human misery. Luther Place had opened its doors to shelter homeless people during this cold Winter and Spring, and my spouse and I were among the volunteers staying in the church with them, eating together and sharing together. The church had been involved in a study of Dorothy Sölle's book *Suffering*,[25] deepening a longing for respite, for justice, for salvation. That Easter morning the church's evening residents returned to the streets, and those who had rested in beds in homes started to arrive for worship. Tired, we settled into the liturgy. As the service moved to the Table, I found myself singing for the first time in months the familiar words:

> This is the feast of victory for our God.
>   Alleluia, alleluia, alleluia.
> Sing with all the people of God,
>   and join in the hymn of all creation:
> Blessing, honor, glory, and might
>   be to God and the Lamb forever. Amen.[26]

Tears ran down my cheeks as this song rose from our chests. In the face of the forces of death, we would sing of our savior, of life's victory, of the promise of salvation. When we commune with Christ, we commune with Christ's—with all of Christ's—with those who had been in church that night as well those who had gathered that morning, with those who had gathered with Jesus before the crucifixion and with those who banquet with Christ in final victory.

The scriptural reference in these lines of the hymn is to Revelation 5:13:

> Then I heard every creature in heaven and on earth and under the earth and in the sea, and all that is in them, singing,
>   To the one seated on the throne and to the Lamb
>   be blessing and honor and glory and might
>   forever and ever!

Every meal is represented here at the Lord's Table, and every creature is represented here at this meal.

EASTER SUNDAY AND EASTER SEASON

This conversation about baptism and Communion at the vigil is pertinent to the rest of worship on Easter Sunday as well as to the entire Easter season. Revelation 5:13, quoted earlier and sung in feast of victory, is included in the reading for the third Sunday of Easter in year C in both lectionaries. Everything said thus far both about the Eucharist and about baptism and baptismal renewal is relevant for the other occasions of worship on Easter Sunday and in the Great Fifty Days of the Easter season, including its concluding finale at the feast of Pentecost. More will be said in the chapters that follow.

For Easter Sunday, though, worship continues with more proclamation and praise. Scripture passages from the lectionaries all proclaim resurrection and restoration. Peter's sermon in Caesarea recounted in Acts 10:34–43 is given by the lectionaries as either the first lesson or the second lesson for the main service of Easter Sunday. Peter begins this sermon to a Gentile audience observing that "God shows no partiality" (vs. 34), and proceeds to declare Christ resurrected as "judge of the living and the dead" (vs. 42). Peter testifies to eating and drinking with the risen Christ. The passage suggested by the lectionaries concludes with verse 43, but the chapter continues with the outpouring of the Holy Spirit on the Gentiles gathered and with their baptism with water! Especially if baptism is being celebrated on Easter when this is read, it would be appropriate to continue reading to this finale of the chapter.

The Revised Common Lectionary suggests readings from the Hebrew Scriptures as the first lesson for the main service of Easter Sunday if the reading from Acts is given as the second lesson: Jeremiah 31:1–6 in year A, Isaiah 25:6–9 in year B, and Isaiah 65:17–25 in year C. Jeremiah promises the people peace and a productive land: "You shall plant vineyards on the mountains of Samaria; the planters shall plant, and shall enjoy the fruit" (Jer 31:5). Isaiah 25 promises life and a joyful feasting in the defeat of disgrace and death: "He will swallow up death forever," it declares and continues as follows: "Then the Lord GOD will wipe away the tears from all faces, and the disgrace of his people he will take away from all the earth, for the LORD has spoken" (Isa 25:8). Isaiah 65 envisions harmony between creatures as God establishes "new heavens and a new earth," characterized by the wolf and the lamb feeding together: "They shall not hurt or destroy on all my holy mountain, says the LORD" (vs. 25).

The Revised Common Lectionary suggests readings from Colossians and 1 Corinthians as the second lesson for the main service of Easter Sunday if Acts 10 is read for the first lesson. 1 Corinthians 15 provides the readings in years B and C. The entire chapter of 1 Corinthians 15 addresses the matter of resurrection—both Christ's and ours. The reading for year B is 1 Corinthians 15:1–11, where Paul attests to Christ having risen and appeared to a sequence of witnesses, including himself. The reading for year C is 1 Corinthians 15:19–26, where Paul describes Christ's resurrection as the "first fruits of those who have died" (vs. 20), and claims Christ will reign until death itself is destroyed (vs. 26). Elsewhere in this fifteenth chapter of 1 Corinthians, Paul explains the resurrection of the body as a matter of different kinds of bodies with different kinds of "glory." His explanation can be as confusing as clarifying with distinctions made between heavenly bodies and earthly bodies, bodies of different kinds of animals, physical bodies, and spiritual bodies, and between perishable and imperishable. Importantly, though, is his insistence on some kind of bodily resurrection as shown by Christ and as expected to be experienced by us.

Bodies are important. That our God would be embodied at all is remarkable! Every moment of Christ's incarnate life challenges our conceptions. Good Friday and Easter Sunday are particularly challenging. The Divine dies, and the Mortal Man who died lives. Docetism is the heresy "prevalent in certain NT [New Testament] times and later, to the effect that Christ had not come in the flesh."[27] "Strictly speaking," writes Daniel A. Smith, "docetism denies the reality or physicality of Jesus' body, not just in the postresurrection appearances, but during his life and career as well."[28] Some of the Easter stories in the New Testament depict the risen Christ in a way that directly refutes this [mis]conception. Jesus, now risen, eats with his disciples on the road to Emmaeus (Luke 24:13–43) and by the Sea of Tiberias (John 21:1–14), and the resurrected Jesus invites his disciples to touch and feel him (Luke 24:39, John 20:24–29). These stories are often read on the evening of Easter Sunday or on the Sundays soon following in the Easter season.

Docetism has its contemporary corollaries—interpretations of Christ's resurrection that reductively spiritualize it in a way that diminishes its earthly and embodied import. Both liberal Christians and more fundamentalist Christians can exhibit such inclinations. The modernist liberal version of docetism is to psychologize the event of Christ's resurrection; the emphasis falls on the psychological effect on the witnesses. Whatever happened, whatever they saw, whatever they heard, their lives were forever changed. The emphasis shifts to the subjective experiences of the believers rather than the earthy reality of the risen Christ. The more fundamentalist version of docetic interpretation spiritualizes resurrection in a dualistic way, and it becomes all about heaven. Jesus may have risen in the flesh momentarily but then takes all his flesh—and we with him eventually—up into heaven and away from this Earth. Both of these interpretive tendencies are faithful witnesses to God's love for God's people, but they do not really do justice to God's love for this Earth and these bodies inhabiting Earth. But the risen Christ was born of this Earth, lived and breathed on this Earth, died an earthly death, and rose an embodied presence to eat and drink with us. We continue with Christ to eat and drink. An ecological interpretation of resurrection needs to recover this embodied emphasis. We need to bring Easter back down to Earth.

Earth participates in resurrection. Matthew's Gospel has Earth quaking with Jesus's resurrection even as it did with his crucifixion (Matt 27:51, 28:2). Inspired by Matthew's account, Norman Habel has written a liturgy moving us to celebrate Easter with Earth. The following is a segment of it, inviting commitment to Earth," from a longer liturgy titled, "Song of Earth." This is written as Habel has provided it, but it would also be possible to reverse the role of "leader" and "all" and use this as a litany with the congregation responding, "On the first day of resurrection Earth quaked" to each of the sections, and the leader then reading all else. Such use of a litany with a simple and repeated congregational response would not require printed or projected text; it would also reinforce for worshipers the realization of Earth's participation in resurrection. The congregational response could be prompted simply with a raised hand. Following the liturgy, this chapter on Easter Sunday concludes with stanzas from Carolyn Winfrey Gillette's hymn of dedication, "You Give Us Hope This Easter Day."

Song of Earth: Commitment[29]

Leader: On the first day of resurrection, Earth quaked
and celebrated with a bright light in the tomb.

All: On this day we celebrate the light,
and promise Earth we will strive to remove
all nuclear darkness and death.

Leader: On the first day of resurrection, Earth quaked
and an angel descended from the sky.

All: On this day we celebrate sky,
and promise Earth we will find new ways
to keep our atmosphere fresh and clean.

Leader: On the first day of resurrection, Earth quaked
and a stone rolled back to reveal a cave.

All: We celebrate our rocks, our soil, our caves,
and we promise Earth we will work
to save its soil from salt and its forests from destruction.

Leader: On the first day of resurrection, Earth quaked
as the sun rose on a very new day.

All: We celebrate our sun, our moon, and our seasons

and we promise Earth to refrain from ripping
into the ozone layer and destroying life on Earth.

Leader: On the first day of resurrection, Earth quaked
and tidal waves swept across the seas.

All: We celebrate our seas with all their glistening life,
and we promise Earth not to deposit more toxins
that kill the creatures of the ocean.

Leader: On the first day of resurrection, Earth quaked
and all life on Earth felt the rumble of Christ rising.

All: We celebrate all life that emerges from Earth,
and we promise Earth that we will work
to save all threatened species, including humans.

Leader: On every day of resurrection, Earth quakes somewhere
reminding us to celebrate and sustain life.

All: We celebrate with all creation,
and we promise Earth to hold life sacred
and find ways that sustain all forms of life.

HYMN: "You Give Us Hope This Easter Day" by Carolyn Winfrey Gillette[30] 8.8.8.8
(May be sung to the tune "O Waly Waly")

You give us hope this Easter Day:
O God, in Christ, you make us new!
As we've been blessed, O Lord, we pray,
May these our gifts bless others, too.

When people flee from drought or storm,
When children cry, in need of bread —
May these our gifts keep victims warm
And see that hungry ones are fed.

When workers suffer, long-oppressed,
When neighbors seek to organize,

When those abused weep in distress —
May these our gifts change people's lives.

When churches seek to tend the earth,
When gardens grow on urban lands —
May these our gifts provide new birth,
Clear-flowing waters, helping hands.

O gracious God, you give us life!
This gift is one we're called to share.
May we now serve the risen Christ
Through these our gifts of love and care.

Chapter 6

Easter Season and Christ's Ascension:
To Fill All Things

Holy Week and the fifty days following Easter constitute the earliest liturgical season observed by the church. Easter and Holy Week were identified with the timing of the Jewish feast of Passover and were accordingly named *Pascha*. "Pentecost" is the Greek word denoting the Jewish feast of Weeks (*Shavuot*), or First fruits, which occurs fifty days following Passover. As previously mentioned, both Jewish festivals are related to natural seasons and to agricultural cycles. Earth's fecundity and salvation history were celebrated. The early church continued this season of celebration of new life, now commemorating Christ's resurrection and the outflowing of the Holy Spirit. The timing also shifted to privilege the first day of the week, Sunday, as the day of resurrection. So in the Christian iteration of the liturgical calendar, both Pascha and Pentecost would fall on Sundays. At one point, the entire period of fifty days was termed Pentecost and constituted a single season inclusive of Christ's resurrection, ascension, and the blessing of the Holy Spirit. Unique to the book of Acts is the specific chronology of the risen Christ appearing to the apostles for forty days before ascending, and the Holy Spirit pouring out on the "day of Pentecost" (Acts 1:3–5; 2:1), presumably the fiftieth day. Eventually, during the fourth century, this chronology became accepted for the church's liturgical season with the feast of Ascension falling on the fortieth day.[1]

EPISTLES: ASCENDED TO REIGN
THROUGHOUT CREATION

The defeat of the principalities and powers is a theme resounding throughout the season of Easter, beginning even earlier with Good Friday. Colossians proclaims this defeat of the *exousia* and the victory of Christ to have occurred in the crucifixion and on the cross: "He disarmed the rulers (*archas*) and authorities (*exousias*) and made a public example of them, triumphing over them in it," that is, in the cross (Col 2:15), and the Gospel of John (19:30) quotes Jesus declaring from the cross, "it is finished," that is, it is accomplished.

On Easter Sunday, Christ's resurrection is proclaimed as a victory over the "principalities and powers," that is over deadly forces inimical to God's reign throughout creation, as well as victory over death itself. Year B of the Revised Common Lectionary for Easter Sunday suggests the reading from 1 Corinthians that declares that Christ must reign until putting all enemies under his feet; explicitly this is after destroying "every ruler (*archēn*) and every authority (*exousian*) and power (*dunamin*)," the last enemy being death itself (1 Cor 15:24–26).

Easter season concludes with the Day of Pentecost, one of the lectionary readings being Romans 8:22–27.[2] This passage has been most suggestive for Christian environmental ethics, saying that "the whole creation has been groaning in labor pains until now" (Rom 8:22). This chapter of Romans continues by proclaiming the resurrection of Christ from the dead, now ascended at God's right hand, and it concludes by announcing the defeat of all powers antithetical to God's love for us in creation:

> It is God who justifies. Who is to condemn? Is it Christ Jesus, who died, yes, who was raised, who is at the right hand of God, who indeed intercedes for us? Will hardship or distress, or persecution, or famine, or nakedness, or peril, or sword? . . . No, in all these things we are more than conquerors through him who loved us. For I am convinced that neither death, nor life, nor angels, nor rulers (*archai*), nor things present, nor things to come, nor powers (*dunameis*), nor height, nor depth, nor anything else in all creation, will be able to separate us from the love of God in Christ Jesus our Lord. (Rom 8:33b–35, 37–39)[3]

The earlier verses about creation groaning in travail should be read while keeping in mind the chapter's conclusion with this defeat of the powers in creation by Christ. Moreover, resurrection—both Christ's and ours—can be seen as referenced in this passage. Paul writes:

> For the creation waits with eager longing for the revealing of the children of God; for the creation was subjected to futility, not of its own will but by the will of the one who subjected it, in hope that the creation itself will be set free from its bondage to decay and will obtain the freedom of the glory of the children of God. We know that the whole creation has been groaning in labor pains until now; and not only the creation, but we ourselves, who have the first fruits of the Spirit, groan inwardly while we wait for adoption, the redemption of our bodies. (Rom 8:19–23)

This is some of the clearest "Mother Earth" imagery in the Bible. Creation groans in travail to give birth to resurrection from within her depths, the redemption of our bodies. Creation participates in this birthing—both in travail and in the "revealing of the children of God." This redemption is creation's own freedom from futility as well as the "freedom of the glory of the children of God." Our confidence and creation's hope lie in Christ crucified, risen, and ascended, who intercedes for us even while we struggle against the principalities and powers that have already been defeated by Christ.

Christ's ascension can be seen as the culmination of the Easter season, with Christ's powerful presence affirmed throughout creation. The Day of Ascension occurs on a Thursday, ten days before Pentecost, but it is often celebrated on the following Sunday, the seventh Sunday of Easter. Even prior to Ascension Thursday, though, on the sixth Sunday of Easter, the Epistle reading for year A in the Revised Common Lectionary is from 1 Peter which presents Christ's death and resurrection as prefiguring our baptism, ". . . as an appeal to God for a good conscience, through the resurrection of Jesus Christ, who has gone into heaven and is at the right hand of God with angels, authorities (*exousiōn*), and powers (*dunamenōn*) made subject to him" (1 Pet 3:21b–22).[4]

On the Day of Ascension, the theme of the ascended Christ's powerful presence throughout creation is announced in the first chapter of Ephesians, which is the epistle reading for year A of the Roman Catholic Lectionary and for each year in the Revised Common Lectionary:

> God put this power to work in Christ when he raised him from the dead and seated him at his right hand in the heavenly places, far above all rule (*archēs*) and authority (*exousias*) and power (*dunameōs*) and dominion (*kuriotētos*), and above every name that is named, not only in this age but also in the age to come. And he has put all things under his feet and has made him the head over all things for the church, which is his body, the fullness of him who fills all in all. (Eph 1:20–23)

The church continues to embody the risen Christ who now claims sovereignty over all competing powers and dominions, and who is revealed as filling and fulfilling all of creation. Two aspects of this proclamation are inexorably related to each other: the defeat of the principalities and powers and the immanent reign of Christ within creation.

The Epistle reading in the Roman Catholic Lectionary for Ascension in year B is from the fourth chapter of Ephesians which similarly emphasizes the immanence of the ascended Christ, that Christ "who descended is the same one who ascended far above all the heavens, so that he might fill all things" (Eph 4:10). On Ascension, Christ's ultimate victory is proclaimed, Christ's dominion is reaffirmed, and Christ's presence throughout creation is reassured. Christ's sovereignty pertains to the world of nature, to the social sphere, and to the spiritual realm; it pertains to both political power and spiritual power. Christ is Lord of all—Christ who fills all in all.

Theology of Ascent and Theology of Descent

The actual image of ascension, though, is difficult for us—the picture presented of Jesus being lifted into the sky and beyond the clouds. The physics of it bothers liberal and rational minds. Even when the ascension is interpreted symbolically as depicting Christ's authority over all, the vertical symbolism of authority can be disturbing to people of egalitarian conscience who are rightfully suspicious of hierarchy and patriarchy. Partially as a result of this disquiet with the image, many Protestant congregations simply forego celebration of the feast of Ascension, despite it being one of the major feast days in Christian tradition (along with Christmas, Epiphany, Easter, and Pentecost). That it traditionally falls on Thursday—forty days after Easter Sunday and ten days before Pentecost Sunday—is another reason for the lack of attention to Ascension in congregations unaccustomed to gathering on Thursdays. Most liturgical calendars have the provision of celebrating Ascension on the seventh Sunday of the Easter season a week prior to Pentecost, but, even so, the theme of ascension is often lacking in many Protestant congregations. When it is celebrated, ironically sermons frequently focus on absence rather than presence of Christ—on leaving rather than ruling in the world. These sermons often presume to take the disciples' bewildered perspective, something like "there he goes! . . . guess it's up to us now," and sermonic attention awaits Pentecost and our receiving, as promised in Luke, "power from on high" (Luke 24:49). But the Gospel lessons, as well as the Epistle lessons for Ascension, actually emphasize the abiding presence of Christ in the world of God's creation.

Christ ascends to the right hand of God—which is placed exactly where—and where not? As Martin Luther puts it, "The right hand of God is everywhere."[5] Following Luther, H. Paul Santmire advocates a "theology of descent" to offer corrective counterbalance to dominant images of a "theology of ascent" in Western theology. Such a theology of descent affirms God's immanence throughout creation and emphasizes Christ's incarnation and sovereign presence. The risen and ascended Christ is everywhere because, being at God's right hand, God is everywhere. Santmire describes Luther's perspective that God is "in, with, and under all things" as applying to "the whole creation and indeed every creature."[6] Santmire quotes Luther, "For God is wholly present in all creation, in every corner, he is behind you and before you," and Luther then asks, "Do you think he is sleeping on a pillow in heaven?"[7]

The omnipresence of Christ at the right hand of God has implications both for the way we regard Christ's sacramental presence in worship and Christ's "sacral" presence in nature. Concerning sacramental presence, Santmire writes:

> The whole Christ sits at the right hand of God, wherever that right hand is—and that is everywhere. Only this way can Luther affirm as consistently and as passionately as he does that in the Eucharist the believer is in communion with the whole Christ, thus encountering "God with us," Immanuel, then and there, really present in the administration of bread and wine.[8]

Concerning Christ's sacral presence in the natural world, Santmire prefers the language of "sacrality" to describe this presence rather than either "sacred" or "sacramental." "Sacred," to Santmire's ears, implies a greater identity of the divine with the natural world and suggests a pantheism that he does not intend. "Sacramental" carries a particular constellation of historical and theological meaning pertaining to God's presence perceived and received in the worship of the liturgical assembly. "Sacral," Santmire suggests describes the presence of Christ in, with, and under the world of nature perceived with the eyes of faith. He explains: "My point is, *nature is sacral to me* when I am gifted in the Spirit to experience it so, because nature is where I encounter the same Christ whom I know personally, by grace alone, in the midst of the [liturgical] assembly."[9]

Finally, for Santmire following Luther, there is both distinction and continuity between the present "ubiquity of the risen and ascended Christ" in the natural world and Christ's promised eschatological reign to make all things new. "Christ who will so publicly claim [this] lordship in the eschaton," writes Santmire, "is the same Christ who is really here, in these times, exercising . . . lordship in hidden ways" discerned with the eyes of faith and disclosed to the faithful through the means of grace in Word and Sacrament.[10]

Santmire urges us to be intentional in using images of descent as well as ascent in public worship so as to reinforce a greater sense of God's abiding presence among us. He notes, for instance, that we continually rehearse an image of ascent when we begin the Eucharist as we do traditionally with the *Sursum corda*, "Lift up your hearts. We lift them up to the Lord." He suggests instead, perhaps substituting, "Open your hearts."[11]

The hymn writer, Brian Wren, has attended particularly to language about God that might broaden our liturgical depiction from vertical images of hierarchy and patriarchy. He playfully spells an acronym that describes these dominant images in our hymnals: "KINGAFAP," which stands for "King-G-d-Almighty-Father-Protector."[12] Alternatively he urges that a greater variety of metaphors be used for naming and addressing God, enriching our understanding while yet in continuity with Trinitarian confession, claiming female imagery while refashioning male images. In particular he advocates as a guideline for choosing such metaphors that they be liberating. As an example he suggests Sallie McFague's "Mother, Lover and Friend."[13] Concerning the Trinity, Wren explains:

> Trinitarian experience is unique to Christianity. Though formed within the KINGAFAP metaphor system, it broke through it, to see God not as a single, isolated being, the mon-arch, but as a complex, coequal unity in relatedness. The Christian experience of God as Trinity is implicitly antipatriarchal and a rich resource.[14]

The variety of liberating metaphors extends to God's ongoing relationship to creation, to "the conviction that the Holy One indwells and permeates all things,"[15] and to the need for human responses of thankfulness and responsibility. Quoting from his own hymn, "Thank You, God, for Water, Soil and Air," Wren pens:

> We need imagery that expresses our gratitude for water, soil, and air, "large gifts supporting everything that lives," for "priceless energy, stored in each atom, gathered from the sun," and especially for God, who has woven nature's life "into a seamless robe, a fragile whole," which we tamper with at our peril.[16]

Wren does not advocate abandoning "KINGAFAP" imagery but rather nuancing it in ways that are more liberating while also bringing other images to expand our understanding and our celebration. Speaking of Christ's ascension in particular, Wren makes five affirmations. He writes:

> One way forward is to analyze KINGAFAP metaphors and reimage from their root intentions. For example, the Ascension story shows the resurrected Crown Prince going up to the heavenly throne and sitting at the right hand of this Father-King-God. The imagery expresses the following convictions:
>
> 1. Jesus is alive forever.
> 2. Jesus is as close to God as it is possible to get, and on the same level, not secondary or subordinate.
> 3. Everything he taught and showed about God is vindicated, and his whole human life is taken into the divine life and experience.
> 4. Jesus, with God, has access to all human life: past, present, and future (in the KINGAFAP system this is expressed as "oversight," control, sovereignty).
> 5. The active presence of the Holy Spirit stems from the closeness of Son and Father.[17]

He composes the hymn, "Jesus is with God," to express these same convictions. The first verse poetically affirms the ascended Christ's abiding presence within creation:

Jesus is with God,
endlessly alive.
All he did and said and suffered,
all he hoped and all he offered
beats with shimmering wings
in the heart of things.[18]

Another contemporary hymn writer, Marty Haugen, similarly emphasizes Christ's abiding presence in our midst, in our world, and in our worship. After singing about Christ's Eucharistic presence in the "wine of compassion" and in "the bread that is you," the third verse of his hymn, "Gather Us In," locates Christ and Christ's reign on Earth:

Not in the dark of buildings confining,
not in some heaven, light-years away,
but here in this place the new light is shining,
now is the Kingdom, now is the day.[19]

An older hymn recommended for Ascension by *Episcopal Hymnal 1982* and *The Presbyterian Hymnal*, and included in many other hymnals, is *Salve Festa Dies*, "Hail Thee, Festival Day," which weaves the story of Christ's crucifixion, resurrection, and ascension with poetic praise from creation. The *Episcopal Hymnal* begins the hymn with this chorus for Ascension:[20]

Hail thee, festival day!
 Blest day to be hallowed forever,
day when the Christ ascends,
 high in the heavens to reign.

The first verse then follows, affirming Christ's reign throughout earthly creation. This is the version from *The Presbyterian Hymnal*:[21]

Christ who was nailed to the cross,
 Is Lord and the Ruler of nature;
All things created on earth
 Sing to the glory of God.

These hymns all use the vertical dimension metaphorically to indicate both Christ's ascension to reign in glory and the participation of Earth and earthlings in this reign. Christ ascends in order to fill and fulfill all things and to bestow broadly the Holy Spirit. Even in ascending, Christ does not abandon Earth and earthlings but perseveres with us and includes us in the journey. But verticality can be problematic, implying separation and hierarchical domination. We can notice two related theological strategies for understanding this tension of separation implied in the vertical metaphor. One strategy represented by Santmire, Wren, and McFague tends to emphasize the earthward direction of Christ's reign even in the portrayal of ascending. Santmire describes this as a "theology of descent."

Alternatively, we have seen in previous chapters, Eastern Orthodox theologians tend to emphasize earthly movement toward God, a participation with Christ ascending toward glory; we have been naming this as transfiguration, glorification, and *theosis* or deification of humanity and of creation. Metropolitan Paulos Gregorios, for instance, writes: "The new creation, into which the whole of humanity has to be reborn through death and resurrection, has already been inaugurated through Christ's death, resurrection, and ascension. He has assumed all humankind into himself, and exalted it to the right hand of God."[22] Not only humanity, but all of creation is included in this exaltation.

Saying that "matter is God's will, [God's] energy, made palpable to our senses," Bijesh Philip cites Metropolitan Paulos Gregorios to insist that we need to "find a new respect for inanimate as well as organic nature." He writes:

> Incarnation of the Son of God, use of nonhuman creation in his life, offering of nature and humanity on the cross, resurrection, and the ascension by which he lifted nature and humanity to heaven, amply assert the spiritual significance of matter. It was also given participation in the redemption. The sacraments, especially the Holy Eucharist respect this significance of matter and nature.[23]

The "spiritual significance of matter" is evident in Christ's physical incarnation, crucifixion, resurrection, and ascension. *Theosis* requires incarnation as well as ascension.

Both metaphorical directions—earthward and heavenward—are continually present through our ongoing participation with Christ and Christ's continuing participation in creation. These are not mutually exclusive or opposed theological strategies. Both affirm a continuing relationship between Earth and Christ, risen and ascended—rather than separation. In the incarnation, life, death, resurrection, and ascension of Christ—in the whole story of shared life and death and new life—the gulf between God and God's creatures is bridged—bridged by Christ and traversed by faith.

The problem of hierarchy is related to the problem of separation. No one can be God except God, and God's sovereignty is unlike any dominion or principality or power that might presume to govern on Earth. The question is, do we experience God's sovereignty as being in solidarity with us, as sharing in our suffering, as both compassionate and liberating? Or do we experience God as despot? At its worst, a hierarchical picture of divine rule can be seen as undergirding or even justifying human inequality and the destruction of the natural world. When pictured well, however, confession of God's sovereignty can be understood as relativizing human power, subverting dominant ideologies, and even overthrowing injustice and oppression. God's sovereignty, moreover, can be our hope for sustaining creation's flourishing and the well-being of Earth's inhabitants. The ascendency of the risen Christ, who lived and died as we do as creatures on Earth, helps us to see God's sovereignty in this more positive light as solidarity with suffering humanity and with creation, and as claiming ultimate victory over powers that divide and demean.

Ascension: The Gospels

The Easter season follows the chronology as interpreted in the book of Acts which states that Jesus appeared alive to the apostles for forty days following the crucifixion before being lifted up beyond their gaze (Acts 1:1–11). This reading from the beginning of Acts is given as the first lesson for Ascension in both the Roman Catholic Lectionary for the Mass and the Revised Common Lectionary for all three years of the cycle. The verses from the end of Luke are also given as the Gospel lesson for Ascension for each year in the Revised Common Lectionary, but the Roman Catholic Lectionary provides for readings from each of the Synoptics for each of the three years: Matthew 28:16–20 in year A, Mark 16:15–20 in year B, and Luke 24:46–53 in year C.

Each of these readings from the Gospels, as well as the Gospel of John, proclaims Christ's ascended reign and continuing presence differently. Curiously the Gospel of Luke concludes with greater ambiguity concerning the timing of Christ's ascension than does Acts, and some ancient manuscripts of Luke even lack the phrase that Jesus was "carried up into heaven" (Luke 24:51). Suggestively, though, the word used for "carried up" (*anapherō*) carries an added connotation of offering up of sacrifice. An emphasis in Luke/Acts is on the divine presence of the Holy Spirit following Christ's ascension—empowering and emboldening the church's witness about Jesus Christ "to the ends of the earth."

In John's Gospel there is no depiction of Christ's ascension, but the Gospel of John portrays Jesus actually speaking about his ascension more than in the other Gospels. After rising from the dead, when Jesus appeared to Mary Magdalene, he cautions her not to hold him "because I have not yet ascended," and he sends her to tell the others: "I am ascending to my Father and your Father, to my God and your God" (John 20:17). Earlier statements about ascending made by Jesus in John's Gospel indicate that this ascension is seen as a return to a divine status enjoyed before the incarnation. This dynamic of descending and ascending is unique to John. "No one has ascended into heaven except the one who descended from heaven, the Son of Man," explains Jesus to Nicodemus, "And just as Moses lifted up the serpent in the wilderness, so must the Son of Man be lifted up" (John 3:13–14). "This is the bread that came down from heaven," Jesus told the disciples, speaking about his own flesh (John 6:58a); hearing this, the disciples grumbled about it being difficult to understand. "Does this offend you?" Jesus challenged them, "Then what if you were to see the Son of Man ascending to where he was before?" (John 6:61b–62). Jerome Neyrey makes the point that these references to ascending by Jesus in John's Gospel use the Greek word *anabainō*, which entails agency by the one speaking. Jesus is the one actively ascending, as opposed to *analambanō*, which is the word used in Acts and which conveys a sense of being acted upon, being lifted.[24] Finally at John's version of the last supper, Jesus prays, "So now, Father, glorify me in your own presence with the glory that I had in your presence before the world existed" (John 17:5).

Matthew's Gospel similarly does not have a depiction of ascension but instead concludes with Jesus claiming "all authority in heaven and on earth," commissioning the disciples to "make disciples of all nations, baptizing them in the name of the Father and of the Son and of the Holy Spirit," and reassuring, "I am with you always, to the end of the age" (Matt 28:20). Quoting this verse from Matthew, Christopher J. H. Wright expounds:

> The whole earth is the field of God's mission, and ours. If God owns the universe, there is no place that does not belong to [God]. There is nowhere we can step off [God's] property, either into the property of some other deity or into some autonomous sphere of our own private ownership. Such claims were made in relation to Yahweh in the Old Testament (for example, Ps 139). But in the New Testament the same claims are made in relation to Jesus Christ. Standing on a mountain with his disciples after his resurrection, Jesus paraphrases [these claims], and calmly applies them to himself; "All authority in heaven and on earth has been given to me" (Matt 28:18 NRSV). The risen Jesus thus claims the same ownership and sovereignty over all creation as the Old Testament affirms for Yahweh.
>
> The whole earth belongs to Jesus by right of creation, by right of redemption, and by right of future inheritance.[25]

Matthew, Luke, and John present Christ assuming authority throughout the earth, empowering the disciples to represent Christ in the world and invoking the Holy Spirit for their earthly mission.

So does the long ending of Mark. While there is a broad consensus among biblical scholars that Mark 16:9–20 is not the original ending to Mark, these verses include an account of the ascension, and Mark 16:15–20 is given in the

Roman Catholic Lectionary as the Gospel reading for the Day of Ascension in year B. These verses are striking in that, "creation" is named as the recipient of the disciples' proclamation of good news: "Go into all the world and proclaim the good news to the whole creation" (Mark 16:15).

Mark is the only Gospel that even uses the word for creation, *ktisis*, and it occurs at two other points—Mark 10:6 and 13:19.[26] In both of these other instances, *ktisis* is spoken from the mouth of Jesus in the phrase, "From the beginning of [the] creation." Mark 10:6 explicitly cites the creation stories in Genesis (1:27 and 2:24) in giving Jesus's answer to a question about divorce. Mark 13:19 is in the context of Mark's version of the Synoptic apocalypse. That Mark is intentionally invoking the idea of creation with this reference is indicated by a redundancy: "In those days there will be suffering such as has not been from the beginning of the creation that God created, until now." The apocalyptic passage concludes with the promise that "after that suffering . . . the powers (*dunameis*) in the heavens will be shaken" and the messiah will come "with great power and glory" (Mark 13:24–25). Mark is voicing an expectation for the messianic reign to be a defeat of powers that are inimical to God's will for creation, and the flourishing of God's reign in creation.

The story of ascension in the longer ending of Mark, although written at a later date than the rest of Mark, is similarly invoking this idea of creation in the commissioning of the disciples to proclaim the gospel "to the whole creation." Indeed the signs that accompany this proclamation demonstrate a resurgence of spiritual power for believers acting in Jesus's name within the world of nature. In addition to speaking in tongues, these signs include casting out demons, healing the sick, being able to pick up snakes, and being able to ingest poison without harm. The power present among the believers is manifest in creation and signifies the ascended Christ's reign in creation through these signs by believers "using my name." The last verse, following Christ's ascension, attests to this power being the continued presence of the ascended Christ, saying, "the Lord worked with them and confirmed the message by the signs that accompanied it."

Mark mentions "signs" (*semeia*) only at two other points in the Gospel: in chapters 8 and 13. Each deserve attention. In chapter 8, a sign from heaven is requested from Jesus "to test him," and Jesus responds negatively for "this generation," sighing and saying: "No sign will be given to this generation," and he then sailed off in a boat (Mark 8:11–13). In Mark's Gospel, not even the sign of Jonah is proffered as it is in the Synoptic parallels (Matt 12:39, 16:4; Luke 11:29). This refusal of a sign for "this generation" is nonetheless sandwiched between the feeding of 4,000 and the giving of sight to one who was blind. This is immediately followed by Peter's confession that Jesus is the Christ and then by Jesus's teaching about the impending suffering, death, and resurrection of the Son of Man. Chapter 8 concludes with further admonition for the current generation and looking ahead to the Son of Man coming "in the glory of his Father with the holy angels" (Mark 8:38).

Mark 13, as we have already noticed, is Mark's iteration of the Synoptic apocalypse in which the idea of creation (*ktisis*) is evoked and the defeat of destructive powers in creation is foretold in conjunction with the coming of the Son of Man to Earth in power and glory. The entire apocalyptic chapter is prefaced with the disciples asking, "What will be the sign that all these things are about to be accomplished?" (Mark 13:4).

The longer ending to Mark also presents signs of messianic presence and power—but now to the next generation.[27] It is not the disciples alone who are to manifest these signs but rather to recipients of their proclamation who believe and are baptized. The signs are to and for the church and all believers who continue to receive and proclaim the gospel to the whole creation. It is as if the author of this longer ending to Mark is intentionally addressing the next generation of readers of Mark, the next generation of believers in the gospel, the next generation for the sake of all creatures.[28]

Some of these miraculous signs may be thought to be referring to events depicted in the book of Acts, such as speaking in tongues (Acts 2:4) and handling venomous snakes (Acts 28:3–6). Moreover, all the other events mentioned in this longer ending to Mark have parallels in each of the three other Gospels.[29] The collation of these events presents a kind of summative conclusion to Mark's Gospel that is very different from the open-ended conclusion at 16:8. The astonished response of the women fleeing from the tomb at verse 8 is by itself awe-inspiring and evocative of readers' responsive engagement with the story and the mystery. The longer ending to Mark, though, provides not just a cumulative conflation of events from other accounts. It places these events into the context of Mark's proclamation of the defeat of inimical powers and the inbreaking of messianic reign throughout creation. It further invites readers to be believers empowered with this proclamation and by this proclamation to participate in the ascended Christ's reign over all the earth and not just beyond the clouds.

Roman Catholics are able to attend to this account from Mark on the Day of Ascension in year B when Mark 16:15–20 is given as the reading from the Gospel. The official Roman Catholic Canon is based on the *Vulgate*, which contains these verses as Mark's ending, included by Jerome even though he was apparently aware of copies of Mark that lacked this ending.[30] The longer ending was known as early as the mid-second century by Tatian, and Irenaeus (180 CE) was also familiar with it.[31] While text criticism now discredits its originality, this was nonetheless the assumed ending of Mark through much of the Christian tradition—for Protestants as well as Catholics. Both Luther and Calvin make substantial reference to it.[32] While text criticism informs us that these verses are not a part of the original Mark and thus amends our contemporary understanding of the biblical canon, they cannot facilely be excised from the Christian tradition. Protestants can choose how best to read these verses liturgically—whether read as the Gospel lesson itself, simply cited in the context of delivering a sermon, or edited into compositions of prayers, hymns, or litanies for corporate worship. This putative ending to Mark does present an opportunity to interpret Christ's ascension with reference to creation, commission, and Christ's power with us in the world.

Ascension: The Psalter

Psalms recommended for liturgical use on the Day of Ascension in both the Roman Catholic Lectionary for the Mass and the Revised Common Lectionary are enthronement psalms which proclaim and celebrate God's universal sovereignty. These are appropriately read on this day when Christ's ascension is understood as enthronement to reign throughout creation. The Roman Catholic Lectionary prescribes Psalm 47, which declares YHWH to be the great ruler over all the earth and calls for praises to be sung to this sovereign God. (Ps 47: 2, 6–7). The psalm begins enjoining, "Clap your hands, all you peoples; shout to God with loud songs of joy," and it concludes affirming, "the shields of the earth belong to God" (Ps 47:9).

According to *Midrash Tehillim* on Psalm 47, the celebratory clap of hands is because "the Holy One, blessed be He, will do away with the dominion of mortals over you, as it is said *The Lord most high is terrible; he is a great king over all the earth* (Ps 47:3)."[33] Far from undergirding human governance over Earth and its peoples, God's sovereignty curtails—even concludes—human pretensions toward dominion. Moreover, the midrash continues with a portrayal of God's justice turning from "terrible" to merciful: "At the sound of the Shofar, [the Holy One] becomes Lord [of mercy] (Ps 47:6), and deals mercifully, for the term Lord connotes mercy, as in The Lord, the Lord . . . Merciful and gracious (Exod 34:6)."[34] The Sovereign God's mercy and grace extend throughout the earth.

The Revised Common Lectionary likewise urges Psalm 47 to be read for Ascension but suggests another enthronement psalm as well, Psalm 93. Even more striking in Psalm 93 is the explicit reference to creation and the recognition of the Sovereign God as Creator. Robed in majesty, God "has established the world," and Psalm 93 declares at the outset that "it shall never be moved" (Ps 93:1). At the same time, invoking imagery of primordial watery chaos, the psalm continues, "The floods have lifted up their roaring" (Ps 93:3). Hearing a tension between creation and chaos in this psalm, Arthur Walker-Jones notes that Psalm 93 places "the stability of the world in parallel with the stability of God's throne," and he finds the psalm affirming, in Walker-Jones's words, "The natural world can be counted on because God is king."

Even more majestic than the pounding tides, thundering waters, and breakers of the sea, invoked in Psalm 93, the psalm acclaims, "majestic on high is the LORD" (Ps 93:4).[35] Sounding ominous, the pounding of the seas in Psalm 93 is subsumed by an overwhelming majesty of God. Alternatively, though, *Midrash Tehillim* on Psalm 93 interprets the sound of the waters in this psalm not as ominous but as the very first voices to sing praise to the Creator in the beginning of God's reign.[36] Other enthronement psalms follow Psalm 93 (Pss 95–99), which continue to amplify creation's voices of praise.

In additional to these enthronement psalms, there are royal psalms which might have been used in a coronation or other ceremony to laud a political regent and to invoke blessing on that regent's reign. These royal psalms might also be interpreted allegorically to refer to the Creator's just rule over nature or, anachronistically, to the ascended Christ's reign to fill and fulfill all things. The enthronement psalms, however, seem more directly to laud the Creator as universal regent rather than any human aspirant.[37] Citing Gerald Wilson's comment that these enthronement psalms might be considered the "theological heart" of the fourth book of the Psalms (Ps 90–106) and even of the entire Psalter, Arthur Walker-Jones suggests, "creation plays such a prominent role in these psalms that one could say that creation lies at the theological heart of the Psalter."[38]

While it is the two particular enthronement psalms, Psalms 47 and 93, that are advocated by the lectionaries for the Day of Ascension, any of the other enthronement psalms, Psalms 95–99, might be read and sung as well. All of them bring our human voices into concert with the rest of creation in ascribing glory to the One who creates and sustains, who judges and justifies. When, as we confess, Christ ascends in order to reign and to fill and fulfill all things, these enthronement psalms ground our worship in the earth and anchor our praise in the sea, even as our voices rise to the skies.

A Dialogical Sermon for Ascension or Easter Season

Beginning from Larry Rasmussen's *Earth Community, Earth Ethics*, I initially prepared this dialogical sermon while serving at the Presbyterian School of Ministry in Aotearoa New Zealand. It was scripted for voices to be read by the Presbyterian ordinands who delivered it at First Presbyterian Church of Otago in Dunedin, New Zealand. Afterward, I edited it so that it can be more easily contextualized to other locals and shared it largely in this form on May 20, 2006 with participants at a National Council of Churches Ecological-Justice Training Event in Saint Paul, Minnesota, titled, "The Church, Climate Change, and God's Creation: How to Live as Faithful Disciples." Any number of readers can take the role of "Voice."

Scripture Lessons:

    Acts 1:1–11

    Romans 8:19–23

Voice: The Day of Ascension in the ecumenical Christian calendar—the culmination of the Season of Easter—is next week. On Thursday or in many congregations on the following Sunday, this passage from Acts is read:

> So when they had come together, they asked him, "Lord, is this the time when you will restore the kingdom to Israel?" He replied, "It is not for you to know the times or periods that the Father has set by his own authority. But you will receive power when the Holy Spirit has come upon you; and you will be my witnesses in Jerusalem, in all Judea and Samaria, and to the ends of the earth." When he had said this, as they were watching, he was lifted up, and a cloud took him out of their sight. While he was going and they were gazing up toward heaven, suddenly two men in white robes stood by them. They said, "Men of Galilee, why do you stand looking up toward heaven?" (Acts 1:6–11a)

Where on Earth did he go? Where else is there?

Voice: About 13.72 billion years ago, scientists tell us,[39] the entire universe began with a massive explosion of all energy and existence—everything hurtling out from this center. For the next 5 billion years, out of this hurtling stuff, stars and galaxies formed which continue to travel out from each other to this very day.[40]

Chorus: *The whole creation has been groaning in travail together until now.*

Voice: About 5 billion years ago, the earth and the rest of the solar system formed in this far corner of the Milky Way galaxy. Earth formed about 4.5 billion years ago developing "an atmosphere, oceans and continents—all wildly different from ours at present—as molten rock cooled over [a period of] several tens of thousands of years."[41]

Chorus: *The whole creation has been groaning in travail together until now.*

Voice: "Roughly 4 billion years ago . . . the first living cell emerged." Between 3.2 and 2.4 billion years ago, the first green plants, microscopic algae, began photosynthesizing energy from the sun.[42]

Chorus: *The whole creation has been groaning in travail together until now.*

Voice: Suddenly, about 580 million years ago, life really blossomed with multicellular life. "Insects, earthworms, corals, sponges, molluscs, and animals with rudimentary backbones . . . appeared." [And] Just as suddenly most of these were eliminated [in the Cambrian extinctions]. Roughly 80–90% of life collapsed forever."[43]

Chorus: *The whole creation has been groaning in travail together until now.*

Voice: "Beginning largely anew, shellfish, finned fish, vertebrates, insects, trees, and reptiles strode on the scene over the next 300 million years, only to experience the Permian extinction of 245 million years ago (75 to 90 percent of all species simply vanished.)"[44]

Chorus: *The whole creation has been groaning in travail together until now.*

Voice: "Life began yet again" Eventually birds and flowers and the first mammals all appeared. "So did the 'Atlantic' Ocean. The mass continent . . . had begun to break up and drift on earth's crustal plates . . . Then 67 million years ago, in the Cretaceous era, more extinctions occurred."[45]

Chorus: *The whole creation has been groaning in travail together until now.*

Voice: "life began (or continued) again. . . . mammals extended their family trees . . . Cats and dogs and apes first appeared (30 million years ago), as did camels, bears, and pigs (only 4.5 million years ago). Grasslands spread. But so did glaciers."[46]

Chorus: *The whole creation has been groaning in travail together until now.*

Voice: While human-like creatures first appeared 2.6 million years ago, our species "*Homo sapiens* first walked tall only very recently—some 200,000 to 400,000 years ago."[47] People have since migrated over the earth. 14,000 to 40,000 years ago, the first 'Americans' crossed the Bering Strait into North America, eventually settling throughout the Americas.

Voice: About 4,000 years ago, our father Abraham migrated from Ur to Canaan.

Voice: Only 1,000 years ago the first canoe of Polynesian voyagers arrived in New Zealand.

Chorus: *The whole creation has been groaning in travail together until now.*

Voice: *"And not only the creation, but we ourselves . . . groan inwardly as we wait for adoption."*

Voice: About 500 years ago, Europeans began settlement of the Americas. They brought with them their technology, their culture and their disease. The result was devastating. Almost 90% of the original human population was destroyed within two centuries.[48]

Chorus: *The whole creation has been groaning in travail together until now.*

Voice: *"And not only the creation, but we ourselves . . . groan inwardly as we wait for adoption."*

Voice: A little more than 200 years ago, the United States purchased the middle of North America from France and organized the "Lewis and Clark Expedition" to explore this territory and to gather information about its inhabitants. President Thomas Jefferson instructed Lewis, "In all your intercourse with the natives, treat them in the most friendly and conciliatory manner which their own conduct will permit."[49]

In the next fifty years, over a 100,000 American Indians from twenty-eight tribes were deported West.[50]

Chorus: *The whole creation has been groaning in travail together until now.*

Voice: *"And not only the creation, but we ourselves . . . groan inwardly as we wait for adoption."*

Voice: The years 1939–1945 saw unprecedented human destruction in Europe: the genocide of 6 million of God's chosen people in the Nazi holocaust. This period of world violence culminated in a holocaust of a different kind—the United States bombing the cities of Hiroshima and Nagasaki with a nuclear fire as if from hell itself. The suffering from those blasts continues to this day.

Chorus: *The whole creation has been groaning in travail together until now.*

Voice: *"And not only the creation, but we ourselves . . . groan inwardly as we wait for adoption."*

Voice: Greenhouse gasses from years of industrialization continue to accumulate in the atmosphere. Some models warn that global temperature will increase 3 degree Celsius in the next 100 years. The sea level will rise due to thermal expansion of the ocean along with melting glaciers and mountain snow and ice perhaps 20 inches by 2100.[51] Which species will evolve quickly enough to survive such rapid environmental change? Which won't?

Chorus: *"For the creation was subjected to futility, not of its own will"*

Voice:

> In the middle of time,
> in a place that was both
> the very center and
> the growing edge of the universe,
> on the first day of the week,
> after a horrifying weekend in which
> the one they had loved,
> the one in whom they had placed their hope,
> had suffered an agonizing death on the cross,
> some women came to the grave and found it open.
>
> The tomb like a womb had brought forth new life,
> nurtured unseen within the damp depths.
> A place of death had become a place of life.
> The grave had given birth to resurrection.

Voice: Fear and faith mingled here—as these women puzzled over these events and began to look for explanations. For forty days, we are told, the one they sought appeared to his friends in places other than this tomb. And since those days, many have continued to try to understand his appearance and disappearance. According to the Gospel of Luke, after forty days, Christ ascended into Heaven, to the right hand of the Ruler of all creation, in order from there, in the words of Ephesians, "to fill all things."

Chorus: *The whole creation has been groaning in travail together until now.*

Voice: What pain is this for which creation groans? This has become something of a prooftext for eco-theology. Is it the pain of the extinction of species which precede us—like the moa or the passenger pigeon—or perhaps the extinction of species which may yet follow?

Voice: Is it the pain of homelessness for refugees or uprootedness for displaced peoples? Is it the pain of people longing for their homeland or of people looking for acceptance and security even within their homeland?

Voice: Is it the pain of hatred, violence and war or even of nuclear nightmare, screams silenced before they've been uttered?

Voice: Is it the pain of pollution, of chemical contaminants, and of radioactive pollution, of pesticides from agricultural climes found in the body tissues of Antarctic penguins?

Voice: Is it the pain of contortion as the very genetic structures of creatures—plants and animals—are mixed and mingled ostensibly to improve the species—to make an herbicide-ready world?

Voice: Is it the pain of heat and melting and climate change: the earth's atmospheric blanket, designed to moderate temperatures and to keep earth habitable—now smothering us with our own greenhouse emissions?

Chorus: *The whole creation has been groaning in travail together until now.*

Voice: It is not the pain of death but the pain of life.

Voice: It is not the pain of killing but of giving birth.

Voice: It is not the pain of dying but of resurrection.

Voice: It is not the pain of despair, or a desperate plea for human rescue. It is a pain of hope in the power of God to sustain, redeem, and resuscitate God's creation!

Voice: Though creations situation is dire, this is not a passage about human desperation but about creation's regeneration and God's generativity.

Voice: This is not just some lifeless grave,

Voice: Not just some desert dust,

Voice: Not just some outer space.

Voice: This is mother Earth,

Voice: Our mother,

Voice: Our body,

Voice: Mother Earth, opening from her depths to give life to the children of God.

Voice: Christ is portrayed here as the first fruits of her soil, the first born of her womb.

Voice: We are her children who also follow from death to life by the power of God at work throughout the universe. Creation herself is to be renewed and we her children with her. We see creation made new. We are not abandoned to the grave; neither are we saved FROM the earth—with creation our home abandoned to decay. Rather both Earth and earthling,

Voice: Both mother and child,
Voice: both creation and creature—
Voice: both are resurrected in new birth,
Voice: in new life,
Voice: *in new creation.*

Chorus: We know that the whole creation has been groaning in travail together until now:

Voice: When we gather in worship, we don't do so as disembodied souls, but as enfleshed souls. We come—body and soul—representing all of creation seeking God's sanctifying grace for ourselves as creatures and for all of creaturely nature. All of nature is represented with us here as we draw on God's redemptive grace.

Voice: Paul writes: "For the creation was subjected to futility, not of its own will but by the will of the One who subjected it in hope; because the creation itself will be set free from its bondage to decay and obtain the glorious liberty of the children of God."

Chorus: *We know that the whole creation has been groaning in travail together until now:*

Voice: "And not only the creation, but we ourselves, who have the first fruits of the Spirit, groan inwardly as we wait for adoption, the redemption of our bodies."

Voice: And of our neighbors

Voice: And of our world.

Chorus: Amen.

Chapter 7

Pentecost

Let Everything that Breathes Praise the LORD

> In the beginning when God created the heavens and the earth, the earth was a formless void and darkness covered the face of the deep, while a wind from God swept over the face of the waters. (Gen 1:1–2)

> When the day of Pentecost had come, they were all together in one place. And suddenly from heaven there came a sound like the rush of a violent wind, and it filled the entire house where they were sitting. (Acts 2:1–2)

Pentecost celebrates the blessing of the Holy Spirit. God's own Spirit, Christ's own Spirit, is bestowed on the church—the whole church—and fills the believers—all believers. And not just the church! God's Spirit enlivens all of creation. On Pentecost Sunday, the Roman Catholic Lectionary for the Mass and the Revised Common Lectionary recommend two passages from the Bible to be read every year across the three-year cycle: Psalm 104 as the psalm and the story in Acts 2 of the sending of the Holy Spirit. They recommend passages from the Gospel of John as the Gospel readings. Psalm 104 effusively includes every part of creation in rendering praise: "When you send forth your spirit (or breath), they are created; and you renew the face of the ground (or earth)" (Ps 104:30). Inspired by this verse, our prayer, "Send forth your Holy Spirit and renew the face of the earth," is often sung as a response between verses of the Psalm 104 as it lyrically celebrates with all of creation. There is a universal vision to the Spirit's presence and the Spirit's work.

The universality of Pentecost is also apparent, at least proleptically, in the reading from Acts. While it is only the believers gathered in Jerusalem who are filled with the Holy Spirit and begin to speak in other languages, it is significant that they do speak in languages from around the world. Also, there is an international crowd gathered in Jerusalem and able to hear about "God's deeds of power" proclaimed in their native tongues (Acts 2:11). Symbolically, the miracle of understanding in different languages demonstrated at Pentecost reverses the confusion of languages and the human division said to have occurred following the tower of Babel. The story of the tower of Babel (Gen 11:1–9) is one of the readings recommended by the lectionaries for Pentecost in order to highlight this movement of the Spirit from confusion to understanding and from division to community amid diversity. The whole globe is represented in the languages voiced and heard at Pentecost.

In particular, though, it is the followers of Jesus who receive this blessing of the Spirit on Pentecost. The Holy Spirit comes upon them, as promised by Christ, in order to empower their witness throughout the world. Earlier, before Christ's ascension, they had been told, "You will receive power when the Holy Spirit has come upon you; and you will be my witnesses in Jerusalem, in all Judea and Samaria, and to the ends of the earth" (Acts 1:8). The world is thus represented symbolically both in the variety of languages and in the direction that this witness will travel—to the ends of the earth. The entire earth, created and enlivened by God's Spirit, is ultimately to be the recipient of the Spirit's message and the Spirit's blessings.

The reading from Acts given in the Revised Common Lectionary is Acts 2:1–21, which includes a quotation from the book of Joel (Joel 2:28–32) in Peter's preaching to the crowd. Peter proclaims:

> This is what was spoken through the prophet Joel: "In the last days it will be, God declares, that I will pour out my Spirit upon all flesh, and your sons and your daughters shall prophesy, and your young men shall see visions, and your old men shall dream dreams. Even upon my slaves, both men and women, in those days I will pour out my Spirit; and they shall prophesy." (Acts 2:16–18)

It is clear that the Spirit proceeds without regard to human differences of age, gender, or social status. While "all flesh," here would seem to refer to human recipients of the Spirit, the blessing as pronounced in Joel is more widely inclusive than human diversity alone. Earlier in the second chapter of Joel, shortly before this quotation, blessing is given to animals as well as to the soil that sustains them:

> Do not fear, O soil;
>   be glad and rejoice,
>   for the LORD has done great things!
> Do not fear, you animals of the field,
>   for the pastures of the wilderness are green;
> the tree bears its fruit,
>   the fig tree and vine give their full yield. (Joel 2:21–22)

There is a sharing in the blessing of the Spirit throughout creation.

Creation spirituality surrounds Pentecost spirituality, and the direction of Pentecost spirituality is toward the renewal of creation. It is the same Spirit of God that blows through the gathered believers that blew over the gathered waters at creation's beginning. The Bible's beginning with the first two verses of Genesis invokes God's Spirit as the wind over the face of the deep, and the conclusion of the Bible in the final verses of Revelation has that same Spirit inviting all to partake of the living water in new creation:

> The Spirit and the bride say, "Come."
> And let everyone who hears say, "Come."
> And let everyone who is thirsty come.
> Let anyone who wishes take the water of life as a gift. (Rev 22:17)

In the meantime, the Spirit moves the church to witness for the sake of the world. As the wind from God moved over creation, it now rushes over the Pentecost gathering, and they are all filled with the Holy Spirit.

SPIRIT, WATER, AND BREATH

In the Gospel of John, the emphasis is placed particularly on the Spirit empowering the witness of believers during a difficult time of persecution, and the timing is different in John than in Luke. In John, Jesus appears to the disciples on Easter, on the very evening following his resurrection, and breathes the Holy Spirit onto them while commissioning them (John 20:19–23). The Holy Spirit is described as the Paraclete, translated as Advocate or Comforter, promised to the disciples by Jesus in his farewell discourse prior to his crucifixion (John 14:16, 26; 15:26; 16:7), who is to teach and guide them in the challenging days ahead. The stark challenge is presented as contention between the faithful followers who are promised peace and the "world" which rejects Jesus and which portends hatred toward his followers. Jesus even refers to an inimical "ruler of this world" but assures "he has no power over me" (John 14:30).

Even with all the worldly animosity toward believers voiced in the farewell discourse, Jesus is presented throughout John's Gospel as having all the real power, and this power extends to the world. Regarding his crucifixion, Jesus willingly lays down his life, assuring, "No one takes it from me, but I lay it down of my own accord. I have power to lay it down, and I have power to take it up again" (John 10:18). Toward the conclusion of the farewell discourse, Jesus prays, acknowledging that now he has been given "power over all flesh" (John 17:2 RSV) to grant eternal life. Famously, the Gospel of John proclaims, "God so loved the world . . . Indeed, God did not send the Son into the world to condemn the world, but in order that the world might be saved through him" (John 3:16a–17). The Gospel of John begins with the creation of the world by the primordial Word and moves toward the cross where the final word from Jesus declares, "It is finished" (John 19:30). The world is the subject of God's salvation.

Preaching from John's Gospel on the role of the Paraclete, the preacher should declare the Spirit's undying support of believers in the face of hatred; this is especially important during a time when violent hatred divides society and personal bigotry as well as structural evil oppresses God's people. At the same time such preaching should not condemn the world but proclaim God's unfailing love for the whole world—for which Christ comes, Christ dies and Christ rises. God sends the Spirit to complete this work of salvation for the world through the witness of the church.

There is a link between water and Spirit in John. Jesus tells Nicodemus, "No one can enter the Kingdom of God without being born of water and the Spirit" (John 3:5). In chapter 7, the Holy Spirit is cryptically promised with reference to living water. Jesus speaks:

> Let anyone who is thirsty come to me, and let the one who believes in me drink. As the scripture has said, "Out of the believer's heart shall flow rivers of living water." Now he said this about the Spirit, which believers in him were to receive." (John 7:37b–39a)

There is no scriptural passage clearly identified as that which Jesus is quoting, but some suggested scriptural allusions[1] carry strong ecological connotations. "Living waters shall flow out from Jerusalem," as envisioned in the apocalyptic final chapter of Zechariah, "And the LORD will become king over all the earth" (Zech 14:8–9). Waters feature prominently in Deutero-Isaiah, which is rich in natural images and which strongly links creation and redemption. "Ho, everyone who thirsts, come to the waters," Isaiah 55:1 invites. Isaiah 44:3–4 promises:

> For I will pour water on the thirsty land,
>   and streams on the dry ground;
> I will pour my spirit (*ruach*) upon your descendants,
>   and my blessing on your offspring.
> They shall spring up like a green tamarisk,
>   like willows by flowing streams.

The Hebrew word, *ruach*, in Isaiah 44, is the same as in Genesis 1 and in Psalm 104 and means both wind and spirit. It blows throughout creation.

Ruach is also one of the Hebrew words signifying breath. The other common Hebrew words for breath are *nephesh* and *neshamah*. All three can be used in the phrase "breath of life" to refer to a living, breathing being. So, for instance, in the story of Noah, all the animals imperiled by the flood and all the animals saved in the ark are said to have *ruach chayyīm*, "breath of life" (Gen 6:17, 7:15). On the sixth day of creation, when God gives plants as food to human beings and to all the animals, the blessing is given to all who have the *nephesh chayah*, the "breath of life" (Gen 1:30). When God breathes the breath of life into Adam, it is *nishmat chayyīm*, and when Psalm 150 summons "everything that breathes to praise the LORD," (Ps 150:6) it is similarly *neshamah*.

All three meanings of *ruach*—wind, breath, and spirit—can be heard in Psalm 104. The psalm in praise of the Creator begins, as in Genesis, with images of primordial creation: light and heavens, waters and earth, and wind:

> You are clothed with honor and majesty,
>   wrapped in light as with a garment.
> You stretch out the heavens like a tent,
>   you set the beams of your chambers on the waters,
> you make the clouds your chariot,
>   you ride on the wings of the wind (*ruach*),
> you make the winds (*ruach* or "spirits") your messengers,
>   fire and flame your ministers.
> You set the earth on its foundations. (Ps 104: 1b–5a)

The psalm glorifies God for creating and sustaining numerous wild and domestic animals throughout the earth: "every wild animal" (vs. 11), wild asses, birds of the air, storks, cattle, wild goats, coneys, "all the animals of the forest" (vs. 20), lions, people, Leviathan, and "creeping things innumerable" in the sea "living things both small and great" (vs. 25). These animals are placed in ecological context, naming their habitats: fields, forests, mountains, the sea, and branches in which birds both sing and nest. Their food is mentioned—prey for predators, and plants—"grass to grow for the cattle, and plants for people to use, to bring forth food from the earth" (vs. 14). "The trees of the LORD are watered abundantly" (vs. 16a), and water is provided for all the animals:

> You make springs gush forth in the valleys;
>   they flow between the hills,
> giving drink to every wild animal;
>   the wild asses quench their thirst.
> By the streams the birds of the air have their habitation;
>   they sing among the branches.
> From your lofty abode you water the mountains. (Ps 104:10–13a)

There is a role for both light and darkness. Noticing nocturnal life, the psalm sings: "The sun knows its time for setting. You make darkness, and it is night, when all the animals of the forest come creeping out" (Ps 104: 19b–20). Life and death both have their place, and *ruach* makes the difference as both God's spirit and our breath: "When you take away their breath (*ruach* or 'spirit'), they die and return to their dust. When you send forth your spirit (*ruach* or 'breath'), they are created and you renew the face of the ground (or earth)" (vss. 29b–30).

Similarly the Greek words for wind (*pnoē*) and spirit (*pneuma*) in Acts 2 are both related to the word for blowing or breathing (*pneō*). Also, the Latin word *spiritus* means both breath and spirit, and our English words for respiration and spirituality are etymologically related. Moreover, taken together these words for "spirit" coincidentally convey gender inclusivity, as *ruach* is feminine, *spiritus* is masculine, and *pneuma* is neuter.

So spirituality at some level is about breath, about respiration. "Let everything that breathes praise the LORD! Praise the LORD!" according to Psalm 150:6, the final word of the Psalms. Everything that breaths, that has the breath of life, is inclusive of all animals. Today, too, we know that plants respirate. Indeed the respiration of plants is responsible both for the supply of oxygen in our air and for the fixation of atmospheric carbon into biomass that helps to curb global warming. Plants really do provide the breath of life. Moreover, as plants and animals respire, the whole earth can be seen to be cycling and recycling oxygen, maintaining life, sharing life, breathing, praising the LORD. This is spirituality on a molecular as well as a planetary level. The wind at Pentecost is the same Holy Spirit enlivening the whole planet.

FIRST FRUITS, DELIVERANCE, AND COMMUNITY

It is perhaps a coincidence that Acts presents the Holy Spirit coming to those gathered on the day of Pentecost, a feast day in the Jewish liturgical calendar. But this timing highlights two dimensions of the Jewish festival that might be relevant for Christian celebrations of Pentecost that are ecologically informed. First is the significance of plants. "Pentecost" is the Greek word denoting the Jewish feast of *Shavuot* or Weeks, which occurs fifty days following Passover. It is also called the festival of First fruits (*Bikurim*) and the festival of the Harvest (Exod 23:16). Shavuot is the harvest festival for wheat, symbolized by the offering and waving of two loaves of bread (Lev 23:15–17), and the harvest festival for "first of all the fruit of the ground" (Deut 26:2). In Deuteronomy 16:9, the countdown to *Shavuot* begins "from the time the sickle is first put to the standing grain," which is the beginning of the harvest of barley. Second, the Jewish feast commemorates God's deliverance of the people from slavery in Egypt to bring them to a "land flowing with milk and honey" (Deut 16:12; 26:8–9).[2] "Honey" (*devash*), Abraham Bloch points out, "has two definitions, the honey of bees and the sap or juice of dates." He interprets the phrase "milk and honey" to refer to agricultural fecundity, "a land rich in meat (cattle), dairy, produce of the soil, and fruit."[3] Plants and the land's productivity figure prominently in traditional Jewish celebrations of Shavuot as a harvest festival and can enter into Christian celebrations of Pentecost as well.

"First fruits" is also the metaphor employed by Paul in Romans 8 to refer to himself and to other believers in Christ as having the "first fruits of the Spirit." This passage was discussed in the previous chapter on Ascension and the Season of Easter, and it is recommended by the lectionaries to be read at Pentecost: "We know that the whole creation has been groaning in labor pains until now; and not only the creation, but we ourselves, who have the first fruits of the Spirit, groan inwardly while we wait for adoption, the redemption of our bodies" (Rom 8:22–23). Our own redemption—bodily as well as spiritually—is presented as first fruits of freedom for the entire creation. Elsewhere in Romans, Paul makes reference to the dough from the offering of first fruits, presumably at Shavuot (Lev 23:17), to describe the believers themselves as presaging the salvation of "all Israel" along with a "full number of the Gentiles" (Rom 11:16–27). Christian Pentecost is often celebrated as the birthday of the church, which it is. Importantly, though, as we see in Romans, the church's birthday recalls our roots not only in the Spirit but in the land. The church is being birthed by the earth and enlivened by the Spirit, into new creation.

As mentioned earlier, the Jewish festival of Weeks or *Shavuot* is not only a festival of harvest and of First fruits but of celebration of God's deliverance of the people from slavery in Egypt. The lectionaries recommend for Pentecost two lessons from the Hebrew Bible pertaining to the exodus, each of which has an earth-related aspect to be noticed. The Revised Common Lectionary recommends Numbers 11:24–30 to be read in year A, and the Roman Catholic Lectionary for the Mass gives verses from Exodus 19 as one of the readings for a Pentecost vigil. In the passage from Numbers, God's Spirit extends beyond Moses to include seventy elders who are gifted with ecstatic prophecy. In the passage from Exodus, God consecrates the entire population of Israelites. In instructing Moses to prepare the people to be consecrated, God declares: "Indeed, the whole earth is mine, but you shall be for me a priestly kingdom and a holy nation" (Exod 19:5b–6a). The priestly people and holy nation represent God's claim on the whole earth.

In the passage from Numbers, God had instructed Moses to gather seventy elders at the tent of meeting, "and I will take some of the spirit that is on you and put it on them; and they shall bear the burden of the people along with you so that you will not bear it all by yourself" (Num 11:17b). Moses does as

God commands, "and when the spirit rested on them, they prophesied" (Num 11:25). Of interest beyond the tent of meeting, though, is the way God's *ruach* reaches Eldad and Medad and a flock of birds. This entire passage about the elders receiving the spirit is surrounded by a story about quails. Prior to the consecration of elders, the people had been complaining about manna being their only food and wanting some meat. Their complaining had been burdensome to Moses, so God had Moses select seventy others to be consecrated as leaders to assist with governance and to attend to the people. Eldad and Medad had been among the select but had failed to show up at the meeting. The spirit rested on them nonetheless, and they prophesied.

> Two men remained in the camp, one named Eldad, and the other named Medad, and the spirit (*ruach*) rested on them; they were among those registered, but they had not gone out to the tent, and so they prophesied in the camp. And a young man ran and told Moses, "Eldad and Medad are prophesying in the camp." And Joshua son of Nun, the assistant of Moses, one of his chosen men, said, "My lord Moses, stop them!" But Moses said to him, "Are you jealous for my sake? Would that all the LORD's people were prophets, and that the LORD would put his spirit (*ruach*) on them!" (Num 11:26–29)

This passage from Numbers has been influential in the development of shared governance in Western Christendom, especially in the Reformed tradition. Even beyond shared governance, however, the vision and hope is expressed that all of God's people would be touched by God's spirit. But not just the people, it would seem. In the next two verses (which are not included in the lectionary), God's *ruach* reaches thousands of birds: "Then a wind (*ruach*) went out from the LORD, and it brought quails from the sea and let them fall beside the camp, about a day's journey on this side and a day's journey on the other side, all around the camp, about two cubits deep on the ground." The breath of God's Spirit blows beyond the prophet Moses to include others in the congregation, and then toward the sea and to the birds of the air.

In 1 Corinthians 12, also recommended by the lectionaries for Pentecost, all believers receive the Holy Spirit, and the Spirit manifests itself in many ways besides prophesy. The community of believers is broad. Early in the chapter, Paul affirms, "No one can say 'Jesus is Lord' except by the Holy Spirit," and the selected verses for Pentecost conclude: "For in the one Spirit we were all baptized into one body—Jews or Greeks, slaves or free—and we were all made to drink of one Spirit" (1 Cor 12:13). Baptism is invoked here as a sign of our unity in the Spirit and of our unity in the body of Christ.

In referencing baptism and unity in 1 Corinthians 12, Paul is returning to themes in the opening of this letter in which he warns against divisions among the believers in Corinthians. Immediately preceding, in 1 Corinthians 11,

Eucharist is the subject. Class divisions in the Corinthian church had become salient in the meal, with some being gluttonous and some going hungry. In correcting the Corinthians, Paul delivers the earliest account in the Bible of Christ's institution of the Eucharist at the last supper, locating this meal and our participation in this meal in the body of Christ: "'This is my body that is for you. Do this in remembrance of me.' In the same way he took the cup also, after supper, saying, 'This cup is the new covenant in my blood. Do this, as often as you drink it, in remembrance of me'" (1 Cor 11:24b–25). When Paul returns to reference drinking in chapter 12, it is to say that "we were all made to drink of one Spirit" (1 Cor 12:13). Both baptism and Eucharist form us, diverse though we are, into the single body of Christ as effected by the Holy Spirit.

Paul affirms our diversity while chiding our division. The metaphor is the many members constituting a single body, which Paul exposits as a diversity of gifts imparted by the one Spirit, with all in one body, serving one Lord. While not an exhaustive listing, Paul names utterance of wisdom, utterance of knowledge, faith, healing, working of miracles, prophecy, discernment of spirits, various kinds of tongues, and interpretation of tongues. Paul repeats, almost like a litany, that these are all given by one and the same Spirit. "To each is given the manifestation of the Spirit for the common good" (1 Cor 12:7). The gifts of the Spirit are for the sake of mutual service, care, and respect for one another in the body of Christ. Paul continues to elaborate on this theme, waxing poetic about the importance of love in chapter 13 and drawing out the implications for corporate worship in chapter 14.

Then in chapter 15 of 1 Corinthians, as discussed in the previous chapter on Ascension and the Season of Easter, Paul strongly proclaims the resurrection of Christ and the supremacy of Christ. In doing so, Paul makes reference to Christ's resurrection as "first fruits" of an ultimately cosmic salvation under Christ's reign:

> But in fact Christ has been raised from the dead, the first fruits of those who have died. . . . Christ the first fruits, then at his coming those who belong to Christ. Then comes the end when he hands over the kingdom to God the Father, after he has destroyed every ruler and every authority and power. For he must reign until he has put all his enemies under his feet. The last enemy to be destroyed is death . . . so that God may be all in all. (1 Cor 15:20a, 23b–26, 28b)

As with Romans discussed earlier, in these passages citing first fruits in 1 Corinthians, Paul is envisioning a universal salvation throughout creation already begun by Christ and at work in believers by the power of the Spirit.

All of the lectionary passages suggested for Pentecost discussed here present God's Spirit extending beyond particular individuals to foster true community and indeed to embrace all creation. After Pentecost, spirituality can no longer be considered something just personal and private; it is corporate. It is about God's Spirit moving through the whole community even as God's Spirit moves through the whole creation, renewing the face of the earth.

GREEN SPIRITUALITY

Pentecost, then, has implications not only for the way we think about church but also for the way we think about spirituality as a whole. "Hildegard of Bingen says there is only one spirit or breath in the universe, and it is God's," according to Matthew Fox, and he adds "We all partake in breathing it in and out." Moreover, Hildegard of Bingen believed all creatures to have *viriditas* or the "greening power of the Holy Spirit that made all things creative and nourishing."[4]

Elizabeth Johnson names a "plethora of images" pictured by Hildegard of Bingen for describing the Holy Spirit in relationship to creation:

> The Spirit, she [Hildegard] writes, is the life of the life of all creatures; the way in which everything is penetrated with connectedness and relatedness, a burning fire who sparks, ignites, inflames, kindles hearts; a guide in the fog; a balm for wounds; a shining serenity; an overflowing fountain that spreads to all sides. She [the Spirit] is life, movement, color, radiance, restorative stillness in the din. Her power makes all withered sticks and souls green again with the juice of life. She purifies, absolves, strengthens, heals, gathers the perplexed, seeks the lost. She pours the juice of contrition into hardened hearts. She plays music in the soul, being herself the melody of praise and joy. She awakens mighty hope, blowing everywhere the winds of renewal in creation.[5]

Elizabeth Johnson herself draws on the biblical wisdom tradition in naming each person of the Trinity with reference to Sophia. Here is her summative celebration of "Spirit-Sophia" who "dwells in the world at its center and at its edges":

> God is God as Spirit-Sophia, the mobile, pure, people-loving Spirit who pervades every wretched corner, wailing at waste, releasing power that enables fresh starts. Her energy quickens the earth to life, her beauty shines in the stars, her strength breaks forth in every fragment of shalom and renewal that transpires in arenas of violence and meaninglessness. From generation to generation she enters into holy souls, and not so holy ones, to make them friends of God and prophets, thereby making human beings allies of God's redeeming purpose.[6]

More will be said about Johnson's Trinitarian understanding of God as Sophia in relation to creation in the next chapter pertaining to Trinity Sunday, which is the Sunday after Pentecost.

We began examining the Lent-Easter-Pentecost cycle on Ash Wednesday with a quote from Wendell Berry meditating on his own bodily mortality in ecological relationship to the life of the soil. As we conclude our reflection on the seasons in this cycle of worship, we conclude with another quote from Berry about creation enlivened by God's Spirit:

> We will discover that the Creation is not in any sense independent of the Creator, the result of a primal creative act long over and done with, but is the continuous, constant participation of all creatures in the being of God. Elihu said to Job that if God "gather unto himself his spirit and his breath; All flesh shall perish together" (Job 34:15). And Psalm 104 says: "Thou sendest forth thy spirit, they are created." Creation is God's presence in creatures. The Greek Orthodox theologian, Philip Sherrard, has written that "Creation is nothing less than the manifestation of God's hidden being." Thus we and all other creatures live by a sanctity that is inexpressibly intimate. To every creature the gift of life is a portion of the breath and spirit of God.[7]

Pentecost, we conclude, points to a spirituality that is not just about the person but about community, and not just about the Christian community but about life. Spirituality is not just about consciousness but about wind and breath, and not just something other-worldly but is profoundly this-worldly.

EARTHLY/SPIRITUAL WORSHIP

Pentecost concludes the Easter Season. It draws us into the resurrected life of Christ and into wider living community. We celebrate the Spirit's presence in creation and new creation, in the birthing of the church and the mission of the church, and in the calling of individuals and the gifting of individuals. Pentecost is an opportunity to affirm the Spirit's power and presence in creation, in the church, and in the lives of persons. Pentecost Sunday is a most appropriate occasion to conduct baptisms, to receive people into church membership, and to remember and renew our baptismal covenant. That is, it is an opportunity to celebrate our rite of passage both into church membership and into new creation.

Pentecost also occurs in proximity to other rites of passage in society. It occurs very close to the end of school years and to the time of graduation ceremonies. Many congregations like to recognize graduates and honor them. Pentecost can help to bring these individual achievements of graduates into the wider contexts of church, society, and creation. Pentecost allows us not only to celebrate these individuals and their achievements but also to participate with them in spiritual discernment of God's calling to service in church and world—their calling and ours! As they graduate, how might they (and we!) be called to work for social justice and for the flourishing of creation? Pentecost presents an opportunity for us to name and affirm the particular gifts of the Spirit that have already blessed us, and to name and pray for those spiritual gifts needed for perseverant and faithful service.

The following liturgy for renewal and celebration can be used in conjunction with either or both of these occasions: the honoring of graduates and/or the celebration or renewal of baptism and church membership.

Litany of Thanksgiving Over the Water

Gather at the baptismal font with water.

Voice: "In the beginning God created the heavens and the earth. The earth was without form and void, and darkness was upon the face of the deep; and the Spirit of God was moving over the face of the waters." (Gen 1:1–2 RSV)

Sung response: **"Send forth your Spirit and renew the face of the earth"**
(or "Come, Holy Spirit, renew the face of the earth." *Both paraphrase Psalm 104:30. There are many musical settings.*)

Voice: Thus says the LORD who made you,
   who formed you from the womb and will help you:
Fear not, O Jacob my servant,
   Jeshurun whom I have chosen.
For I will pour water on the thirsty land,
   and streams on the dry ground;
I will pour my Spirit upon your descendants,
   and my blessing on your offspring.
They shall spring up like grass amid waters,
   like willows by flowing streams. (Isa 44:2–4 RSV)

Sung response: **"Send forth your Spirit and renew the face of the earth"**

Voice: [Jesus] cried out, "Let anyone who is thirsty come to me, and let the one who believes in me drink. As the scripture has said, 'Out of the believer's heart shall flow rivers of living water.'" Now he said this about the Spirit, which believers in him were to receive. (John 7:37b–39a)

Sung response: **"Send forth your Spirit and renew the face of the earth"**

Voice: The Spirit and the bride say, "Come."
And let everyone who hears say, "Come."

And let everyone who is thirsty come.
Let anyone who wishes take the water of lie as a gift. (Rev 22:17)

HYMN: "Spirit of God" by Marty Haugen, © Copyright © 1987 GIA Publications, Inc. GIA Publications[8]

Spirit blowing through creation,
Spirit burning in the skies,
let the hope of your salvation fill our eyes;
God of splendour, God of glory,
You who light the stars above,
all the heavens tell the story of your love.

As you moved upon the waters,
As you ride upon the wind,
Move us all, your sons and daughters, deep within;
As you shaped the hills and mountains
Formed the land and filled the deep
Let your hand renew and waken all who sleep.

Refrain: Spirit renewing the earth,
renewing the hearts of all people;
burn in the weary souls, blow through the silent lips,
come now awake us, Spirit of God.

Love that sends the rivers dancing,
love that waters all that lives,
love that heals and holds and rouses and forgives,
You are food for all your creatures,
You are hunger in the soul,
in your hands the brokenhearted are made whole.

All the creatures you have fashioned,
All that live and breathe in you,
Find their hope in your compassion, strong and true;
You, O Spirit of salvation,
You alone, beneath, above,
Come, renew your whole creation in your love.

Refrain: Spirit renewing the earth,
renewing the hearts of all people;
burn in the weary souls, blow through the silent lips,
come now awake us, Spirit of God.

Baptismal Renewal For Spiritual Mission In The World

Reading: Paul tells us: "For just as the body is one and has many members, and all the members of the body, though many, are one body, so it is with Christ. For in the one Spirit we were all baptized into one body—Jews or Greeks, slaves or free—and we were all made to drink of one Spirit." (1 Cor 12:12–13)

Call to Prayer for the gifts and fruit of the Spirit in ourselves as Christ's church:

God's Spirit calls us to be church.

We are called, gifted and sent as Christians to be the body of Christ.

What fruit or gifts of the Spirit have you been given that you would want to name and claim, that you bring as part of the body of Christ? What spiritual gifts do you see in others that knit us together as one body in the Spirit? Reflect on these gifts, the gifted and the Giver, naming these gifts in your hearts or sharing them with one another.

Bring your petitions for gifts and thanksgiving for gifts to the Spirit in prayer—silent or spoken.

brief prayerful silence (Naming of gifts can occur differently in different contexts of worship: silent naming, vocal sharing in the congregation, or divided into pairs or small groups for sharing.)

Action with water, such as splashing, pouring into the font, or lightly sprinkling the people.

Leader: Remember your baptism and be thankful.

Reading: Paul tells us "the fruit of the Spirit is love, joy, peace, patience, kindness, generosity, faithfulness, gentleness, and self-control." (Gal 5:22)

Call to Prayer for the gifts and fruit of the Spirit for social justice and peace:

God's Spirit calls us toward liberation and justice.

We are called, gifted and sent as human beings to seek social justice and to make peace.

What fruit or gifts of the Spirit have you been given that you would want to name and claim, that can contribute to greater justice in society? What fruit or gifts do you see in others that can be employed, working together, to help end inequality and oppression and to further the cause of justice? Reflect on these gifts, the gifted and the Giver, naming them in your hearts or sharing them with one another.

Bring your petitions for gifts and thanksgiving for gifts to the Spirit in prayer—silent or spoken.

brief prayerful silence (Naming of gifts can occur differently in different contexts of worship: silent naming, vocal sharing in the congregation, or divided into pairs or small groups for sharing.)
Action with water, such as splashing, pouring into the font, or lightly sprinkling the people

Leader: Remember your baptism and be thankful.

Reading: Paul envisions, "the creation itself will be set free from its bondage to decay and will obtain the freedom of the glory of the children of God. We know that the whole creation has been groaning in labor pains until now; and not only the creation, but we ourselves, who have the first fruits of the Spirit, groan inwardly while we wait for adoption, the redemption of our bodies. For in hope we were saved." (Rom 8:21–24a)

Call to Prayer for the gifts and fruit of the Spirit for creation's flourishing:

God's Spirt creates and renews creation.

We are called, gifted and sent as God's creatures to tend and keep the garden of the earth, to care for creation, to guard the conditions of flourishing for God's myriad creatures.

What fruit or gifts of the Spirit have you been given that you would want to name and claim to promote the well-being of creation? What fruit or gifts do you see in others that can be employed, working together, to help ensure a sustainable future? Reflect on these gifts, the gifted and the Giver, naming them in your hearts or sharing them with one another.

Bring your petitions for gifts and thanksgiving for gifts to the Spirit in prayer—silent or spoken.

Brief prayerful silence (naming of gifts can occur differently in different contexts of worship: silent naming, vocal sharing in the congregation, or divided into pairs or small groups for sharing.)

Action with water, such as splashing, pouring into the font, or lightly sprinkling the people

Leader: Remember your baptism and be thankful.

Chapter 8

Trinity

The Dance of Life

I bind unto myself today
the strong Name of the Trinity,
by invocation of the same,
the Three in One, and One in Three.

I bind unto myself today
the virtues of the star-lit heaven,
the glorious sun's life-giving ray,
the whiteness of the moon at even,
the flashing of the lightning free,
the whirling wind's tempestuous shocks,
the stable earth, the deep salt sea,
around the old eternal rocks.

Christ be with me,
Christ within me,
Christ behind me,
Christ before me,
Christ beside me,
Christ to win me,
Christ to comfort and restore me,
Christ in danger,
Christ in hearts of all that love me,
Christ in mouth of friend and stranger.

I bind unto myself the Name,
the strong Name of the Trinity,
by invocation of the same
the Three in One, and One in Three.

> Of whom all nature hath creation,
> eternal Father, Spirit, Word:
> praise to the Lord of my salvation,
> salvation is of Christ the Lord.
>
> att. Saint Patrick[1]

The first Sunday in "ordinary time" after Pentecost Sunday is Trinity Sunday. The conclusion of the Easter season with the celebration of the outpouring of the Holy Spirit at Pentecost moves us to deepening reflection about the reality of God at work in the world, centered so sharply on Christ and dispersed so broadly in the Spirit. Trinity Sunday is an opportunity for such deepening reflection and celebration, even as we move into ordinary time. Moreover, it is an opportunity to celebrate the work of the Trinity in creation.

We are rich with liturgical resources—both ancient and recent—for inspiring worship at this time. The hymn of Saint Patrick quoted above is an example. The Trinity is invoked at the beginning without being explained, and again at the end with the further attribution, "Of whom all nature hath creation." The body of the hymn shines with the stars, the sun, the moon, and lightning; and the sea, the earth, and the air are all illumined in the singing. The interlude confesses Christ—also without theological explanation—but with repeated confident declaration of Christ's abiding presence and omnipresence. Throughout the hymn, creation shimmers in the mystery of Trinity.

When preachers turn from poetry to prose, however, we can sometimes lose the luster of this mystery. We get tripped up by arithmetic and by physics. So too, actually, did theologians of the church's first centuries. We also get tripped up by psychology. The language of three "persons" is confusing to common sense understandings of a "person" in modern, Western culture. Catherine Mowry LaCugna has argued that Enlightenment reasoning and modern psychologies have tended to focus on the "person" as an individual, autonomous "self."[2] Even when it is recognized that this is an abstraction and that individual selves cannot exist apart from community, the idea of a "person" still connotes individuality, independence, and consciousness, which further exacerbates the difficulty in affirming the unity of three "persons" in the Triune Godhead.[3] Despite the arithmetic and psychologizing difficulties, I will continue to speak of numbered "persons" of the Trinity because of the gender inclusivity of this language and because of its historical precedent and general acceptance. With regard to the language of "persons," Elizabeth A. Johnson wryly quotes Anselm of Canterbury with approval, "Anselm of Canterbury will even speak of 'three something-or-other,' 'three I know not what' (*non nescio quid*),"[4] the latter English phrase being a literal translation. This chapter will first examine some of the biblical lections suggested for Trinity Sunday before examining further some of the Trinitarian metaphors offered by theologians with implications for an ecological reading and ecological worship.

LECTIONS FOR TRINITY SUNDAY

While it is anachronistic to read back into Scripture post-canonical conceptions of the Trinity, the biblical witness is even more varied than the historic creeds that summarily reflect it. Regarding the role of the whole Trinity in creation and new creation, Geoffrey Wainwright states:

> Though we may distinguish within the divine activity towards the world and ascribe certain functions to one Person by appropriation, we may not *oppose* the roles of the Persons; for there is harmony, not discord, with the Blessed Trinity, and in their activity towards the world the divine Persons actively cooperate.
>
> In the areas that are going to interest us particularly, namely creation and re-creation, we find Scripture suggesting that both the Second and the Third Persons of the Trinity play an active part.[5]

Wainwright gives as an example, Psalm 33:6, where both the second Person as the Word of God and the third Person as the Breath of God can be inferred as creatively active along with the first Person. The psalm sounds God's praise throughout the earth, sky, and sea:

> ...the earth is full of the steadfast love of the LORD.
> By the word of the LORD the heavens were made,
>   and all their host by the breath of his mouth.
> He gathered the waters of the sea as in a bottle;
>   he put the deeps in storehouses.
> Let all the earth fear the LORD;
>   let all the inhabitants of the world stand in awe of him.
> For he spoke, and it came to be;
>   he commanded, and it stood firm. (Ps 33:5b–9)

Psalm 33 is given as the psalm for Trinity Sunday in year B by the Roman Catholic Lectionary for the Mass.[6]

The Epistle lesson for Trinity Sunday in year B given by both lectionaries is Romans 8:12–17, which names all three persons of the Trinity as active in effecting our redemption:

> For all who are led by the Spirit of God are children of God. For you did not receive a spirit of slavery to fall back into fear, but you have received a spirit of adoption. When we cry, "Abba! Father!" it is that very Spirit bearing witness with our spirit that we are children of God, and if children, then heirs, heirs of

God and joint heirs with Christ—if, in fact, we suffer with him so that we may also be glorified with him. (Rom 8:14–17)

As we know from discussing Romans 8 in previous chapters, Paul continues to speak of the whole creation cooperating with the Spirit to bring forth bodily as well as spiritual redemption: "We know that the whole creation has been groaning in labor pains until now; and not only the creation, but we ourselves who have the first fruits of the Spirit, groan inwardly while we wait for adoption, the redemption of our bodies" (Rom 8:22–23). The whole Trinity and the whole creation are involved in this redemption. It is not only the Second Person of the Trinity who is the Redeemer.

The other lectionary readings for Trinity Sunday in year B also declare God's sovereignty, glory, or salvation throughout the natural world. The Roman Catholic Lectionary for the Mass gives Deuteronomy 4:32–34, 39–40, which recalls the exodus and the giving of the law and declares, "So acknowledge today and take to heart that the LORD is God in heaven above and on the earth beneath; there is no other" (Deut 4:39). The first lesson in the Revised Common Lectionary for year B is Isaiah 6:1–8, the call of Isaiah, in which Isaiah in a vision hears one seraph calling to another before God enthroned, "Holy, holy, holy is the LORD of hosts; the whole earth is full of his glory" (Isa 6:3). The Gospel lessons for Trinity Sunday are Matthew 28:16–20 or verses from John 3 in either year A or B in both lectionaries. John 3:16–17 famously presents "the Son" as sent out of God's love for the whole world:

> For God so loved the world that he gave his only Son, so that everyone who believes in him may not perish but may have eternal life. Indeed, God did not send the Son into the world to condemn the world, but in order that the world might be saved through him.

Matthew 28:16–20 is the conclusion of the Gospel of Matthew and the great commission in which the risen Christ claims "all authority in heaven and on earth" and sends the disciples to "make disciples of all nations, baptizing them in the name of the Father and of the Son and of the Holy Spirit," and he assuredly promises, "remember, I am with you always, to the end of the age." The mission for the sake of the world is presented in terms of baptizing—and baptizing in the "name" which became our traditional baptismal formula for naming God as Trinity.

In year A, the Revised Common Lectionary gives this passage from Matthew as the Gospel lesson and also provides other readings from the Hebrew Bible that ring with creation themes: Genesis 1:1–2:4a as the first lesson and Psalm 8 as the Psalter (which it recommends for year C as well). The reading from Genesis is the entire first creation story, which begins with God's *ruach* blowing and God's word speaking, "Let there be. . . ." It lends itself to a Trinitarian interpretation, obviously anachronistic though it may be. By bringing such an interpretation to the text, however, the presence and agency of Word and Spirit in creation are highlighted, that is the Second and Third Persons of the Trinity and not just the First are active in creating. Psalm 8 poetically recounts God's creation of the heavens and the heavens' inhabitants of moon and stars. Inexplicably, the psalm presents humans inhabiting the earth as recipients of God's favor and "crowned with glory and honor" that is little less than these heavenly beings. Humans are given "dominion" over other inhabitants of the earth, of the seas, and of the air below the heavens. The difficulties and possibilities of the biblical idea of dominion from an ecological standpoint have been discussed previously in the chapter on Lenten beginnings. In this context it should be noted, though, that it is God's sovereignty throughout the earth—and not really human dominion—that is celebrated and praised in this psalm. In the face of God's sovereignty and creation's marvels, human dominion seems enigmatic: "What are humans that you are mindful of them, mortals that you care for them?" The psalm begins and ends with praise of our Creator who remains Sovereign over all the earth: "O LORD, our Sovereign, how majestic is your name in all the earth!" (Ps 8:1, 9).

The Roman Catholic Lectionary for the Mass also prescribes Psalm 8 for use in year C, but in year A the Roman Catholic Lectionary instead gives part of a hymn from the deuterocanonical additions to Daniel (3:52–55) as the psalter. This is the beginning of the song of praise by Shadrach, Meshach, and Abednego from the fiery furnace, "*Benedicite, omnia opera*" ("Bless the Lord, all you works"), discussed previously in the context of the Easter vigil. When excerpted out of Daniel as an apocryphal book, it is titled simply the "Song of the Three"[7] and the reading would be verses 29–33. As mentioned earlier, this Song as a whole, found in Daniel 3:52–90, contains some of the richest creation imagery in the Bible, but here the Roman Catholic Lectionary provides for reading just the first four verses, which only begin to describe the first of God's creative acts with the "firmament of heaven." But the hymn continues for thirty-four verses, calling on "all you works of the Lord" to laud and bless their Creator, naming them throughout the earth, the heavens and the seas. Writing about this Song from near the center of the Pacific Ocean, George Knight, then the Principal of the Pacific Theological College in Fiji, hears all of creation summoned to sing of its Creator, who is:

God who **lookest upon the deeps** (vs. 32), the "waters under the firmament" (Gen 1:7; cf. Exod 20:4)—a phrase which pictorializes the chaos out of which God brings forth order, salvation, and light.

Thereafter the Song becomes a summons to all creatures in heaven and earth, animate and inanimate, to **bless the Lord**.[8]

Many Christian renditions of this canticle for liturgical use append a closing Trinitarian benediction that is not original to the text and certainly not strictly necessary for Christian worship, but nonetheless appropriate for Trinity Sunday: "Let us bless the Father, the Son and the Holy Spirit: Praise and exalt our God forever."[9]

Both lectionaries urge Proverbs 8: [1–4], 22–31 be read as the first lesson for Trinity Sunday in year C. Some of these verses were also suggested by the Revised Common Lectionary for Easter and this entire passage was discussed earlier concerning the Easter vigil. Here now, though, for Trinity Sunday, the most creation-oriented verses are included for reading. I refer the readers to the previous material on the vigil—or even better, to Proverbs 8 directly—to hear those words of God's delight in Wisdom and in creation. Significantly this passage verbalizes a woman's speech in the Trinity's voice, as God's Wisdom personified as a woman declares her work in creation from the very beginning. Her name is *Chochma* in Hebrew and *Sophia* in Greek. Her voice of Wisdom can be heard to resound back to the blowing of God's Spirit at creation, and to echo forward through the eons to find expression in the word spoken by John about the Word spoken by God—through whom all things came into being and who took on flesh and dwelt among us. Wisdom's voice sounds like the Second Person of the Trinity as well as the Third.

The next Proverb, Proverbs 9, is also about Wisdom, or Sophia, personified as a woman, and it includes the enigmatic line, "the fear of the LORD is the beginning of wisdom." This oft-repeated line in Proverbs and Psalms strikes contemporary worshipers as enigmatic, paradoxical, or even contradictory. Notice the tension in the two differing nuances of "fear" mentioned earlier in this chapter when discussion of Psalm 33:8a, "Let all the earth fear the LORD," was followed in the next paragraph by reference to Romans 8:15, "You did not receive a spirit of slavery to fall back into fear." Fear is frightening, but the Wisdom Woman is awe-inspiring. Inspired by her image in the context of Trinity, I am moved to provide the following lines that can be sung to the tune *Sanctissimus*:

> The fear of the LORD, the beginning of Wisdom,
>   Through her our God gives life to this world.
> Incarnate in Christ she was raised high on Golgotha,
>   God in God's Spirit, God's Wisdom, God's Word.

This can be sung as an antiphonal response for any of the psalms that also refer to the "fear of the LORD." After select verses of a psalm, the first two lines of this can be chanted antiphonally between leader and congregation, with the congregation singing: "Through her our God gives life to this world." The entire stanza can then be sung at the conclusion of the psalm with congregation singing the final two lines of acclamation and praise ending "God in God's Spirit, God's Wisdom, God's Word."

TRINITY, EUCHARIST, AND CREATION

Historically our understanding of Trinity grew out of debates about Christology and how Jesus Christ is related to the Divine. So the basic question was, Who is Jesus Christ? In debating this question, attention turned to our very conceptualization of God—both our ideas about God in Godself and about God in relation to us. The two basic perennial questions, then, are as follows: Who is God? and What is God doing? Conceptions of the Trinity tend to focus on whichever of these two questions comes to the fore. If focusing on the question of God in Godself, we are talking about the immanent Trinity. If focusing on the question of God in relation to God's works, we are talking about the economic Trinity. The distinction is not so clear-cut, though, since whatever we might affirm about our belief in God is inferred from the ways God is revealed to us, or self-disclosed, in creation, in Christ, and in the Holy Spirit's witness through the inspiration of Scripture and the inspired hearts and minds of believers.[10]

The increasingly prevalent practice of referring to the Trinity as Creator, Redeemer, and Sanctifier exemplifies this apprehending of God through reception of God's works. We are the result of God's creation, the beneficiaries of God's redemption, and the subjects of God's sanctifying grace. This "formula" has the benefit of gender inclusivity, so as not to reinforce patriarchal categories and assumptions. However, oft-repeated use of this phrase entails the disadvantage of reinforcing a narrow functionalist interpretation of God and of God's activity, so that only the First Person is clearly affirmed as Creator, the Second Person as Redeemer, and the Third Person as Sanctifier. This apparent mutual exclusivity between the persons of the Trinity is certainly not logically necessitated by use of this formula, but it can be the unintended conceptual result inferred from frequent liturgical repetition. If so, the divine creative activity of Christ and of the Holy Spirit are not fully acknowledged, conceptualized, or celebrated; creation becomes conceptually relegated to the First Person—a kind of deism.

This narrative of the First Person creating, the Second Person redeeming, and the Third Person sanctifying is told in the recitation of the Apostles' Creed developed in baptismal contexts, "I believe in God, the Father almighty, creator of heaven and earth."[11] and the others follow. The Nicene Creed, developed in the context of the Christological controversies, is more explicit regarding the role of both Christ and the Holy Spirit in creation: "We believe in one Lord, Jesus Christ, the only Son of God, eternally begotten of the Father, . . . of one Being with the Father; through him all things were made. . . . We believe in the Holy Spirit, the Lord, the giver of life."[12] Both of these Trinitarian creeds are appropriate for use in Christian worship every Sunday and especially on Trinity Sunday. The Apostles' Creed, perhaps read responsively, is most appropriate when baptisms are being celebrated. The Nicene Creed, though, makes the relationship between the persons of the Trinity more explicit and, importantly for the relationship between Trinity and creation, it names the activity of each of the persons in the creative activity of God.

The Nicene Creed as we know it today (titled more accurately, the Nicene-Constantinopolitan Creed) is associated with the Council of Constantinople in 381. At that Ecumenical Council, the Holy Spirit in particular received attention, and an earlier version of the Nicene Creed from the Council at Nicea in 325 was amended to affirm the Holy Spirit as "the Lord and Giver of Life . . . who with the Father and the Son together is worshiped and glorified." All three were "declared to be consubstantial and of equal dignity."[13] Influential on the doctrinal and creedal developments of Trinitarian theology at the Ecumenical Council in 381 were the so-called Cappadocian Fathers: Gregory of Nyssa, Gregory Nazianzus, and Basil (the Great) of Caesarea who further developed the Trinitarian understanding of God as one *ousia* and three *hypostaseis*, which became translated into Latin as one *substantia* and three *personae*.[14]

Basil especially is noted for developing a Trinitarian understanding of the divinity of the Holy Spirit. Elizabeth Johnson, who draws on the biblical and deuterocanonical Sophia tradition, quotes Basil with approval in describing the Holy Spirit. "The Spirit is much more than the stereotypical, patriarchal feminine," she writes, "she is, in the words of one early Christian theologian, 'intelligent, boundless in power, of unlimited greatness, generous in goodness, whom time cannot measure.[15] Basil modified the liturgical doxology to emphasize the Spirit's divinity as well as Christ's, from the original "Glory be to the Father through the Son" to "Glory be to the Father with the Son and with the Holy Spirit." Eventually the church settled on the familiar Trinitarian wording, "Glory be to the Father, and to the Son and to the Holy Spirit," which according to Leonardo Boff, "gives full expression to the simultaneity of the divine nature-communion of the divine Three."[16]

Eucharistic prayers attributed to Basil in the fourth century have been of great influence on Eucharistic prayer today in Orthodox, Catholic, and ecumenical Protestant churches alike. These prayers are notably Trinitarian, addressing the First Person of the Trinity, remembering the Second Person of the Trinity, and invoking the Third Person of the Trinity. John

Baldovin describes Basil's Eucharistic prayer known as "Alexandrian Basil" as "clearly" and "deliberately" Trinitarian in this way.[17]

In the Alexandrian Basil, not only is each Person of the Trinity named and affirmed in God's divinity, but they are also each active in creation and sanctification. The prayer begins, after the opening dialogue, addressed to "I AM" in praise for creation and acclaiming Christ primordially active in creation:

> It is fitting and right, fitting and right, truly it is fitting and right, I AM, truly Lord God, existing before the ages; you dwell on high and regard what is low; you made heaven and earth and the sea and all that is in them. Father of our Lord and God and Savior Jesus Christ, through whom you made all things visible and invisible . . .

The prayer concludes with an epiclesis, invoking the Holy Spirit to sanctify the gathering and the gifts that "your Holy Spirit may descend upon us and upon these gifts that have been set before you, and may sanctify them and make [Greek, *anadeixai* = 'reveal'] them holy of holies."[18]

A "Common Eucharistic Prayer" developed ecumenically and used with some variation in a number of ecumenical Protestant denominations, including Episcopal, United Methodist, Evangelical Lutheran, and Presbyterian Church (USA), is even more closely based on the Alexandrian Basil.[19] This prayer amplifies creation's participation in receiving blessing and in giving thanks and praise. Addressed to the First Person of the Trinity, it acclaims: "Fountain of life and source of all goodness, you made all things and fill them with your blessing; you created them to rejoice in the splendor of your radiance."[20] Introducing the *Sanctus*, "every creature under heaven" joins with human and angelic worshipers in rendering praise:

> Countless throngs of angels stand before you to serve you night and day; and, beholding the glory of your presence, they offer you unceasing praise. Joining with them, and giving voice to every creature under heaven, we acclaim you, and glorify your Name.[21]

Further, in remembering the saving work of Christ, salvation extends to all creation: "To fulfill your purpose he gave himself up to death; and, rising from the grave, destroyed death and made the whole creation new."[22] Human dominion is mentioned in this prayer, but in a way that is defined by care for creation and service toward fellow creatures: "You formed us in your own image, giving the whole world into our care, so that, in obedience to you, our Creator, we might rule and serve all your creatures."[23]

Nearly all Eucharistic prayers in wide usage by the ecumenical churches, though, follow the basic Trinitarian structure. The World Council of Churches' document on *Baptism, Eucharist and Ministry* discusses the Eucharist with reference to these Trinitarian headings: "The Eucharist as Thanksgiving to the Father," "The Eucharist as Anamnesis or Memorial of Christ," and "The Eucharist as Invocation of the Spirit."[24] The Presbyterian Church (USA) and the Presbyterian Church of Aotearoa New Zealand, which maintain a "free prayer" tradition along with the use of prepared liturgies, advocate Eucharistic free prayer to follow this pattern as well, suggesting: "The prayer begins with thankful praise to God"; "The prayer continues with thankful recalling of the acts of salvation in Jesus Christ"; "The Holy Spirit is called upon."[25] Creation is particularly celebrated in the first part of the prayer offering praise to God, but creation is a theological theme that can occur explicitly throughout Eucharistic prayer.

A more recent Eucharistic prayer with this structure, composed by Robert J. Daly, SJ[26] and shared for ecumenical consideration, omits any reference to human dominion but quotes from Genesis 2:15, concerning the human vocation to till and keep the garden of God's creation. The concluding epiclesis and solemn petition invokes the Holy Spirit:

> Send down on us and on these gifts full portions of your Holy Spirit who with your Word and before all time brought forth the galaxies, breathed over the primal waters, came upon the prophets and hovered over Mary's womb.
>
> Send on us now that same Spirit that we may know our place in this your universe, on this your earth, and in this your Church, so that in and through our living, dying, and rising with your Son we may learn to till and keep this earth with the same love with which you till and keep us.[27]

This entire Eucharistic prayer has been informed by an ecological understanding of earthly life and by theological affirmation of the Trinity active throughout the created universe. Daly exclaims that "the Trinitarian Christology of the early ecumenical councils literally screams from the great anaphoras of Chrysostom and Basil,"[28] and he carries that Trinitarian emphasis and Eucharistic structure into this contemporary prayer. The first half of the prayer lauds the Creator for the whole physical universe and for all earthly history, moving sequentially from cosmos to biological life to humanity to Jewish and Christian History. The second half of the prayer, revolving around worshipful remembrance of God's saving presence in Christ, is more integrative, striving to portray, in Daly's words, "interrelated aspects of a unified, eschatological, Trinitarian Eucharistic Christ-event that has already begun but is not yet fully accomplished."[29] Ecology rings throughout. So, for instance, following the opening dialogue and preface, the prayer launches forth:

> With joy we give you thanks and praise. Where once was nothing, your love brought matter into being and motion, thus creating time itself,

and countless galaxies, each with its countless stars, and, to prepare a home for us, delicately circling round one single star, this one small globe, our mother earth. And on this globe, aeons later, you brought forth, infinitely small, but inexorably growing, the beginnings of the life we share with all that lives. And then, past more billions of years, past aeons of seemingly random developments, past the seeming chaos of countless extinctions—but springing from those deaths ever new forms of life—your Word breathed not just life but Spirit too into man and woman, your image and likeness. Past further countless generations you lovingly watched us grow, becoming part of the life-death-life of all that lives and grows on earth, until finally, you made rainbow covenant with us.[30]

This Eucharistic prayer follows the Trinitarian pattern already noted of being addressed to the First Person, in worshipful remembrance of the Second Person, and invoking the Third Person in blessing.

The prayer begins, though, with a Trinitarian litany of praise for the universe, for ecological life, and for salvation:

> Father, we praise you, with all your creatures
> great and small,
> from measureless galaxy
> to tiniest particle.
> They all came forth from your hand.
> Filled with your presence,
> they are signs of your undying love:
> Praise be to you!
> **A. Praise be to you!**
>
> Word of God, Jesus, we praise you.
> Through you all these things were made
> and have their being.
> And when you took your bodily shape
> in the womb of Mary our mother,
> you entered into the chaos of our lives
> to bring us to the beauty of your love:
> Praise be to you!
> **A. Praise be to you!**
>
> Holy Spirit, we praise you,
> who breathed over the primal chaos,
> spoke to us through the prophets' voices,
> hovered over Mary's womb
> and made us temples of your love:

Praise be to you!
A. Praise be to you!

Triune God, we praise you,
you who knew us all,
each and every one,
Even before the stars were born,
calling us with deathless love
always to come back to you
A. Praise be to you![31]

This prayer addresses the First Person of the Trinity as "Father." A friend of mine, Olivia Warren, changed this opening to be more gender inclusive, though, praying: "God who is like a mother and father, a God who transcends gender, we praise you, with all your creatures great and small."[32] This expansive address opens then to the wide expanse of creation that follows in prayer.

TRINITARIAN METAPHORS AND ECOLOGY

A diversity of metaphors for naming the persons of the Trinity are in theological parlance today as well as in liturgical use. A number of theologians have provided fertile understandings of the Trinity that have branched forth with ecological ramifications for theology and worship. Among them are Norman Pittenger, Sallie McFague, Jürgen Moltmann, Leonardo Boff, Matthew Fox, and Elizabeth Johnson. These will be summarily reviewed here, without attempt to reconcile them, but with the intent to note the ecological implications of their respective conceptions of Trinity.

Norman Pittenger

Norman Pittenger names God as "always Love,"[33] or stated actively as the "cosmic Lover."[34] In naming God as Love, Pittenger is inspired by one of Augustine's formulations of Trinity as "lover, the loved one, and the loving relationship between the first two," which form a unity amid these distinctions.[35] Preferring the language of Triunity rather than Trinity, Pittenger describes the one God interpreted threefold in relationship to creation as "Creative Source, Self-Expressive Act, and Responsive Movement."[36] Writing within a framework of process theology, he explains:

> We wish to speak of God as the everlastingly creative agency who works anywhere and everywhere, yet without denying the reality of creaturely freedom—hence we point toward God as Parent. We wish also to speak of God as

so working that he acts with and besides his creation, by luring it and attracting it toward realizing its possibilities and thereby achieving the fulfillment or satisfaction which is its aim—hence we point toward God as Self-Expressive Word. And we wish finally to speak of God as active in and through his creation in its accepting or "prehending" the lure or attraction which is offered to it . . . hence we point toward God as the Responsive Agency who is the Holy Spirit.[37]

This triune God is "inexhaustible" in creativity and in love, with each person of the Triunity active within creation.[38] As a process theologian, Pittenger is in keeping with the philosophy of organism developed by Alfred North Whitehead and the "natural theology" espoused by Charles Hartshorne.[39] The universe and the natural world are taken seriously from the outset in seeking to talk about God in a way that is consistent with scientific understandings of physical reality and of natural existence.

Sallie McFague

Also writing within a process framework, ecofeminist theologian, Sallie McFague, is intentionally metaphoric in her theological construction. Her intention is to speak of God in ways that are not only consistent with a nondualist ecological understanding of earthly life but also take seriously the threat's to Earth's ecology posed by humanity's power to destroy. She is seeking alternative metaphors that do not undergird this patriarchal and hierarchical power. She emphasizes the relational nature of God to all earthly reality. She develops the metaphors of Mother, Lover, and Friend to name God and to indicate God's love toward and within creation.[40] As our Mother, God creates all existence and brings to life all living creatures, expressing her agapeic love for us. The metaphor of mother also includes the idea of fatherhood but recovers a needed emphasis on loving paternity rather than dominating patriarchy.[41] Citing Norman Pittenger, McFague also describes God as Lover.[42] With *eros*, God as our lover is incarnate with us to bring salvation to all creation and healing to a suffering world. McFague explains:

> God as lover is interested not in rescuing certain individuals from the world but in saving, making whole, the entire beloved cosmos that has become estranged and fragmented, sickened by unhealthy practices, and threatened by death and extinction. God as lover finds all species of flora and fauna valuable and attractive, she finds the entire, intricate evolutionary complex infinitely precious and wondrous.[43]

As Friend, God sustains and companions all creatures: "God's sustaining love (philia) underscores the joy of all forms of life as companions united with one another and with the source of their life."[44] The entire world McFague describes as God's body, emphasizing God's immanence and loving presence with us in creation.[45] This theological model of God has ethical content from the start, in that McFague is seeking theological language alternative to that which undergirds patriarchy, hierarchy, and dualism. The model further invites an ethical response for us to participate with God in living into this alternative vision for holistic planetary life. She writes: "The model of God as mother, lover, and friend of the world presents us with an ethic of response and responsibility toward other human beings and other forms of life, in which our deep parental, erotic, and companionable instincts can be socialized and politicized." In a subsequent book, *Super, Natural Christians: How We Should Love Nature*, McFague further fleshes out that ecological ethic.[46]

Jürgen Moltmann

Jürgen Moltmann describes his own position as panentheist (distinct from pantheist) with the Trinitarian God's very essence being creative. "Creation is a fruit of God's longing for 'his Other,'" and for that Other's free response to the divine love," writes Moltmann in his influential *The Trinity and the Kingdom*, "That is why the idea of the world is inherent in the nature of God himself from eternity."[47] Internally God's love is expressed reciprocally between the persons of the Trinity in intimate and empathic perichoresis, that is, in love. Moltmann explains perichoresis as

> the circulatory character of the eternal divine life. An eternal life process takes place in the triune God through the exchange of energies. The Father exists in the Son, the Son in the Father, and both of them in the Spirit, just as the Spirit exists in both the Father and the Son. By virtue of their eternal love they live in one another to such an extent, and dwell in one another to such an extent, that they are one. It is a process of most perfect and intense empathy.[48]

But yet God's love must reach out beyond the divine self. God makes space for creation; in Christ, God brings creation into being; and by the Spirit, God enlivens and in-lives creation. Citing Proverbs 8, Moltmann interprets Christ as Sophia, eternal Wisdom, as the divine mediator of creation and in creation.[49] Subsequently in his Gifford Lectures, *God in Creation*, Moltmann further develops this doctrine of Trinity in ecological direction as follows:

> The Christian doctrine of creation takes its impress from the revelation of Christ and the experience of the Spirit. The One who sends the Son and the Spirit is the Creator—the Father. The One who gathers the world under his liberating lordship, and redeems it, is the Word of creation—the One who gives life to the world and allows it to participate in God's eternal life is the creative Energy—the Spirit. The Father is the creating origin of creation, the Son its shaping origin, and the Spirit its life-giving origin.

Creation exists in the Spirit, is molded by the Son and is created by the Father. It is therefore from God, through God and in God.[50]

Leonardo Boff

Leonardo Boff particularly draws on a perichoretic understanding of Trinity to inform a theology of creation. Referring to the three persons of the Trinity, he describes perichoresis in his book *Trinity and Society*, "the Three live in eternal perichoresis, being one in the others, through the others, with the others and for the others," and moreover, "since this union is eternal and infinite, we can speak of one God."[51] This has implications for both liberation and ecology, as the divine communion of the Trinity is reflected in the creative work of the Trinity, expressing a kind of perichoresis among God's creatures. Considering "perichoretic communion and love" to be "the very essence of the three divine Persons," Boff explains:

> Creation, without being necessary (nothing is imposed on God), is con-natural with the divine essence. This means it is also free. It prolongs and reflects the outpouring of life and love that eternally constitute the being of Father, Son and Holy Spirit. To use anthropomorphic language: the Trinity does not wish to live alone in its splendid Trinitarian communion; the three divine Persons do not love just one another, but seek companions in communion and love. Creation arose from this wish.[52]

Derivatively Boff sees the universe itself and human society within it "as a process of communication, communion and union through the interpenetration of creatures with one another (perichoresis)." This idea supports the cause of liberation of the poor from oppression, "so that there can be greater sharing and communion."[53]

In a subsequent book, *Cry of the Earth, Cry of the Poor*, Boff further develops the ecological implications from this Trinitarian theology. He begins by noticing an interrelatedness between all aspects of the cosmos which he describes as perichoresis—from the physical forces of the universe to the ecological relationships of life on Earth. This perichoretic interrelationship in creation is a reflection of the Trinitarian perichoresis of its Creator. The whole Trinity creates. In *Trinity and Society*, Boff concisely conveys an historic conception of "creation by the Father through the Son in the Holy Spirit."[54] He elaborates upon this "co-creation" by the three persons in *Cry of the Earth*:

> By reason of co-creation all things possess a mysterious depth coming from the mystery of the Father (where the Trinity reveals its unfathomability). But there is a dimension of light and intelligibility, for creation is projected by the Son, which is where the Trinitarian mystery reveals its light and its wisdom. Finally,

there is a perspective of communion and love, for it is loved in the Holy Spirit which is where love and communion are revealed.[55]

Speaking of the deep perichoretic relationship between Creator and creation, Boff describes the Trinity as "theosphere," as "the common sphere of all beings and entities." He writes, "The Trinity helps us to delve deeper into understanding our common home, planet Earth, the universe, and its future, because they are all woven of the most intricate and open relationships, in the likeness of the Trinity."[56]

Citing Boff, Loida I. Martell-Otero finds the idea of perichoresis to resonate with Latina *evangelica* theology. She observes:

> Perichoresis is a term that literally signifies "to dance around" and in the tradition became synonymous with "interpenetration" and "interdependence." I believe that the Spanish word *vinculo* (literally, intimate ties that bind) captures this well. The Three are so intimately involved in a dance of love that they are one, yet not so involved that they cannot invite others to dance as well. We, and all of creation, are invited to dance with God.[57]

Martell-Otero finds that a perichoretic understanding of Trinity displays the One God's own "diversified and intimate community." This draws us beyond individualistic anthropology and soteriology to celebrate our diversity and community as "God's intention for creation."[58]

Matthew Fox

Matthew Fox writes of the need for a "cosmic and creativity-oriented understanding of the Trinity based on the expanding cosmos within and without us."[59] He is inspired by Hildegard of Bingen who described the Trinity as a brightness flashing forth with fire. The First Person is the "'living' light," the Second Person is the "flash of light," and the Third Person is the "fire."[60] The divine fire of God burns in all of life throughout the universe. Matthew Fox quotes Hildegard of Bingen:

> I [God] remain hidden in every kind of reality as fiery power. Everything burns because of me in such a way as our breath constantly moves us, like the wind-tossed flame in a fire. All of this lives in its essence and there is no death in it. For I am life.[61]

Elsewhere, Fox himself discusses the Trinity as "First Person: Creator of the Cosmos," "Second Person: The Logos of Liberation," and "Third Person: The Spirit of Sophia." All three as One are deeply involved in creation. This corresponds with a trinity of human response as "Cosmology, Liberation, and

Wisdom." With respect to the First Person, Fox writes: "The Creator is the one who fills the cosmos everywhere with beauty and power, light and darkness in an ongoing act of creation. Cosmology is the human effort to understand and enter the cosmos by way of science, mysticism, and art."[62] Attending to the Second Person as the Logos of Liberation, revealed in the person Jesus and present throughout creation as the Cosmic Christ, Fox speaks of the scope of the need for liberation as "good news to the poor" understood as

> the children and grandchildren to come. They are poor if the earth they will inherit is diminished in its health and beauty. Among the poor are the rain forests and the seas, the soil and the air, the winged creatures and the finned ones, the four-legged and the two-legged.[63]

The Third Person is the Spirit of Sophia. She is "the fecund spirit, the spirit of generativity, the spirit who broods over the fetal waters of birth, of transformation and of Pentecost, the spirit of the elements of the universe, the cosmic spirit of all nations of the earth."[64] Fox acknowledges, too, that the Second Person of the Trinity as well as the Third can be interpreted as Sophia, as a development of the biblical tradition presenting Wisdom as active throughout creation. In fact, Fox interprets Sophia/Wisdom as the very "matrix" of the Triune God:

> She lies at the heart of the creative process, a co-creator of the ongoing process of the universe. It is Sophia who teaches holy ways of living in the universe; she is the matrix for all three persons of the Trinity for she is present as Creator, as Prophet, and as Spirit making all things new.[65]

Elizabeth Johnson

Elizabeth A. Johnson has particularly developed an understanding of Trinity focused on Sophia/Wisdom, with each of the three persons of the Trinity understood as Sophia intimately involved with all of creation. "By wisdom God founded the earth," Johnson quotes Proverbs 3:19, and then she proceeds to examine Proverbs 8 and 9 as well as other canonical and deuterocanonical strands of the wisdom tradition. Johnson is persuaded, "Sophia is a female personification of God's own being in creative and saving involvement with the world."[66] She writes of God as Mother-Sophia, "abyss of livingness, Holy Wisdom unknown and unknowable . . . the matrix of all that exists, mother and fashioner of all things, who herself dwells in light inaccessible." She writes of God as Jesus-Sophia: " . . . Jesus Christ. Sophia child and prophet, and yes Sophia herself personally pitching her tent in the flesh of humanity to teach the paths of justice. . ." And she writes of God as Spirit-Sophia, "the mobile, pure, people-loving Spirit who pervades every wretched corner, wailing at the waste, releasing power that enables fresh starts. Her energy quickens the earth to life."[67] However the three are named, Johnson believes, "there is reflected a livingness in God, a beyond, a with and a within to the world and its history; a sense of God as from whom, by whom, and in whom all things exist, thrive, struggle toward freedom, and are gathered in."[68]

Moreover, "the threes keep circling round," says Johnson referring to *perichoresis* from Eastern theology which "signifies a cyclical movement, a revolving action such as the revolution of a wheel."[69] She further explains:

> Each person encompasses the others, is coinherent with the others in a joyous movement of shared life. Divine life circulates without any anteriority or posteriority, without any superiority or inferiority of one to the other. Instead there is a clasping of hands a pervading exchange of life, a genuine circling around together that constitutes the permanent, active, divine *koinōnia*.[70]

This perichoretic Trinitarian movement embraces us, too, and encircles all of creation.

The previous chapter on Pentecost elaborated Elizabeth Johnson's affirmation of Sophia-Spirit's vivifying, renewing, and gracing activity within creation. Here we might further hear her words about God's Word as Sophia in Christ in creation. Johnson quotes Augustine regarding Wisdom's incarnation in Christ, "But she is sent in one way that she may be with human beings; she has been sent in another way that she herself might be a human being."[71] Describing the wider ecological significance of this she writes:

> A relation to the whole cosmos is already built into the biblical wisdom tradition, and this orients Christology beyond the human world to the ecology of the earth, and indeed to the universe, a vital move in this era of planetary crisis. As the embodiment of Sophia who is fashioner of all that exists, Jesus the Christ's redeeming care intends the flourishing of all creatures and the whole earth itself.[72]

In her subsequent book, *Creation and the Cross*, Johnson further develops her understanding of Sophia Christology as deep incarnation, deep cross, and deep resurrection in creation. Sharing in creaturely flesh comprised of the elements of the universe, "Jesus was a complex living unit of minerals and fluids, an item in the carbon, oxygen, and nitrogen cycles," writes Johnson and continues:

> The atoms comprising his body were once part of other creatures. The genetic structure of the cells in his body were kin to the flowers, fish, frogs, finches, foxes, the whole community of life that descended from common ancestors in the ancient seas. And by the nature of living things he was going to die.[73]

Indeed, she observes that nature itself is "cruciform." Sharing with all living creatures both in life and in suffering and death, Christ's creaturely solidarity extends as well to resurrected life and to the unimaginable renewal of all creation. Johnson affirms, ". . . deep resurrection encourages us to include every creature of flesh in the hoped for future," and adds, "Each will be blessed according to its own nature as part of the whole creation that will be made new."[74]

Speaking of deep incarnation and deep resurrection, Johnson quotes Pope Francis from *Laudato Si'*:

> Pope Francis writes beautifully along these lines in *Laudato Si'*. In the days of his flesh, "the gaze of Jesus" looked on the natural world with an attention full of fondness and wonder. Now risen from the dead, Christ, who took unto himself this material world, is intimately present to each creature, "surrounding it with his affection," illuminating it, and directing it toward fullness in God. Indeed, "The very flowers of the field and the birds which his human eyes contemplated and admired are now imbued with his radiant presence." Speaking oracles of promise like the prophets of old, Francis proposes a wonderful vision of where this is all going. "At the end we will find ourselves face to face with the infinite Beauty of God." Rather than enjoying this by ourselves, "eternal life will be a shared experience of awe in which each creature, resplendently transfigured, will take its rightful place." All creation "will share with us in unending plenitude."[75]

Pope Francis also quotes Proverbs 3:19, "the Lord by wisdom founded the earth," and draws on the biblical wisdom tradition but uses masculine-gendered language in speaking about God rather than "Sophia." His Trinitarian prayer concluding *Laudato Si'* is faithful in its invocation of Trinity and inspiring in its inclusion of the natural world in the life of God and inclusion of the life of God in the natural world. Titled, "A Christian prayer in union with creation," it might well be prayed in congregations—not just Roman Catholic—on Trinity Sunday and on any occasion.

A Christian Prayer in Union with Creation[76]

> Father, we praise you with all your creatures.
> They came forth from your all-powerful hand;
> they are yours, filled with your presence and your tender love.
> Praise be to you!
>
> Son of God, Jesus,
> through you all things were made.
> You were formed in the womb of Mary our Mother,
> you became part of this earth,
> and you gazed upon this world with human eyes.
> Today you are alive in every creature

in your risen glory.
Praise be to you!

Holy Spirit, by your light
you guide this world toward the Father's love
and accompany creation as it groans in travail.
You also dwell in our hearts
and you inspire us to do what is good.
Praise be to you!

Triune Lord, wondrous community of infinite love,
teach us to contemplate you
in the beauty of the universe,
for all things speak of you.
Awaken our praise and thankfulness
for every being that you have made.
Give us the grace to feel profoundly joined
to everything that is.

God of love, show us our place in this world
as channels of your love
for all the creatures of this earth,
for not one of them is forgotten in your sight.
Enlighten those who possess power and money
that they may avoid the sin of indifference,
that they may love the common good, advance the weak,
and care for this world in which we live.
The poor and the earth are crying out.
O Lord, seize us with your power and light,
help us to protect all life,
to prepare for a better future,
for the coming of your Kingdom
of justice, peace, love and beauty.
Praise be to you!
Amen.

As a final benediction, this chapter closes with the Epistle lesson for year A in both lectionaries. It is 2 Corinthians 13:11–13, the last verse of which is this Trinitarian benediction:

> The grace of the Lord Jesus Christ,
> the love of God,
> and the communion of the Holy Spirit
> be with all of you.
> Go in Peace.

Part II

DIVINE NATURE IN FLESH LIKE OURS

Advent/Christmas/Epiphany

Chapter 9

Interlude

Reign of Christ Sunday

The last Sunday in ordinary time focuses on the theme of the Reign of Christ. This is the Sunday just prior to Advent and the beginning of the Christian year. As such, it anticipates a major theme of that liturgical season. Advent is about the advent of the Messiah and the expectation of Christ's messianic reign throughout the earth. The season of Advent begins with hope and longing for the Messiah, and it concludes with Christmas and the celebration of the Messiah's birth. The season is about expectations and beginnings. But just before this exciting season of expectation, the Reign of Christ Sunday reminds us of all that we already affirm about this Sovereign Christ. It introduces the season of Advent much like Transfiguration Sunday introduces the seasons of Lent and Easter and anticipates Christ's passion, resurrection, and ascension.

Reign of Christ Sunday echoes some of the themes of Christ's sovereignty that had been remembered and celebrated during Holy Week and the season of Easter, even as it introduces Advent and Christmas. The one expected during Advent and the one to be born at Christmas is also the one who is proclaimed regent on Calvary, who triumphs over contending powers and dominions on the cross and in the resurrection, who in glory fills all creation with sovereign presence, and whose reign is being perfected in new creation. We have already seen how the entire earth participates in the reign of Christ through each of these moments. Reign of Christ Sunday reiterates this sovereignty.

The Gospel readings for years B and C for both the Roman Catholic and the Revised Common Lectionary present Christ proclaimed as regent in the passion accounts of John and Luke, respectively. The Gospel of Luke portrays Jesus crucified with an inscription proclaiming, "This is the King of the Jews" and with soldiers challenging this claim and mocking him. Luke uniquely provides the confession and plea from one of those crucified alongside, "Jesus, remember me when you come into your kingdom" (Luke 23:36–38, 42). This encounter is immediately followed in Luke by the whole earth darkening in participatory response to the crucifixion, giving an earthly amen to the criminal's confession of Christ's realm.

The Gospel reading from John for year B is the interrogation of Jesus by Pilate in which Pilate asks if Jesus is King of the Jews, and Jesus responds, "My kingdom is not from this world. If my kingdom were from this world, my followers would be fighting. . . . But as it is, my kingdom is not from here." Pilate clarifies, "So you are a king?" To which Jesus responds, "You say that I am a king." But Jesus further connects this avowedly other-worldly regency with his nativity and earthly incarnation: "For this I was born, and for this I came into the world to testify to the truth" (John 18:33–37). The other lectionary readings for this day in year B (especially in the Roman Catholic Lectionary which are also the alternate readings in the Revised Common Lectionary) further bring this heavenly reign back down to Earth. The Epistle lesson is the beginning of Revelation in which John greets the churches with grace and peace "from Jesus Christ . . . the ruler of the kings of the earth" and further ascribes to Christ who "made us to be a kingdom," "glory and dominion forever and ever" (Rev 1:4–6).

Psalm 93, an enthronement psalm discussed in the chapter on Ascension, is recommended for this day in year B by both lectionaries. It begins by declaring God's sovereignty over the entirety of this world: "The LORD is king, he is robed in majesty; the LORD is robed, he is girded with strength. He has established the world; it shall never be moved" (Ps 93:1). The Roman Catholic Lectionary omits the following, but the alternate Revised Common Lectionary continues:

> The floods have lifted up, O LORD,
>   the floods have lifted up their voice;
>   the floods lift up their roaring.
> More majestic than the thunders of mighty waters,
>   more majestic than the waves of the sea,
>   majestic on high is the LORD! (Ps 93: 3–4)

The sound of the pounding surf is drowned out by God's majesty, and the flooding waters are themselves overwhelmed. The waters which represent contending chaos are contained and constrained to contribute to praise of God's overarching rule throughout the world.

Other psalms recommended for this day for all three years—A and C as well as B—are rich with imagery of God's reign on Earth and over the processes of nature. "Make a joyful noise to the LORD, all the earth!" begins

Psalm 100 for year A in the Revised Common Lectionary, and affirms that the LORD is God who "made us *and not we ourselves*" (Ps 100:1, 3).[1] The alternative psalm is Psalm 95 which acclaims God's sovereignty over the heights and depths of the earth and sea and over any contending forces or gods throughout:

> For the LORD is a great God,
>   and a great King above all gods.
> In his hand are the depths of the earth;
>   the heights of the mountains are his also.
> The sea is his, for he made it,
>   and the dry land which his hands have formed.
> O come, let us worship and bow down,
>   let us kneel before the Lord our Maker! (Ps 95: 3–6)

Psalm 46, recommended as the alternate psalm by the Revised Common Lectionary for year C, dramatically presents God's exercise of sovereignty both over tumultuous natural forces and over humanity's warring nature.

> God is our refuge and strength,
>   a very present help in trouble.
> Therefore we will not fear, though the earth should change,
>   though the mountains shake in the heart of the sea;
> though its waters roar and foam,
>   though the mountains tremble with its tumult.
>   *Selah*
>
> There is a river whose streams make glad the city of God,
>   the holy habitation of the Most High.
> God is in the midst of the city; it shall not be moved;
>   God will help it when morning dawns.
> The nations are in an uproar, the kingdoms totter;
>   he utters his voice, the earth melts.
> The LORD of hosts is with us;
>   the God of Jacob is our refuge.
>   *Selah*
>
> Come, behold the works of the LORD;
>   see what desolations he has brought on the earth.
> He makes wars cease to the end of the earth;
>   he breaks the bow, and shatters the spear;
>   he burns the shields with fire. (Ps 146:1–9)

And the psalm then calls for stillness in the face of God's exultation amid the nations and throughout the earth:

> Be still and know that I am God!
> I am exalted among the nations,
> I am exalted in the earth. (Ps 46:10)

So often in worship, we may chant the line "Be still and know that I am God" without necessarily connecting our inner prayerful stillness with the heaving of land and sea and with the breaking forth of earthly peace despite our violence.[2] But this psalm explicitly connects our personal stillness with God's sovereign activity and with Earth's dynamic exaltation.

All of these psalms refer to the LORD as sovereign God. Predating Jesus's advent, none of them refer to the sovereignty of Christ specifically. Read in the context of Christian worship, however, and on the particular Sunday celebrating the reign of Christ, they evoke for Christian worshipers a deeper awareness of Jesus Christ's exercise of sovereignty within the Godhead and throughout creation. Read in conjunction with the Gospel lessons and the Epistle lessons for this Sunday, worshipers are able to connect these songs celebrating God's rule in creation with Christ's victory on the cross and with Christ's enthronement in Ascension. Moreover, read on this Sunday preceding Advent and Christmas, these psalms incline worshipers to anticipate the Advent hope for such a messianic ruler and the Christmas celebration of that Regent being born on Earth.

As with the reading from Revelation assigned to year B discussed earlier, the Epistle lections for years A and C also celebrate Christ's reign over any and all contending forces or powers in creation. These readings are Colossians 1:11–20 for year C in both lectionaries, 1 Corinthians 15:20–26, 28 for year A in the Roman Catholic Lectionary, and Ephesians 1:15–23 for year A in the Revised Common Lectionary. The entire Christological story involving incarnation, crucifixion, resurrection, and ascension is invoked in these readings as they declare Christ's realm in creation. They each, though, might be seen to provide a particular emphasis within this overall narrative. The reading from Colossians emphasizes "making peace by the blood of the cross" (Col 1:20); the reading from 1 Corinthians emphasizes Christ's resurrection as first fruits until all is made subject, and Ephesians 1 emphasizes Christ's ascension to "fill all" and to reign over all other putative dominions.

The Epistle reading for year C is Colossians 1:11–20, verses 15–20 of which comprise an ancient Christological hymn celebrating Christ's divine sovereignty. It depicts Christ as Creator as well as incarnate, crucified and resurrected, and it pronounces Christ's victory over all contending forces in creation. Because this victory is declared to occur on the cross and reiterated in resurrection, these verses from Colossians were discussed earlier in the material pertaining to Good Friday and Easter. But the cross and Christ's victory, it should be recalled, are presented here in continuity with Christ's creative activity from the primordial beginning and with Christ's continuing presence holding creation together.

> He is the image of the invisible God, the firstborn of all reaction; for in him all things in heaven and on earth were created, things visible and invisible, whether thrones or dominions or rulers or powers—all things have been created through him and for him. He himself is before all things, and in him all things hold together. He is the head of the body, the church, he is the beginning, the firstborn from the dead, so that he might come to have first place in everything. For in him all the fullness of God was pleased to dwell, and through him God was pleased to reconcile to himself all things, whether on earth or in heaven, by making peace through the blood of his cross. (Col 1:15–20)

This hymn confesses faith in Christ's sovereignty made known in creation, cross, resurrection, and ascension. On Reign of Christ Sunday, verses preceding this hymn explicitly introduce it in the context of our inclusion in Christ's redeemed realm: "He has rescued us from the power of darkness and transferred us into the kingdom of his beloved Son" (Col 1:13). Liturgically, this ancient hymn might have been used as a confession of faith, and it can still serve that liturgical role. The *United Methodist Hymnal* 888 combines it with verses from 1 Corinthians 15 as an affirmation of faith to be read in congregational worship. But it also can be read in its given form in Scripture, perhaps with a worship leader introducing it by reading verses 13 and 14 and with the whole congregation together reading verses 15 through 20.

The Epistle lessons for year A also celebrate Christ's reign over any contending forces or powers in creation. The Roman Catholic Lectionary lists 1 Corinthians 15:20–26, 28 as the Epistle reading. The Revised Common Lectionary recommends Ephesians 1:15–23. The passage from 1 Corinthians begins, "But in fact Christ has been raised from the dead," and presents Christ's reign in the context of Christ's resurrection, enthronement, and second coming. The resurrection is the sign of ultimate victory, and it marks the current period in which contending forces are brought into subjection under Christ's reign until such time as the fullness of God's realm is to be realized. The resurrection of Christ inaugurates a sequence:

> But each in his own order: Christ the first fruits, then at his coming those who belong to Christ. Then comes the end, when he hands over the kingdom to God the Father, after he has destroyed every ruler and every authority and power. For he must reign until he has put all his enemies under his feet. The last enemy to be destroyed is death. (1 Cor 15:23–26)

Death-dealing forces are eliminated throughout the world. The resurrection becomes the sign and promise of the renewal and enlivening of the entire creation so that, as the passage concludes, "God may be all in all" (1 Cor 15:28).

The reading from Ephesians similarly moves from Christ's resurrection to Christ's ascension and universal reign over all contending power.

> God put this power to work in Christ when he raised him from the dead and seated him at his right hand in the heavenly places, far above all rule and authority and power and dominion, and above every name that is named not only in this age but also in the age to come. And he has put all things under his feet and has made him the head over all things for the church, which is his body, the fullness of him who fills all in all. (Eph 1:20–23)

Because the image of ascension is vividly presented, this passage was discussed in the chapter regarding the feast of Ascension during the Easter season. Though the picture is of Christ high and above all, this ascendency is in order for Christ to reign and fill all. This is earthly as well as heavenly. It is about here and now as well as "the age to come." All other claims to power being subordinated, Christ's reign fills heaven and earth.

These Epistle lessons present the messianic reign as universal and extending throughout the earth, the heavens, and all of creation. As earlier in discussing Christ's defeat of the *exousia*, it is not always clear whether these powers and dominions are earthly or heavenly, material or spiritual, demonic or human; it is clear, though, that this language points to a universal messianic reign over any contending powers. These powers involve both the spiritual realm and the social realm. Moreover and importantly, as the psalms for this Sunday particularly illustrate, these powers involve not only the spiritual and social but inevitably earthly processes and forces of nature as well. All is claimed within Christ's reign.

Similarly, Daniel 7, which is the first lesson for year B, envisions the advent of this messianic reign over all dominions:

> I saw one like a human being
>   coming with the clouds of heaven.
> And he came to the Ancient One
>   and was presented before him.
> To him was given dominion
>   and glory and kingship,
> that all peoples, nations, and languages
>   should serve him
> His dominion is an everlasting dominion
>   that shall not pass away.
> and his kingship is one
>   that shall never be destroyed. (Dan 7:13b–14)

Finally, this discussion of the lectionary readings for Reign of Christ Sunday concludes with attention to Ezekiel 34, which is the first lection for year A. The central metaphor in this passage pertains to sheep and shepherds rather than universal powers. But the metaphor is addressing the problem of leadership for the Hebrew people at the time of the Babylonian exile and the "scattering of the sheep" among the nations. The leaders are excoriated for feeding themselves off the flock rather than feeding the flock and caring for them. God promises to become their Shepherd, to "judge between sheep and sheep," to gather the flock together, and to establish justice. The Roman Catholic Lectionary is Ezekiel 34:11–12, 15–17; the Revised Common Lectionary is Ezekiel 34:11–16, 20–24 and concludes: "I will set up over them one shepherd, my servant David, and he shall feed them: he shall feed them and be their shepherd. And I, the LORD, will be their God, and my servant David shall be prince among them; I, the LORD, have spoken" (Ezek 34:23–24) While these two lectionaries each provide a slightly different selection of verses from Ezekiel, curiously they both omit verses 18 and 19. With an ecological concern in mind, though, these verses really should be included in our reading. Verses 18 and 19 reveal the ecological dimensions of the leaders' injustice that Ezekiel is criticizing. In addition to avarice and bullying, these leaders are pictured as contaminating the environment, degrading the land and polluting the water.

> Is it not enough for you to feed on the good pasture, but you must tread down with your feet the rest of your pasture? When you drink of clear water, must you foul the rest with your feet? And must my sheep eat what you have trodden with your feet, and drink what you have fouled with your feet? (Ezek 34:18–19)

Reign of Christ Sunday reminds us that the one expected in Advent is the one who brings good news to the whole earth and for the whole earth. "The LORD reigns, let the earth be glad!" Psalm 97 exclaims.[3] Our hope and our confession is that Christ is sovereign. The reign of Christ calls us to faithful living that challenges all lesser loyalties. We are called to political life that seeks an end to oppression with the establishment of justice and that seeks violence to cease with peace. We are called to challenge economic realms of inequality that magnify wealth for some and impoverish millions, and to work instead for the wealth and well-being of all. The reign of Christ calls us now, as at the beginning, to respect God's own claim of sovereignty throughout creation and to live and work for the health of the earth so as to sustain the flourishing of our fellow creatures. Our hope is in the advent of Christ who will establish this reign throughout the world.

Before moving to the next chapters on Advent, though, this chapter concludes with three verses from Brian Wren's hymn, "Christ is Alive."[4] Wren places Christ's reign here, invoking justice for people divided and for "earth and sky and ocean."

> Not throned afar, remotely high,
> Untouched, unmoved by human pains,
> But daily in the midst of life,
> Our Savior in the Godhead reigns.
>
> In every insult, rift, and war,
> Where color, scorn, or wealth divide,
> Christ suffers still, yet loves the more,
> And lives where even hope has died.
>
> Christ is alive, and comes to bring
> Good news to this and every age,
> Till earth and sky and ocean ring
> With joy, with justice, love, and praise.

Chapter 10

Early Advent

Longing for Wholeness

> The wolf shall live with the lamb,
> the leopard shall lie down with the kid,
> the calf and the lion and the fatling together,
> and a little child shall lead them.
>
> They shall not hurt or destroy in all my holy mountain;
> for the earth will be full of the knowledge of the LORD
> as the waters cover the sea.
> (Isaiah 11:6, 9)

ENTERING ADVENT

Advent begins with biblical readings that promise the inbreaking of God's justice on Earth. Whether biblical prophecies or apocalyptic writings, as Christian worshipers we hear these readings with hearts longing for messianic fulfillment and with faith that Christ's birth represents that promise and that fulfillment. They point us both back to the nativity, which we celebrate at Christmas, and ahead to Christ's second coming, which we await. Not all of these readings sound hopeful, however. There is an emphasis on God's judgment breaking into earthly life to effect justice—whether in the affairs of nations or in an apocalyptic Day of the Lord. There are images of violence as well as a promise of peace. Correlatively, we find images of both environmental destruction and ecological flourishing.

This presents us with a particular challenge for attending to the earth's well-being in our Advent expectations. Images of judgment and of apocalypse are particularly prominent earlier in Advent, especially but not exclusively on the first Sunday of Advent. Later in Advent, the readings anticipate the birth of Christ as embodying our Advent hope and, as Christmas unfolds, enfleshing God's very presence on Earth. In the middle of Advent, John the Baptist appears and mediates this transition, proclaiming repentance from sin in making ready a people prepared for God's judgment and pointing toward Jesus as the one being expected.

Of the greenery adorning the sanctuary in Advent, the Advent wreath in particular centers our attention on Advent as a season of expectant waiting. Four candles mark each of the four Sundays of Advent, with perhaps a Christ candle in the center of the wreath. The light from the wreath grows over the course of Advent as a new candle is lit on each consecutive Sunday, often culminating with the lighting of the Christ candle on Christmas Eve. According to Laurence Hull Stookey, this is the central significance of the Advent wreath: "The accumulation of light reminds us of the ever closer approach of the Light of the World, both at Bethlehem and in glory at the end of the age."[1] The light signifies both the eschatological expectations of early Advent and the tightening focus on the "light of the stable"[2] in later Advent. Light and fire also brilliantly symbolize creation and creation's continuance. Energy as light received from the sun by green plants is cycled throughout animate life. In ecological perspective, the Advent greenery and the light of the wreath constitute a symbolic unity, plants being the means by which light energizes life on the biosphere.

Beyond the marking of time as we move through Advent expectations to Christmas realization, the symbolism of the Advent wreath is open. The symbolic openness is due to the fairly recent history of liturgical use of the wreath in congregational worship. Having originated as a domestic practice in the homes of people of northern Europe, it gained in popularity for congregational use only in the second half of the twentieth century.[3] The individual four candles do not necessarily represent any particular theme for a given Sunday, but there are a number of popular designations for them. Stookey cautiously explains some of these:

> There has emerged the practice of giving a separate significance to each candle, so that the first represents, faith; the second, hope; the third, love; the fourth, joy. Or, faith, hope, love, and peace. Or humility, gentleness, patience and kindness. Or various other sets of abstract virtues. Yet another system asserts that the first candle represents Mary and Joseph, the second the angels over Bethlehem's plain, the third the shepherds, and the fourth the Magi.[4]

Stookey cautions against this practice of individualizing the meaning of each candle, so as not to "obscure the basic symbol of accumulating light."[5]

Symbols, though, are not mutually exclusive; they can be polyvalent with multiple levels of meaning. One meaning does not necessarily obscure another but might actually illumine it—or illuminate certain facets of the symbol in order to broaden the spectrum of meaning. The "abstract virtues" remembered on a given Sunday in Advent can take on concrete meaning if contextualized to earthly realities—to earthly faith, hope, love and peace. Rather than abandoning these symbolic designations, an alternative is to embrace the openness of the symbolism of the wreath so as to bring an ecological appreciation and apprehension of light's perception and of Christ's reception. Each of these virtues acquire meaning not in the abstract but in lived earthly reality.

The first series of liturgies for wreath lighting provided here in these first two chapters on Advent is based on the sequence of faith, hope, love and peace, with these virtues interpreted as ecologically relevant. Kathryn D. Blanchard and Kevin J. O'Brien have brought an ecological perspective to virtue ethics, and quotations from their thought introduce some of the liturgies that follow.[6] The liturgy for each Sunday of Advent weaves together an ecological insight, quotations from the lectionary readings, and images of light—together with the named virtue on that Sunday. One symbol does not displace the others, it is hoped, but rather the interweaving of them allows for an enriched integration of meaning for each Sunday of Advent.

Additionally, these liturgies bring prayer of confession into the ceremony. In some churches, Advent was once more of a penitential season in preparation for the celebration of Christmas, much like Lent is for Easter. The penitential character of Advent was softened after Vatican II, but there are nonetheless strong penitential themes in the lectionary readings for Advent, such as John the Baptizer's summons to repent in preparation for the coming of Christ. The joy of expectant celebration around the Advent wreath need not be negated by communal confession. Again the combination of symbolic action can serve to welcome us into confession and pardon as well as to deepen our Advent hopes and expectation. The time of confession concludes with words of assurance and declaration of pardon. Care should be taken to respect particular ecclesial traditions regarding the voicing of forgiveness in Christ.

A second set of liturgies for wreath lighting that is based on the canticles in the first chapter of Luke follows below in Chapter 12 on "Turning to the Children: Ecological Threat and Hope in Advent."

FIRST SUNDAY IN ADVENT

First Sunday in Advent: First Lections

Advent begins with the longing of Earth for peace and justice and with the messianic vision of a just world at peace. The imagery of the vision varies, but hope is resilient in the longing. Especially in the lessons from the Old Testament in the lectionary, earthy images project a picture of nature receiving and participating in a new era of peace and justice. Nature is seen to participate in the hoped-for restoration of Jerusalem and to celebrate in the promised enlightenment of the nations.

In year A, the first lection in both the Roman Catholic Lectionary and the Revised Common Lectionary is the promise from Isaiah 2:1–4 that in days to come all nations and peoples will flow to God's holy mountain, and "they shall beat their swords into plowshares, and their spears into pruning hooks; nation shall not lift up sword against nation, neither shall they learn war anymore." The same passage is found in Micah 4:1–3, but Micah continues with a simple but rich metaphor showing human life in peace with both nature and neighbor: "But they shall all sit every one under their vines and under their own fig trees, and no one shall make them afraid" (Mic 4:4a). The picture is of peace between peoples, the productivity of plants, and the economic security and peace of mind of each person on his or her property. The promise is at once global and local, economic and ecological.

The first lection for year C for the first Sunday of Advent in both lectionaries is Jeremiah 33:14–16, which promises a branch to spring from David. The promise is to the land as well as to the people:

> The days are surely coming, says the LORD, when I will fulfill the promise I made to the house of Israel and the house of Judah. In those days and at that time I will cause a righteous Branch to spring up for David; and he shall execute justice and righteousness in the land. In those days Judah will be saved and Jerusalem will live in safety. And this is the name by which it will be called: "The LORD is our righteousness." (Jer 33:14–16)

That the whole land is intended as the subject of God's righteousness is evidenced by the verses preceding this selection. Twice, in verse 10 and again in verse 12, Jeremiah laments the fact that the land is "waste, without human beings or animals." Sandwiched between these verses is the stated promise to the land, "For I will restore the fortunes of the land as at first, says the LORD." Of explicit concern in the verses that follow are domesticated animals and pasture in particular, but the vision is of ecologically healthy and productive land capable of supporting life (Jer 33:12–13). Moreover, while Judah is particularly named in verses 13 and 14, preceding verses also make explicit concern for the whole earth as well as both Judah and Israel. All nations of the earth are to turn toward Jerusalem as a source of joy: "And this city shall be to me a name of joy, a praise and a glory before all the nations of the earth who shall hear of all the good that I do for them" (Jer 33:9a). It is the same word (*eretz*) translated as "earth" in verse 9 that is translated as "land" in verses 11, 13, and 15 that follow. At the conclusion of chapter 33, it is translated as "earth" again in verse 25:

> Thus says the LORD: Only if I had not established my covenant with day and night and the ordinances of heaven and earth, would I reject the offspring of Jacob and of my servant David and not choose any of his descendants as rulers over the offspring of Abraham, Isaac, and Jacob. For I will restore their fortunes, and will have mercy upon them. (Jer 33:25)

God covenants with day and night as well as with Israel and Judah! Jeremiah 33 concludes with this explicit link between God's enduring love for the people of the lands of Israel and Judah and God's universal care for the heavens and the earth as Creator and Sovereign.

For year B the first lection for the first Sunday of Advent in the Revised Common Lectionary is Isaiah 64:1–9. These verses are part of a longer song of lament, Isaiah 63:7–64:12. The song rues the devastation wrought in Jerusalem and in the Jewish community by the Babylonian exile, and it expresses a longing for restoration.[7] God's agency for both judgment and renewal is affirmed. The plea is put to God to shake the earth as God had done in the past and to overturn the political order:

> O that you would tear open the heavens and come down,
>   so that the mountains would quake at your presence—
> as when fire kindles brushwood
>   and the fire causes water to boil—
> to make your name known to your adversaries,
>   so that the nations might tremble at your presence!
> When you did awesome deeds that we did not expect,
>   you came down, the mountains quaked at your presence. (Isa 64:1–3)

Confession of sin follows, and then confession of faith:

> We all fade like a leaf,
>   and our iniquities, like the wind, take us away.
> There is no one who calls on your name,
>   or attempts to take hold of you;
> For you have hidden your face from us,
>   and have delivered us into the hand of our iniquity.
> Yet, O LORD, you are our Father;
>   we are the clay, and you are our potter;
>   we are all the work of your hand. (Isa 64:6b–8)[8]

The metaphor of potter and clay are placed here in the context of global history and international affairs. God is affirmed as the Potter, the Creator.

"We are the clay," but this is not only about individual souls seeking to be refashioned. Everything and everyone is clay. The people as a whole are here confessing iniquity and seeking forgiveness and restoration, acknowledging the Potter's ability to do so. All the nations are also clay in the Potter's hands, making such restoration possible. And, indeed, the whole universe is presented as malleable to this Potter: tearing heavens, quaking mountains, churning water.

Reading these first lections in the context of Christian assemblies on the occasion of the first Sunday in Advent, they all broaden and deepen our expectation for the coming Messiah. The hope of the Hebrew people for restoration and their prayer for God's reign to establish justice and peace are framed within the faith that the God who makes covenant with them is the Creator and Sovereign of the entire world. This natural world of God's creation must participate in the advent of God's justice—whether through quaking in anticipation or through bucolic greening in reception. As Advent unfolds, Christian expectations will increasingly focus on the Christ child as embodying these hopes and as incarnating God's response to Earth's longing. It is as if in answer to the prayer in Isaiah 64:1 that the heavens might open and the divine come down. Moreover, as that child matures, and as Christmas merges into Epiphany and the celebration of Christ's baptism, we will see and hear, as petitioned in Isaiah 64:1, the heavens torn open as well as the waters moving, a dove descending, and a voice sounding, "This is my beloved."

First Sunday of Advent: Gospel Readings

The reading from the Gospel of Luke for the first Sunday of Advent in year C echoes the reverberations of the universe in anticipating the establishment of messianic reign. Sun, moon, stars, earth, and sea all resound.

> There will be signs in the sun, the moon, and the stars, and on the earth distress among nations confused by the roaring of the sea and the waves. People will faint from fear and foreboding of what is coming upon the world, for the powers of the heavens will be shaken. They will see the Son of Man coming in a cloud with power and great glory. (Luke 21:25–27)

Matthew and Mark in parallel with Luke also have heavenly powers being shaken and the heavenly bodies of sun, moon, and stars giving signs. Only Luke, though, gives voice to the roaring of the sea's waves and the distress this causes on Earth. It is as if the last throes of primordial chaos are being confronted and confounded by the coming of the Christ.

All three Gospel readings provided by the Lectionaries for the first Sunday in Advent are excerpted from the respective narratives of the Synoptic apocalypse. The focus in each of these Gospel readings is on the coming of the Son of Man, which in Christian tradition is interpreted as the second coming of Christ. Advent anticipates the coming of the Messiah—both the birth of the Messiah confessed as Jesus the Christ and the culmination of the Messiah's reign symbolized as Christ's second coming. That this consummation of Christ's rule is vehemently in antithesis to the ways in which worldly power is construed and wielded is symbolized by the dynamic potency of the signs in heaven, earth, and sea. That these tumultuous signs are actually presaging the good news of redemption, though, is made clear by Luke: "Now when these things begin to take place, stand up and raise your heads, because your redemption is drawing near" (Luke 21:28).

The two other Gospel readings in years A and B for the first Sunday of Advent are also taken from the Synoptic apocalypse, but provide material in each reading that is unique to the apocalypse in that particular Gospel. Mark concludes the apocalyptic discourse with a parable about a homeowner leaving servants in charge of the estate until returning (Mark 13:33–37). In Mark the parable is starkly about vigilance, "Therefore, keep awake—for you do not know when the master of the house will come" (Mark 13:35a). Matthew and Luke expand on this parable as a frame for expounding the parable of the talents (Matt 25:14–30; Luke 19:12–27), but there are no talents or reckoning of talents in Mark's telling of this story. Moreover, when Mark's Jesus says that the homeowner left the servants "in charge," the word being translated for this authority is *exousia*, and the word for the "master" is *kurios*. Especially occurring as it does at the conclusion of this apocalyptic discourse, it reads as reassurance of the restoration of the Lord's rule over the whole of God's creation, retrieving power that may have been otherwise wielded during an interim period awaiting resolution.

The reading from Matthew for year A similarly warns, "Keep awake, therefore, for you do not know on what day your lord is coming" (Matt 24:42). This is preceded, though, by invoking the memory of Noah: "For as the days of Noah were, so will be the coming of the Son of Man" (Matt 24:37). The same material occurs elsewhere in Luke (Luke 17:11–37), but Matthew places it here. The coming of the Son of Man is likened to the unexpected coming of the flood in Noah's lifetime, interrupting the normal pattern of life. There is clearly a warning delivered; the passage continues: "Then two will be in the field; one will be taken and one will be left. Two women will be grinding meal together; one will be taken and one will be left" (Matt 24:40–41). At the same time, by remembering Noah, we also recall that a covenant with all flesh—animals as well as humans—emerged after the destruction of the flood. There is a promise implied for earthly life, even as a dire warning is given to "keep awake." When read in conjunction with other readings for the first Sunday in Advent, that promise for the earth in the Messiah's rightful reign is made liturgically explicit and becomes salient for worshipers.

The first Sunday of Advent focuses generally on messianic expectation—both prophecies for earthly redemption and apocalyptic visions of the inbreaking of divine judgment. There is a summons to "Keep Awake," which is also a call to prepare our lives and our hearts for the coming of God's justice. The second Sunday of Advent starts to sharpen the focus of that messianic expectation on the person of Jesus even while amplifying the call to repentance.

First Advent Candle Lighting Ceremony: Faith

A thought for the bulletin:

Speaking of faith in God as both an ecological and a social virtue, Kathryn D. Blanchard and Kevin J. O'Brien write:

> Faith in God means not just individual change but also a new kind of community. Christian conversion to live more responsibly on earth should therefore involve communities, seeking not only to reduce our own negative impacts on the earth but also to inspire our churches and our neighborhoods to conversion as well.[9]

Voice: As people of faith, on this first Sunday of Advent, we turn in faith to God and to God's promise to establish peace and justice on Earth. Hear this prophecy from Isaiah (Isa 2:4–5):

> For out of Zion shall go forth instruction,
>   and the word of the LORD from Jerusalem.
> He shall judge between the nations,
>   and shall arbitrate for many peoples;
> they shall beat their swords into plowshares,
>   and their spears into pruning hooks;
> nation shall not lift up sword against nation,
>   neither shall they learn war any more.
> O house of Jacob,
>   come, let us walk
>   in the light of the LORD!

(*Light first Advent candle*)

Litany of Confession

> *One:* Let us turn to God in faith, seeking forgiveness and restoration. Let us pray: Giver of life, our faith wavers in the face of worldly temptations. We are slow to take your instruction to heart and to embrace holy and healthy lifestyles.

Response: "Restore us, O God; let your face shine that we may be saved." (Ps 80:3)

One: Giver of life, our faith wavers in the face of social turmoil. We are slow to take your love to heart and to bridge divisions of race, language, culture, poverty and privilege.

Response: "Restore us, O God; let your face shine that we may be saved." (Ps 80:3)

One: Giver of life, our faith wavers in the face planetary danger. We are slow to join with others to protect Earth's health for the well-being of all creatures below the sky.

Response: "Restore us, O God; let your face shine that we may be saved." (Ps 80:3)

One: Giver of Life, our faith wavers in the face of violence and war. We are slow to promote peace and to challenge the assumption that violence makes us secure.

Response: "Restore us, O God; let your face shine that we may be saved." (Ps 80:3)

One: Giver of Life, our faith wavers as we face the long wait for your justice on Earth. We are slow to proclaim your promise of renewed creation even as we herald your Messiah's advent.

Response: "Restore us, O God; let your face shine that we may be saved." (Ps 80:3)

Words of Assurance: "The night is far gone, the day is near. Let us then lay aside the works of darkness and put on the armor of light." (Rom 13:12)

Pardon: In the name of Jesus Christ, you are forgiven. . . . Glory to God! Amen.

Sung Response: "Jesus is Coming Again," verse 2

> Forest and flower exclaim,
>   Mountain and meadow the same,
> All earth and heaven proclaim:
>   Jesus is coming again![10]

OR "The King Shall Come" verse 1

> The King shall come when morning dawns
>   and light triumphant breaks,
> when beauty gilds the eastern hills
>   and life to joy awakes.[11]

SECOND SUNDAY IN ADVENT

Second Sunday of Advent: First Lections and the Gospel

Gospel readings for the Second Sunday of Advent portray John the Baptist summoning people to repentance while indicating that he is but the forerunner of the one expected. While the Revised Common Lectionary cycles through the Synoptic parallels for each of the three years, the Roman Catholic Lectionary for the Mass has Luke 3:4–6 every year. All the Gospel lections for the second Sunday of Advent for all three years quote Isaiah 40:3 in presenting John the Baptist, though Isaiah 40:1–11 is given as the first lection only in year B. Luke gives the most extensive quotation from Isaiah, concluding with salvation appearing to "all flesh."

The voice of one crying out in the wilderness:

> Prepare the way of the Lord,
>   make his paths straight.
> Every valley shall be filled,
>   and every mountain and hill shall be made low,
> and the crooked shall be made straight,
>   and the rough ways made smooth;
> and all flesh shall see the salvation of God. (Luke 3:4b–6, quoting Isa 40:3–5)

For some reason, the NRSV translates the Hebrew *kol basar* in Isaiah 40:5 as "all people" but translates *pasa sarx* in the Greek translation quoted in Luke 3:6 as "all flesh." "All flesh," however, is the literal translation in each instance. It is the same expression as found in the ninth chapter of Genesis where God covenants with "every creature of all flesh" (Gen 9:15), which is explicitly inclusive of animals as well as humanity.[12] There are contexts where this phrase seems to be signifying humans in particular even though it is literally more inclusive of animal life, but it is generally a good practice to read it literally as "all flesh," letting the attentive listener discern the meaning in context, else we may inadvertently obscure from the proclamation its possible inclusion of animals.

In the context of Isaiah 40, there is ambiguity about "all flesh." It is "my people" (*ami*) who are specifically addressed in the opening line, "Comfort, O comfort my people says your God" (Isa 40:1). So in verse 5, it makes sense to consider "all flesh" as again referring to people in particular. As we continue to read, though, both "all flesh" and "the people" are considered as withered grass:

> A voice says, "Cry out!"
>   And I said, "What shall I cry?"
> [All flesh is] (*kol habasar*) grass,
>   their constancy is like the flower of the field.
> The grass withers, the flower fades,
>   when the breath of the LORD blows upon it;
>   surely the people (*ha'am*) are grass. (Isa 40:6–7)

People are included here along with the rest of all flesh as being like plants. Plants, animals, and humans are united in their mortality and in their dependence on God for their being and continuance.

Isaiah 40 marks the beginning of the writings of Deutero-Isaiah understood by most to have been written during the Babylonian exile. These chapters in the book of Isaiah are remarkable for the depth of creation theology and for the detail of poetic imagery of creation. Chapter 40 continues with declaration of God's mighty acts in creation and asking if any can compare:

> Who has measured the waters in the hollow of his hand
>   and marked off the heavens with a span,
> enclosed the dust of the earth in a measure,
>   and weighed the mountains in scales
>   and the hills in a balance? (Isa 40:12)

Against this creative and sovereign power, "all the nations are as nothing" (Isa 40:17), and all of Earth's inhabitants are likened to grasshoppers:

> Have you not known? Have you not heard?
>   Has it not been told you from the beginning?
>   Have you not understood from the foundations of the earth?
> It is he who sits above the circle of the earth,
>   and its inhabitants are like grasshoppers,
> who stretches out the heavens like a curtain,
>   and spreads them like a tent to live in;
> who brings princes to naught,
>   and makes the rulers of the earth as nothing. (Isa 40:21–23)

So "all flesh" in this chapter of Isaiah, and by inference echoed in Luke's remembrance of this chapter, might indeed refer to people—but to people as but one iteration of all flesh likened to grasshoppers, indeed likened to grass. With this in mind, the forecasted messiah in Luke is coming to the earth—to every hill and valley—and bringing salvation for all flesh: "and all flesh shall see the salvation of God" (Luke 3:6).

The first lections for the other two years for the second Sunday in Advent similarly combine messages of expectation for salvation with images of nature receiving that saving presence. Year C in the Roman Catholic Lectionary prescribes a reading from the deterocanonical book of Baruch (Bar 5:1–9).[13] Echoing the imagery in Isaiah 40 of leveled mountains and filled valleys, Baruch announces:

> For God has ordered that every high mountain and the everlasting hills be made low
> > and the valleys filled up, to make level ground,
> > so that Israel may walk safely in the glory of God.
> The woods and every fragrant tree
> > have shaded Israel at God's command. (Bar 5:7–8)

Here the leveling of mountains and hills prepares the way explicitly for Israel to walk, perhaps a walk of freedom returning from captivity, under the glory of God and under the shade of trees. Forests and trees as well as hills and valleys are presented as participating in God's glory and sharing in Israel's safety.

Year A for the second Sunday in Advent in both lectionaries has Isaiah 11:1–10 as the first lection, which begins famously with the messianic prophecy for a shoot from the stump of Jesse:

> A shoot shall come out from the stump of Jesse,
> > and a branch shall grow out of his roots.
> The spirit of the LORD shall rest on him,
> > the spirit of wisdom and understanding,
> > the spirit of counsel and might,
> > the spirit of knowledge and the fear of the LORD. (Isa 11:1–2)

This heir to David is to take delight "in the fear of the LORD," and to exercise judgment for the poor and the "meek of the earth" with righteousness and equity (Isa 11:3–5). This passage concludes with a vision of peace enveloping the entire world, including both wild and domestic animals and human beings:

> The wolf shall live with the lamb,
> > the leopard shall lie down with the kid,

> the calf and the lion and the fatling together,
>   and a little child shall lead them.
> The cow and the bear shall graze,
>   their young shall lie down together;
>   and the lion shall eat straw like the ox.
> The nursing child shall play over the hole of the asp,
>   and the weaned child shall put its hand on the adder's den.
> They will not hurt or destroy on all my holy mountain;
> for the earth will be full of the knowledge of the LORD
>   as the waters cover the sea. (Isa 11:6–9)

The vision is one of a restored wholeness to creation, freed from violence. This is not the same as ecological health in which there is a cycling of nutrients and elements in the patterns of consumption between predators and prey and among animals, plants, and decomposers. This is poetry rather than science, but it does point to the realization of hope for a world at peace inclusive of all that live "and a little child shall lead them."

The "nursing child" in verse 8 may or may not refer to the same individual as the shoot from the stump of Jesse prophesied in the opening of Isaiah 11. But read together during the season of Advent, they suggest for us a portrait of the Christ child awaited—and the transformed world awaited. This is to be a world safe for children. It is to be a world, moreover, safe for wildlife.

The richness of vocabulary in this passage and in Isaiah as a whole underscores the importance given to both children and animals. John W. Olley notes that there are three different words[14] for child employed in this passage—all different from the common word for child (*yeled*) used elsewhere in Isaiah such as in Isaiah 9:6, "For a child has been born for us, a son given to us." Moreover, Olley finds the book of Isaiah to be replete with images of animals, naming at least 160 different kinds of animals or terms for animals.[15] In addition, these references to animals tend to be respectful and appreciative of them rather than disparaging or pejorative. "The wonder is that animals are included in the 'knowledge of YHWH' (Isaiah 11:9)," Olley marvels. "'Harmful' animals are not banished," he specifies, rather they share in the transformation with humans." While not ecologically correct, the vision of Isaiah 11 does suggest the interconnectedness of species and the inclusion of diverse species in Earth community. Noting this inclusion of animal species, Olley writes, "the vision of the future involves transformation . . . of a total real world, not only of human society, and not into a spiritual realm where animals have no place." That inclusive place includes our life of worship as well as our earthly existence. Olley concludes:

> Throughout the book of Isaiah animals are more than recognized as part of the Earth community. Whether wild or domestic, their integrity and diversity

is affirmed. The vision of the future worshipping life on the holy mountain includes animals.[16]

For, as the passage concludes, the earth itself, the whole earth, "will be full of the knowledge of the LORD as the waters cover the sea" (Isa 11:9b).

The first readings from the lectionaries for the second Sunday in Advent present a vision for a world of peace and justice inclusive of all earthly life. Our messianic hope is for one to lead us into such a world. Our faith is that the birth of Jesus Christ presents to us just such a one, and the proclamation of John the Baptist also read on this day points in Christ's direction.

Second Sunday in Advent: The Psalter

The psalms for the second Sunday in Advent also resound with this hope for peace and justice on Earth. Most notably, Psalm 85, in year B, brings these together in a kind of earthly embrace:

> Steadfast love and faithfulness will meet;
> > righteousness and peace will kiss each other.
> Faithfulness will spring up from the ground,
> > and righteousness will look down from the sky. (Ps 85:10–11)

The word translated "ground" is *eretz*, so verse 11 could also read "faithfulness will spring up from the earth." This translation might be especially fitting read next to the parallel image of righteousness looking down "from the sky." The word *eretz* appears at four different points in this psalm. Also, *tsedeq* translated as "righteousness" is sometimes translated as "justice." Earth and sky together are presented as participating in peace and justice, in righteousness and truth, in God's steadfast love.

The psalter for year C in the Revised Common Lectionary is actually the Song of Zechariah from the Gospel of Luke (1:68–79). There Zechariah sings of his newborn son, John the Baptist, that he will "guide our feet into the way of peace," so that we might serve God "without fear, in holiness and righteousness . . . all our days" (Luke 1: 75a, 79). At the conclusion of Zechariah's song, the first chapter of Luke summatively concludes concerning John: "The child grew and became strong in spirit, and he was in the wilderness until the day he appeared publicly to Israel" (Luke 1:80). John the Baptist, who was to call the people to repentance, and who was to point the way to righteousness and peace, and who was to prepare the way for the messiah coming after him, was formed for this ministry in the wilderness, in untamed nature.

Instead of the Song of Zechariah, the Roman Catholic Lectionary has Psalm 126 for the psalter on the second Sunday of Advent.[17] Rather than the image of wilderness, an agricultural image is invoked. This psalm is a prayer for restoration that concludes with celebration of the abundance of grain:

> Those who go out weeping,
>   bearing the seed for sowing,
> shall come home with shouts of joy,
>   carrying their sheaves. (Psalm 126:6)

This psalm is the inspiration for the hymn "Bringing in the Sheaves."

Agricultural images are also vivid in Psalm 72, which is the psalm listed for the second Sunday in Advent for year A in both lectionaries. Psalm 72 is a prayer of blessing for a righteous regent, and it presents the earth as participating in this blessing with agricultural bounty being a part of that blessing. "May there be abundance of grain in the land," verse 16 prays and, "may it wave on the tops of the mountains." The psalm unites images of just rule with earthly peace and productive land. Verse 7 petitions, "In his days may righteousness flourish and peace abound, until the moon is no more." The psalm concludes, "Blessed be his glorious name forever; may his glory fill the whole earth. Amen and Amen" (Ps 72:19). Read in the context of Advent during congregational worship, it points us toward our messianic hope for Christ to establish such a reign of justice, peace, and ecological wholeness. This psalm is also listed by both lectionaries as the psalter for the feast of Epiphany, and it will be discussed further in the chapter on Epiphany.

Second Sunday in Advent: Epistle Lections

The Epistle lessons in years B and C for the second Sunday of Advent point to the second coming of Christ. The first chapter of Philippians, read in year C, expresses confidence "that the one who began a good work among you will bring it to completion by the day of Jesus Christ" (Phil 1:6) and further links this day with a "harvest of righteousness": "That in the day of Christ you may be pure and blameless, having produced the harvest of righteousness that comes through Jesus Christ for the glory and praise of God" (Phil 1:10b–11). Writing to believers in Philippi, Paul would be referring to the completion and culmination of Christ's work of furthering righteousness in and through them who believe and through us who continue to believe and to wait.

One of the most troubling lections in Advent, especially from the standpoint of the creation, is 2 Peter 3:8–15a, which is the Epistle lesson in year B for the second Sunday in Advent.[18] We need to examine it and the context of 2 Peter at greater length with creation in mind. Continuing the apocalyptic theme from the first Sunday in Advent, 2 Peter 3:8ff looks toward the coming of the "day of the Lord" but with frightening images of Earth's destruction. There is an apocalyptic scenario which sounds bizarre to contemporary ears:

> With the Lord one day is like a thousand years, and a thousand years are like one day. The Lord is not slow about his promise, as some think of slowness, but is patient with you, not wanting any to perish, but all to come to repentance. But the day of the Lord will come like a thief, and then the heavens will pass away with a loud noise, and the elements will be dissolved with fire, and the earth and everything that is done on it will be disclosed.
>
> Since all these things are to be dissolved in this way, what sort of persons ought you to be in leading lives of holiness and godliness, waiting for and hastening the coming of the day of God, because of which the heavens will be set ablaze and dissolved, and the elements will melt with fire? But, in accordance with his promise, we wait for new heavens and a new earth, where righteousness is at home. (2 Pet 3:8b–13)

Beyond other-worldly, this passage sounds anti-worldly. We are right to be suspicious about the story and interpretations of it that would eclipse earthly hopes rather than illumine them.

There is very little that seems saliently ecological when first encountering this passage. The images of destruction in 2 Peter 3, though, are surprisingly prefaced with confidence expressed in God's power exhibited in creation and reiterated at the time of Noah: ". . . by the word of God heavens existed long ago and an earth was formed out of water and by means of water, through which the world of that time was deluged with water . . ." (2 Pet 3:5–6). By reminding hearers of God's power in creation, 2 Peter seems to be cautioning against a complacency in creation's continuance, and warns that "judgment and the destruction of the godless" is also within this God's power (2 Pet 3:7).

The promise of "new heavens and a new earth" in 2 Peter 3:13 seems to be a phrase quoted from Isaiah 65:17 and 66:22. In Isaiah, the vision is not of devastation but of the restoration of well-being throughout creation, as *The Oxford Annotated Bible* puts it, "not the destruction but the renewal and transformation of the universe."[19] Douglas Harink interprets the language in 2 Peter similarly—to refer not to the devastation but the transformation of earthly existence.

Focusing on some of the more problematic verses in 2 Peter with regard to Earth's continuance (2 Pet 3:10–12), Harink argues that the phrase "the elements (*stoicheia*) will be dissolved" should refer not to material elements but to the elemental forces inimical to right living and well-being, such as the *stoicheia* referenced in Galatians 4:3–9.[20] In Galatians, the warning against being enslaved by the elements (*stoicheia*) is voiced in conjunction with an affirmation of Christ's incarnation "born of a woman" and of our own adoption as heirs of the promises of God. The warning against the elements is consistent with an affirmation of bodily existence. The warning in both Galatians and 2 Peter is against succumbing in our life and our loyalties to that which is contrary to God's promised intent for us.

Harink notes also that contemporary text critics tend to favor a reading of 2 Peter 3:10 where "the earth and everything done on it will be disclosed (*heurethēsetai*)" (NRSV as quoted earlier) as opposed to "burned up" (*katakaēsetai*). There is still fire burning in 2 Peter, but Harink likens this fire not to a literal conflagration but symbolically to creation's Pentecost as we experience our transfiguration. "The point is this," he insists, "while the transformation of all creaturely being in the parousia of God will be radical beyond imagining, it will nonetheless be a transfiguration *of creaturely being*, including human beings and the many works that they have done and will do on the face of the earth." He concludes with this verse from the Advent reading: ". . . we wait for new heavens and a new earth, where righteousness is at home" (2 Pet 3:13).[21]

The Epistle lesson in year A for the second Sunday of Advent is Romans 15:4–13 in the Revised Common Lectionary.[22] The first lection in year A is the reading from Isaiah 11 discussed earlier, and it is echoed in this Epistle lesson. Verse 12 of Romans 15 quotes Isaiah 11:10 saying, "The root of Jesse shall come." At the beginning and end of this reading from Romans are two benedictions. Either or both of these blessings can be given as congregational benedictions on the second Sunday of Advent, even if the Epistle lesson as a whole is not read. This subchapter prayerfully closes with these benedictions:

> May the God of steadfastness and encouragement grant you to live in harmony with one another, in accordance with Christ Jesus, so that together you may with one voice glorify the God and Father of our Lord Jesus Christ. (Rom 15:5–6)

> May the God of hope fill you with all joy and peace in believing, so that you may abound in hope by the power of the Holy Spirit. (Rom 15:13)

Second Advent Candle Lighting Ceremony: Hope

A thought for the bulletin:

Kathryn D. Blanchard and Kevin J. O'Brien write about hope as an "environmental virtue":

> When facing the realities of environmental degradation, we should add hopes for the rest of creation: hope for healthy ecosystems to nurture ourselves, our human neighbors, and other species; and hope for the diversity of creation to reveal God's glory.[23]

Voice: On this second Sunday in Advent, we light a candle in hope. "For whatever was written in former days was written for our instruction," wrote Saint Paul, "so that by steadfastness and by the encouragement of the scriptures we might have hope" (Rom 15:4).

(*Light first two candles*)

Today, with John the Baptist, we hope that, in the light of God's reign drawing near, "all flesh shall see the salvation of God" (Luke 3:6).

Prayer of Confession

> *Voice:* Hearing John the Baptizer's call to repent, let us turn to the source of our hope in prayer.
>
> Creator of light and darkness,
> > of time and eternity,
> > of life on earth and in the sea:
>
> Your promise of salvation to us and to all flesh shines through our gloom. The threats to your creation seem so complex, so menacing, so recalcitrant, that we have been tempted to lose hope. We vacillate between a disheartened lethargy of defeat and a Pollyanna optimism of denial. We confess to you our
> > laziness in lifestyle, thinking we can't make a difference,
> > inaction in politics, thinking it can't matter, and
> > isolationism in our spiritual life, disengaged from your living presence
> > > in our midst,
> > > among our neighbors,
> > > throughout the whole diversity of earthly creatures.
>
> Forgive us. Enlighten and enliven us for faithful and fruitful service
> > throughout the human race,
> > throughout the living planet.
>
> Through Christ, our Dayspring from on high,
> Amen.

Words of Assurance

> "The woods and every fragrant tree have shaded Israel at God's command. For God will lead Israel with joy, in the light of his glory." (Bar 5:8–9)
>
> OR
>
> "May the God of hope fill you with all joy and peace in believing, so that you may abound in hope by the power of the Holy Spirit." (Rom 15:13)

Pardon: In the name of Jesus Christ, you are forgiven. . . . Glory to God! Amen.

Sung Response from "All Hail to God's Anointed" (based on Ps 72)

You shall come down like showers upon the fruitful earth;
    love, joy, and hope, like flowers, spring in your path to birth.
Before you on the mountains shall peace, the herald go,
    and righteousness in fountains from hill to valley flow.[24]

Chapter 11

Late Advent

God's Promised Presence

> Drop down dew from above, you heavens,
> and let the clouds rain down the Just One;
> let the earth be opened and bring forth a Savior.[1]

As Advent progresses, our messianic hope and expectation for restoration throughout the earth becomes increasingly focused on the coming of the Christ child. Gospel readings for the third Sunday in Advent develop John the Baptist's proclamation of the one who will come after. There continues to be a tension or a balance between this messianic expectation as frightening and as hopeful. Indeed in Luke's Gospel, John the Baptist's dire declaration of judgment is proclaimed as "good news." Speaking of the coming Christ, he says:

> "He will baptize you with the Holy Spirit and fire. His winnowing fork is in his hand, to clear his threshing floor and to gather the wheat into his granary; but the chaff he will burn with unquenchable fire."
> So, with many other exhortations, he proclaimed the good news to the people. (Luke 3:16b–18a)

The "good news" or "gospel" (*euangelion*) is a peculiar word that takes on a particular set of meanings in the Greek Testament. Etymologically, though, it refers to the proclamation of victory by a monarch or commander. Judgment and celebration are united in John's proclamation of good news, because the one awaited "who is more powerful than I" is righteous, and the awaited outcome is justice restored.

In Luke's Gospel, the "good news," the *euangelion* announced by an angel, is the proclamation of Christ's birth soon to be heralded at Christmas celebrations: "Do not be afraid; for see—I am bringing you good news of great joy for all the people: to you is born . . ." (Luke 2:10b–11a). Gospel readings for the fourth Sunday of Advent give either Matthew's account of Christ's birth (in year A) or readings from the first chapter in Luke (in years B and C) focusing on Mary's conception and gestation of Jesus: the Annunciation, the visit with Elizabeth, and the Magnificat. The psalter also gives the opportunity during these two Sundays to sing the Magnificat as well as the song of Zechariah.

THIRD SUNDAY IN ADVENT

The first lections and psalms from the Hebrew Scriptures during the second half of Advent present the whole earth and all of nature participating in God's redemptive inbreaking. On the third Sunday of Advent in year A, Isaiah 35:1–10 heralds this inbreaking marked by a return of exiles to Zion and a celebratory blooming of life in the wilderness through which they pass. It begins as follows:

> The wilderness and the dry land shall be glad,
>   the desert shall rejoice and blossom;
> like the crocus it shall blossom abundantly,
>   and rejoice with joy and singing. (Isa 35:1)

It concludes as follows:

> And the ransomed of the LORD shall return,
>   and come to Zion with singing;
> everlasting joy shall be upon their heads;
>   they shall obtain joy and gladness,
>   and sorrow and sighing shall flee away. (Isa 35:10)

Walter Brueggemann refers to the message here as a kind of "gospel," a proclamation of good news that God is active redemptively in both history and nature, restoring people to their home and productivity to the land:

> The arid soil will astonishingly produce vegetation and flowers, so much so that the land itself will break out in singing. The imagery concerns a personalized creation that has languished in despair, but now, by the power of Yahweh, is raised to new life and therefore must sing praise to Yahweh the giver of life.[2]

In the heart of this passage, according to Brueggemann, is the promise of God's vengeance:

> Be strong, do not fear!
> Here is your God.

> He will come with vengeance,
> with terrible recompense.
> He will come and save you. (Isa 35:4b)

Similar to the complementarity between judgment and celebration in John the Baptist's proclamation of "good news," here in Isaiah is a complementarity between God's vengeance and the good news of creation enlivened and people restored. The good news is that God claims sovereignty over both nature and history. "The term 'vengeance' includes a quite negative connotation that we readily assign to it," Brueggemann explains, "but it also includes the positive dimension that God will come to right wrong, to order chaos, to heal sickness, to restore life to its rightful order."[3]

The psalm accompanying Isaiah 35 suggested by the lectionaries for the third Sunday of Advent in year A is Psalm 146 which also declares at once God as the upholder of social justice and God as the Creator of earth, sky, and sea. "Happy are those whose help is the God of Jacob," the psalm proclaims, "whose hope is in the LORD their God, who made heaven and earth, the sea, and all that is in them" (Ps 146: 5–6a). The psalm continues lauding God for establishing justice for the oppressed, giving food to the hungry, setting prisoners free, giving sight to the blind, lifting the lowly, watching over aliens, and upholding widows and orphans. The psalm concludes:

> . . . but the way of the wicked he brings to ruin.
> The LORD will reign forever,
> your God, O Zion, for all generations.
> Praise the LORD! (Ps 146 9b–10)

As with the reading from Isaiah and as with the proclamation of John the Baptist, this psalm unites an affirmation of God's sovereignty over all creatures with celebration of God's vindication of the downtrodden in society "for all generations." The psalm clearly parallels themes voiced by Mary in the Magnificat, also suggested to be sung on the third Sunday in Advent: scattering the proud and bringing down the powerful, but lifting up the lowly and filling the hungry "from generation to generation" (Luke 1:46–55).

Similarly in year B for the third Sunday in Advent, the first lesson which is from Isaiah 61 demonstrates this complementarity of God's "vengeance" and "good news," and it parallels the themes of justice and liberation as voiced by Mary in the Magnificat. The start of Isaiah 61 is the famous announcement, the beginning of which was read by Jesus at the outset of his ministry in Luke 4:16–19:

> The spirit of the Lord GOD is upon me,
> because the LORD has anointed me;

> he has sent me to bring good news to the oppressed,
> > to bind up the brokenhearted,
> to proclaim the year of the LORD's favor,
> > and the day of vengeance of our God. (Isa 61:1–2b)

The chapter concludes with images of Earth's fecundity as symbolic of the establishment of righteousness and praise before all nations, likened to a garden:

> For as the earth brings forth its shoots,
> > and as a garden causes what is sown in it to spring up,
> so the Lord GOD will cause righteousness and praise
> > to spring up before all the nations. (Isa 61:11)

In year C for the third Sunday in Advent, the readings from the Hebrew Bible show the whole earth bearing witness to the good news of a promised renewal and restoration of the Hebrew people, voiced in martial language as "victory." The first lesson is from the conclusion of Zephaniah:

> The LORD, your God, is in your midst,
> > a warrior who gives victory;
> he will rejoice over you with gladness,
> > he will renew you in his love;
> he will exult over you with loud singing
> > as on a day of festival
> I will remove disaster from you,
> > so that you will not bear reproach for it.
> I will deal with all your oppressors at that time.
> And I will save the lame
> > and gather the outcast,
> and I will change their shame into praise
> > and renown in all the earth.
> At that time I will bring you home
> > at the time when I gather you;
> for I will make you renowned and praised
> > among all the peoples of the earth. (Zeph 3:17–20b)

The suggested canticle for the third Sunday in Advent for year C is Isaiah 12:2–6, which similarly proclaims salvation to be made known throughout the whole earth. "Sing praises to the LORD, for he has done gloriously," it chants, "let this be known in all the earth" (Isa 12:5). Clean water is the metaphor for this salvation: "With joy you will draw water from the wells of salvation" (Isa 12:3).

The Epistle lessons for the third Sunday in Advent point toward the second coming of Christ, awaited to fulfill the promise of salvation. In year A, James 5:7–10 likens this wait to a farmer's expectation for seasonal rain to sprout and grow the crop. "Be patient, therefore, beloved until the coming of the Lord," James urges, "The farmer waits for the precious crop from the earth, being patient with it until it receives the early and the late rains" (James 5:7). In years B and C, Saint Paul exhorts the churches in Thessalonica and Philippi respectively to rejoice and to pray as they await Christ's return (1 Thess 5:16–20; Phil 4:4–7). "Rejoice in the Lord always; again I will say, Rejoice," Paul enjoins in Philippians (4:4)—a phrase that can serve as a contemporary call to worship or a chorus of praise. He continues urging the believers to exercise "gentleness" beyond their own community "to everyone,"[4] and reminds that "the Lord is near"[5] (Phil 4:5). He then calls on the Philippians to continue with prayer, supplication, thanksgiving, and requests to God. To the church in Thessalonica, he similarly exhorts, "Rejoice always, pray without ceasing, give thanks in all circumstances" (1 Thess 5:16–18a). Both of these passages conclude by invoking peace and by offering a blessing that can be used as a benediction in congregational worship. This discussion of the readings for the third Sunday in Advent concludes receiving these blessings:

> May the God of peace himself sanctify you entirely; and may your spirit and soul and body be kept sound and blameless at the coming of our Lord Jesus Christ. (1 Thess 5:23)

> And the peace of God, which surpasses all understanding, will guard your hearts and your minds in Christ Jesus. (Phil 4:7)

Third Advent Candle Lighting Ceremony: Love

A thought for the bulletin:

Kathryn D. Blanchard and Kevin J. O'Brien write about love for all humanity and all creation:

> the fact remains that in a global ecosystem under conditions of environmental degradation, it is only possible to love God and the neighbor if we also care for the creation God has given us to live in, the creation upon which our neighbor's life depends.
> . . . Christian virtue calls people of faith to love creation: to understand its concrete reality, to know and honor its creator, and to care for all God's children who depend upon it.[6]

God's light and God's love extend to all the earth, and so might ours.

Voice: Hear these words from the Gospel of John:

> There was a man sent from God, whose name was John. He came as a witness to testify to the light, so that all might believe through him. He himself was not the light, but he came to testify to the light. The true light, which enlightens everyone, was coming into the world. (John 1:6–9)

On this third Sunday in Advent, glimpsing the true light coming into the world, we light this candle out of love for all for whom that light shines.

(*Light first three candles*)

Prayer of Confession

> Hearing John the Baptizer's call to repent, let us turn toward the Light in prayer.
>
>> Compassionate and merciful God,
>> we thank you for your steadfast love, revealed in Christ, radiant in creation, illumined in our hearts.
>> Inspired by your love, we yet fall short. As passionately as we love some people and some animals, we nonetheless find that we love narrowly. We often fail even to know our neighbors—let alone to love them as ourselves. We love domesticated pets, but are unaware of the wild creatures they displace. We love beautiful gardens, but often dismiss native plants that feed and sustain all surrounding life.
>> Forgive us, we pray, and magnify your love within us, that we might love all your children, indeed all your creatures.
>> In the light of Christ, Amen.

Words of Assurance

> "May the God of peace . . . sanctify you entirely," Paul blesses us in 1 Thessalonians, "and may your spirit and soul and body be kept sound and blameless at the coming of our Lord Jesus Christ." (1 Thess 5:23)
>
> OR

"Strengthen your hearts," exhorts James, "for the coming of the Lord is near." (James 5:8b)

Pardon: In the name of Jesus Christ, the true light, your sins are forgiven. . .
   Glory to God. Amen.

Sung Response from "The Baptist Shouts on Jordan's Shore" (verse 2):

> The earth and sky and sea now feel
> that which their Author will reveal:
> The Child now leaping in the womb
> as God does human form assume.[7]

OR "People, Look East"[8] (In sequential verses, the advent of "Love" is invoked as "Guest," "Rose," "Bird," "Star," and "Lord." Here are the birds.)

> Birds, though you long have ceased to build,
> guard the nest that must be filled.
> Even the hour when wings are frozen
> God for fledging-time has chosen.
> People, look east, and sing today:
> Love, the Bird is on the way.
> Fourth Sunday in Advent

Fourth Sunday in Advent: First Lessons and Gospels

The first lections from the Hebrew Bible suggested by the lectionaries for the fourth Sunday in Advent make reference to God's promise to maintain or to restore the Davidic line of reign. Messianic expectations focus on the restoration of that reign with implications both for the whole earth as well as for the life of the Hebrew people in the affairs of nations. The suggested psalms for the fourth Sunday of Advent further declare the inclusion of the whole earth in God's salvific work. The Gospel lessons sharpen the focus of that promise of salvation on the gestation and birth of Jesus.

The first lection in year B for the fourth Sunday in Advent are verses from 2 Samuel 7:1–17, which is God's promise to establish David's throne through his descendants "forever." This passage finds resonance with the prophecies in Isaiah 7 and Micah 5, which are read as the first lections in years A and C, respectively. After King David offered to build a house for God, the prophet Nathan voiced God's response to David in 2 Samuel, offering instead to establish David's house:

> Thus says the LORD of hosts: I took you from the pasture, from following the sheep to be prince over my people Israel; and I have been with you wherever you went, and have cut off all your enemies from before you; and I will make for you a great name, like the name of the great ones of the earth. And I will appoint a place for my people Israel and will plant them, so that they may live in their own place and be disturbed no more; and evildoers shall afflict them no more, as formerly, from the time that I appointed judges over my people Israel; and I will give you rest from all your enemies. Moreover the LORD declares to you that the LORD will make you a house. When your days are fulfilled and you lie down with your ancestors, I will raise up your offspring after you, who shall

come from your body, and I will establish his kingdom. He shall build a house for my name, and I will establish the throne of his kingdom forever. I will be a father to him, and he shall be a son to me. . . . Your house and your kingdom shall be made sure forever before me; your throne shall be established forever. (2 Sam 7:8b–14a, 16)

The first lection for year A for the fourth Sunday in Advent is from Isaiah 7 and dates from the time of the reign of Ahaz in Judah when Assyria was the superpower threatening the stability of all other kingdoms. The lection for year C is from Micah 5, and it reads as if it is from the same period. During this time the continuance of both the southern and the northern kingdoms was in doubt. The prophets decry injustice and infidelity among the Hebrew people and their leaders, and they envision that a new leader will arise in keeping with the Davidic covenant. Micah announces:

> But you, O Bethlehem of Ephrathah,
>   who are one of the little clans of Judah,
> from you shall come forth for me
>   one who is to rule in Israel,
> whose origin is from of old,
>   from ancient days.
> Therefore he shall give them up until the time
>   when she who is in labor has brought forth;
> then the rest of his kindred shall return
>   to the people of Israel.
> And he shall stand and feed his flock in the strength of the LORD,
>   in the majesty of the name of the LORD his God.
> And they shall live secure, for now he shall be great
>   to the ends of the earth;
> and he shall be the one of peace. (Mic 5:2–5a)

Bethlehem is associated with David, and the messianic language of one who "shall come forth" is reminiscent of 2 Samuel 7:12 concerning one who would come forth from David's body. As the prophecy continues, the reference to "one who is to rule in Israel... from ancient days" continues to remind of 2 Samuel 7.[9] The vision is of a peaceful world "to the ends of the earth." Matthew quotes this passage from Micah as pertaining to the birth of Jesus in Bethlehem (Matt 2:6) and the subsequent visit of magi from the East who represent that wider world coming to pay homage. The lectionaries place this reading from Matthew at the time of Epiphany rather than here on the fourth Sunday of Advent, though many congregations read it at this time or at Christmas as part of the whole story of nativity.

The first lesson for the fourth Sunday of Advent in year A is the famous passage in Isaiah 7 giving the sign of Immanuel, "God with us." The verse about Immanuel is quoted in the Gospel of Matthew (1:23), and the lectionaries call for this lesson from Matthew to be read on this same Sunday as well. The reading from Isaiah 7 is also reminiscent of 2 Samuel 7, but there is a portentous turn of a phrase. Whereas in 2 Samuel 7:16 Nathan promises King David affirmatively, "Your house and your kingdom shall be made sure forever before me," Isaiah now warns King Ahaz conversely, "If you do not stand firm in faith, you shall not stand at all" (Isa 7:9).[10]

In the context of Isaiah, the sign of Immanuel would have been heard soberly. It was a pronouncement of God's judgment as well as a promise of God's presence.[11] The inbreaking of both God's sovereign judgment in human affairs and the expression of a hopeful promise of renewal and restoration, we have already seen, is characteristic of the readings for Advent. Here, that combination comes to sharp focus in the sign of Immanuel. The king of Judah at the time, Ahaz, was the recipient of Isaiah's pronouncement of judgment for his lack of faithfulness to God in the face of international threats to Judah's welfare. The looming threat to both Judah and Israel was the Assyrian empire, but the immediate threat was the prospect of an attack on Jerusalem by Israel (also called Ephraim) and Syria (also called Aram) in order to coerce Ahaz to bring Judah into their alliance against Assyria. Against this idea of a military alliance, Isaiah urged calm and trust in God. Referring to the kings of Israel and Syria, Isaiah was told by God to tell Ahaz: "Take heed, be quiet, do not fear, and do not let your heart be faint because of these two smoldering stumps of firebrands, because of the fierce anger of Rezin and Aram and the son of Remaliah" (Isa 7:4).

The good news to Ahaz in this message was that the alliance immediately threatening Jerusalem would not stand as long as Ahaz could trust in God's deliverance rather than in a military response, but, "if you do not stand firm in faith," the prophecy warned, "you shall not stand at all" (Isa 7:9b). The reassurance to Ahaz and to Judah in the face of the immediate threat by Israel and Syria, however, was overshadowed by the greater threat of Assyria which is interpreted as unavoidable due to God's own claim of sovereignty in the affairs of nations and in the earth itself. This is news that Ahaz did not want to hear, and so he resisted, asking for a sign. Against Ahaz's resistance, Isaiah declared that God nonetheless was giving him a sign that a child already conceived, to be named Immanuel, would be born, indicating both God's presence and judgment in the affairs of nations:

> For before the child knows how to refuse the evil and choose the good, the land before whose two kings you are in dread will be deserted. The LORD will bring on you and on your people and on your ancestral house such days as have not come since the day that Ephraim departed from Judah—the king of Assyria. (Isa 7:16–17)

This is devastating news for the land as well as the civilizations dwelling on these lands. Speaking of Judah as well as of Israel and Syria, Isaiah 7 concludes:

> On that day every place where there used to be a thousand vines, worth a thousand shekels of silver, will become briers and thorns. With bow and arrows one will go there, for all the land will be briers and thorns; and as for all the hills that used to be hoed with a hoe, you will not go there for fear of briers and thorns; but they will become a place where cattle are let loose and where sheep tread. (Isa 7:23–25)

Lands which had been vineyards and cultivated fields are said now to become fallow and overgrown, used only for grazing by ruminants which were to be the source of food, along with hunted game, for the surviving human population. This is not really bad news for the wild plants that continue to grow or the animals that make this their habitat, but the relationship between productive agriculture and the civilizations supported by it and dependent on it is disrupted.

Chapter 7 of Isaiah also begins with an inferred threat to Jerusalem's water supply. When God sends Isaiah and his son, Shearjashub, to confront Ahaz with this prophecy, they are sent to "the end of the conduit of the upper pool on the highway to the Fuller's Field" (Isa 7:3), which was a supply of water for the city and which Ahaz may have been guarding in anticipation of an attack.[12] The prospect of war threatens the ecological carrying capacity supporting the urban civilization. The divine promise as well as judgment in this scenario is symbolized by the names of both children mentioned: Immanuel, ostensibly Ahaz's yet-to-be-born son, whose name means "God is with us," and Shearjashub, Isaiah's son, whose name means "a remnant shall return." The devastation will occur but a remnant will survive and rebuild, and God is present in all of it.

The specific land of Judah during the reign of Ahaz is the subject of this prophecy, and Ahaz's dilemma is presented with reference to both Judah's natural environment and international political context. The affirmation of God's sovereignty over both nature and nations amid Judah's plight seems both dire, even harsh, in terms of God's judgment and at the same time hopeful in terms of God's promise. It is hard, though, for Ahaz—and even for contemporary readers—to hear the promise amid the gloom. But Isaiah's message is both damning and promising because of this confidence that the God of Judah and of Israel is also the God of all nations and is the Creator and Sovereign over all the earth.

When Matthew quotes from Isaiah concerning Emmanuel in speaking about the new child, Jesus, there is a similar interplay between judgment and restoration but with emphasis on the latter. Sin is recognized and named but in order to proclaim the promise of forgiveness. In Matthew's Gospel, it is Joseph who is visited by an angel who declares concerning Mary's pregnancy, "the child conceived in her is from the Holy Spirit. She will bear a son, and you are to name him Jesus, for he will save his people from their sins"

(Matt 1:20b–21). Emmanuel means "God is with us," the Gospel of Matthew reminds us (Matt 1:23) when quoting Isaiah 7:14. Before and after the quotation from Isaiah about Emmanuel, though, Matthew clearly states the actual name of the child to be Jesus (Matt 1:21, 25). God is with us in Jesus, and this is good news for the world.

Fourth Sunday in Advent: Psalter

The psalms recommended by the lectionaries for the fourth Sunday of Advent invoke images of creation in anticipation of the establishment of God's justice throughout the earth that would be in keeping with the Davidic covenant. Both lectionaries urge Psalms 80 and 89 be brought into worship at this time, and the Roman Catholic Lectionary for the Mass also prescribes Psalm 24 for liturgical use in year A.

Psalm 24 begins with words that perennially inspire people of ecological and ecumenical conscience:[13]

> The earth is the LORD's and all that is in it,
> > the world, and those who live in it;
> for he has founded it on the seas,
> > and established it on the rivers. (Ps 24:1–2)

In a chapter titled "The Earth is the LORD's," Christopher J. H. Wright quotes this verse and explains that God's ownership of the earth suggests something like a landlord-tenant relationship, where human beings are the tenants and accountable to God for the ways in which we treat the earth. He identifies four "ethical and missional implications":[14]

- God's creation is good.
- God's creation is distinct from, but dependent on, God the creator.
- The whole earth is the field of God's mission, and ours.
- God's glory is the goal of creation.

The Hebrew word translated earlier in Psalm 24:1 as "and all that is in it," or literally, "and all its fullness," denotes the entirety of creation.[15] " 'The fullness of the earth' is a way of talking about the whole rich abundance of the created order, especially the non-human creation," declares Wright, explaining that "the earth is full of God's glory because what fills the earth constitutes (at least one dimension of) God's glory."[16]

Also quoting this verse, David Gushee similarly points to the importance of God's continued claim on all the earth. "Human beings must respect and care for creation precisely because it is God's creation," he says and elaborates,

"God is the *source* of creation; it is [God's] amazing handiwork, and to God belongs *ownership* and *rule* over what [God] has created."[17] Bruce C. Birch and Larry L Rasmussen, too, quote this verse and affirm, "Nature is itself God's creation and has intrinsic worth before God apart from relationship to the human." Moreover, they add that Psalm 24:1 represents the proclamation of ancient "Israel at worship."[18]

Psalm 24 was probably sung in worship as a song of celebration or triumphal entry into the temple. "There is no question but that the psalm is liturgical, celebrating the victory process of the LORD into the sanctuary," Allen P. Ross avers.[19] Following the initial verse proclaiming that "the earth is the LORD's," there is a dialogue of liturgical question and response: "Who shall ascend the hill of the LORD? . . ." answered by, "Those who have clean hands and pure hearts. . . (Ps 24:3a, 4a)" The psalm concludes with the command to the gates to open "that the King of glory may come in" and further call and response: "Who is this King of glory? The LORD of hosts, he is the King of glory. (Ps 24:7b, 10)" This psalm continues to draw us into worship and praise and can be chanted as a call to worship or sung as an opening hymn today.

Ross also suggests that the reference in verse 2 to having "founded the earth on the seas, and established it on the rivers" might be a polemic claiming the LORD's sole creativity and sovereignty in contradistinction to Canaanite mythology. "In Canaanite mythology the forces of nature were deified, two of them identified as Prince Sea (*Yam*) and Judge River (*Nahar*), the precise words used in the verse," Ross writes, "but to the Israelites they were simply forces of nature that God had created and controlled when he established the land." Ross further speculates that the image of the land being established upon the waters would help conceptualize the presence of life-sustaining groundwater: "we have a picture of the inhabitable earth being created over waters and currents, perhaps a way to explain the fountains, springs, and rivers under the ground."[20]

Michael S. Northcott meaningfully links the images of creation in this psalm with its original and continuing context in worship, saying that "the just and holy treatment of creation is predicated on the priority given to the worship and the love of God among the people of God," and he concludes that "from right worship, and right relationship to God, flows the recognition that 'the earth is the LORD's.'"[21]

Psalms 80 and 89 look back toward David's reign and ahead toward universal justice.[22] At the same time, and in keeping with the tension in Advent, these psalms both express hope and pronounce judgment. Both psalms come from the third book of the Psalms that reflect the realities, hopes, and disappointments in the years of the divided kingdom between the time of Solomon's reign and the Babylonian exile.[23] Psalm 89 concludes this collection of psalms on a dire note, remembering the promises to David and bewailing the end of his reigning line with the exile. "You have removed the scepter from his hand, and hurled his throne to the ground," the psalm decries and continues, "You have cut short the days of his youth; you have covered him with shame" (Ps 89:44–45). Nevertheless, earlier Psalm 89 extols God as Creator and as Sovereign over nations and nature:

> You rule the raging of the sea;
>   when its waves rise, you still them.
> You crushed Rahab like a carcass;
>   you scattered your enemies with your mighty arm.
> The heavens are yours, the earth also is yours;
>   the world and all that is in it—you founded them.
> The north and the south—you created them...
> Righteousness and justice are the foundation of your throne;
>   steadfast love and faithfulness go before you. (Ps 89:9–12a, 14)

The psalm depicts God's primordial act of creation in bringing order from chaos. After quoting this psalm, Bruce C. Birch comments on God's continuing power in creation and the ongoing implications for ordering a just society:

> It is important to note that the role of God as the source of order and the enemy of chaos is not limited to primordial times. Since chaos is not removed but controlled, God's activity in restraining chaos and sustaining order is a dimension of God's work in every generation. Whenever the order of things seems threatened and confusion or purposelessness reigns it is to trust in God's power as Creator, the source of order and meaning, that the community of faith must turn.[24]

Turning, or repenting, is a theme and a refrain in another psalm suggested by the lectionaries for the fourth Sunday in Advent, Psalm 80, a communal lament. The refrain repeated thrice is, "Restore us, O LORD God [of hosts]; let your face shine, that we may be saved" (Ps 80:3, 7, 14). The word "restore," addressed to God, is the same word that means to turn or to repent; the prayer is for God to "cause us to return."[25] The petition shifts in verse 14 to a plea to God Godself to turn, which Denise Dombkowski Hopkins considers the "theological center"[26] of the psalm: "Turn again, O God of hosts: look down from heaven, and see" (Ps 80:14a,b). God is addressed as the agent throughout the psalm, but the focus centers on asking God to turn, to change in regarding the Hebrew people with renewed favor.

Verse 14 is also centered in the middle of a metaphor in which God's chosen people are likened to a vine and God is addressed as the Vinedresser or Gardener. The passage is laced with imagery of both creation and exodus:

> You brought a vine out of Egypt;
>   you drove out the nations and planted it.
> You cleared the ground for it;
>   it took deep root and filled the land.
> The mountains were covered with its shade,
>   the mighty cedars with its branches,
> it sent out its branches to the sea,
>   and its shoots to the River.
> Why then have you broken down its walls,
>   so that all who pass along the way pluck its fruit?
> The boar from the forest ravages it,
>   and all that move in the field feed on it.
> Turn again, O God of hosts;
>   look down from heaven, and see;
> have regard for this vine,
>   the stock that your right hand planted.
> They have burned it with fire, they have cut it down.
>   may they perish at the rebuke of your countenance.
> But let your hand be upon the one at your right hand,
>   the one whom you made strong for yourself. (Ps 80:8–17)

Arthur Walker-Jones considers this passage and this metaphor "significant from the perspective of Earth."[27] While recognizing that the portrayal of wild animals as enemy is problematic, he nonetheless affirms as important the portrayal of God who gets God's "hands dirty" in the soil God has planted:

> This is an image of God who is present and involved, getting hands dirty in the work of creation. The metaphor could help overcome the separation between humanity and nature by focusing on the identification of humans and nature. Nations, like plants, rely on the providential presence of God in creation to flourish. Like plants, people and nations are dependent on water, fertile soils, and other natural resources. Human societies are interdependent and interrelated with all of Earth community. The metaphor can speak to God's involvement in nature and history.[28]

Before the final refrain, Psalm 80 concludes with petitions referencing both the restoration of Davidic reign and the giving of life itself—both nature and history:

> But let your hand be upon the one at your right hand,
>   the one whom you made strong for yourself.
> Then we will never turn back from you;
>   give us life, and we will call on your name. (Ps 80:17–18)

Give Us Life!

Anachronistically in Christian tradition, it is easy to imagine Jesus Christ when hearing the phrase, "the one at your right hand," especially if the next line is translated, "the son of man you have raised up for yourself" (Ps 80: 17b NIV). The identity of the one at the right hand is not named in the text itself. It may be humanity or the Hebrew people as a whole, but it seems to refer to national sovereignty and to a particular regent or to the Davidic line generally. The particular historical challenge being faced is also not explicated in the psalm, and there is no scholarly consensus with regard to the dating of it.[29] But there is a tradition of associating it with the threat from Assyria near the time of Isaiah, and Denise Dombkowski Hopkins creatively imagines this psalm being sung in that context. The associative intertextual link is the emphasis on turning and returning in Psalm 80 and the use of that same word for turning in the name of Isaiah's son, Shearjashub, meaning "a remnant shall return." She imagines what it would be like for Shearjashub to pray this psalm while accompanying his father to confront King Ahaz at Jerusalem's water supply in the face of immediate threats from Syria and the northern kingdom of Israel and the larger looming threat of Assyria. She wonders how he might ponder the identity of the one mentioned in verse 17 who is at God's right hand and whom God makes strong. With him and with her, we also wonder. Is it his father? Is it his king? Is it himself? Is it his future? Is it our future? Dombkowski Hopkins concludes her commentary on Psalm 80 quoting Jacqueline E. Lapsley with reference to the names in Isaiah and to the children themselves:

> Shear-jashub expresses "the importance of children in God's economy." The children in Isaiah (see also "Immanuel, God with us") not only convey the message; "they themselves are part of the message: children, children, children . . . essential to salvation. . . . How children are treated, both in the present and in the future, is essential to the divine vision of what God would have for Israel."[30]

And, we might add, the divine vision of what God would have for us. How do we imagine continuing to sing this psalm in Advent, adding its voice and ours to those also singing: Gabriel, Mary, Zechariah?

Epistle of Romans: Opening and Closing in Blessing

"Grace to you and peace from God our Father and the Lord Jesus Christ," Paul addresses the Romans and continues to bless us (Rom 1:7b). This blessing and greeting is part of the reading from Romans given by both lectionaries for the fourth Sunday of Advent in year A. These words, like

Psalm 24, can be announced as a Call to Worship or at other moments of greeting in a service of worship. While the Book of Romans opens with these words, it concludes with a doxology that is given by the lectionaries as the epistle reading for the fourth Sunday of Advent in year B. A service of worship can close with this extensive and profound committal as benediction. We close with it now:

> Now to God who is able to strengthen you according to my gospel and the proclamation of Jesus Christ, according to the revelation of the mystery that was kept secret for long ages but is now disclosed, and through the prophetic writings is made known to all the Gentiles, according to the command of the eternal God, to bring about the obedience of faith—to the only wise God, through Jesus Christ, to whom be the glory forever! Amen. (Rom 16:25–27)

Fourth Advent Candle Lighting Ceremony: Peace

Voice: From the prophet Micah, we hear:

> But you, O Bethlehem of Ephrathah,
>   who are one of the little clans of Judah,
> from you shall come forth for me
>   one who is to rule in Israel,
> whose origin is from of old,
>   from ancient days.
> Therefore he shall give them up until the time
>   when she who is in labor has brought fourth;
> then the rest of his kindred shall return
>   to the people of Israel.
> And he shall stand and feed his flock in the strength of the LORD,
>   in the majesty of the name of the LORD his God.
> And they shall live secure, for now he shall be great
>   to the ends of the earth;
> and he shall be the one of peace. (Mic 5:2–5a)

We light this fourth candle praying for peace, claiming the promised peace, striving to promote peace.

(*Light four candles*)

Voice: So what is the nature of this peace and security covering all the earth? The prophet Micah's vision of shalom, like Isaiah's prophecy which was read at the very beginning of Advent, is for ecological wholeness, economic well-being, cessation of war, and universal security:

> He shall judge between many peoples,
>> and shall arbitrate between strong nations far away;
> they shall beat their swords into plowshares,
>> and their spears into pruning hooks;
> nation shall not lift up sword against nation,
>> neither shall they learn war anymore;
> but they shall all sit under their own vines and under their own fig trees,
>> and no one shall make them afraid;
>> for the mouth of the LORD of hosts has spoken. (Mic 4:3–4)

Prayer of Confession

> Creator and Preserver,
> Though you send light and rain earthward to grow plants that feed all living beings,
>> we pollute the air and foul the waters and gouge the land
>> so that all life is threatened.
> Though you generously provide enough for all to flourish,
>> we allow some to live and die in poverty
>> while others consume in wasteful excess.
> Though you would lift the lowly,
>> we preserve power and privilege.
> Though you would judge between nations,
>> we jealously guard national self-interest.
> Though you have promised peace,
>> we embrace fear and resort to war and violence.
> Forgive us and heal us, that we might gratefully share of your bounty
>> and become makers of peace
>>> between neighbors,
>>> between nations, and
>>> between humanity and all life on your planet.
> In the name of Christ, the Prince of Peace, we pray. Amen

Words of Assurance: "The earth is the LORD's and all that is in it, the world, and those who live in it." (Ps 24:1)

Pardon: In the name of Jesus Christ, God with us, you are forgiven. . . .
Glory to God! Amen.

Sung Response from "O Loving Founder of the Stars" (verse 1):

> O Loving founder of the stars,
>> to all of faith light without end,
> O Christ, redeemer of us all,
>> to earnest prayers your mercy lend.[31]

> OR *"Toda la Tierra"*[32]

Chapter 12

Turning to the Children
Ecological Threat and Hope in Advent

In late Advent, the lectionaries focus on Mary's conception and gestation of Jesus both in the Gospel lessons and in the psalter's canticles. There are opportunities to remember and sing the Magnificat and the Song of Zechariah as found in Luke's Gospel. There is much in the first chapter of Luke, however, that is not included in the lectionary readings for Advent and, moreover, does not appear at all in the lectionaries for any Sunday. The omitted material from the lectionary, though, is most appropriate for any Sunday in Advent and can be included by worship leaders in either the liturgies or the sermons preached during Advent. Some of this material has import for interpreting the infancy narratives with closer attention to the promised salvation for all of creation. Notably, Zechariah as the father of John the Baptist is remarkable for the role his silence plays in the unfolding of the story. In this chapter, therefore, we listen to Zechariah's silence amid the proclamations of the angel, the acclamations of the women, and the witness of those yet to be born.

TURNING THE HEARTS OF FATHERS

The Gospel of Luke begins with an angel appearing to Zechariah while he is attending to priestly duties in the temple to announce the imminent conception and birth of his son, John. Zechariah finds this announcement incredible because of the advanced age of himself and his wife, Elizabeth. In response to his incredulity and skepticism, the angel silences Zechariah "until the day these things occur" (Luke 1:20). The announcement to Zechariah begins as a blessing in answer to Zechariah's prayer for a son, but it proceeds in a direction that has ramifications for all parents and children:

> . . . and he will be filled with the Holy Spirit, even from his mother's womb. And he will turn many of the sons of Israel to the Lord their God, and he will go before him in the spirit and power of Elijah, to turn the hearts of the fathers to the children and the disobedient to the wisdom of the just, to make ready for the Lord a people prepared. (Luke 1:15b–17 RSV)

The first mention of the Holy Spirit in the Gospel of Luke is this word that an unborn child rather than his priestly father will be filled with the Holy Spirit. Moreover, this Spirit-filled child will "turn the hearts" of other fathers "to the children."

We are accustomed to thinking of paternal love, and of parental love generally, as the most natural of affections, infinitely precious but hardly a miracle. Our lived experience, however, is often otherwise. This promised turning to the children is deeply needful—for healthy families and the well-being of children themselves, for social justice where every child is cared for and valued, and for environmental sustainability extending into future generations of our children's children who will depend on the natural resources bequeathed to them by fathers and mothers today. There is a need to turn to the children not just for familial nurture but for societal justice and a sustainable future. This will be discussed briefly before looking at the original context of the phrase "turn the hearts of fathers to the children." This phrase is not original to Luke but is a quotation from Malachi as well as from the deuterocanonical book of Ecclesiasticus (also called Sirach or Wisdom Ben Sira), and these earlier contexts of the phrase provide praise for the goodness of God's creation and a promise for the land's health.

SUSTAINING THE CHILDREN'S FUTURE

One of the most important norms for ecological ethics developed in the past century is the idea of environmental sustainability—that the "carrying capacity" of the planet should be preserved and extended for future generations. The idea is that the size of the human population and our rate of using natural resources be brought into synch with the capacity of those natural resources to be renewed. This means both a diminished rate of use of nonrenewable resources and a pacing of use of renewable resources such that they can be replenished. This includes limiting environmental pollution, so that clean air and water will be available well into the future. It also includes wise preservation and development of land and water resources, so that both productive agriculture is able to meet the needs of society and preserved natural habitat is available for other species.

Ecumenically, the phrase "just and sustainable" society was coined in 1974 at a conference in Bucharest sponsored by the World Council of Churches.

The conference was the culmination of an unprecedented five-year study program involving economists, scientists, and theologians at a time when there was increasing global awareness of the limits of natural resources and the hazards of environmental pollution. The next year, at the General Assembly of the World Council of Churches in Nairobi in 1975, the Assembly issued a call for a "just, participatory and sustainable society." International development agencies took this teaching seriously and began to discuss environmental sustainability as a necessary corollary to economic development when addressing the problem of human poverty.[1] Sustainability is a practical norm for social planning and public policy to help ensure human welfare into the future. It has implications for social organization and economic practice at local, national, and international levels. It does not address other ecotheological concerns, though, such as the question of intrinsic as opposed to instrumental value of nature or the question of a sacred presence in nature. But it clearly points to the need at every level of society to preserve the planet's capability to care for future generations of children. In a global economy increasingly driven by consumption and consumerism, sustainability continues to be of critical relevance and importance. How can our hearts, our lifestyles, and our social structures be turned to truly care for the children of the future?

Part of the conversation about Earth's carrying capacity is a concern about human population growth—that the level of human population be maintained in balance with a sustainable use of resources. In the previous generation, some ardent proponents of limiting population proposed draconian measures to ensure or even coerce limits on human reproduction.[2] China's one-child policy from 1980 to 2015 horrifyingly implemented some of these measures on a wide scale, an assault on women's autonomy resulting in a documented practice of regular late-term abortions and forced sterilizations.[3] Others, though, have noted more modestly and more compassionately that when people have access to options and resources for family planning, they are better able to voluntarily determine the number of children they want and for whom they can best provide. In particular, when women have access to reproductive healthcare options and are so empowered, they choose to limit their number of children in order to better secure a flourishing future for the children they do have, and thus there is a move toward a more environmentally sustainable rate of reproduction. Robert Engleman of Population Action International and of Worldwatch Institute has demonstrated this trend occurring in cultures around the world and finds a "three-way connection between individual women's lives, world population, and the health of the planet."[4]

Still others have emphasized a reverse direction of causality—not just that population growth increases the stress on natural resources and on the social processes that ensure well-being but also that increased human well-being diminishes people's perceived need for large families. Arthur Dyck describes this understanding that unfavorable socioeconomic conditions might lead to pressures for larger families:

> . . . illiteracy (especially of women), high infant mortality rates, extremely unjust distributions of income, lack of governmental social security systems, underemployment, and poor production in agriculture are some of the most important socioeconomic conditions that contribute to high fertility rates and rapid population growth.[5]

The turning of parental hearts to the children is not just a personal stance or a matter held within nuclear families. The whole society is challenged to make this turn toward promoting the well-being of all society's children now and into the future.

In addition to issues of poverty and neglect, we see actual violence systemically conducted against children by governments which should be guarding their welfare. The southern border of the United States is a horrifying example. In a recent paper, Denise Dombkowski Hopkins provides a chilling summary:

> In our recent history, children have been recruited to serve in rebel armies and young girls have been sexually abused by soldiers. Modern examples of children caught in the cross hairs of political strife abound—in Mali, the Sudan, the former Yugoslavia, and most recently, at the Mexican border with the United States.
>
> The president of the American Academy of Pediatrics (AAP), Colleen Kraft, is calling the separation of immigrant children from their parents at the U.S.-Mexican border a form of "sweeping cruelty." According to a news report, 2,342 children have been separated from 2,206 parents at the US-Mexico border between May 5 and June 9 [2018] as part of the Trump administration's "zero tolerance" policy of prosecuting people who cross the border illegally.[6]

Separations of immigrant children from their guardians continued into 2019, particularly when guardians are not the children's biological parents but rather other family members. It should be noted that these "illegal" crossings are often people seeking the legal recourse of sanctuary and expecting a legal proceeding to adjudicate their legitimate request.

This disregard for children's well-being and these overtly violent trends seem to be premised on the perception of children as problem rather than as promise or as blessing. Earlier, when looking at Genesis 1, we noticed the blessing of fertility given to all of humanity and to all of animate life that swims in the waters and flies through the air. It is universally given to entire species, including humanity: "Be fruitful and multiply" (Gen 1:22, 28). This original blessing is not bestowed exclusively on individual persons any more than it is bestowed on individual carp. It is given to the entire species as a part of the goodness of the entire creation. Children are not a problem; they are a blessing. And they are not a privatized blessing to select individuals, but rather each child is a blessing to all of us. They are all our children, all our future. Furthermore, this is not a command to procreate but rather a blessing broadly bestowed. Those of us who do not bear children might experience deep grief or loneliness as a result, but we are not bereft of the blessing since we are part of an entire community blessed with children. All children are our children.

The other half of this blessing is food. Originally, the food given to all animate life on the sixth day, including people, was vegetarian:[7]

> God said, "See, I have given you every plant yielding seed that is upon the face of all the earth, and every tree with seed in its fruit; you shall have them for food. And to every beast of the earth and to every bird of the air and to everything that creeps on the earth, everything that has the breath of life, I have given every green plant for food." And it was so. (Gen 1:29–30)

Food is universally given to all Earth's children. Humanity has partitioned and divided this blessing, distinguishing between our lands and theirs, between our resources and theirs, our food supply and theirs, our wealth and theirs, our children and theirs, legitimate children and illegals. We have alienated the blessing.

Returning to the question of carrying capacity with this theological perspective in mind, we see the challenge is not just survival but generosity and justice. The disparity between rich and poor has been steadily widening both nationally and internationally. In the United States, the richest 0.00025 percent of the population now own more than the poorest 60 percent, a majority of the population.[8] Internationally, Oxfam has reported that the twenty-six richest people own as much wealth now as the poorest half of the world's population.[9] This growing disparity can hardly be sustainable in a world with limited carrying capacity of environmental services and supplies of natural resources. Nonrenewable resources are finite, and renewable resources cannot be stressed beyond their ability for regeneration.

The ecological challenge is a social, economic, and political one—to organize economic existence such that all people can have access to the necessities for life without overtaxing the ecological systems that support life for all children and for all species. Sufficient food, potable water, and clean air are fundamental for both ecological health and human flourishing. The challenge is to organize human society in ecologically sustainable patterns so that all children—and indeed all species—have access to God's universal blessing of fertility and food, of life and that which sustains life, for generations now and for generations to come.

MALACHI

The challenge is to "turn the hearts of the fathers to the children, and the disobedient to the wisdom of the just. . ." (Luke 1:17b RSV). With these words from the angel to Zechariah, Luke is beginning literally where the Christian order of books in the Old Testament leaves off. The final verses are Malachi 4:5–6:

> Behold, I will send you Elijah the prophet before the great and terrible day of the LORD comes. And he will turn the hearts of fathers to their children and the hearts of children to their fathers, lest I come and smite the land with a curse.

The "curse" refers to things devoted to a ban and marked for destruction, and it is clearly something to be avoided.[10] The "land" here could also be translated as "earth," and the passage is unclear as to whether the whole earth is intended or the vicinity surrounding Jerusalem. Elijah is invoked as the prophet presaging the day of the Lord in which God will bring justice to the earth. The hope being expressed is that this divine justice will result in restoration rather than destruction, with the turning of the hearts of fathers to the children and of the children to the fathers.

The sense of urgency to avoid doomsday on the earth conveyed in this conclusion to Malachi resonates with our contemporary urgency to avoid ecological calamity by ordering life more sustainably and justly. The focus is both on the present need to establish justice and on the impending future that requires right relationships for the earth's continuance and children's well-being. The people being addressed in the book of Malachi are the Hebrew people who recently returned to Judah from exile in Babylon. In resettling the land, they faced economic hardships, social disruption, and the ecological challenge of producing enough food from land that may have been left untended. They faced economic scarcity and ecological vulnerability.[11]

The ending to Malachi appears to be an appended ending to conclude the book and perhaps to conclude the collection of twelve minor prophets or even to conclude the whole collection of prophets in the Bible.[12] Its immediate context, though, is the book of Malachi itself which begins the third chapter with the promise, "See, I am sending my messenger to prepare the way before me. . ." (Mal 3:1a). These words are quoted in all three Synoptic Gospels as pertaining to John the Baptist (Matt 11:10; Mark 1:2; Luke 1:76, 7:27) and are given by the lectionaries as the Gospel lessons at various points in the season of Advent. Only Luke, however, also quotes this conclusion to Malachi concerning the hearts of the fathers at the end of chapter 4 (Mal 4:6). Between these two verses, in chapter 3, Malachi raises issues of both economic justice and right religious practice, calls for repentance, and offers the prospect of blessings on the land in response:

> Bring the full tithe into the storehouse, so that there may be food in my house, and thus put me to the test, says the LORD of hosts; see if I will not open the windows of heaven for you and pour down for you an everflowing blessing. I will rebuke the locust for you, so that it will not destroy the produce of your soil; and your vine in the field shall not be barren, says the LORD of hosts. Then all nations will count you happy, for you will be a land of delight, says the LORD of hosts. (Mal 3:10–11)

The offenses which the prophet names and seeks to correct include economic injustices against workers, widows, orphans, and aliens. Giving voice to God's judgment, the prophet writes:

> . . . I will be swift to bear witness against the sorcerers, against the adulterers, against those who swear falsely, against those who oppress the hired workers in their wages, the widow and the orphan, against those who thrust aside the alien, and do not fear me, says the LORD of hosts. (Mal 3:5)

Moreover, the people's sin against God in their religious practice is also interpreted in economic terms as robbery: "Will anyone rob God? Yet you are robbing me! But you say, 'How are we robbing you?' In your tithes and offerings!" The people are accused of bringing animals of marginal worth, lame and sick animals, and polluted food, to offer to God instead of the best of their flocks (Mal 1:7–13).

Two classes of people in particular are singled out in judgment: the priests who are not faithful in their duties and show partiality in their instruction (Mal 2:7–9) and men who are not faithful to their wives. Both are interpreted with reference to the need for covenantal faithfulness to the Creator who is Father of all, women and men:

> Have we not all one father? Has not one God created us? Why then are we faithless to one another, profaning the covenant of our ancestors? . . . And this you do as well: You cover the LORD'S alter with tears, with weeping and groaning because he no longer regards the offering or accepts it with favor at your hand. You ask, "Why does he not? Because the LORD was a witness between you and the wife of your youth, to whom you have been faithless, though she is your companion and your wife by covenant. Did not one God make her? Both flesh and spirit are his. And what does the one God desire? Godly offspring. So look to yourselves, and do not let anyone be faithless to the wife of his youth. (Mal 2:10, 13–15)

A woman abandoned by her husband would be in the same economically vulnerable and precarious position as the widows and orphans mentioned earlier.[13] Specific condemnation is made of those who would abandon their wives in favor of "the daughter of a foreign god" (Mal 2:11). Indeed, a challenge facing the returning exiles was to maintain their covenantal faithfulness and identity while still negotiating life among the people encountered upon their return. But there is actually very little explicit xenophobia expressed in this book. To the contrary, there is explicit affirmation of the universal sovereignty of this one God who claims men and women alike as offspring and who is God over all other nations as well: "For from the rising of the sun to its setting my name is great among the nations, and in every place incense is offered to my name, and a pure offering; for my name is great among the nations, says the LORD of hosts" (Mal 1:11).

The language of judgment in Malachi is graphic and harsh, and the references to "curse" are troubling. There is even an ancient Jewish tradition of reading verse 4:5 after verse 4:6 so that the book does not end with this threat of curse being the last word.[14] The language of curse in Malachi is intentionally troubling, but the book as a whole begins with God's profession of God's love to God's people, and this is the premise for the expectation of greater covenantal faithfulness in return. The book begins:

> An oracle. The word of the LORD to Israel by Malachi. I have loved you, says the Lord. But you say, 'How have you loved us?" (Mal 1–2a)

The sovereignty of this God throughout creation is the reason that the plants on the earth and the rains in the heavens respond to the need for justice. The love of this God is why the hope is expressed that the land will be turned from curse to blessing, even as the hearts of the fathers are turned to the children—and to these children's God.

Malachi contains the additional phrase of turning the "hearts of children to their fathers," which is not included in the words from the angel to Zechariah in Luke's Gospel. Speculation about the meaning of this phrase has tended to focus on restoring respectful relationship—whether in families or between generations or toward the ancestral heritage of covenantal faithfulness. It may be, though, that this first generation of young people returning from Babylonian exile was experiencing cultural dislocation that follows the path of refugees and other immigrants. The children of missionaries often experience such dislocation and alienation when they return to the land and the culture of their parents. An entire generation had been raised in Babylon into adulthood, perhaps speaking Aramaic rather than Hebrew.

There is no explicit evidence for this interpretation in the rest of Malachi, but other books of the Bible from the post-exilic period do present such a generational divide. Notably in rebuilding the foundation of the temple, younger and older generations responded differently, with joy and sadness respectively. The book of Ezra recalls:

> And all the people responded with a great shout when they praised the LORD, because the foundation of the house of the LORD was laid. But many of the priests and Levites and heads of families, old people who had seen the first house on its foundations, wept with a loud voice when they saw this house, though many shouted aloud for joy, so that the people could not distinguish the sound of the joyful shout from the sound of the people's weeping, for the people shouted so loudly that the sound was heard far away. (Ezra 3:11b–13)

Both generations, though, were heard in the shout. Furthermore, both generations continued to rebuild the temple, and both generations celebrated Passover when it was completed.

Also, the book of Nehemiah recounts a service of worship that occurred after the completion of rebuilding the wall around Jerusalem. Ezra read from the book of the law of Moses, and there were thirteen Levites named who provided interpretation. "So they read from the book, from the law of God, with interpretation," according to Nehemiah 8:8, explaining that "they gave the sense, so that the people understood the reading." Whether this was sermonic interpretation or translation into Aramaic is unclear, but the need to make the meaning known to a new generation is apparent. Then, after completing the wall, the people made booths and celebrated Sukkot within.

Perhaps the turning of the hearts of children to the fathers in Malachi 4:5 speaks to such a bridging of generational divide, as a generation raised in Babylon learns again from their elders the laws, customs, and ceremonies of a people chosen by God. Verse 4:4 of Malachi begins this concluding section of the book, reminding: "Remember the teaching of my servant Moses, the statutes and ordinances that I commanded him at Horeb for all Israel." Then follows the final two verses with the promise of Elijah and the turning of hearts.

SIRACH

In Luke's Gospel, however, instead of the turning of children's hearts to the fathers, the angel continues by telling Zechariah that the child will turn "the disobedient to the wisdom of the righteous" (Luke 1:17). This phase evokes a combination of covenantal obedience and attention to wisdom, and it is more reminiscent of another context in the wisdom literature in which the turning of the father's heart to the child is quoted.

The deuterocanonical book of Ecclesiasticus or Sirach, the full title of which is "The Wisdom of Jesus the Son of Sirach," seems to cite Malachi when writing of the prophet Elijah:

> . . . you who are ready at the appointed time, it is written,
>   to calm the wrath of God before it breaks out in fury,
> to turn the heart of the father to the son,
>   and to restore the tribes of Jacob.
> Blessed are those who saw you,
>   and those who have been adorned in love;
>   for we also shall surely live. (Sir 48:10–11 RSV)

Writing at a later time, in the second century BCE,[15] the author, Ben Sira, is remembering the promise in Malachi to send Elijah for this turning of the heart. The focus of Sirach, though, is on wisdom. In particular, Sirach weaves an understanding of wisdom that is at once sourced in the One God revealed to the Hebrew people in sacred tradition and also readily apparent throughout creation in all God's works. The book begins:

> All wisdom is from the Lord,
>   and with him it remains forever.
> The sand of the sea, the drops of rain,
>   and the days of eternity—who can count them?
> The height of heaven, the breadth of the earth,
>   the abyss, and wisdom—who can search them out?
> Wisdom was created before all other things,
>   and prudent understanding from eternity.
> The root of wisdom—to whom has it been revealed?
>   Her subtleties—who knows them?
> There is but one who is wise, greatly to be feared,
>   seated upon his throne—the Lord.
> It is he who created her;
>   he saw her and took her measure;
>   he poured her out upon all his works,
> upon all the living according to his gift;
>   he lavished her upon those who love him. (Sir 1:1–10)

The verses about Elijah are part of a longer hymn (Sir 42:15–50:29), extolling the virtues of myriad patriarchs that begins with Abraham.

Prefacing this litany praising patriarchs from the past, though, is a hymn celebrating the wisdom of God visible in the works of God's creation (Sir 42:15–43:33). "He has set in order the splendors of his wisdom," Ben Sira writes (Sir 42:21a) and exclaims:

> How desirable are all his works,
>   and how sparkling they are to see!
> All things live and remain forever;
>   each creature is preserved to meet a particular need. (Sir 42:22–23)

The hymn continues, beautifully singing praise for the magnificence of the sun, the moon, the stars, the rainbow, lightning, clouds, wind, snow, frost, icicles, dew, the sea, the islands in the sea, and the creatures in the sea. "We could say more but could never say enough," the hymn moves toward its finale and professes, "let the final word be: 'He is the all'" (Sir 43:27). The last verse reiterates, "For the Lord has made all things, and to the godly he has given wisdom" (Sir 43:33).

In Malachi, the reference to Elijah coming to turn the hearts of the fathers to the children occurs within a larger theological context where both the welfare of the people and the productivity of the land are seen as dependent on and responsive to the sovereign God's desire for justice and faithfulness. In Sirach, the reference to Elijah coming to turn the heart of the father to the child occurs within an even wider, cosmic theological context where God's wisdom is made known in the entirety of visible creation and in the entirety of the history of the Hebrew people with the faithful witnesses from the past. The hope is expressed in this turning, "that we also shall surely live" (Sir 48:11b).

In Luke, we can read the angel's words that John will come "with the spirit and power of Elijah . . . to turn the hearts the hearts of the fathers to the children" (Luke 2:17) and to "make ready a people prepared" with the broader biblical contexts of Malachi and Sirach in mind. It is not just this one child to be born of Elizabeth, but there is one to follow born of Mary. And it is not just for these two children but for all children and their parents that we are called to turn from disobedience to the wisdom of the righteous. And it is not just for that time, or even for this time, but for all time. Children must have a future. Justice and faithfulness are the response incumbent on each generation. Our hope is in the One who promises to bring rain to make the earth productive. It is in the One whose primordial and ongoing works throughout the earth, heavens, and seas reveal wisdom. The universe is gathered in witness, as we turn to see the children.

In our own time, the turning is urgent. Children suffer from neglect and abuse, from poverty and war, and from our turning away at the borders of our conscience. A generation ago, modern scientists, economists, and prophets warned that well-being in society and in the depends on our turning to a sustainable use of natural resources, a just distribution of economic resources, and an ecological frame for political life and public policy. A generation later, we now hear the angel's words on a hotter planet, underneath a hole in the atmospheric ozone, and with an unprecedented division between wealth and poverty. The words of "the messenger" point to our present and to our children's future. They point to our hope that justice will yet prevail to provide for a sustainable world, preserved by its Creator's sovereignty, providence, and love. We are called to faith and to faithful living.

The angel told Zechariah that his son would be "filled with the Holy Spirit" even within the womb (Luke 1:15). Zechariah had a hard time believing this messenger and was silenced until he could see the evidence coming to birth. In the meantime, as we read Luke, Mary too is promised a child and told, "The Holy Spirit will come upon you" (Luke 1:35). Then in the next turn of the story, when Mary visits Elizabeth and greets her, and as Elizabeth's child then "leaped within her womb," we read: "And Elizabeth was filled with the Holy Spirit and exclaimed with a loud cry, 'Blessed are you among women, and blessed is the fruit of your womb" (Luke 1:41–42). Mary responds in praise, "My soul magnifies the Lord." All the women and children surrounding Zechariah are being filled with the Holy Spirit and prophesying through leaps and shouts and magnificent praise, while Zechariah remains silent. Only after the birth of the baby, and only after Zechariah confirms in writing the words of his wife that the child's name is John, is Zechariah also then "filled with the Holy Spirit" and prophesies (Luke 1:67).

It would likely surprise Ben Sira, after he had written eight-and-a-half chapters in praise of the patriarchs, to read this story in Luke. Beginning with the same quote from Malachi about turning the hearts of the fathers to the children, we see the turn taking place. The patriarch Zechariah is silenced, while it is the women and children who receive the Holy Spirit and prophesy. Finally, Zechariah too is filled with the Holy Spirit and allowed to speak, and he confirms what the women already knew and made known. His words are worth the wait, and he expresses the hope and promise for the future for the giving of "light to those who sit in darkness and in the shadow of death, to guide our feet into the way of peace" (Luke 1:79).

Advent Wreath Lighting Liturgies
Based on a Sequence of Readings from Luke 1

First Sunday of Advent: Turning to the Children

Voice: The Gospel of Luke begins with Zechariah,
       soon to become the father of John the Baptizer,
       lighting incense in the temple.

(Light first candle)

> So now we begin this season of Advent lighting this candle,
> remembering the angel's promise to Zechariah of that child,
> remembering the angel's continuing promise
> that we turn to the children in wisdom and justice:
>
>> And you will have joy and gladness,
>> and many will rejoice at his birth;
>> for he will be great in the sight of the Lord,
>> and he shall drink no wine nor strong drink,
>> and he will be filled with the Holy Spirit,
>> even from his mother's womb.
>> And he will turn many of the [people] of Israel to the Lord their God,
>> and he will go before him in the spirit and power of Elijah,
>> to turn the hearts of the fathers to the children,
>> and the disobedient to the wisdom of the just,
>> to make ready for the Lord a people prepared. (Luke 1:14–17 RSV[16])

Prayer of Confession

> Humbly, let us pray:
>
> God of our ancestors and of our progeny:
> We confess that we have turned away in the narrowness of our faith.
>> Inspired by your saints of old, we hesitate to be your saints today.
>> Celebrating the past, we fear for the future.
>> Cherishing our families,
>>> we exclude from our love those we do not know.
>>
>> Enjoying the abundance of Earth's resources,
>>> we fail to conserve Earth's life and richness for those who will come after us.
>
> Forgive us and turn our hearts to the children,
>> to those who are here and those who are far,
>> to those who receive presents and those who go begging,
>> to those who are present and those who are our future.
>
> Grant us wisdom and make us a people prepared to receive your justice,
> now and for all generations.
>
> Amen.

Words of Assurance from Malachi (Mal 4:2):

> "But for you who revere my name the sun of righteousness shall rise,
> with healing in its wings. You shall go out leaping like calves from the stall."

Pardon:

> In the name of Christ, expected and promised,
> your sins are forgiven. . . . Glory to God! Amen.

Hymn: "Christ Whose Glory Fills the Skies"

Another hymn that echoes some of the Advent themes of this passage from Luke—our hope for wisdom and for the inbreaking of God's justice on Earth—is "God of Grace and God of Glory" by Harry Emerson Fosdick which is not often sung in Advent. The meter (87 87 87), though, is very similar to the Advent hymn, "Come, Thou Long-Expected Jesus" (87 87 D). If the last line of a verse of "God of Grace" is repeated, it can be appended as a verse to the more common hymn for Advent. For example, to HYFRYDOL or a tune of similar meter:[17]

> Come, thou long-expected Jesus,
>   born to set thy people free;
> from our fears and sins release us,
>   let us find our rest in thee.
> Israel's strength and consolation,
>   hope of all the earth thou art;
> dear desire of every nation,
>   joy of every longing heart.
>
> Cure thy children's warring madness,
>   bend our pride to thy control;
> shame our wanton, selfish gladness,
>   rich in things and poor in soul.
> Grant us wisdom, grant us courage,
>   lest we miss thy kingdom's goal,
> Grant us wisdom, grant us courage,
>   lest we miss thy kingdom's goal.

Second Sunday of Advent: The Annunciation

[This may also be used for the fourth Sunday of Advent in year B if following the lectionaries, which give this pericope, Luke 1:26–38, as the reading for that Sunday.]

Voice: On this second Sunday of Advent we remember an angel visiting Mary and announcing:

> "Greetings, favored one! The Lord is with you." But she was much perplexed by his words and pondered what sort of greeting this might be. The angel said to her, "Do not be afraid, Mary, for you have found favor with God. And

now, you will conceive in your womb and bear a son, and you shall name him Jesus. He will be great, and will be called the son of the Most High, and the Lord God will give to him the throne of his ancestor David. He will reign over the house of Jacob forever, and of his kingdom there will be no end." (Luke 1:28b–33)

We ignite this candle, as a sign of God's power overshadowing that one young woman and illumining a portent for all the earth.

(*Light first two candles*)

The angel said to her, "The Holy Spirit will come upon you, and the power of the Most High will overshadow you; therefore the child to be born will be holy; he will be called the Son of God." . . . "For nothing will be impossible with God." Then Mary said, "Here am I, the servant of the Lord: let it be with me according to your word." (Luke 1:35, 37–38a)

Prayer of Confession

Hopefully and expectantly, let us pray:

God Most High and Most Present: We confess that we may feel too small to claim your power, or too inexperienced to proclaim your word, or too troubled to trust in you wholly. Enlighten us to see the power of your Holy Spirit at work in us and to perceive your life enlivening the whole world—both around us and within us. Embolden us to live into your possible, that we might find in Mary an inspiration and an example for our own life, witness and service. Amen.

Assurance and Pardon:

"For nothing will be impossible with God," declares the angel. In the name of Christ, conceived of Mary, eternally of God, your sins are forgiven. . . . Glory to God! Amen.

Third Sunday of Advent: The Magnificat

[This may also be used for the fourth Sunday of Advent in year C if following the lectionaries, which give these verses about Mary's visit to Elizabeth, as the reading for that Sunday.]

Voice:

In those days Mary set out and went with haste to a Judean town in the hill country, where she entered the house of Zechariah and greeted Elizabeth. When Elizabeth heard Mary's greeting, the child leaped in her womb. And Elizabeth was filled with the Holy Spirit and exclaimed with a loud cry,

"Blessed are you among women, and blessed is the fruit of your womb. And why has this happened to me, that the mother of my Lord comes to me? For as soon as I heard the sound of your greeting, the child in my womb leaped for joy. And blessed is she who believed that there would be a fulfillment of what was spoken to her by the Lord." (Luke 1:39–45)

(Light first three candles)

We light this third candle of Advent, celebrating with Elizabeth and with Mary the joy of salvation already begun and the hope of salvation promised to all generations—casting down the powerful and lifting up the downtrodden. With Mary we acclaim:

Congregation reading together:

My soul magnifies the Lord,
    and my spirit rejoices in God my Savior,
for he has looked with favor on the lowliness of his servant.
    Surely, from now on all generations will call me blessed;
for the Mighty One has done great things for me,
    and holy is his name.
His mercy is for those who fear him
    from generation to generation.
He has shown strength with his arm;
    he has scattered the proud in the thoughts of their hearts.
He has brought down the powerful from their thrones,
    and lifted up the lowly;
he has filled the hungry with good things,
    and sent the rich away empty.
He has helped his servant Israel,
    in remembrance of his mercy,
according to the promise he made to our ancestors,
    to Abraham and to his descendants forever. (Luke 1:46b–55)

Fourth Sunday of Advent: Song of Zechariah

Voice: On this fourth Sunday of Advent, still looking toward the birth of Christ, we celebrate the birth of John the forerunner—who was born to call the people to repentance and to point the way to salvation in Christ, "to give light to those who sit in darkness and in the shadow of death, and to guide our feet into the way of peace" (Luke 1:79). We light this light symbolizing that light.

(Light all four candles)

With John's father we bless God who blesses us:

Blessed be the Lord God of Israel,
   for he has looked favorably on his people and redeemed them.
He has raised up a mighty savior for us
   in the house of his servant David,
as he spoke through the mouth of his holy prophets from of old,
   that we would be saved from our enemies
   and from the hand of all who hate us.
Thus he has shown the mercy promised to our ancestors,
   and has remembered his holy covenant,
the oath that he swore to our ancestor Abraham,
   to grant us that we, being rescued from the hands of our enemies,
might serve him without fear, in holiness and righteousness
   before him all our days.
And you, child, will be called the prophet of the Most High;
   for you will go before the Lord to prepare his ways,
to give knowledge of salvation to his people
   by the forgiveness of their sins.
By the tender mercy of our God,
   the dawn from on high will break upon us,
to give light to those who sit in darkness and in the shadow of death,
   to guide our feet into the way of peace. (Luke 1:68–79)

Sung Response: "O Come, O Come, Emmanuel," verse 6
   "O come, thou Dayspring, come and cheer
      our spirits by thine advent here;
   disperse the gloomy clouds of night,
      and death's dark shadows put to flight.
   Rejoice! Rejoice! Emmanuel
      shall come to thee, O Israel.

Chapter 13

Christmas
Birthed and Embodied

There are two stories of Jesus's birth in the Gospels—one in Matthew and one in Luke. They can both be read on Christmas, but the lectionaries provide for Matthew 1:18–24 to be read on the fourth Sunday of Advent and for Luke's nativity narrative to be read on Christmas Eve and Christmas Day.[1] The lectionaries also provide for the option of reading the prologue to John as a Gospel lesson at Christmas. These passages and their parallel lessons in the lectionaries will all be discussed in this chapter. The next chapter on Epiphany will look at the beginning of Mark's Gospel and at Mathew's account of the visit of the magi as epiphanies.

Theologically, the central focus on Christ's incarnation affirms God's immanence in the baby born and throughout the world. With our ecological concern in mind, Christmas celebrates God's presence on Earth and in earthly life. Christ enters creation, and creation welcomes the Christ. In Trinitarian language, creation is not just a matter pertaining to the First person of the Trinity, but we find creation's intimate and deep relationship with the Second person of the Trinity—the Word through whom all things were made in the beginning, the Word made incarnate and present among us, and the final Word that will bring all things to fulfillment. In Christ, God takes on the flesh of animate life with us and, indeed, shares with us in the physical nature of the universe. The baby Jesus is incarnate in flesh like us, metabolizes like us, breathes the same air, is replenished by the same water, and ingests the same nutrients. His metabolizing provides the same natural by-products as us, sending water, nutrients, and carbon dioxide back into the environment to be shared by other living creatures in the natural cycles of life.

CHRISTMAS EVE AND CHRISTMAS DAY

There are three sets of readings given by the lectionaries to be read on Christmas Eve or Christmas Day. The first lessons are from the book of Isaiah. The particular verses vary slightly between the two lectionaries, but the readings are from chapters 9, 52, and 62 of Isaiah. The psalms provided by the lectionaries are three enthronement psalms: Psalms 96–98. These psalms are rich in imagery of creation and God's sovereignty within the natural world. The readings from Isaiah are not as replete with images of nature, but each of them projects a universal vision of restoration and renewal under divine rule. Read together, the psalms concretize and enflesh this vision of salvation within earthly reality. For Christians reading these scriptures on Christmas, the earthward direction of this message of salvation finds exclamation in Christ's incarnation.

The first of the lessons from Isaiah urged by the lectionaries to be read on Christmas Eve or Christmas Day is Isaiah 9:1–7: The poetry of this passage begins with the entrance of light: "The people who walked in darkness have seen a great light; those who lived in a land of deep darkness—on them light has shined" (Isa 9:2). The passage proceeds to the proclamation of a child to become monarch resulting in peace with justice:

> For a child has been born for us,
>   a son given to us;
> authority rests upon his shoulders;
>   and he is named
> Wonderful Counselor, Mighty God,
>   Everlasting Father, Prince of Peace.
> His authority shall grow continually,
>   and there shall be endless peace
> for the throne of David and his kingdom.
>   He will establish and uphold it
> with justice and with righteousness
>   from this time onward and forevermore.
> The zeal of the LORD of hosts will do this. (Isa 9:6–7)

Sometimes this passage is read concluding with verse 6 naming the "Prince of Peace," but then the explicit promulgation of endless peace, justice, and righteousness is omitted. Verse 7 should be read and "justice with righteousness" declared. Moreover the pairing of justice and righteousness, or God's judgment and righteousness, is explicitly promised in each of the three enthronement psalms given for Christmas as well (Pss 96:13, 97:2, 98:10).[2]

In between the beginning of this passage in Isaiah 9 with the light shining in the darkness and its conclusion with the child establishing endless peace, two kinds of celebration are poetically invoked: a joyous harvest and a celebration of military victory. "You have multiplied the nation, you have increased its joy," verse 3 begins and continues, "they rejoice before you as with joy at the harvest." The picture of joyful harvest is immediately followed by lines portraying military victory and liberation from oppression:

> as with joy at the harvest,
> as people exult when dividing plunder.
> For the yoke of their burden,
> and the bar across their shoulders,
> the rod of their oppressor,
> you have broken as on the day of Midian.
> For all the boots of the tramping warriors
> and all the garments rolled in blood
> shall be burned as fuel for the fire.
> For a child has been born for us. (Isa 9:4b–6a)

While dividing plunder is clearly a violent image, the occasion being portrayed is that of cessation of war, securing of liberation, and establishment of lasting peace. The image of a joyful harvest of cultivated plants is joined with the image of a victory bonfire burning bloodstained garments and warriors' boots. In the juxtaposing of these two contexts of celebration, once again we see a conceptual linkage between the welfare of the land and the establishing of political justice. Both are simultaneous indications of God's sovereignty expressed throughout the social and natural world.

Peace is represented both in the burning of boots and in the healthy harvest. When people fight, the land suffers. Moreover, productive agricultural land depends on people to tend it and care for it. Biblical scholar Ellen F. Davis, makes a further point that she learned from engaging in Bible study with farmers. "It's obvious," she declares, "when humans are disconnected from God, the soil will be the first to suffer." "Land degradation," she cautions, "is a sure sign that humans have turned away from God. Conversely, the flourishing of the land" she continues, "marks a return to God."[3] Quoting Davis in this regard, and citing Isaiah 9, Patricia K. Tull notes, moreover, that in Isaiah "responsibility for both ecological and economic health lies not simply with the people as a whole but most urgently with their leaders."[4] In this instance, the light of God's sovereignty is refracted through Davidic rule resurgent in both power and peace in the promise of a child.

Probably the child being born and destined to rule in Isaiah 9 is the same child named by Isaiah as Immanuel earlier in Isaiah 7 and likely referenced again in Isaiah 11 as a "shoot from the stump of Jesse" (Isa 11:1). All three of these passages from Isaiah seem to refer to the coming of a king that would rule more effectively than Ahaz who was king of Judah at the time of these prophecies. It is good news in these passages that a remnant shall survive the international turmoil of the time and the looming threat from Assyria.

The other two passages from Isaiah provided by the lectionaries to be read on Christmas Eve or Christmas Day are from later in the book of Isaiah and address a later period in the history of the Hebrew People. In Isaiah 52 and 62, the good news is not about liberation from Assyria but that a remnant should return from exile in Babylon. These three passages put forward by the lectionaries to be read at Christmas were originally addressing two different historic situations with hope for salvation. Further Christian interpretation through the millennia has also found in these ancient expressions of salvific hope language to denote and to declare Jesus Christ as Prince of Peace.

Hilary Marlow notes that "motifs of creation" are prominent throughout the book of Isaiah. She finds only two chapters (chapters 20 and 39) in the first half of Isaiah (Isa 1–39) that contain no reference to "non-human creation," and only two chapters (chapters 52 and 63) in the rest of Isaiah that contain no such references, though a few other chapters in the later chapters in Isaiah (including chapter 62), she adds, have a "negligible amount" of such material about the natural world.[5] It just happens, though, that two of these chapters (chapters 52 and 62) with little or no reference to the natural world are provided by the lectionaries to be read on Christmas Eve or Christmas Day. Both of these chapters from the second half of Isaiah do, however, present a global picture of announced salvation. Salvation is promised to Jerusalem or to Zion but with worldwide implications. The lection from Isaiah 52 begins with a promise of peace:

> How beautiful upon the mountains
>   are the feet of the messenger who announces peace,
> who brings good news,
>   who announces salvation,
>   who says to Zion, "Your God reigns." (Isa 52:7)

The lection concludes with the whole earth bearing witness to this salvation:

> The LORD has bared his holy arm
>   before the eyes of all the nations;
> and all the ends of the earth shall see
>   the salvation of our God. (Isa 52:10)

Similarly, Isaiah 62 declares "to the end of the earth" in verse 11:

> The LORD has proclaimed
>   to the end of the earth:
> Say to daughter Zion,

> "See, your salvation comes;
> his reward is with him,
> and his recompense before him." (Isa 62:11)

These verses in Isaiah 52 and 62 are written with immediate reference to the return of the Hebrew people from Babylonian exile to a land that had been left forsaken. The salvation of God's particular people is presented as being of global import. As Isaiah 62:7 puts it, God "establishes Jerusalem and makes it a praise in the earth" (Isa 62:7 RSV).

Proclaimed in Christian celebrations at Nativity, the references to earth are enriched and embellished liturgically by the imagery in the psalms provided by the lectionaries for Christmas. Psalms 96–98 are enthronement psalms as discussed previously in the chapter pertaining to Christ's Ascension. Referring to the declaration in Isaiah 52:7, "Your God reigns," and to the promise of peace and salvation that follows, Claus Westermann points to the significance of Psalms 93–99 for clarifying and celebrating the "importance even in Israel's worship of such extolling of God's kingship."[6] These psalms elaborate the themes of creation, the Creator's continuing sovereignty throughout creation, and creation's praise of the Sovereign Creator.[7] Creation's voice in praise of the Sovereign Creator resounds ever louder as one reads through the enthronement psalms. Psalm 96 begins, "O sing to the LORD a new song; sing to the LORD, all the earth" (Ps 96:1), and then summons the whole creation—the sea, the earth, the heavens, the fields, and the trees of the forest—to shout and sing and dance for joy before the Creator who reigns in judgment and truth:

> Let the heavens be glad, and let the earth rejoice;
> let the sea roar, and all that fills it;
> let the field exult, and everything in it.
> Then shall all the trees of the forest sing for joy
> before the LORD; for he is coming,
> for he is coming to judge the earth.
> He will judge the world with righteousness,
> and the peoples with his truth. (Ps 96:10–13)

Moreover, in Psalm 96 images of earthly creation consistently occur along with declarations of God's glory.[8] God's glory is invoked in this psalm in verses 3, 7, and 8. God's glory is presented earth-wide, to all peoples and nations. We are told to declare God's glory among the nations (Ps 96:3), and all "families of the peoples" are called to "Ascribe to the Lord the glory due his name" (Ps 96:7–8). So, as the psalm proceeds with the heavens being glad, the earth rejoicing, the sea roaring, the fields exulting, and the trees singing, all of nature is participating in this global glorification of God.

Psalm 97 opens similarly with pronouncement and summons: "The LORD is king! Let the earth rejoice" (Ps 97:1a) and then proclaims God's power present in the forces of nature both in and above the earth:

> His lightnings light up the world;
>   the earth sees and trembles.
> The mountains melt like wax before the LORD,
>   before the Lord of all the earth.
> The heavens proclaim his righteousness;
>   and all the peoples behold his glory. (Ps 97:4–6)

Psalm 97 sings God's glory with lightnings firing and mountains melting.

Psalm 98 declares, in language similar to Isaiah 52:10 quoted earlier, "All the ends of the earth have seen the victory of our God" and continues by exhorting, "Make a joyful noise to the LORD, all the earth, break forth into joyous song and sing praises" (Ps 98:4). Then reverberating with verse as sung in Psalm 96, Psalm 98 concludes:

> Let the sea roar, and all that fills it;
>   the world and those who live in it.
> Let the floods clap their hands;
>   let the hills sing together for joy
> at the presence of the LORD, for he is coming
>   to judge the earth.
> He will judge the world with righteousness,
>   and the peoples with equity. (Ps 98:7–9)

Here, watery forces that might have been considered symbols of chaos or even of competing deities, according to Dianne Bergant, are presented as joining "with the mountains and the inhabitants of the earth in rejoicing in anticipation of the arrival of the divine king, who will come in justice."[9] The celebration of enthronement includes all creation. Jonathan Magonet compares this reference to rivers and mountains in Psalm 98 with the reference to productive fields and trees of the forest in Psalm 96:12, and concludes, "Between them the two psalms cover all of nature, both cultivated and uncultivated."[10]

Psalm 98 was the inspiration for Isaac Watts's hymn, "Joy to the World"[11] that we sing at Christmas, and there are also more contemporary musical renderings of this psalm that lend themselves well to worship. Psalm 98 can be chanted, for instance, with the refrain, "All the ends of the earth have seen the power of God," sung as written by David Haas and Marty Haugen.[12] David Haas's lyrics paraphrase the first six verses of Psalm 98 but conclude before the sea roars and the hills start singing with the floods' clapping. Another lively and singable paraphrase is "All the Ends of the Earth" by Bob Dufford, SJ, which declares in its refrain:

> All the ends of the earth, all you creatures of the sea,
>   lift up your eyes to the wonders of the Lord.
> For the Lord of the earth, the master of the sea,
>   has come with justice for the world.[13]

We behold God's glory on Earth again in the Gospel readings given by the lectionaries for Christmas Eve and Christmas Day from Luke 2 and John 1. In Luke 2, the "glory of the Lord" shines around shepherds and sheep in the field as an angel announces to them of a Messiah born in the city of David and lying in a manger, and as a choir of heavenly host sing: "Glory to God in the highest heaven, and on earth peace, good will among people!" The shepherds then go with haste to see this child in the manger and respond by "glorifying and praising God" (Luke 2:8–20). Glory is given and peace proclaimed on Earth, beginning with shepherds and sheep.

In the Gospel of John, both the universality and the particularity of this glory are shown incarnate in the Word active in creation, embodied in time and space on Earth. The Gospel begins "in the beginning" with the Word, creation, light, and life:

> In the beginning was the Word, and the Word was with God, and the Word was God. He was in the beginning with God. All things came into being through him, and without him not one thing came into being. What has come into being in him was life, and the life was the light of all people. (John 1:1–4)

In verse 14, this divine Word of God takes on flesh and lives with us, revealing the very glory of the Creator within creation: "And the Word became flesh and lived among us, and we have seen his glory, the glory as of the Father's only Son, full of grace and truth" (John 1:14).

Finally, the ascription of God's glory to the Son, active in creation and throughout creation, finds parallel expression in the Epistle reading from the first chapter of Hebrews that is paired with John's Gospel for Christmas:

> In these last days [God] has spoken to us by a Son, whom he appointed heir of all things, through whom he also created the worlds. He is the reflection of God's glory and the exact imprint of God's very being, and he sustains all things by his powerful word. (Heb 1:2–4)

Lessons and Carols

A service of lessons and carols is a joyous part of Christmas worship in many congregations. The service, begun in 1880 in Truro, England, was adapted for use at King's College in Cambridge in 1918. There have since been many variations following the basic pattern from Kings College. Traditionally there have been nine lessons and carols, though the number can vary. It is usually celebrated on Christmas Eve, bringing us from Advent expectation into Christmas wonder, and it can conclude with a Christmas Eve candlelight ceremony. The readings typically begin with the Fall in Genesis 3, move into prophetic expectation for the coming of a savior, and conclude with proclaiming and celebrating the nativity of Christ.

Genesis 3 is hard on the land (and on women!), however, and some literalist interpretations of the "curse" of the ground undermine appreciation for the continued goodness of creation and our continued charge to till and keep the garden—despite its "thorns and thistles." Wesley Granberg-Michaelson has offered this more earth-friendly interpretation:

> What these verses point to is a distortion in humanity's relationship to creation, and in particular to the ground, which results from humanity's rebellious inclinations. There is no suggestion that all the creation has lost its inherent goodness. The earth is not suddenly made evil. Such interpretations extend far beyond what is found in this text, and conflict with countless other scriptures testifying to creation's capacity and purpose to show forth God's glory.[14]

Some services of lessons and carols begin instead with the story of Adam and Eve and the charge to "till and keep" in Genesis 2 before moving into the account of the Fall in Genesis 3.[15] This provides a broader context affirming creation but does not negate the more disparaging and damning interpretation of curse that worshipers might bring to a hearing of the story. It is possible, of course, to compose a different progression of readings with different theological nuance. One possibility that would emphasize deep incarnation of the cosmic Christ in the baby born on Earth might be to start with the first chapter of Genesis and God's Spirit blowing over the deep, move to the woman's voice of Wisdom speaking throughout creation in Proverbs 8, and conclude with the Incarnate Word in John.

If one does choose to read about the Fall and the "curse" in Genesis 3, it is important that the rest of the service proclaim redemption from curse and salvation from sin heralded in the one being born. A good hymn to follow a reading of Genesis 3 might be Charles Wesley's original version of "Hark, How All the Welkin Rings" (known more popularly as "Hark, the Herald Angels Sing"), suggested below as one of the carols. The longer version of this hymn addresses clearly the union of divine with earthly nature in the incarnation effecting our restoration. Referring to human nature after the Fall, a little-known verse implores:

> Now display thy saving power,
> Ruined nature now restore,

> Now in mystic union join
>   Thine to ours, and ours to thine.
> Adam's likeness, Lord, efface,
>   Stamp thine image in its place,
> Second Adam from above,
>   Reinstate us in thy love![16]

The following sets of lessons and carols, however, do not include Genesis 3, as this service is based simply on the Lectionary Readings for late Advent and Christmas Eve and Christmas Day. Ecologically relevant aspects of these readings have already been discussed in this and in the previous chapters. The carols chosen to accompany these readings are hymns both old and more recent. In each instance, verses or phrases are highlighted which connote some aspect of the natural world or of the earth itself responding to or participating in the good news of Christ's birth.

Liturgists may substitute readings and carols as seems best for the particular occasion of worship planned and for the people gathering. There is something to be said simply for singing old favorites. And there is something that is lost when we scrupulously avoid singing about the nativity during Advent. When we refrain from singing Christmas carols in Advent, little time is left to enjoy them before Christmas concludes. Moreover, with the secularization of Christmas, it is the more banal ditties rather than the reverent carols that are repeatedly played in stores and public places. As people of faith, we need to find opportunities to sing!

First Lesson: Isaiah 62:(1–5) 6–12 or Isaiah 52:7–10 [situates the beginning of the service with the Advent image of watching for God's salvation to be proclaimed to the ends of the earth][17]

Carol: "Watchman, Tell Us of the Night" [which declares in dialogue:

> Watcher, will its beams alone gild the spot that gave them birth?
> Traveler, ages are its own; see, it bursts o'er all the earth![18]]

OR "Go Tell it on the Mountain"

Second Lesson: Isaiah 11:1–9 [which begins with the branch sprouting from the stump of Jesse and concludes with a picture of peace between the wolf, lamb, leopard, kid, calf, lion, fatling, snake and little child]

Carol: "Isaiah the Prophet Has Written of Old"[19] [begins with a promise of "new creation," invoking images from Isaiah 11:6–9, moves to confession that "nations still prey on the meek" and that "people despoil all sweetness of earth," and concludes praying, "God, bring to fruition your will for the earth"]

OR "Lo! How a Rose E'er Blooming" [the rose being both Jesse's branch and Mary's child]

Third Lesson: Isaiah 7:10–14

Carol: "Hark, How All the Welkin Rings" [This is the early first line of the hymn by Charles Wesley commonly known as "Hark, the Herald Angels Sing." "Welkin" denotes the entire sky or firmament and not just angels, which in the hymn declares "peace on earth." Earth and sky and "universal nature" are named in these earlier opening verses. Subsequent verses in the longer version of this hymn refer to a joining of divine nature with ours. Immanuel is invoked, not in an overly sentimentalized way but in a manner consistent with the prophetic call for God's justice among all Earth's nations. Here are the opening lines.]

> Hark, How All the Welkin Rings,
> Glory to the King of kings,
> Peace on earth, and mercy mild,
> God and sinners reconciled!
> Joyful all ye nations rise,
> Join the triumph of the skies,
> Universal nature say
> "Christ the Lord is born today!"[20]

Fourth Lesson: Psalm 98 or Psalm 96 or Psalm 97

Carol: "Joy to the World" [Isaac Watts based this hymn on Psalm 98.[21] "Let heaven and nature sing" is the refrain of the first verse as usually sung, followed by the earth itself singing with joy in the second verse as follows.]

> Joy to the earth! the Savior reigns;
> Let all their songs employ;
> While fields and floods, rocks, hills and plains
> repeat the sounding joy[22]

Fifth Lesson: Matthew 1:18–25

Carol: "O Little Town of Bethlehem" ["abide with us, our Lord Emmanuel!"]

Sixth Lesson: Luke 2:1–7

Carol: "Jesus, Our Brother, Strong and Good"[23] also titled, "The Friendly Beasts" [Of course there were animals near the manger, but popular imagination has filled in the blanks in the biblical narrative. Saint Francis, who respected animals as kin, is said to have produced the first live Christmas manger scene in Europe and to have brought ox and donkey along.[24] Saint Bonaventure recalls how Saint Francis:

> made ready a manger, and bade hay, together with an ox and an ass, be brought unto the spot. The Brethren were called together, the folk assembled, the wood echoed with their voices, and that august night was made radiant and solemn with many bright lights, and with tuneful and sonorous praises. The man of God, filled with tender love, stood before the manger, bathed in tears, and overflowing with joy.[25]

Regarding Francis's regard for animals generally, moreover, Bonaventure writes that Saint Francis:

> would call the dumb animals, howsoever small, by the names of brother and sister, forasmuch as he recognised in them the same origin as in himself. Yet he loved with an especial warmth and tenderness those creatures that do set forth by the likeness of their nature the holy gentleness of Christ.[26]

The Christmas carol, "The Friendly Beasts," fancifully puts worshipful words in the mouths of those animals.]

Seventh Lesson: Luke 2:8–21

Carol: "O Holy Night!" [The last verse begins as follows.]

> Truly He taught us to love one another;
>   His law is love and His gospel is peace;
> Chains shall He break, for the slave is our brother,
>   and in His name all oppression shall cease.[27]

Eighth Lesson: John 1:1–5, 14

Carol: "Of the Father's Love Begotten" [Be sure to use a copy that includes the following amazing verse.]

> By his Word was all created;
>   he commanded; it was done:
> heaven and earth and depths of ocean,
>   universe of three in one,
> all that sees the moon's soft shining,
>   all that breathes beneath the sun.[28]

Ninth Lesson: Hebrews 1:1–4

Carol: "Who Would Think That What Was Needed"[29] [This carol begins:

> Who would think that what was needed to transform and save the earth
> might not be a plan or army, proud in purpose, proved in worth?
> Who would think, despite derision, that a child would lead the way?

It continues with traditional images surrounding the nativity, and concludes recognizing the ambiguity of our more scientific age, and still confesses, "God surprises earth with heaven, coming here on Christmas Day."]

CHRISTMAS SEASON

Following all the pageantry leading up to Christmas morning, the longer season of Christmas presents opportunity to reflect more deeply on the awesome significance of Christ and the incarnation of Creator in creation. The lections for the Sundays in Christmas season present several theological images that resonate with ecological wonder: plants and gardens, the incarnation of God in animate flesh, the praise of God by all creation, and the defeat of contending powers and the universality of God's salvation.

As the Christmas season proceeds, the Gospel lections continue with accounts of Jesus's childhood in the second chapters of Matthew and Luke for the first Sunday after Christmas Day. On the second Sunday after Christmas Day, the Gospel lesson returns to the very beginning with creation and the incarnation of the Word as disclosed in the first chapter of John. Many congregations following the lectionary, though, will celebrate Epiphany on the second Sunday in Christmas and read the lections that are discussed in the following chapter on Epiphany. Moreover, many years will have only one Sunday between December 25 and the actual feast of Epiphany on January 6.

First Sunday after Christmas Day

Luke's Gospel has the holy family of Mary, Joseph, and Jesus traveling to Jerusalem to present Jesus in the temple. There they hear the testimonies of Simeon and of the prophet Anna concerning the child. The Song of Simeon, or *Nunc Dimittis*, succinctly intones some of the themes already discussed as having ecological import in the readings for Christmas Day: peace, light, glory, and salvation "in the presence of all peoples":

> Now you are dismissing your servant in peace,
>   according to your word;

> for my eyes have seen your salvation,
>> which you have prepared in the presence of all peoples,
> a light for revelation to the Gentiles
>> and for glory to your people Israel. (Luke 2:29–32)

This canticle can be sung in corporate worship not only during the Season of Christmas but throughout the year and in personal devotion as well.

God's glory declared "above earth and heaven" is celebrated throughout creation in Psalm 148, which is the psalm given for the first Sunday after Christmas Day in the Revised Common Lectionary. Psalm 148 is effusive with praise to God both from all the heavens and from all the earth and seas. The first verse begins by invoking heavenly praise, "Praise the LORD! Praise the LORD from the heavens" and then the following verses issue a call to praise from all beings pictured as residing in the heavens: angels, host, sun, moon, and shining stars. Even the primordial watery chaos is presented as part of God's creation and called on to offer praise:

> Praise him, you highest heavens,
>> and you waters above the heavens!
> Let them praise the name of the LORD,
>> for he commanded and they were created.
> He established them forever and ever;
>> he fixed their bounds, which cannot be passed. (Ps 148:4–6)

Next, the psalm continues with praise from below the heavens, from the earth and the ocean: sea monsters and deeps, fire, hail, snow, frost, stormy wind, mountains, hills, fruit trees, cedars, wild animals, cattle, creeping things, and flying birds. People too, of every station and gender and age are included:

> Kings of the earth and all peoples,
>> princes and all rulers of the earth!
> Young men and women alike,
>> old and young together!
> Let them praise the name of the LORD,
>> for his name alone is exalted;
>> his glory is above earth and heaven.
> He has raised up a horn for his people. (Ps 148:11–14a)

Hearing this psalm in the season of Christmas, the horn raised up in verse 14 reminds us of Zechariah's song proclaiming that God "has raised up a horn of salvation for us" (Luke 1:68), whom we now confess as Christ. God's glory above all of heaven and earth and proclaimed throughout heaven and earth in Psalm 148 is seen reflected in the Song of Simeon as well as in the heavenly praise proclaimed to sheep and shepherds at Christ's birth, "Glory to

God in the highest and on earth peace" (Luke 2:14). God's glory throughout the heavens and the earth finds a home on this earth in the childhood of the one worshiped as Christ. Psalm 148 can be chanted with a *Gloria* from one of the Christmas carols sung as a response. Also the hymn "All Creatures of our God and King," originally written by Saint Francis, is often associated with this psalm and can be sung along with it, with their respective choruses of praise from all parts of creation.[30]

"When the fullness of time had come," we are told in Galatians 4:4–7, which is one of the Epistle lessons for the first Sunday after Christmas Day in the Revised Common Lectionary, "God sent his Son, born of a woman." In Galatians, though, immediately preceding the lectionary's selection of verses declaring Christ's birth, there is given the context of our enslavement to the "*stoicheia tou kosmou*," the elements of the universe (Gal 4:3). Guardianship under the law is described as an example of such bondage to the elements. The law which was given for the good purpose of guiding us until the promise of faith was revealed in Christ, nonetheless, becomes for us a restraint that must give way. The guardian also becomes our prison, and we are likened to minors in need of such guardianship until the advent of Christ and our justification by faith. Christ enters our world, assumes our flesh, and is born under the law in order to liberate us from the law and from all *stoicheia*, so that by the Spirit of Christ we are adopted as God's progeny and heirs. The selection from the lectionary concludes: "God has sent the Spirit of his son into our hearts, crying, 'Abba! Father!'" So you are no longer a slave but a child, and if a child then also an heir, through God" (Gal 4:6b–7). Then the next two verses also give the context of liberation from the *stoicheia* as the import of our adoption: "Formally, when you did not know God, you were enslaved to beings that by nature are not gods. Now, however, that you have come to know God, or rather to be known by God, how can you turn back again to the weak and beggarly elemental spirits (*stoicheia*)?" (Gal 4:8–9). Our personal redemption, effected by Christ born among us, is presented as taking place within God's cosmic victory over contending powers in creation. God in Christ, claiming creation, declares us heirs in God's reclaimed order.

It is clear that the *stoicheia* are a broader category than the law alone, and that bondage to and liberation from them is not just a matter pertaining to Jewish observance of the law. Jew and Gentile alike are addressed in this famous passage at the conclusion of the preceding third chapter of Galatians:

> As many of you as were baptized into Christ have clothed yourselves with Christ. There is no longer Jew or Greek, there is no longer slave or free, there is no longer male and female, for all of you are one in Christ Jesus. And if you belong to Christ, then you are Abraham's offspring, heirs according to the promise. (Gal 3:27–29)

Also, following the verses selected by the lectionary, the elements are identified with the turning of seasons and years, which earthly rhythms would have been linked with movements of heavenly bodies. There are several associations possible for the meaning of *stoicheia*, all of which might be inferentially present in Paul's use of the term: rudiments of learning, heavenly bodies associated with the zodiac; elemental spiritual beings; and worldly "elements" understood as earth, air, fire, and water.[31] These can be conceptually related, since both the earthly elements and the heavenly bodies might have been worshiped as spiritual beings or as representing deities. The law, which is of both earthly and spiritual import, is also discussed by Paul as a kind of rudiment of learning in the progression of faith. Those under the law are likened to minors receiving guidance and tutelage until maturing with faith as heirs of the promises of God. Indeed all the earthly and heavenly *stoicheia* might be considered similarly—as creations of the Creator given for good purpose but distorted in their purpose when overly empowered or even deified by us. But with our liberation in Christ these *stoicheia* are returned to their proper place, considered now to be "weak and beggarly," and we ourselves are established as heirs with Christ within creation.

"Creation" is not explicitly named in these verses of Galatians but may be inferred in the language about "elements" which necessarily would refer to creatures—whether earthly, heavenly, spiritual, or physical—and whether serving obediently in their created purposes or representing idolatrous antagonism to those purposes. Creation is more explicitly referenced, however, in Hebrews 2:10–18, which is another Epistle lesson given by the Revised Common Lectionary for the first Sunday after Christmas Day. The lesson begins:

> It was fitting that he, for whom and through whom all things [*ta panta*] exist, in bringing many children to glory, should make the pioneer of their salvation perfect through sufferings. For the one who sanctifies and those who are sanctified are all of one [*ex enos*]." (Heb 2:10–11a)

The one "for whom and through whom all things exist" would be the Creator of all, and the "pioneer" of our perfection would be Jesus Christ. Mary Ann Beavis and HyeRan Kim-Cragg consider the phrase denoting the union of sanctifier and sanctified as "most likely referring to the divine source of all creation."[32] Moreover, at the very beginning of the book of Hebrews, the Creator is identified with "the Son."

> In these last days he has spoken to us by a Son, whom he appointed heir of all things, through whom he also created the worlds. He is the reflection of God's glory and the exact imprint of God's very being, and he sustains all things by his powerful word. (Heb 1:2)

This one named as Jesus and identified with God's glory also identifies deeply with us in mortal life and death. We read in verse 2:14 of Christ sharing with us in "flesh and blood . . . so that through death he might destroy the one who has the power of death, that is, the devil and free those who all their lives were held in slavery by the fear of death." The argument here in Hebrews is similar to that in Galatians where Jesus is born human and under the law in order to liberate humanity from bondage to *stoicheia*. In Hebrews, though, it is not the elements that are presented as enslaving, but rather it is the devil and death from which freedom is gained through Christ's incarnation and suffering. This Christ, who was active throughout creation, enters into creation as flesh and blood, and through suffering defeats inimical power and champions life. The whole of creation and of life itself is the context for our personal salvation and sanctification. Already during the Christmas season, this passage anticipates Good Friday, Easter, and Ascension. We are prompted to remember that the baby born among us is also the one who suffers mortally with us and who lives eternally as our great high priest.

Second Sunday after Christmas Day

The New Testament readings for the second Sunday after Christmas Day, given in both lectionaries, further amplify these same themes of incarnation and the inclusion of "all things" in the creative and salvific work of Christ. The Gospel lesson is from the first chapter of John. With the beginning of John's Gospel there is an opening of our vista to encompass the cosmos. The baby Jesus who has been our focus during Christmas is like a microcosm for the universe, the Word made flesh, Creator and Pantocrator within creation, eternity instantiated in time. There is momentous conceptual balance between the tiny and the infinite, the temporal and the eternal, the numinous and the earthy.

The epistle lesson is from the first chapter of Ephesians which declares: "With all wisdom (*pasē sophia*) and insight he has made known to us the mystery of his will, according to his good pleasure that he set forth in Christ, as a plan for the fullness of time, to gather up all things (*ta panta*) in him, things in heaven and things on earth" (Eph 1:8b–10). All things are gathered together in Christ, explicitly all things on earth as well as in heaven. Curiously, though, these particular verses are omitted from the Roman Catholic Lectionary for the Mass, which jumps from Ephesians 1:3–6 to verses 15–18, even though this reference to "all things" gathered in Christ to God with "all wisdom" fits nicely with the logos theology in the prologue to John as well as with the Old Testament lesson from the deuterocanonical book of Sirach (Sir 24:1–4, 12–16), both of which are prescribed as readings in the Roman Catholic Lectionary for the Mass. Sirach 24:1–12 is also an optional reading in the Revised Common Lectionary. Sirach or Ecclesiasticus, the long title of which is "The Wisdom of Jesus Son of Sirach," presents Wisdom poetically speaking with a woman's voice intoning the universal breadth of her presence throughout creation.

The wisdom tradition, represented by Sirach and other deuterocanonical books, as well as by the book of Proverbs, is fully formative of the understanding of logos presented in John. Elizabeth A. Johnson writes, "Virtually every attribute and activity of the Word in the prologue [to John] come from rich Wisdom sources in the Christian Old Testament," which for Johnson includes the deuterocanonical books. Citing this chapter of Sirach together with Proverbs 8 and the deuterocanonical books of Baruch and The Wisdom of Solomon, she reminds, "It is important to remember that the wisdom tradition also carried the impulse to bring Wisdom to earth." Johnson refers to a "flowering" of identification between conceptions of Jesus with wisdom in the late first century, so that the "hymns of Colossians (1:15–20) and Hebrews (1:2–3) and the gospel of John just about take it for granted." It is important, though, that we not take it for granted. "The importance of this connection cannot be overstated," Johnson continues and that "it configured . . . Jesus, the crucified prophet from Nazareth, to Wisdom's universal role in creating, saving, and making holy the world." Moreover, with Christ's incarnation, "God's presence abides not only in and for the world but goes deep down to the point of identity as *part* of the world."[33] Echoing Niels Gregersen's language of "deep ecology," Johnson describes Christ's incarnation in creaturely flesh in contemporary terms:

> Jesus was a complex living unit of minerals and fluids, an item in the carbon, oxygen, and nitrogen cycles. The atoms comprising his body were once part of other creatures. The genetic structure of the cells in his body were kin to the flowers, fish, frogs, finches, foxes, the whole community of life that descended from common ancestors in the ancient seas. And by the nature of living things he was going to die.[34]

One might note further that the bodily elements expelled or exhaled by Jesus in his eating and breathing among us are still being cycled through our own bodies and over all the planet.

In Sirach, Wisdom speaks of her all-encompassing presence throughout the earth and seas, the abyss below, and the heavens above:

> I came forth from the mouth of the Most High,
>   and covered the earth like a mist.
> I dwelt in the highest heavens,
>   and my throne was in a pillar of cloud.
> Alone I compassed the vault of heaven

>   and traversed the depths of the abyss.
> Over waves of the sea, over all the earth,
>   and over every people and nation I have held sway. (Sir 24:3–6)

Then from all the breadth of creation and all the depth of time, she locates herself in special relationship with the line and lands of Jacob:

> Then the Creator of all things gave me a command,
>   and my Creator chose the place for my tent.
> He said, "Make your dwelling in Jacob,
>   and in Israel receive your inheritance."
> Before the ages, in the beginning, he created me
>   and for all the ages I shall not cease to be. (Sir 24:8–9)

Wisdom moves to the metaphor of plants and sings of taking root in Jacob. The selection of verses given by the Roman Catholic Lectionary for the Mass concludes with a whole litany of plants. Wisdom grows tall like trees throughout the region: a cedar in Lebanon, a cypress on the heights of Hermon, a palm tree in Engedi, rosebushes in Jericho, olive tree and "a plane tree beside water" (Sir 24:13–14). Wisdom perfumes the air with a potpourris of fragrant plants: cassia, camel's thorn, myrrh, galbanum, onych, and stacte (Sir 24:15). The selection of verses concludes simply with botanical beauty, "Like a terebinth I spread out my branches, and my branches are glorious and graceful" (Sir 24:16). But the reading could continue, as Wisdom buds and blossoms like a vine bearing fruit in verse 17. Actually, though, this entire passage pertaining to plants is only in the Roman Catholic Lectionary for the Mass; the Revised Common Lectionary concludes with verse 12. But the Revised Common Lectionary includes the wide vista of earth, seas, heavens, and abyss of verses 5–6, which are omitted in the Roman Catholic Lectionary for the Mass. All of these verses extolling Wisdom as God's work throughout creation, though, can be grafted into our liturgies and sermons in Christmas season.

Plants sprout up in other readings from the Old Testament given by the lectionaries for this season. Jeremiah 31:7–14 is the non-apocryphal Old Testament lesson offered by the Revised Common Lectionary for the Second Sunday after Christmas Day, and it promises the exiles returning from Babylon and from around the world that they will return walking "by brooks of water" (31:9). Upon their return they are likened to a watered garden and blessed with bountiful harvest:

> They shall come and sing aloud on the height of Zion,
>   and they shall be radiant over the goodness of the LORD,
> over the grain, the wine, and the oil,

> and over the young of the flock and the herd;
> their life shall become like a watered garden,
> > and they shall never languish again. (Jer 31:12)

The image of garden is also present in Isaiah 61:10–62:3, which is given by the Revised Common Lectionary for the first Sunday after Christmas Day in year B:

> For as the earth brings forth its shoots,
> > and as a garden causes what is sown in it to spring up,
> so the Lord GOD will cause righteousness and praise
> > to spring up before all the nations. (Isa 61:11)

This verse was also included in the selection from Isaiah that had been read for the third Sunday in Advent in year B. The returned exiles themselves are pictured here as a garden growing fruits of righteousness, even as the earth itself sprouts green growth.

Psalm 147 beginning at verse 12 is given by both lectionaries as the psalm for the second Sunday after Christmas Day. It promises Jerusalem:

> [God] grants peace within your borders;
> > he fills you with the finest of wheat.
> He sends out his command to the earth;
> > his word runs swiftly. (Ps 147:14–15)

The selection of verses in the Revised Common Lectionary continues:

> He gives snow like wool;
> > he scatters frost like ashes.
> He hurls down hail like crumbs—
> > who can stand before his cold?
> He sends out his word, and melts them;
> > he makes his wind blow, and the waters flow. (Ps 147:16–18)

The Roman Catholic Lectionary for the Mass omits this celebration of the seasons of Winter and Spring. But the wintery image aligns well with the climate in many parts of the Northern Hemisphere in the season of Christmas, and the anticipation of Spring is warming. Also, both lectionaries omit verses earlier in this psalm that sing thanksgiving to God for watering the earth and providing food for animals:

> Sing to the LORD with thanksgiving;
> > make melody to our God on the lyre.
> He covers the heavens with clouds,

> prepares rain for the earth,
> makes grass grow on the hills.
> He gives to the animals their food,
> and to the young ravens when they cry. (Ps 147:7–9)

These verses in Psalm 147 that sing of God's care for creatures should be included in our liturgies.

Arthur Walker-Jones finds an emphasis on the "intrinsic worth and voice of creation" characteristic of the fifth book of Psalms (107–150) reaching a "crescendo" in the final six psalms, including Psalm 147.[35] Walker-Jones refers to the expression of "creational justice" in this Psalm. Psalm 147 is remarkable in alternating between expressions of God's care for creation that extends beyond humanity and God's concern for human well-being, justice, and peace. So for instance, these verses (7–9) that speak of God providing water for earth and food for animals are preceded by a statement of justice for the oppressed in society: "The LORD lifts up the downtrodden; he casts the wicked to the ground" (Ps 147:6). And following the feeding of young ravens in verse 9, there is a tacit criticism of using animals for warfare and a call for hoping in God's steadfast love: "His delight is not in the strength of the horse, nor his pleasure in the speed of a runner; but the LORD takes pleasure in those who fear him, in those who hope in his steadfast love" (Ps 147:10–11). "Since the horse was a weapon of war," Walker-Jones suggests, "this could be understood as subverting military claims to divine authorization." Moreover, Walker-Jones points to a balance in the way God's word is spoken at the conclusion of this psalm—speaking both a word of the law to Jacob (verse 19) and, in verse 18 quoted earlier, a word to creation that brings melting snow, winds to blow, and waters that flow.[36]

Psalm 147, as with Psalm 148, can be chanted with or without refrains as provided in multiple psalters, and there are old and new paraphrases available as hymns and songs. One such, by Brenton Brown, Keith Getty, and Stuart Townend, begins by exclaiming, "The universe resounds with praise" to God who "brings the sun and rain" and "calls each star by name."[37] Liturgical resources based on deuterocanonical writings such as Sirach, however, are less accessible especially for those Protestants who do not consider Apocryphal writings to be part of sacred Scripture. Nevertheless, they are still a part of sacred tradition and can be folded into liturgies as we do with other reverent writings. When doing so, it helps congregants to enter into worship with these materials if explanation is given and exposition offered. The season of Christmas presents an opportunity to do so and to pair the wisdom tradition with the New Testament's proclamation of incarnate Logos. Liturgically, one might juxtapose verses from Sirach with proclamation from John in responsive reading. Here is one possibility for scripting such a responsive reading.

Reader: Sirach 24:1–2

Congregation: In the beginning was the Word, and the Word was with God, and the Word was God. He was in the beginning with God. All things came into being through him, and without him not one thing came into being. (John 1:1–3a)

Reader: Sirach 24:3–6

Congregation: What has come into being in him was life, and the life was the light of all people. The light shines in the darkness, and the darkness did not overcome it. (John 1:3b–5)

Reader: Sirach 24:7–11

Congregation: The true light, which enlightens everyone, was coming into the world. He was in the world and the world came into being through him; yet the world did not know him. (John 1:9–10)

Reader: Sirach 24:12–17

Congregation: And the Word became flesh and lived among us, and we have seen his glory, the glory as of a father's only son, full of grace and truth. (John 1:14)

Reader: Sirach 24:19–22

This is a long reading which covers twenty-two verses of Sirach 24, but it can be broken into segments to provide for shorter moments, such as a call to worship or a briefer act of praise. The parade of plants alone at the end of the chapter (Sir 24:12–17, 19–20) invites praise, wonder, and thanksgiving (though difficult for liturgists to pronounce)! If all twenty-two verses of Sirach were to be read in this manner with responses given from the prologue to John, the verses from John can be sung antiphonally perhaps using a lyrical paraphrase. The song "In the Beginning" by Joel Payne,[38] for instance, is energetic, can be arranged for either choir or praise band, and would sound enlivening in this liturgy with each of four verses from the song interspersed with the readings from Sirach.

It is possible as well to integrate the voice from Ephesians which explicitly speaks of God's "wisdom" when proclaiming "the word of truth" about Christ. Here, for instance, to conclude this chapter, is a possible call to worship harmonizing voices from Sirach, John, and Ephesians:

John's voice: In the beginning was the Word, and the Word was with God, and the Word was God. He was in the beginning with God. All things came into being through him, and without him not one thing came into being. (John 1:1–3a)

Sophia's voice:

> Wisdom praises herself,
>   and tells of her glory in the midst of her people.
> In the assembly of the Most High she opens her mouth,
>   and in the presence of his hosts she tells of her glory:
> "I came forth from the mouth of the Most High,
>   and covered the earth like a mist.
> I dwelt in the highest heavens,
>   and traversed the depths of the abyss.
> Over waves of the sea, over all the earth,
>   and over every people and nation I have held sway." (Sir 24:1–6)

John's voice: And the Word became flesh and lived among us, and we have seen his glory, the glory as of a father's only son, full of grace and truth. (John 1:14)

Ephesians' voice: With all wisdom and insight [God] has made known to us the mystery of his will, according to his good pleasure that he set forth in Christ, as a plan for the fullness of time, to gather up all things in him, things in heaven and things on earth." (Eph 1:8b–10)

Chapter 14

Epiphany

God Manifest on Earth

Epiphany means manifestation. In Christian witness it is the manifestation of Jesus born of Mary as the Christ for the world. Earth receives this epiphany. In worship we celebrate and proclaim it. Traditionally, the feast of Epiphany is celebrated as the conclusion of the Christmas season on January 6. It might even be thought of as the finale of Christmas, bringing deeper meaning to our confession of Christ and Christ's divinity. All Christmas season, though, affirms Jesus as the Christ and celebrates both Christ's humanity and Christ's divinity. So it is as well with Epiphany.

Christ's humanity and the mystery of incarnation are often at the forefront of Christmas celebrations. The significance of Christ's incarnation as divine solidarity with all flesh was discussed in the previous chapters. The incarnation does not eclipse but rather reveals God's glory on Earth. Similarly at Epiphany, Christ's divinity is revealed in a way that does not overshadow Earth but rather illumines God's earthly immanence and the divine presence amid our earthly realities.

Each of the four Gospels attests differently to the manifestation of God's presence on Earth in Christ. Each of the Gospels begins differently and witnesses to this epiphany with varying initial stories illustrating God's glory made known in Christ on Earth. For Luke, the birth itself is epiphanic, as the extended birth narrative in Luke makes clear. From the angel's proclamation to Zechariah, through Mary's exclamation of praise, to the angels declaring among shepherds: "Glory to God in the highest and on earth peace. . .! (Luke 2:14)" This is followed in Luke by two other epiphanic stories—that of Simeon and that of Anna recognizing in Jesus the long-awaited Christ.

Matthew's Gospel alone provides the story of magi traveling from around the world, guided by a star, to find Jesus and worship him as Christ. Matthew's story of the magi, while often read throughout Christmas and integrated into

Christmas pageants, is the traditional text for Epiphany read on January 6 or on the Sunday preceding. Both the Revised Common Lectionary and the Roman Catholic Lectionary have this reading for Epiphany, Matthew 2:1–12; they each also provide for parallel readings from Psalm 72, Ephesians 3, and Isaiah 60:1–6.

John's Gospel declares at the outset Christ's divinity as the Word of God and Light of the world, active in the very beginning of the universe with creation itself. John's Gospel alone also provides the story of Jesus's first miracle at the wedding in Cana of Galilee. Turning water into wine, John writes, Jesus ". . . manifested his glory, and his disciples believed in him" (John 2:11 RSV).

Mark's Gospel begins more abruptly without any story of the birth but instead moves immediately to Christ's baptism at the River Jordan and the heavenly voice declaring, "You are my Son, the Beloved" (Mark 1:11). All of these stories are epiphanies, portraying Jesus as Christ and revealing God's glory. All these stories are also earthy, sparking recognition of heavenly glory within earthly life—with Jesus providing the locus and focus for this divine presence on Earth.

The tradition of celebrating Epiphany on January 6 historically predates the celebration of Christ's Nativity on December 25, but by the end of the fourth century both feasts were celebrated.[1] The Eastern churches, however, have continued to place a greater emphasis on Epiphany, often called Theophany (Manifestation of God). Whereas the Western churches that celebrate Epiphany tend to highlight Matthew's story of the visit of the magi, the Eastern churches give prominence to the baptism of Christ. Eastern liturgies on this day involve a blessing of waters that is rich with images of God's manifestation not only as revealed at Christ's baptism but as shown throughout salvation history and in the world of creation.

This chapter explores ecological dimensions of both approaches to Epiphany. After looking at the suggested Gospel reading and psalm for Epiphany in the Roman Catholic and the Revised Common Lectionaries, attention will be given to the Baptism of Christ, our own baptism, and the blessing of the waters. Roman Catholic congregations and Protestant congregations following the calendar of the Revised Common Lectionary celebrate the Baptism of Christ every year on the first Sunday after Epiphany.

MAGI, JUST RULE, AND CREATION'S FLOURISHING

Magi were scientists of their time, attending to natural phenomena. In particular, the magi traveling to pay homage to Jesus were studying astronomic occurrence. They have been described by some as astrologers, but there was no difference at the time between astrology and astronomy. They are presented in Matthew's Gospel with little other detail. Nothing is said about their number or their countries of origin other than that they were from the East. As foreigners, though, they represent the rest of the world coming to acknowledge the special presence of this child whom they name as both messiah and king. In their visit from parts unknown, guided by the light in the sky, heaven, and earth can be seen as participating in this witness.

The word "magi" forms the root of the word "magician," and indeed there was an element of mystery entailed in their arts and science even in the ancient world. At the same time, though, their scholarly knowledge and wisdom were recognized. Philo, a Jewish philosopher who lived at the same time as Jesus's birth, describes the magi as a learned group "investigating the works of nature for the purpose of becoming acquainted with the truth."[2]

In interpreting the witness of the magi in Matthew 2 as epiphany for our time, we might ask how the "works of nature" today demonstrate God's sovereignty or attest to—God's glory. How do earth and sky reveal the presence of Christ? Conversely, how does the presence of God, acclaimed now in Christ, manifest the holy in the midst of our earthly and natural realities?

While the Magi represent "wise" ones in Matthew's telling of the story, a long tradition also refers to these visitors as "kings." The kings named in this story, however, are simply two—the child Jesus and the regent Herod. These are contrasted, with Herod portrayed ignobly as frightened by the prospect of a rival king and villainously responding in anger by slaughtering all male children under two years of age within the vicinity of Bethlehem. The lectionary for Epiphany deepens the contrast between just and unjust rule by suggesting Psalm 72 be read on this occasion along with the reading from Matthew. Psalm 72 portrays a just king whose justice encompasses the natural world and the poor of the land.[3]

Psalm 72 is recommended in both the Roman Catholic Lectionary (Ps 72:1–2, 7–8, 10–11, 12–13) and the Revised Common Lectionary (Ps 72:1–7, 10–14) for use in worship on Epiphany. Ecological images and images of royal dominion are interwoven in this psalm which offers prayer for God's justice on Earth to be established through right rule. Social justice and environmental health are interconnected in this vision, with a productive land lending prosperity to the people. God's own justice and righteousness is the source of these virtues for the earthly ruler as portrayed in the psalm. "Psalm 72 pictures the king responding to God's gifts of judgment and righteousness by displaying the same attributes to his people," explains Anne Gardner, and "mountains and hills in turn are said to bring peace and righteousness."[4] Earth it would seem responds to justice with its own flourishing as well as rewards justice with increased productivity. An expressed concern in this psalm is that the right rule benefit the poor in particular,[5] and the prayer of the psalm is that "justice will fill both society and nature (vs. 3)."[6]

Presented here are both the promise of ecological health and the apparent subjection of natural processes to human purposes and power represented in the ruler. As elsewhere in Scripture with regard to the theme of dominion, there is ambiguity with this interweaving. In his *Green Psalter*, Arthur Walker-Jones notes that the image of the just ruler in Psalm 72 has been used by some environmentally concerned interpreters of Scripture as a point of comparison with Genesis 1:26–27 to advocate for an ecologically beneficent exercise of human dominion within creation, but even such an ecologically beneficent dominion carries the burden of assuming human separation from and power over nature.[7] Norman Gottwald earlier voiced a related suspicion concerning political justice and the imperialist pretensions apparent in this psalm "that the Israelite king by force of arms will impose justice in the earth."[8] Suspicion of centralized political power is important as a liberationist hermeneutical principle and as a check against the abuse of power—whether power over nature or power over peoples. Still, Psalm 72 is remarkable for the degree to which just rule is portrayed, especially justice toward the poor, and the natural world is seen to participate in this justice and to flourish accordingly.

The psalm begins as follows:

> Give the king your justice, O God,
>   and your righteousness to a king's son.
> May he judge your people with righteousness
>   and your poor with justice.
> May the mountains yield prosperity for the people,
>   and the hills, in righteousness.
> May he defend the cause of the poor of the people,
>   give deliverance to the needy,
>   and crush the oppressor.
>
> May he live while the sun endures,
>   and as long as the moon, throughout all generations.
> May he be like rain that falls on the mown grass,
>   like showers that water the earth.
> In his days may righteousness flourish
>   and peace abound, until the moon is no more.
>
> May he have dominion from sea to sea,
>   and from the River to the ends of the earth.
> May his foes[9] bow down before him,
>   and his enemies lick the dust.
> May the kings of Tarshish and of the isles
>   render him tribute,

> may the kings of Sheba and Seba
>   bring gifts.
> May all kings fall down before him,
>   all nations give him service.
>
> For he delivers the needy when they call,
>   the poor and those who have no helper.
> He has pity on the weak and the needy,
>   and saves the lives of the needy.
> From oppression and violence he redeems their life;
>   and precious is their blood in his sight.
>
> Long may he live!
>   May gold of Sheba be given to him. (Ps 72:1–15a)

And the psalm continues with a picture of environmental health contributing toward human prosperity.

> May there be abundance of grain in the land;
>   may it wave on the tops of the mountains;
>   may its fruit be like Lebanon;
> and may people blossom in the cities
>   like the grass of the field. (Ps 72:16)

The final verses of this psalm conclude this entire section of psalms with a doxology recognizing that God alone is responsible for establishing such justice on Earth.

> Blessed by the LORD, the God of Israel,
>   who alone does wondrous things.
> Blessed by his glorious name forever;
>   may his glory fill the whole earth.
>   Amen and Amen.
> The prayers of David son of Jesse are ended. (Ps 72:18–20)

    Marvin Tate enumerates three corollary areas of petition in this psalm constituting a prayer for shalom: justice for the poor, life for the land, and the hope that this power for justice and life might extend to the ends of the earth. "When the king gives the life of God's justice to the people, then the blessings of fertile land and far-reaching power follow," Tate explains. "All these themes add up to the biblical concept of *shalom* ('peace/well-being')," he summarizes concluding, "*Shalom* is the salvation which embraces all creation."[10]

    In a similar vein, Norman Habel interprets Psalm 72 as a royal psalm representing the category of "land as the source of wealth" in his typology of six biblical land ideologies. He notes this psalm's universalism, the linkage between the land's health and human well-being, and the representative nature of the earthly monarch with God's own just reign. "Through the monarch," he writes, "the blessings of fertility, wealth, and peace are to be mediated to the land and the people (Ps 72:3, 5–7, 15–17)."[11] Psalm 72 envisions all kings and all nations rendering tribute to the just ruler, with the land participating in that universal justice.

The universalist imagery in Psalm 72 provides part of the rhetorical fit with the Epiphany story of visitors from the East paying homage to the one born king of the Jews (Matt 2:2). When read in conjunction with the second chapter of Matthew at the time of Epiphany, Psalm 72 brings especial salience to two theological points pertaining to the recognition of the child Jesus as Christ and Sovereign. The first is to notice that the universality of this confession of Christ might include the ecological health and life of the land that grounds all human societies. The star points not just heavenward but earthward. The second point, as the story unfolds, is to notice the contrast between the just ruler of Psalm 72 and Herod's unjust reign vilified in the Gospel with the slaughter of the innocents in Bethlehem. This counterpoint of Herod's villainy serves to highlight the hope pronounced in Psalm 72 for the Hebrew people's well-being, the land's health, and the expansion of justice to all nations and throughout the earth. That hope, in this story, rests on this child. This is our epiphany.

BAPTISM OF CHRIST, OUR BAPTISM, AND THE BLESSING OF WATERS

Orthodox Theophany

While the visit of the magi is the central text for Epiphany in the Western churches, the baptism of Christ is central for the Eastern churches on the feast of Epiphany on January 6, often called Theophany. For these churches (e.g., Greek Orthodox, Russian Orthodox, Armenian Apostolic), January 6 is an even more important festive occasion than the Nativity on December 25 and is the occasion for celebrating the whole story of Jesus's birth, the visit of magi, and Jesus's baptism. Recounting Christ's baptism, these churches engage in a liturgical blessing of the waters. The liturgies for the blessing of the waters can be elaborate and invoke all the stories of epiphany from the Gospels. Most notable in some of these liturgies is the degree to which the natural world is pictured participating in epiphany—receiving and celebrating the salvation being made known in Jesus Christ for all of creation.

In fact, remembering the heavens opening and the Holy Spirit descending like a dove, the whole service portrays the intermingling of heaven and earth in Jesus's baptism. The waters, both of Christ's baptism and of ours, provide the symbolic locus for this joining of heaven and earth. The spiritual pervades the natural. "Today," proclaims the Orthodox liturgy of St. Sophronius, "the whole universe is refreshed with mystical streams." "Today," the liturgy continues, "the heavenly dwellers rejoice with those of the earth, and the dwellers of the earth with those of heaven."[12] Here is a longer quotation of the same liturgy demonstrating this rich intermingling imagery of the natural and the numinous:

> Today the grace of the Holy Spirit, in the form of a dove, comes down upon the waters.
>
> Today there shines the Sun that never sets, and the world is sparkling with the light of the Lord.
>
> Today the moon shines upon the world with the brightness of its rays.
>
> Today the glittering stars adorn the universe with the radiance of their twinkling.
>
> Today the clouds from heaven shed upon [hu]mankind a shower of justice.
>
> Today the Uncreated One willingly permits the hands of his creature to be laid upon Him.
>
> Today the Prophet and Forerunner comes close to the Master, and he stands in awe, a witness of the condescension of God toward us.
>
> Today through the presence of the Lord the waters of the Jordan River are changed into remedies.
>
> Today the whole universe is refreshed with mystical streams.
>
> Today the sins of [hu]mankind are blotted out by the waters of the Jordan River.
>
> Today paradise has been opened to [hu]mankind, and the Sun of righteousness has shone upon us.
>
> Today the bitter water, as once with Moses and the people of Israel, is changed into sweetness by the presence of the Lord.
>
> Today we are delivered from the ancient mourning, and, like a new Israel, we are saved.

Today we escape from darkness and, through the light of the knowledge of God, we are illumined.

Today the darkness of the world vanishes with the appearing of our God.
Today the whole creation is brightened from on high.

Today errors are canceled, and a way of salvation is prepared for us by the coming of the Lord.

Today the heavenly dwellers rejoice with those of the earth, and the dwellers of the earth with those of heaven.

Today the noble and eloquent assembly rejoices, the assembly of those of the true faith.

Today the Lord comes to be baptized, so that [hu]mankind may be lifted up.

Today the One who never has to bow inclines Himself before his servant so that He may set us free from bondage.

Today we have acquired the kingdom of heaven: for the Lord's kingdom shall have no end.

Today the land and the sea divide between them the joy of the world, and the world is filled with gladness.

The waters saw You, O God, the waters saw You and shuddered.

The Jordan River turns back its course as it beholds the fire of the Godhead coming down upon it and entering it in the flesh.

The Jordan River turns back its course as it beholds the Holy Spirit descending in the form of a dove, and hovering above it.

The Jordan River turns back its course as it beholds the Invisible made visible, the Creator existing in the flesh, and the Master in the form of a servant.

The Jordan River turns back its course, and the mountains shout with glee as they behold God in the flesh.

And the clouds give voice, and are filled with awe by the One who is coming, Light of light, true God of true God, for today in the Jordan River they saw the triumph of the Master. They saw Him drown in the Jordan River the death of sin, the thorn of error, and the bond of Hades, and bestow upon the world the baptism of salvation.

So also am I, your unworthy and sinful servant, encompassed by fear as I proclaim your great wonders; and I cry out reverently to You, and say:

The priest then says in a louder voice:

GREAT ARE YOU, O LORD, AND MARVELOUS ARE YOUR WORKS AND NO WORD IS SUFFICIENT TO PRAISE YOUR MARVELS.

GREAT ARE YOU, O LORD, AND MARVELOUS ARE YOUR WORKS AND NO WORD IS SUFFICIENT TO PRAISE YOUR MARVELS.

GREAT ARE YOU, O LORD, AND MARVELOUS ARE YOUR WORKS AND NO WORD IS SUFFICIENT TO PRAISE YOUR MARVELS.

For by your divine will You brought forth all things out of nothing into being; by your might you control all creation; by your providence You govern the universe, O You who made the whole world out of four elements and crowned the cycle of the year with four seasons.

The immaterial powers tremble before You;

the sun praises You;

the moon glorifies You;

the stars bless You;

the light obeys You;

the tempests tremble,

and the springs adore You.

You have spread out the heavens like a tent-cloth;

You fixed the earth upon the waters;

You have walled about the sea with sand;

You let the air flow about for our breathing.[13]

Protestant and Catholic churches might receive inspiration from this rich imagery in the Orthodox tradition and let it inform liturgies for the Day of Epiphany, for the first Sunday following Epiphany when Christ's baptism is commemorated, and for baptisms generally.

Roman Catholic and Protestant churches often include blessings over the water at the time of a baptism, typically recounting biblical stories in which water was a vehicle of salvation or redemption: primordial creation dividing the waters, rescuing all flesh from the flood with Noah, exodus from slavery through the parting of the waters, and Christ's own baptism from John in the Jordan.[14] Natural images are also frequently included, such as celebrating our own birth from the waters of the womb and thanksgiving for the continued watering of rains upon the earth. To these, though, might be added Orthodox-inspired images where nature and natural entities receive the sanctifying presence, participate in the baptismal blessing, and praise God together with both human and celestial voices.

Gordon Lathrop's *Holy Ground* and the Hole in the Sky

Lutheran liturgical theologian, Gordon Lathrop, similarly advocates a diversity and depth of images from Earth and indeed from the cosmos be incorporated into our baptismal prayers. These images allow us to conceptualize our natural world within God's saving activity and see ourselves included within that world of God's epiphany. He suggests:

- As the community gives thanks and beseeches God over the water, consider shaping the prayer so that the vastness of the universe and both the marginality and the preciousness of our watery planet are recalled.[15]

- As they [baptismal candidates] learn these patterns of prayer, join with them in praying for other species of life than merely our own, in commending to God the diversity and well-being of these species, in thanking God for their existence. Perhaps even mountains and rivers and seas—even solar systems and galaxies—could enter our prayers. Baptism must not be about saving us from this company, but with this company. Yet learn together again the prayer for needy humanity as well.[16]

Lathrop maps a "liturgical cosmology" in his book *Holy Ground* that begins not just with the ground but with the waters of Christ's baptism and with the hole in the heavens through which the Voice and the Dove descend.

Drawing heavily on the Gospel of Mark's depiction of the scene, Lathrop places us with Christ in the waters of Jordan, at the outset of this "liturgical cosmology." Entering the image of the tearing of the heavens at Jesus's baptism, Lathrop finds in this hole in the sky a generative metaphor for opening our understanding at several levels. An epiphany of the divine in Christ, it is also an indicator of our incorporation and participation in this divine presence in our own baptism. Moreover, it provides a new orientation for us to God's presence throughout creation. This new orientation to the world, entered into at baptism, is renewed in the ongoing liturgical life of communities of faith as we rehearse that which we receive in the hearing of the gospel. Reading Mark's Gospel, Lathrop explains:

> . . . the hearers of the Gospel book, along with Jesus, "see" the heavens torn (1:10), and the "son of God" is not the sphere of the sky but is among us, sharing our death (1:1, 15:39), becoming our life.
>
> A hole in the heavens, a tear in the perfect fabric of the perfect sphere, then the Spirit descending like a dove at the end of the flood and a voice coming from the heaven: there at the outset of the book (1:9–11), is an image of the Markan cosmology.[17]

As the events in Mark's Gospel unfold toward the cross and the empty tomb, the meaning of this baptism—both Christ's baptism and ours who are baptized into Christ—becomes increasingly apparent to the worshiping community. Lathrop continues:

> The Gospel book itself read in the assembly, is the resurrection appearance. The whole assembly comes into the hidden meaning of the story, the now manifest, risen identity of the Crucified One. The whole assembly becomes the locus for seeing the torn heavens, receiving the Spirit, hearing the voice of God, being reoriented in the world.[18]

The reorientation in the world, according to Lathrop, is our entering into an entire cosmological perspective exemplified by this story—the opening of the heavens, the inbreaking of the voice, and the descending of the Spirit with Christ at the waters of Jordan. Read and remembered within the entire biblical narrative of Christ's life, death, and resurrection, Christ's baptism displays an alternative cosmology to established order.

This alternative cosmology is characterized by God's care for all of God's creatures, including the most marginalized in human societies. There is a rupturing of established patterns and hierarchical constructions that we now receive and enter through the hearing of the Word and the liturgical enacting of that reception. Lathrop generalizes this reversal of cosmologies, epitomized by the baptism of Christ, to other biblical accounts and images. The biblical presentation offers the opportunity for such a reversal of hierarchical expectations to the worshiping community. That listening and worshiping community, then, empowered by the Holy Spirit, has the opportunity for further redefining our own identity and our view of the world. Lathrop explains:

What can be found, widespread in the cosmic accounts of the Bible, is the critique and reversal in these accounts, the hole in any perfect cosmic sphere. For the Scriptures, none of the various candidates for a central cosmic principle can be adequate—not the perfect sphere, not the ruling planets, not the conquering god, not the dominant role of humanity, not the end of time, not the Logos, not the Son of Man, not the tree of life. But the cosmologies suggested by all of these can be received if they are turned, if their terms are reused to speak of the living God, if the community encounters that living God through all the gaping holes in their cosmological fabric. For Christians, that encounter is with the triune God, with the Spirit and Voice presenting Jesus through the tear in the heavens, with the day of the resurrection as an eighth day, with the Crucified One as Logos or as tree of life or as Son of Man, holding all things into mercy, known and tasted in the power of the Spirit. For Christians, that encounter with the triune God takes a communal, liturgical form.[19]

The fact that the biblical story is read in the liturgical assembly, rehearsed and enacted communally through liturgical expression, is the key for understanding the broader import connecting our life together as church with our participation in Christ and cosmos.

Psalm 29, often read on the Sunday celebrating Christ's baptism, might be viewed this way as well. Psalm 29 is considered to be a presentation of a nature theophany, or more precisely a storm theophany. "Biblical theophanies have long been acclaimed as bold representations of God's revelation through creation or the forces of nature," Norman Habel and Geraldine Avent explain, and elaborate: "God is said to use everything from a small spring to a massive mountain, from a human form to a thunderstorm, to mask—yet reveal—the divine self."[20] The rhetorical coincidence between Psalm 29 and the theophany at Christ's baptism is the resounding of God's voice. "The voice of the LORD is over the waters; the God of glory thunders, the LORD, over mighty waters" (Ps 29:3). In Psalm 29, God's voice sounds seven times in conjunction with different stormy phenomena; in addition to the waters, God's voice breaks cedars, flashes fire, shakes wilderness, and causes oaks to whirl.

Biblical commentators have noticed the affinity of this psalm with other ancient literature extolling a Canaanite storm god.[21] God seems to be present behind the violence of nature and is presented as frighteningly powerful. Lathrop notices, though, that two elements "reorient the meaning of the psalm" and alter the cosmological perspective. These are the name of YHWH and the final verse which is a prayer for peace and for the people's empowerment: "May the LORD give strength to his people: May the LORD bless his people with peace!" (Ps 29:11).[22] We see a cosmological turning of emphasis from exalting divine dominance to celebrating empowerment and a turn from fearing the violence in nature to propounding peace.

Finally, another liturgical suggestion pertaining to baptism advocated by Lathrop is to enrich the diversity of our language with reference to gender. He writes:

> As these candidates are actually baptized, use words that help us all to understand that God is a flowing, communal reality, holding all things in mercy, under the hole in the heavens, not a patriarchal monarchy, with the authority inherited along a masculine line of succession. While the words from Matthew 28:19 will be used in most of the churches, they may be introduced and surrounded by other words that expand and deepen the understanding of the Trinity and connect this linguistic usage to Jesus' baptism in the Jordan and to the revelation there of the sphere-breaking mercy that is saving all things.[23]

The suggested liturgy at the conclusion of this chapter attempts to do as Lathrop is asking. Though it recites language from Matthew 28:19 as water is applied at baptism, that liturgical moment is surrounded by other words and biblical images that offer an expansive understanding of God—with regard to both gender and God's salvific work in the cosmos and on earth.

WATER AND WISDOM

Roman Catholic theologian, Linda Gibler, provides a deeply reflective integration of ecology, scientific cosmology, and baptism in her book *From the Beginning to Baptism: Scientific and Sacred Stories of Water, Oil, and Fire*. She looks in turn at water, oil, and fire—each of which is used for baptism in Roman Catholic celebrations—attending to their history in the universe, in natural history, and in sacred story. Water is celebrated with reference to the presence of hydrogen in the universe, the occurrence of water in the solar system, the formation of a watery earth, the production of plants, the birthing of animals, and the continuous aqueous composition of human bodies. Water is remembered in connection to the biblical stories of creation, the primordial flood, the exodus, the crossing of Jordan, the baptism of Jesus, the wedding at Cana, and the water and blood flowing from Christ at Calvary. Gibler composes this prayer which might be offered at a baptismal font, titled simply "A Blessing of Water."[24]

> Blessed are you, Ever-Present God,
>   Creator of the Universe,
>   Through you we have the gift of water for baptism.
>
> Water that formed in the remnants of ancient stars
>   and brought our Day Star to birth.

> Water that cooled the nascent Earth.
>> Rising from deep within and carried by comets,
>> your water drenched our young planet
>> and covered it in oceans.
> Water that birthed the first life on Earth
>> and each life thereafter
>> Water that fills and flows within every living being.
>
> This water of Stars, Earth, and Life you give
>> to bring us into fullness of life in you.
> This is the water over which your Spirit hovered at the Beginning,
>> the water that cleansed the Earth in Noah's day,
>> through which the Israelites passed unharmed in Moses's day,
>> and in which Jesus was baptized.
>
> This is the water Jesus calmed,
>> the water he turned into wine in Cana,
>> and that flowed from his side on Calvary.
>
> Ever-Present God, your Spirit continuously moves within water.
>> Enliven the water in this font and in us
>> so we may remember that all water flows
>> with your holy presence.
>
> Blessed are you, Ever-Present God,
>> Creator of the Universe,
>> Through you we have the gift of water for baptism.

Finally, note should be made of the Epistle reading for the Day of Epiphany on January 6. Wisdom and creation are both invoked along with "the unfathomable riches of Christ" in the third chapter of Ephesians, which is suggested as the Epistle reading for the Day of Epiphany in the Revised Common Lectionary.[25] The text reads:

> . . .this grace was given, to preach to the Gentiles the unfathomable riches of Christ, and to bring to light what is the administration of the mystery which for ages has been hidden in God who created all things; so that the manifold wisdom of God might now be made known through the church to the rulers and the authorities in the heavenly places. (Eph 3:8b–10 *New American Standard Bible*)[26]

Wisdom, *sophia* in Greek or *chochma* in Hebrew, as discussed in previous chapters, is often personified in the wisdom literature of the Old Testament and portrayed as speaking with a woman's voice. *Sophia*, God's Wisdom, is active in creation and throughout creation from the beginning of time. She is associated both with God's own Spirit, *ruach* (also a word of feminine gender), which blew over the primordial waters at creation's beginning (Gen 1:2), and with God's *logos*, the Word "in the beginning," identified with God, incarnate in Christ, and through whom all things were made (John 1:1–3, 14).

The confluence of these ideas in the third chapter of Ephesians—Christ, Creation, and *Sophia*—provides an invitation at the time of Epiphany to incorporate some of the images of creation from the wisdom tradition into our liturgies and preaching at this time. The following liturgy for baptism attempts to do this, drawing on a diversity of images from Scripture with regard to both gender and creation. This chapter concludes with this liturgical blessing, which might mark the beginning of a child's epiphanic journey with Christ on this watery world.

Epiclesis:

> God, as your Spirit moved over the waters at creation,
>   birthing and sustaining all life on earth,
> And as your Spirit moved like a dove over the Jordan River
>   alighting on Jesus your Beloved,
> so have her now move over this water
>   and rest her sacred presence on us
>   gathered across generations.

Thanksgiving over the water (Prov 8:23–24, 27–29a *Inclusive Bible*):

From the beginning, God's Wisdom raises her voice: AuQ 1

> "I have been from everlasting,
> in the beginning, before the world began.
> Before the deep seas, I was brought forth,
> before there were fountains or springs of water. . .
>
> I was there when the Almighty created the heavens,
> and set the horizon just above the ocean,
> set the clouds in the sky,
> and established the springs of the deep,
> gave the seas their boundaries
> and set their limits at the shoreline."

> We now give thanks to you, O God, for the gift of water,
>   for all water and for this water,
>   for the fecundity of Earth giving birth to life,
>   for the waters of our birth and the waters that sustain us daily,

for Christ before us and like us, nurtured in the waters of the womb,
and for this child and for these waters which we now apply.

As you've blessed us with water through the ages,
    and as you've blessed us with life and birth,
    so pour out your blessing on us now gathered here with this water
    that our actions might reflect your generativity and love
    for this child, for your whole church, and for all creation.
Amen.

Words at baptism:

Name, I baptize you in the name of the Father, and of the Son, and of the Holy Spirit, One God, Mother of us all.[27]

Blessing of the child at baptism (based on Deut 32:11):

Name, as God like a Mother Eagle watches over her young,
so may She guard you in love and guide you all your days,
that nested in the fellowship of the church,
you may grow as a disciple of Jesus Christ for the world.
Amen.

Postlude

Conclusion

And so we come full circle. We hear the same words and the same voice at Christ's baptism that we hear at Christ's transfiguration: "This is my Beloved." Baptized, Christ proceeds from the River Jordan into the wilderness to be with the wild beasts (Mark 1:13). We journeyed with him there at the beginning of Lent, where we began this book—with Transfiguration Sunday, Ash Wednesday, and the first Sunday in Lent. This has been an earthly journey with Christ, God becoming an earthling among us. Creation responds with each step and each moment of Christ's journey. Our worship during these liturgical seasons steps with Christ and within creation.

We have seen in Christ's transfiguration the promise of a transfigured creation, and we have glimpsed the deeper reality of creation radiant with the glory of God. As human creatures, we participate in this process of transfiguration in Christ. And as worshiping creatures, we find ourselves awesomely privileged to represent all creation in eucharistic prayer and praise.

In Lent we have heard a call both to repent and to celebrate. We have celebrated our mortal nature—a nature Jesus has shared with us. We are flesh and blood. With Jesus we breathe the same air that is still circulating around us and that is recycled by plants. We drink the same water that constituted Christ's very body as well as ours. We live on this earth, and we die on this earth. The reality of death—and the universality of death—reminds us how rich a blessing biological life is! We celebrate and claim this mortal life as a gift from God.

But if ever a generation is called to repent, ours is. Within living memory we have harnessed unprecedented power with destructive results. This generation sees the results of climate change, global warming, and rising sea levels from years of consumption of fossil fuels and deforestation. We see an exponential increase in the extinction of other species due to habitat destruction and environmental pollution. Our use of petrochemicals and our nuclear technology has produced elements and substances never before known and for which there is no ecological home. The widening economic gap between the haves and the have-nots disproportionately burdens the poor with adverse environmental effects, food insecurity, and vulnerability to disease without adequate health care. Our nations continue to wage war and to kill. During Lent and at all times, we are called to turn toward peace between peoples, justice for all humanity, and ecological sustainability throughout the ecosphere. We are called to strive for the dignity due all people created in God's likeness and for the well-being and flourishing of all species created in God's love.

Our Lenten journey has taken us with Jesus into Jerusalem, as he rode with the cooperation of an untamed and unbroken beast of burden. We welcomed Jesus as royalty by waiving tree branches and chanting Hosanna from Psalm 118. Our shouts of Hosanna echoed with the voices of those before us—not only those who were in Jerusalem with Jesus on that very day but also with generations of others who have waived branches and chanted Hosanna in Sukkot prayers for restoring rains and productive harvest. Earth received these saving rains, as Earth received this Savior riding.

On Maundy Thursday, at the last supper with Jesus, we hear him say as he breaks bread, "This is my body." In hearing these words, we realize that this is not the last but rather every communion meal—and indeed every meal shared and eaten. We continue to break bread and to repeat those words, "This is my body." The body is Christ's flesh on the cross, yes, and it is also the body of Christ—ourselves as Christ's church. And it is every morsel of wheat, every drop of rain, and every ounce of soil in that wheat, and every creature on Earth, and even Earth itself. "This is my body."

On Good Friday, we witnessed the culmination of Christ's complete identification with earthly flesh. Christ died. Earth itself quaked in deep sympathy, as life and death shook at its core. At the same time, we confess, we saw the principalities and powers that are inimical to life in God's creation humbled, even defeated, through Christ's death. As the earth held lifeless Christ's mortal body, it also held in waiting the promise for Christ's resurrection and the renewal of creation.

We watched from creation's primordial beginnings through the Easter vigil to behold Earth convulsing with new life and Christ's tomb emptying. We peer into that tomb with the first women to witness the depth of creation's glory in giving birth to resurrection. We sing in ancient verse the *Exsultet*:

> *Rejoice, O earth, in shining splendor...*
> *This is the night truly blessed when heaven is wedded to earth,*
> *and all creation is reconciled with God...*

May the Morning Star which never sets find this flame still burning:
Christ, that Morning Star, who came back from the dead,
and shed peaceful light on all creation.[1]

We watched Christ ascend to God's right hand in order to fill and fulfill all creation. With Martin Luther we confessed, "the right hand of God is everywhere."[2]

On Pentecost, we celebrated the church being energized and gifted by the same Spirit of God that blew at the very beginning of creation—and the same Spirit of God that continues to breathe through all life. We celebrated our spirituality as circulating within the spirituality of everything that respirates, all animals and plants. Everything that has the breath of life shares in God's Spirit and in God's praise.

On Trinity Sunday we celebrated the interrelatedness of the three persons of the Trinity in creation. Not just the First Person is the Creator, as the creed begins, but the Second and Third Persons as well. Christ is the Word through whom all things were made. The Spirit is the wind that blew at creation's beginning and who continues to renew the face of the earth.

We entered Advent with the messianic longing that "the earth will be full of the knowledge of the LORD as the waters cover the sea" (Isa 11:9b). We heard the birth of John the Baptist foretold as one who would "turn the hearts of the fathers to the children," and we heard his birth announced as one who would "guide our feet into the way of peace" (Luke 1:79b). From the waters of the Jordan River and from across the ages, we heard him calling us to repent and to prepare. Even still from yet another river, he calls us to turn to the children!

We heard the birth of Jesus foretold, his own mother declaring that he would scatter the proud and lift up the lowly. We heard his birth announced as "God with Us" (Matt 1:23b), and we came to hear of him as the very Word uttered at creation and resounding throughout the cosmos. We regarded him in earthly flesh, like each of ours, born amid animals of earthly flesh, and we worshiped God among us.

Our journey ends and begins with the Epiphany of this Incarnate One as the Anointed One and, indeed, as the Divine One. The magi, scholars of natural phenomena, saw the signs and bore witness. John the Baptist recognized Jesus as Christ at the waters, while the sky itself openly declared it. In Cana of Galilee, as even today when the faithful assemble in worship, water and wine bear witness to God's abiding earthly presence and to our earthly hope in Christ.

Notes

INTRODUCTION

1 World Council of Churches, "Season of Creation," https://www.oikoumene.org/node/6282 (accessed April 28, 2021); see also U.S. Conference of Catholic Bishops, "The Season of Creation," https://www.usccb.org/issues-and-action/human-life-and-dignity/environment/upload/WDPCC-Bulletin-Insert.pdf; Anglican Communion Environmental Network; and https://seasonofcreation.org/about/ (accessed April 28, 2021).

2 *The Book of Common Prayer and Administration of the Sacraments and Other Rites and Ceremonies of the Church . . . According to the use of The Episcopal Church* (The Church Hymnal Corporation and The Seabury Press, 1979); Presbyterian Church (USA), *Book of Common Worship* (Louisville, KY: Westminster John Knox, [1993] 2018); *Evangelical Lutheran Worship: Leaders Desk Edition* (Minneapolis, MN: Augsburg Fortress, 2008); *The United Methodist Book of Worship* (Nashville, TN: The United Methodist Publishing House, 1993).

CHAPTER 1

1 Bonaventure, *Sermon I for the Second Sunday of Lent* (IX, 218), quoted by Zachary Hayes in *The Gift of Being: A Theology of Creation* (Collegeville, MN: Liturgical Press), 106–107.

2 Pierre Teilhard de Chardin, *Hymn of the Universe* (New York: Harper & Row, 1961), 24. https://archive.org/details/HymnOfTheUniverse (accessed March 9, 2018).

3 Ibid., 28.

4 Baptist theologian Mark S. Medley examines *theosis* in the writings of four Baptist theologians, including Douglas Harink's interpretation of 2 Peter, and concludes concerning transfiguration:

Significant attention to the transfiguration (as well as ascension) by Baptist theologians has the possibilities of leading to a more robust incarnational Christology. Also, attention to the transfiguration of Jesus can possibly give a greater and fuller accent to the apocalyptic nature of God's gospel in christological construction. Lastly, engaging the transfiguration of Jesus can facilitate a greater dialogue with the Christology of the patristic era in general and the Eastern tradition in particular.

"Participation in God: The Appropriation of Theosis by Contemporary Baptist Theologians," chapter 8 in *Theosis: Deification in Christian Theology*, vol. 2, edited by Vladimir Kharlamov (Eugene, OR: Pickwick, 2011), 205–246, 238.

5 Douglas Harink, *1 & 2 Peter, Brazos Theological Commentary on the Bible* (Grand Rapids, MI: Brazos, 2009), 155.

6 John Chryssavgis, "The World of the Icon and Creation: An Orthodox Perspective on Ecology and Pneumatology," in *Christianity and Ecology: Seeking the Well-Being of Earth and Humans*, edited by Dieter T. Hessel and Rosemary Radford Ruether (Cambridge, MA: Harvard University Center for the Study of World Religions and Harvard University Press, 2000), 87, citing Psalm 19 (18).

7 Ibid., 86.

8 The apocalyptic scenario in 2 Peter will be discussed more fully in the chapter on Advent.

9 K. M. George, "Towards a Eucharistic Ecology," in *Justice, Peace and the Integrity of Creation: Insights from Orthodoxy*, edited by Gennadios Limouris (Geneva: WCC, 1990), 45–55, 52.

10 Matthew Fox, *The Coming of the Cosmic Christ* (San Francisco, CA: Harper & Row, 1988), 102.

11 Ibid., 103, quoting Nicolas Berdyaev, "Salvation and Creativity: Two Understandings of Christianity," chapter 3 in *Western Spirituality: Historical Roots, Ecumenical Routes*, edited by Matthew Fox (Santa Fe, NM: Bear & Co., 1981), 115–139, 123.

12 Stephen Finlan and Vladimir Kharlamov, eds., *Theosis: Deification in Christian Theology* (Eugene, OR: Pickwick, 2006), 7–8.

13 Hjalmar Torp, "Preface," in *The Uncreated Light: An Iconographical Study of the Transfiguration in the Eastern Church*, by Solrunn Nes (Grand Rapids, MI: Eerdmans, 2007), xvii, referring to Gregory Palamas and the Hesychast movement.

14 Finlan and Kharlamov, 7.

15 Zizioulas, Metropolitan John of Pergamon, "Man the Priest of Creation: A Response to the Ecological Problem," chapter 10 in *Living Orthodoxy in the Modern World: Orthodox Christianity and Society*, edited by Andrew Walker and Costa Carras (Crestwood, NY: St. Vladimir's Seminary Press, 2000), 183.

16 Leontius of Cyprus, *Apologetic Sermon 3, On the Holy Icons* (Migne, J. P., *Patrologia Graeca*, PG 93.1604ab), quoted by Chryssavgis, "The World of the Icon and Creation," 86; also quoted by Archimandrite Kallistos Ware, "The Value of the Material Creation," *Sobornost*, 6, no. 3 (1971): 154–165, 156–157, quoted by Stanley S. Harakas, "The Integrity of Creation: Ethical Issues," in *Justice, Peace and the Integrity of Creation: Insights from Orthodoxy*, edited by Limouris, 75; see also

The Orthodox Fellowship of the Transfiguration, http://www.orth-transfiguration.org/resources/library/writings-of-the-saints/st-leontios-cyprus-556-634/ (accessed March 21, 2018).

17 John Zizioulas, "Priest of Creation," chapter 24 in *Environmental Stewardship: Critical Perspectives—Past and Present*, edited by R. J. Berry (New York: T & T Clark, 2006), 278.

18 George, "Towards a Eucharistic Ecology," 48–49.

19 Ibid., 53.

20 See Douglas Harink, *1 & 2 Peter*, 140–141.

21 George, "Towards a Eucharistic Ecology," 50.

22 Ibid., 46.

23 Harakas, "The Integrity of Creation: Ethical Issues," 72.

24 Metropolitan Tryphon (Turkestanov), *Ikos* 3 from "An Akathist in Praise of God's Creation," in SYNDESMOS, The World Fellowship of Orthodox Youth, *Orthodoxy and Ecology Resource Book*, Annex 1, *Orthodox Services for the Creation* (Bialystok, Poland: Orthdruk Orthodox Printing House, 1996), 19–25, 21, adapted for responsive reading. See also Greek Orthodox Archdiocese of America, https://www.goarch.org/chapel/texts/-/asset_publisher/ulcNzWPdScz6/content/an-akathist-in-praise-of-god-s-creati-2/ (accessed January 11, 2019). See also Eastern Orthodox Logos: Greek Orthodox website and web radio, posted on October 22, 2013 by Eleftherios Nikolaou, "Prayers: An Akathist in Praise of God's Creation," Metropolitan Tryphon (Turkestanov), 1934, https://orthodoxlogos5.wordpress.com/2013/10/22/prayers-an-akathist-in-praise-of-gods-creation/ (accessed January 15, 2019).

25 Original verses by Joseph E. Bush, Jr.

26 Original material by Joseph E. Bush, Jr.

CHAPTER 2

1 Wendell Berry, "A Native Hill," *The Hudson Review*, 21, No. 4 (Winter 1968–1969): 601–634, 634.

2 *Evangelical Lutheran Worship: Leaders Desk Edition* (Minneapolis, MN: Augsburg Fortress, 2006), 617.

3 James F. White notes that Lent had become generalized as a time of preparation for all Christians by the time of Augustine [*Introduction to Christian Worship*, 3rd ed. (Nashville, TN: Abingdon, 2000), 56.

4 James F. White, *Introduction to Christian Worship*, 56, citing Thomas J. Talley, *Origins of the Liturgical Year* (New York: Pueblo, 1986), 194–203; http://www.calendarpedia.com/when-is/lent.html and http://www.calendarpedia.com/when-is/orthodox-easter.html (accessed January 31, 2019); see also Susan Briehl, Liv Larson Andrews, Mark Mummert, Gail Ramshaw, and Ben Stewart, *Worship Guidebook for Lent and the Three Days* (Minneapolis, MN: Augsburg Fortress, 2009), 20, citing Thomas J. Talley, *Origins of the Liturgical Year*, 2nd amended ed. (Collegeville, MN:

Liturgical Press, 1991), 224; Christopher Seitz, *Joel* (New York: Bloomsbury T&T Clark, 2016), 86.

5 The Prayer continues: "Create and make in us new and contrite hearts, that we, worthily lamenting our sins and acknowledging our wretchedness, may obtain of you, the God of all mercy, perfect remission and forgiveness; through Jesus Christ our Lord, who lives and reigns with you and the Holy Spirit, one God, for ever and ever. Amen." *The Book of Common Prayer and Administration of the Sacraments and Other Rites and Ceremonies of the Church According to Use of The Episcopal Church* (The Church Hymnal Corporation and Seabury Press, 1979), 264; *From Ashes to Fire: Services of Worship for the Seasons of Lent and Easter with Introduction and Commentary*, Supplemental Worship Resources 8 (Nashville, TN: Abingdon, 1979), 35; also amended and quoted in *Evangelical Lutheran Worship: Leaders Desk Edition*, 615; also quoted by Seitz, *Joel* (New York: Bloomsbury T&T Clark, 2016), 89.

6 Paul K.-K. Cho, "Job the Penitent: Whether and Why Job Repents (Job 42:6)," in *Landscapes of Korea/Korea-American Biblical Interpretation, International Voices in biblical Studies 10*, edited by John Ahn (Atlanta, GA: SBL, 2019), 145–174, 151–152, https://www.sbl-site.org/assets/pdfs/pubs/9780884143796_OA.pdf; https://www.sbl-site.org/assets/pdfs/pubs/9780884143796_OA.pdf (accessed July 22, 2020); Cho provides a thorough review of the discussion concerning whether or not Job repents and the possible objects for repentance.

7 David G. Horrell, Cherryl Hunt, and Christopher Southgate, *Greening Paul: Reading the Apostle in a Time of Ecological Crisis* (Waco, TX: Baylor University Press, 2010), 172, 187.

8 Pope Francis, *Encyclical Letter* Laudato Si' *of the Holy Father Francis: On Care For Our Common Home* (May 24, 2015), para. 218, quoting the Australian Catholic Bishops' Conference, *A New Earth—The Environmental Challenge* (2002), http://www.vatican.va/content/francesco/en/encyclicals/documents/papa-francesco_20150524_enciclica-laudato-si.html#_ftn153 (accessed August 3, 2020).

9 Francis, *Encyclical Letter* Laudato Si', paras. 8–9, quoting Patriarch Bartholomew, Message for the Day of Prayer for the Protection of Creation (September 1, 2012); Address in Santa Barbara, California (November 8, 1997); Lecture at the Monastery of Utstein, Norway (June 23, 2003); "Global Responsibility and Ecological Sustainability," Closing Remarks, Halki Summit I, Istanbul (June 20, 2012).

10 Dom Gregory Dix, *The Shape of the Liturgy* (London: Dacre Press, Adam and Charles Black, 1960), 355–356.

11 *Evangelical Lutheran Worship: Leaders Desk Edition*, 615.

12 Benjamin M. Stewart, "Wisdom's Buried Treasure: Ecological Cosmology in Funeral Rites," in *Full of Your Glory: Liturgy, Cosmos, Creation*, edited by Teresa Berger (Collegeville, Minnesota: Liturgical Press Academic, 2019), 353–377: 363.

13 Ame Tugaue, "Dust of the Ground and the Breath of God: A Theological Exploration into the Relation of the Land and the Spirit of God," M.Th. thesis (Suva: Pacific Theological College, 1994), 4–5, 12; discussed in Joseph E. Bush, Jr., "The *Vanua* is the LORD's," *The Pacific Journal of Theology*, 2, no. 13 (1995): 75–87, 81–82; grammatical "gender" in Fijian is not categorized by male, female, and neuter,

as in Western languages, but by the categories of edible, drinkable, familiar and neutral. While some nouns such as the food *dalo* may be modified by either edible or neutral pronouns, depending on whether or not the *dalo* is to be consumed, Tugaue finds significance in the fact that *qele* (soil) usually takes only the edible. G. B. Milner, *Fijian Grammar* (Suva: Government Press, 1990): 65–66.

14 Ginny Stibolt and Sue Reed, "A Primer on Soil Carbon and Ecosystems," in *Climate-Wise Landscaping: Practical Actions for a Sustainable Future* (Gabriola Island, BC, Canada: New Society Publishers, 2018), 133.

15 Benjamin M. Stewart, *Watered Garden: Christian Worship and Earth's Ecology* (Minneapolis, MN: Augsburg Fortress, 2011), 6.

16 Ibid., 46.

17 Bernard Anderson, "Creation and Ecology," in *Creation in the Old Testament* edited by Bernard Anderson (Philadelphia, PA: Fortress, 1984), 167, cited by George H. Kehm, "The New Story: Redemption as Fulfillment of Creation," in *After Nature's Revolt: Eco-justice and Theology*, edited by Dieter T. Hessel (Minneapolis, MN: Fortress, 1992), 93; Kehm adds that the Noahic covenant makes "unambiguous the divine commitment to the preservation of creation that was only implicit and ambiguous in God's recognition of the original creation as 'very good'."

18 Bruce Vawter, *On Genesis: A New Reading* (Garden City, NY: Doubleday, 1977), 115; John H. Marks, "The Book of Genesis," in *The Interpreter's One-Volume Commentary on the Bible*, edited by Charles M. Laymon (Nashville, TN: Abingdon, 1971), 1–32, 2.

19 Odil Hannes Steck, *World and Environment*, Biblical Encounters Series (Nashville, TN: Abingdon, 1980), 57–113.

20 Ibid., 107.

21 Norman C. Habel, "The Challenge of Ecojustice Readings for Christian Theology," *Pacifica* 13, no.2 (June 2000): 140.

22 I developed this argument of double irony in Genesis earlier in Joseph Bush, "Natural Ambivalence," *Stimulus: The New Zealand Journal of Christian Thought and Practice*, 8, no. 4 (November 2000): 2–6, and some of the material in this chapter first appeared there.

23 Leander E. Keck, *Paul and His Letters*, Proclamation Commentaries, 2nd ed. (Philadelphia, PA: Fortress, 1988), 116.

24 A. J. M. Wedderburn, *The Reasons for Romans* (Minneapolis, MN: Fortress, 1991), 152–153.

25 Sharon H. Ringe, *Luke* (Louisville, KY: Westminster John Knox, 1995), 60.

26 Susan R. Garrett, *The Temptations of Jesus in Mark's Gospel* (Grand Rapids, MI: Eerdmans, 1998), 58.

27 Ibid.

28 Ibid., note 19.

29 J. Jeremias, "*Adam*," in *Theological Dictionary of the New Testament*, edited by Gerhard Kittel, translated by Geoffrey W. Bromiley, 10 vols., vol. 1 (Grand Rapids, MI: Eerdmans's Publishing Co, 1979 [1964]), 141–3:141.

30 Ernest Best, *The Temptation and the Passion: The Markan Soteriology* (Cambridge: Cambridge University Press, 1965), 8, citing Jeremias, "*Adam*," also citing J. Schniewind, *Das Evangelium nach Markus* (Göttingen, 1952).

31 Jeffrey B. Gibson, *The Temptations of Jesus in Early Christianity* (Sheffield, UK: Sheffield Academic Press, 1995), 65–69.

32 Garrett, *The Temptations of Jesus in Mark's Gospel*, 58–59.

33 Ringe, *Luke*, 60–61.

34 *Evangelical Lutheran Worship: Leaders Desk Edition*, 615, modified by Benjamin Stewart, "Wisdom's Buried Treasure: Ecological Cosmology in Funeral Rites," 363.

35 United Nations Environment Programme, *Only One Earth* (New York: UN Environment Programme, 1990), reproduced by Washington Interfaith Power and Light, https://earthministry.org/the-united-nations-environmental-sabbath-service/ (accessed January 15, 2021).

36 Translation of verses 13–14 from "The Anglican Church of Canada, A Liturgical Psalter: General Synod 2016 Edition: The Psalter of The Book of Alternative Services Emended for Contemporary Liturgical Use," 96, https://www.anglican.ca/wp-content/uploads/GS2016-Liturgical-Psalter-2016-05-04.pdf (accessed January 15, 2021).

CHAPTER 3

1 G. B. Caird interprets Mark's account of Jesus riding into Jerusalem on a colt that had never been ridden (Mark 11:2) as one of several stories in Mark indicating "Jesus' power extended over the world of nature." [*Principalities and Powers* (London: Oxford University Press, 1956), 71]. Luke follows Mark's account with regard to the unbroken colt (Luke 19:30). Matthew (21:2–5) and John (12:14–15), however, present Jesus riding on a donkey without specifying that it was unbroken and, unlike Mark and Luke, citing this as fulfillment of prophecy in Zechariah 9:9.

2 Much of this section was originally presented to the Ecology and Liturgy Seminar of the North American Academy of Liturgy on January 7, 2017.

3 Marilyn J. Salmon, *Preaching Without Contempt: Overcoming Unintended Anti-Judaism* (Minneapolis, MN: Fortress, 2006), 37.

4 Abraham P. Bloch, *The Biblical and Historical Background of Jewish Customs and Ceremonies* (New York: KTAV Publishing, 1980), 181.

5 Carmine Di Sante, *Jewish Prayer: The Origins of Christian Liturgy* (Mahwah, NJ: Paulist Press, 1985), 192.

6 Bloch, *The Biblical and Historical Background of Jewish Customs and Ceremonies*, 185–186.

7 Ibid., 183, 250.

8 Ibid., 183–184.

9 Ibid., 194.

10 Ibid., 192.

11 Ibid., 192, 194.

12 Ibid., 195; A differing interpretation of the relationship of the four species to the productivity of land was suggested by Maimonides and is cited by Arthur Schaffer in a paper on "The Agricultural and Ecological Symbolism of the Four Species of Sukkot." [*Tradition: A Journal of Orthodox Thought*, 20, no. 2 (Summer 1982)] Schaffer quotes Maimonides: "I believe that the four species

are a symbolical expression of our rejoicing that the Israelites changed the wilderness, 'no place of seed, or of figs, or of vines, or of pomegranates, or of water to drink' (Num 20:5), for a country full of fruit trees and rivers" (p. 130).

13 Ibid., 131–132, 134.

14 Ibid., 136–139.

15 Bloch, *The Biblical and Historical Background of Jewish Customs and Ceremonies*, 187–188.

16 Schaffer, "The Agricultural and Ecological Symbolism of the Four Species of Sukkot," 134; Bloch, *The Biblical and Historical Background of Jewish Customs and Ceremonies*, 187.

17 Ibid., 188.

18 Ibid., 202.

19 Ibid., 201.

20 Psalm 118:25–27 reads: "Save us, we beseech you, O LORD! O LORD, give us success! Blessed is the one who comes in the name of the LORD. We bless you from the house of the LORD. The LORD is God, and he has given us light. Bind the festal procession with branches up to the horns of the altar."

21 *Siddur Lev Shalem for Shabbat and Festivals* (New York: The Rabbinical Assembly, 2016), 382. www.rabinicalassembly.org.

22 Ibid., 394.

23 Gale A. Yee, *Jewish Feasts and the Gospel of John* (Wilmington: Michael Glazier, 1989), 16–21. The interpretation of John here is very much indebted to Yee's keen analysis and is gratefully acknowledged, but I reach a different conclusion concerning the relationship between the two religious communities in John's Gospel that has important implications for interreligious relationship today. Yee states her conclusions in a way that I think falls into supersessionism, saying on pages 25–26, "the Johannine Jesus now nullified and replaced all the Jewish liturgical institutions," and on page 27, "Jesus replaces and abrogates the traditional feasts of the Jews." If we follow Marilyn Salmon's analysis, Yee's conclusion would seem to be based on an anachronistic assumption that reads back into the Johannine Jewish community a greater separation between Christian and Jew that eventually followed. I am suggesting instead a parallel response to the challenge of the temple's destruction from both the Johannine Jewish community and the Pharisaic Jewish community that became rabbinic Judaism. That worship in each community took different forms does not imply that worship in the alternative community is necessarily nullified or abrogated. In fact I am arguing, or at least hoping, for the opposite—that 2,000 years later, living religious communities, each engaged in true worship, can learn from their respective understandings of a common heritage and similar liturgical practices. The challenge is to do so in a way that is respectful and not supersessionist or hegemonic.

24 See e.g. *The Presbyterian Hymnal* (Louisville, KY: Westminster/John Knox, 1990), 232.

25 Leviticus 23:40.

26 Psalm 118:25.

27 Psalm 118:25–26a.
28 Psalm 118:26a.

CHAPTER 4

1 Brian Wren, "Lord God, Your Love Has Called Us Here," Words: Brian Wren © 1975 Hope Publishing Company, Carol Stream, IL 60188. All rights reserved. Used by permission. Verse 4, *United Methodist Hymnal* 579; https://www.hopepublishing.com/find-hymns-hw/hw2596.aspx.

2 Joseph Sittler, "A Theology for Earth," in *Evocations of Grace: The Writings of Joseph Sittler on Ecology, Theology, and Ethics* (Grand Rapids, MI: Eerdmans, 2000), 30.

3 Patriarch Bartholomew, Address during the environmental symposium in Santa Barbara, CA (November 8, 1997), in *Cosmic Grace, Humble Prayer: The Ecological Vision of the Green Patriarch Bartholomew I*, edited by John Chryssavgis (Grand Rapids, MI: Eerdmans, 2003), 219.

4 John Chryssavgis, "The World of the Icon and Creation: An Orthodox Perspective on Ecology and Pneumatology," in *Christianity and Ecology: Seeking the Well-Being of Earth and Humans*, edited by Dieter T. Hessel and Rosemary Radford Ruether (Cambridge, MA: Harvard University Center for the Study of World Religions and Harvard University Press, 2000), 92.

5 Geoffrey Wainwright, *Eucharist and Eschatology* (London: Epworth Press, 1971), 104.

6 Pope Francis, Encyclical Letter *Laudato Si'* (May 24, 2015), ¶236–7, pp. 171–172, http://w2.vatican.va/content/dam/francesco/pdf/encyclicals/documents/papa-francesco_20150524_enciclica-laudato-si_en.pdf (accessed February 13, 2019), citing John Paul II, Encyclical Letter *Ecclesia de Eucharistia* (April 17, 2003), 8; *Acta Apostolicae Sedis* 95 (2003): 438.

7 Ibid., citing Patriarch Bartholomew, "Global Responsibility and Ecological Sustainability," Closing Remarks, Halki Summit I, Istanbul (June 20, 2012).

8 *1552 Book of Common Prayer* quoted in *The Oxford American Prayer Book Commentary* by Massey Hamilton Shepherd, Jr. (New York: Oxford University Press, 1973 [1950]), 81.

9 *John Wesley's Sunday Service of the Methodists in North America*, Methodist Bicentennial Commemorative Reprint (Nashville, TN: The United Methodist Publishing House and the United Methodist Board of Higher Education and Ministry, 1984), 136.

10 *The Book of Discipline of the African Methodist Episcopal Church 2008*, 48th ed. (Nashville, TN: AMEC Sunday School Union, 2009), 499; *The Book of Discipline of the African Methodist Episcopal Church Zion* (Charlotte, NC: A.M.E. Zion Publishing House, 2012), 379; see also https://milewis.wordpress.com/2017/02/08/epiclesis-body-blood-word-sprit/.

11 Quoted by Massey Hamilton Shepherd, Jr., *The Oxford American Prayer Book Commentary* (New York: Oxford University Press, 1963), 81.

12 John Wesley, "A Letter to A Person Lately Joined with the People Called Quakers. In Answer to a Letter Wrote by Him," Bristol, February 10, 1747–1748, *The*

Works of John Wesley, 3rd ed., vol. 10 *Letters, Essays, Dialogs, Addresses* (Peabody, MA: Hendrickson, 1984), 185.

13 John Wesley, *Journal*, Saturday June 16, 1764, *The Works of John Wesley*, 3rd ed., vol. 3 *Journals from May 6, 1760 to September 12, 1773* (Peabody, MA: Hendrickson, 1984), 183.

14 J. Ernest Rattenbury, *The Eucharistic Hymns of John and Charles Wesley* (London: Epworth Press, 1948), 61–78.

15 John Wesley and Charles Wesley, *Hymns on the Lord's Supper* (Madison, NJ: the Charles Wesley Society, 1995), a facsimile of the first edition (Bristol: Felix Farley, 1745), 87; Rattenbury, *The Eucharistic Hymns of John and Charles Wesley*, 73–74, 227.

16 Wesley and Charles Wesley, *Hymns on the Lord's Supper*, 99; Rattenbury, *The Eucharistic Hymns of John and Charles Wesley*, 232.

17 Hoyt L. Hickman, *Worshiping With United Methodists: A Guide for Pastors and Church Leaders* (Nashville, TN: Abingdon, 2007), 109.

18 Ibid.

19 Laurence Hull Stookey, *Eucharist: Christ's Feast With the Church* (Nashville, TN: Abingdon, 1993), 16–17.

20 Ibid., 17.

21 Ibid., 25.

22 Ibid., 26.

23 Ibid., 107–108.

24 "This Holy Mystery: A United Methodist Understanding of Holy Communion," adopted by the 2004 General Conference of the United Methodist Church (Nashville, TN: General Board of Discipleship of the United Methodist Church, 2004), 36 (downloaded February 18, 2019), http://s3.amazonaws.com/Website_Properties/what-we-believe/documents/this-holy-mystery-communion.PDF.

25 Susan Briehl, Liv Larson Andrews, Mark Mummert, Gail Ramshaw, and Ben Stewart, *Worship Guidebook for Lent and the Three Days* (Minneapolis, MN: Augsburg Fortress, 2009), 108.

26 ECLA, *Evangelical Lutheran Worship: Leaders Desk Edition* (Minneapolis, MN: Augsburg Fortress, 2006), 329.

27 Ibid., 332.

28 Ibid., 335.

29 Marva Dawn summarizes the debate in *Powers, Weakness, and the Tabernacling of God* (Grand Rapids, MI: Eerdmans, 2001), 10–34.

30 G. B. Caird, *Principalities and Powers: A Study in Pauline Theology: The Chancellor's Lectures for 1954 at Queen's University, Kingston Ontario* (London: Oxford at the Clarendon Press, 1956), 56–57.

31 Ibid., 57.

32 Ibid., 74.

33 Ibid., 85.

34 Ibid., 97.

35 Ibid., 84.

36 Ibid., 101.

37 Ibid., 65–66.

38 Ibid., 65.

39 Ibid.

40 Ibid., 68.

41 Ibid., 101.

42 The non-canonical Gospel of Peter 6:21, however, has an interesting parallel: "And then they drew out the nails from the hands of the Lord and laid him upon the earth. And the whole earth was shaken and there came a great fear."

43 William Baird, "The Gospel According to Luke" in *The Interpreter's One-Volume Commentary on the Bible* (Nashville, TN: Abingdon, 1971), 704; Carroll Stuhlmueller, "The Gospel According to Luke," chapter 44 in *The Jerome Biblical Commentary*, vol. 2 The New Testament and Topical Articles (Englewood Cliffs, NJ: Prentice-Hall, 1968), 160.

44 Stuhlmueller, "The Gospel According to Luke," 160.

45 Anne F. Elvey, *An Ecological Feminist Reading of the Gospel of Luke: A Gestational Paradigm* (Lewiston, NY: Edwin Mellen, 2005), 195.

46 Ibid., 181–189.

47 Ibid. See also pages 132-33. Mary's gestation of Jesus is invoked in this exchange and points to another chiasmus or shifting of meaning concerning Mary's body earlier in Luke's narrative. Initially Mary is "keeping" within her womb the gestating child, and then subsequently she is "keeping" within her heart the messages of mystery and majesty of this child. Immediately following Christ's birth and the pronouncement of "Glory to God in the highest, and on earth peace," perceived and proclaimed by shepherds, Luke writes: "Mary kept all these words and pondered them in her heart" (Luke 2:19). The narrative continues with the naming of the child "Jesus" at the time of circumcision, "the name given by the angel before he was conceived in the womb" (Luke 2:21b). Moreover, the second chapter of Luke concludes saying that Mary "his mother treasured all these things (words, *rhemata*) in her heart" after describing two visits of the holy family to the temple in Jerusalem. The first visit found Simon and Anna giving testimony after meeting the infant Jesus, and the second visit found the child Jesus among the teachers in the temple. Elvey notes that there is a transposition of Mary's interior keeping of Jesus from her womb to her heart. Both womb and heart are bodily images of interior keeping and gestating, the first giving birth to the child, and the second yet waiting for the time that that same child's full life will be revealed for the world awaiting.

48 Available at http://folksong.org.nz/haere_mai/ (downloaded September 21, 2018) quoting "Karanga" in *Traditional Songs of the Maori* by Mervyn McLean and Margaret Orbell (Auckland: Auckland University Press, 1975); see 2004 edition, pp. 244–245.

49 ELCA, *Evangelical Lutheran Worship: Leaders Desk Edition*, 637.

50 Ibid., 641.

51 They read as follows: "I grafted you into the tree of my chosen Israel, and you turned on them with persecution and mass murder. I made you joint heirs with them of my covenants, but you made them scapegoats for your own guilt." [*From Ashes to Fire*, Supplemental Resources 8 (Nashville, TN: Abingdon, 1980), 158, 161; *The United Methodist Book of Worship* (Nashville, TN: United Methodist Publishing House, 1992), 364; PC (USA), *Book of Common Worship* (Louisville, KY: Westminster/John Knox, 1993), 290].

52 J. D. Crichton, "Tenebrae," in *The New Westminster Dictionary of Liturgy and Worship*, edited by J. G. Davies (Philadelphia, PA: Westminster Press, 1986), 503.
53 Hoyt L. Hickman, Don E. Saliers, Laurence Hull Stookey, and James F. White, *The New Handbook of the Christian Year* (Nashville, TN: Abingdon, 1992), 178–179; *From Ashes to Fire*, 140–141.
54 White, *The New Handbook of the Christian Year*, 176; *From Ashes to Fire*, 136–137.
55 *The United Methodist Book of Worship*, 354, crediting "A Service of Tenebrae (including Dismissal by Don Saliers)" (Nashville, TN: Abingdon, 1986), also crediting J. H. Charlesworth's English translation of "The Passion of Jesus Christ" (Princeton, NJ).
56 *From Ashes to Fire*, 126–136, quoting John T. Townsend, *A Liturgical Interpretation of Our Lord's Passion in Narrative Form* (New York: National Conference of Christians and Jews); White, *The New Handbook of the Christian Year*, 170–175.

CHAPTER 5

1 "Easter Proclamation" [Exsultet], in *Worship Guidebook for Lent and the Three Days*, 155.
2 James F. White, *Introduction to Christian Worship*, 3rd ed. (Nashville, TN: Abingdon, 2000), 50; R. F. Buxton, "Sunday," in *The New Westminster Dictionary of Liturgy and Worship*," edited by J. G. Davies (Philadelphia, PA: Westminster Press, 1986), 499–500, 500.
3 J. D. Crichton, "Paschal Vigil," in *The New Westminster Dictionary of Liturgy and Worship*, 425; White, *Introduction to Christian Worship*, 54–55; Peter G. Cobb, "The History of the Christian Year," in *The Study of Liturgy*, edited by Cheslyn Jones, Geoffrey Wainwright, and Edward Yarnold (New York: Oxford University Press, 1978), 407. Paul F. Bradshaw and Maxwell E. Johnson, *The Origins of Feasts, Fasts and Seasons in Early Christianity* (Collegeville, MN: Liturgical Press, 2011), 39–59.
4 Crichton, "Paschal Vigil," 425; *From Ashes to Fire*, 166–167; this resource also suggests different liturgical structures for utilizing the Exsultet which are especially helpful if introducing it for the first time to congregations, pp. 188–194.
5 Rita Ferrone, "Virgil and the Vigil: The Bees Are Back in the Exsultet," *Commonweal*, 136, no. 7 (April 10, 2009): 12–13, 13.
6 "Easter Proclamation" [Exsultet], in *Worship Guidebook for Lent and the Three Days*, 155. This quotation is from worship materials for ELCA; there are slight differences in both content and English translation of the Exsultet between different churches' liturgies; see *United Methodist Book of Worship* (Nashville, TN: United Methodist Publishing House, 2012), 372; *The Book of Common Prayer . . . According to the use of The Episcopal Church* (The Church Hymnal Corporation and The Seabury Press, 1979), 286–287, and http://www.usccb.org/prayer-and-worship/liturgical-year/easter/easter-proclamation-exsultet.cfm (accessed March 6, 2019).

7 "Easter Proclamation" [Exsultet], in *Worship Guidebook for Lent and the Three Days*, 157.

8 Rita Ferrone, "Virgil and the Vigil," 13.

9 *Gelasian Sacramentary: Liber sacramentorum Romanae Ecclesiae*, edited by Henry Austin Wilson (Oxford: Clarendon Press, 1894), 80–81, https://books.google.com/books?id=S-20jhQQZBMC&printsec=frontcover&dq=subject:%22Sacramentarium+Gelasianum%22&as_brr=1#v=onepage&q=apes&f=false (accessed March 12, 2019); also quoted by Louis Duchesne, *Christian Worship: Its Origin and Evolution: A Study of the Latin Liturgy Up to the Time of Charlemagne* (Society for Promoting Christian Knowledge, 1910), 253, note 2, https://books.google.com/books?id=q1dHAQAAMAAJ&dq=conditor+apes&source=gbs_navlinks_s (accessed March 12, 2019).

10 Virgil, *Georgic IV*, written 29 BCE, http://classics.mit.edu/Virgil/georgics.4.iv.html (accessed March 12, 2019).

11 Dave Goulson, Elizabeth Nicholls, Cristina Botías, and Ellen L. Rotheray, "Bee Declines Driven by Combined Stress from Parasites, Pesticides, and Lack of Flowers," *Science*, 347, no. 622927 (March 2015), http://science.sciencemag.org/content/347/6229/1255957 (accessed March 12, 2019).

12 Warren Cornwall, "Common Weed Killer—Believed Harmless to Animals—May Be Harming Bees Worldwide," *Science* (September 24, 2018), https://www.sciencemag.org/news/2018/09/common-weed-killer-believed-harmless-animals-may-be-harming-bees-worldwide (accessed March 12, 2019).

13 *The Book of Common Prayer . . . According to the use of The Episcopal Church*, 287.

14 *Worship Guidebook for Lent and the Three Days*, 178.

15 Ibid., 159, 163; *United Methodist Book of Worship*, 373; *The Book of Common Prayer . . . According to the use of The Episcopal Church*, 288–289; http://catholic-resources.org/Lectionary/1998USL-Easter.htm (accessed March 12, 2019). While all four services mandate a reading from Exodus 14, and while all four services recommend the first reading from Genesis, only the ELCA service explicitly indicates the reading from Genesis should not be omitted.

16 The full title is often given as "Song of the Three Young Men" or "Song of the Three Holy Children."

17 Philip H. Pfatteicher, *Commentary on the Lutheran Book of Worship: Lutheran Liturgy in Its Ecumenical Context* (Minneapolis, MN: Augsburg Fortress, 1990), 282.

18 *Worship Guidebook*, 144, 145.

19 Ibid., 174, quoting Samuel Torvend, "Easter Vigil," in *Homilies for the Christian People*, assigned to Gail Ramshaw (New York: Pueblo Publishing, 1989), 261.

20 *Worship Guidebook*, 174, quoting *Evangelical Lutheran Worship*, see *Leaders Desk Edition* (Minneapolis, MN: Augsburg Fortress, 2008), 589.

21 *Worship Guidebook*, 176.

22 *Evangelical Lutheran Worship, Leaders Desk Edition*, 285.

23 Ibid., 288.

24 Ibid., 291.

25 Dorothy Sölle, *Suffering* (Philadelphia, PA: Fortress Press, 1975).

26 "This Is the Feast of Victory," translated by John W. Arthur (1970) from Latin, *"Dignus est Agnus"* (1970), © 1978 Lutheran Church in America, The American Lutheran Church, The Evangelical Lutheran Church in Canada, and The Lutheran Church—Missouri Synod, https://hymnary.org/text/worthy_is_christ_the_lamb_who_was (accessed April 16, 2021).

27 J. Knox, s.v. "Docetism," in *Interpreter's Dictionary of the Bible*, vol. 1 (Nashville, TN: Abingdon, 1982), 860.

28 Daniel A. Smith, *Revisiting the Empty Tomb: The Early History of Easter* (Minneapolis, MA: Fortress Press, 2010), 110, https://core.ac.uk/download/pdf/215392265.pdf (downloaded April 21, 2021).

29 Norman C. Habel, "Song of Earth" from *Seven Songs of Creation: Liturgies Celebrating and Healing Earth* (Cleveland, OH: Pilgrim Press, 2004). Thanks to Rev Beth Heller for bringing this liturgy to my attention.

30 Copyright © 2013 by Carolyn Winfrey Gillette. All rights reserved. Written for One Great Hour of Sharing, http://www.carolynshymns.com/you_give_us_hope_this_easter_day.html (accessed 23, April 2021); Carolyn Winfrey Gillette has written many hymns for creation care, and graciously makes many of these available for congregational use, see http://www.carolynshymns.com/lect_earthcare.html. My thanks to Rev. Joshua Gillen for making me aware of Carolyn Winfrey Gillette's great hymns!

CHAPTER 6

1 Dom Gregory Dix, *The Shape of the Liturgy* (London: Dacre Press, Adam & Charles Black), 1960 (1945), 335–359; James F. White, *Introduction to Christian Worship*, 3rd ed. (Nashville, TN: Abingdon, 2000), 60–61; Hoyt L. Hickman, *United Methodist Worship* (Nashville, TN: Abingdon, 1991), 80; Peter G. Cobb, "The Calendar: The History of the Christian Year," chapter 6.1 in *The Study of Liturgy*, edited by Cheslyn Jones, Geoffrey Wainwright, and Edward Yarnold, SJ (New York: Oxford University Press, 1978), 403–419, 411.

2 Given as the reading for Year B in the Revised Common Lectionary and for all three years in a Pentecost vigil in the Roman Catholic Lectionary for the Mass.

3 NRSV alternate reading of verse 34 as interrogative.

4 The Roman Catholic Lectionary also has a reading from 1 Peter 3 for this day but stops short of this verse.

5 *Dextera Dei ubique est*. Martin Luther, "That These Words, 'This is my Body,' Etc. Still Stand against the Fanatics," in *Luther's Works*, edited by Robert H. Fischer (Philadelphia, PA: Muhlenberg, 1961), 37, 62, quoted by H. Paul Santmire, *Ritualizing Nature: Renewing Christian Liturgy in a Time of Crisis* (Minneapolis, MN: Fortress, 2008), 115–116.

6 Santmire, *Ritualizing Nature*, 115–116.

7 Martin Luther, "Two Lenten Sermons, 1518," in *Luther's Works*, edited by John W. Doberstein (Philadelphia, PA: Muhlenberg, 1959), 51, 63, quoted by Santmire, *Ritualizing Nature*, 282 note 9.

8 Santmire, *Ritualizing Nature*, 116.

9 Ibid., 123.

10 Ibid., 118.

11 Ibid., 162.

12 Brian Wren, *What Language Shall I Borrow? God-Talk in Worship: A Male Response to Feminist Theology* (London: SCM, 1989), 119.

13 Ibid., 130–134, 143, citing Sallie McFague, *Models of God: Theology for an Ecological, Nuclear Age* (Philadelphia, PA: Fortress, 1986).

14 Wren, *What Language*, 134.

15 Ibid., 149.

16 Ibid., 148, quoting "Thank You, God, for Water, Soil and Air," Words: Brian Wren © 1975 Hope Publishing Company , Carol Stream, IL 60188. All rights reserved. Used by permission. in *Faith Looking Forward: The Hymns and Songs of Brian Wren* (Carol Stream, IL: Hope Publishing Co., 1983), no. 7.

17 Wren, *What Language*, 227.

18 Ibid., 228, quoting "Jesus Is with God," Words: Brian Wren © 1986 Hope Publishing Company, Carol Stream, IL 60188. All rights reserved. Used by permission. in *Praising a Mystery: 30 New Hymns by Brian Wren* (Carol Stream, IL: Hope Publishing Col, 1986), no. 17.

19 Marty Haugen, "Gather Us In" (GIA Publications, 1982), https://www.giamusic.com/store/resource/gather-us-in-print-g2651 (accessed March 18, 2019). Copyright © 1982 GIA Publications, Inc. quoted with permission.

20 *Episcopal Hymnal 1982* (New York: The Church Hymnal Corporation, 1985), 216.

21 *The Presbyterian Hymnal* (Louisville, KY: Westminster John Knox, 1990), 120. The original hymn contained more than 100 lines in Latin, and contemporary English versions select and amend from the original. Some versions elucidate the relation between ascension and the natural world more clearly than others, and some present a more anthropocentric rendering. The United Methodist version (#324 in *The United Methodist Hymnal*), The ELCA version (#394 in *Worship*), and the more recent PCUSA version (#277 in *Glory to God*), for instance, all translate *deus ecce per omnia regnat* as "Ruler and Lord of all people," while the older Presbyterian version quoted here and the Episcopal Church's version (#216 in *The Hymnal 1982*) have "Lord and the Ruler of nature."

22 Paulos Gregorios, *The Human Presence: An Orthodox View of Nature* (Geneva: WCC, 1978), 67, summarizing Gregory of Nyssa, *De Hominis Opificio* 16, PG 44, 185B–D.

23 Bijesh Philip, *Theosis and Mission: An Orthodox Perspective of Christian Spirituality in the Age of Globalisation* (Nagpur: Theosis Books, 2004), 71, also reproduced in Bijesh Philip, "The Human Presence for a Sustainable Eco System; Gregorian Insights," http://paulosmargregorios.in/Gregorian_Studies/Gregorian_Studies/studies-FrBijesh-human.htm (accessed March 21, 2019).

24 Jerome H. Neyrey, *The Resurrection Stories* (Wilmington: Michael Glazier, 1988), 73–74.

25 Christopher J. H. Wright, "'The Earth Is the LORD's': Biblical Foundations for Global Ecological Ethics and Mission," chapter 9 in *Keeping God's Earth: The Global Environment in Biblical Perspective*, edited by Noah J. Toly and Daniel I. hBlock (Downers Grove, IL: IVP, 2010), 216–241, 222.

26 Harold Riley, *The Making of Mark: An Exploration* (Macon, GA: Mercer University Press, 1989), 117, 156; use of the phrase "the gospel" in the absolute sense is also unique to Mark among the Gospels but typical of Paul's writings, ibid., 5, 163, also Willi Marxsen, *Mark The Evangelist: Studies on the Redaction History of the Gospel* (Nashville, TN: Abingdon, 1969), 126–127 citing Adolf von Harnack, *The Constitution and Law of the Church in the First Two Centuries*, translated by F. L. Pogson (London: Williams and Norgate, 1910), 201 note 1.

27 Henry Barclay Swete, *The Gospel According to St. Mark: The Greek Text with Introduction Notes and Indices* (London: Macmillan, 1927), 405.

28 Eugene LaVerdiere, *The Beginning of the Gospel: Introducing the Gospel According to Mark*, vol. 2, Mark 8:22–16:20 (Collegeville, MN: Liturgical Press, 1999), 325–359.

29 John Painter, *Mark's Gospel* (London: Routledge, 1997), 216.

30 Donald H. Juel, *A Master of Surprise: Mark Interpreted* (Minneapolis, MN: Fortress, 1994), 16.

31 Painter, *Mark's Gospel*, 215.

32 Juel, *A Master of Surprise*, 16–17, citing *Calvin's Commentaries: Harmony of Matthew, Mark, and Luke*, translated by Rev W. Pringle (Grand Rapids, MI: Baker, 1979), 16:38, 17:347; also citing Martin Luther, "The Small Catechism," *The Book of Concord*, translated by and ed. Theodore Tappert (Philadelphia: Fortress, 1959), 349.

33 *Midrash Tehillim*, Psalm 47, in *The Midrash on Psalms*, 2 vols, vol. 1, translated William G. Braude (New Haven, CT: Yale University Press, 1959), 458.

34 Ibid., 459, R. Judah bar Nahman speaking in the name of R. Simeon ben Lakish.

35 Arthur Walker-Jones, *The Green Psalter: Resources for an Ecological Spirituality* (Minneapolis, MN: Fortress, 2009), 134; oceanic imagery is from Walker-Jones's translation of Psalm 93:3–4.

36 *Midrash Tehillim*, Psalm 93, §2, translated by Braude 1959:125, quoted by Peter L. Trudinger, "Friend or Foe? Earth and *Chaoskampf* in the Psalms," in *The Earth Story in the Psalms and the Prophets, The Earth Bible* vol. 4, edited by Norman C. Habel (Cleveland, OH: Pilgrim, 2001), 29–41: 41.

37 Norman K. Gottwald, *All the Kingdoms of the Earth*, 197.

38 Walker-Jones, *The Green Psalter*, 91, citing Gerald H. Wilson, "The Use of Royal Psalms at the 'Seams' of the Hebrew Psalter," *Journal for the Study of the Old Testament* 35 (1986): 92; quoted in J. Clinton McCann, Jr., *A Theological Introduction to the Book of Psalms: The Psalms as Torah* (Nashville, TN: Abingdon, 1993), 662.

39 Lawrence M. Krauss, *A Universe From Nothing: Why There is Something Rather than Nothing* (New York: Free Press, 2012), 3, 187.

40 Larry L. Rasmussen, *Earth Community, Earth Ethics* (Maryknoll, NY: Orbis, 1997), 25; also personal correspondence, June 23, 2018.

41 Ibid.
42 Ibid.
43 Ibid., 25–26.
44 Ibid., 26.
45 Ibid.
46 Ibid.
47 Ibid.
48 Colin G. Calloway, *First Peoples: A Documentary Survey of American Indian History* (New York: Bedford/St. Martins, 1999), 67–69.
49 Colin G. Calloway, *First Peoples: A Documentary Survey of American Indian History* (New York: Bedford/St. Martins, 1999), 225, citing James P. Ronda, *Lewis and Clark among the Indians* (Lincoln: University of Nebraska Press, 1984), 1; see https://lewisandclarkjournals.unl.edu/item/lc.sup.lavender.01.app1 (downloaded June 18, 2018).
50 Peter Nabokov, ed., *Native American Testimony: A Chronicle of Indian-White Relations from Prophecy to the Present* (New York: Penguin, 1991), 148.
51 Helen Willetts, "Global Warming—an Overview," http://www.bbc.co.uk/weather/features/global_warming1.shtml.

CHAPTER 7

1 *Old Testament Quotations in the New Testament*, edited by Robert G. Bratcher (London: United Bible Societies, 1961), 23, note 2.
2 Abraham P. Bloch, *The Biblical and Historical Background of Jewish Customs and Ceremonies* (New York: KTAV Publishing, 1980), 183–184.
3 Ibid., 194.
4 Matthew Fox, *Sins of the Spirit, Blessings of the Flesh* (New York: Harmony Books, 1999), 105, citing Hildegard of Bingen; see *Illuminations of Hildegard of Bingen: Text by Hildegard of Bingen with Commentary by Matthew Fox* (Santa Fe, NM: Bear & Co., 1985), 30–33.
5 Elizabeth A. Johnson, *She Who Is: The Mystery of God in Feminist Theological Discourse* (New York: Crossroad, 1999), 127–128, citing Hildegaard [*sic*] of Bingen, *Scivias* (New York: Paulist 1990), chapter 1, note 122, p. 190 and passim.
6 Johnson, *She Who Is*, 213.
7 Wendell Berry, "Christianity and the Survival of Creation," in *Sex, Economy, Freedom and Community: Eight Essays* (New York: Pantheon Books, 1993), 97–8, quoting Philip Sherrard, *Human Image. World Image* (Ipswich, Suffolk, England: Golgonooza Press, 1992), 152; see also https://crosscurrents.org/berry.htm (downloaded March 4, 2021), http://www.ecofaithrecovery.org/wp-content/uploads/2012/09/BerryWendell_ChristianitySurvivalCreation.pdf.
8 Available at https://www.giamusic.com/store/resource/spirit-of-god-print-g3098; to listen: https://www.youtube.com/watch?v=GZK_W06 HBM4 (accessed March 17, 2021).

CHAPTER 8

1 Patrick (att.), *The Hymnal 1982 According to the Use of The Episcopal Church*, translated by Cecil Frances Alexander (New York: The Church Hymnal Corporation, 1985), 370, vss. 1, 4, 6, 7.

2 Catherine Mowry LaCugna, *God for Us: The Trinity and the Christian Life* (San Francisco, CA: HarperCollins, 1992), 250–251.

3 Gustaf Aulen, *The Faith of the Christian Church*, translated by Eric H. Wahlstrom (Philadelphia, PA: Muhlenberg Press, 1962), 227–228.

4 Elizabeth A. Johnson, *She Who Is: The Mystery of God in Feminist Theological Discourse* (New York: Crossroad, 1999), 203, citing Anselm, *Monologion* 78, in *Saint Anselm: Basic Writings* (see chapter 1, note 12), 142.

5 Geoffrey Wainwright, *Eucharist and Eschatology* (London: Epworth Press, 1978), 96.

6 The Revised Common Lectionary recommends Psalm 29 for Trinity Sunday in year B, which it also recommends for the first Sunday after Epiphany for all three years; it is discussed in the chapter on Epiphany.

7 The full title is often given as "Song of the Three Young Men" or "Song of the Three Holy Children."

8 George A. F. Knight, "The Prayer of Azariah and The Song of the Three Young Men," in *Interpreter's One-Volume Commentary on the Bible* (Nashville, TN: Abingdon, 1971), 582.

9 The Church of the Province of New Zealand, *A New Zealand Prayer Book* (Auckland: William Collins, 1989), 103.

10 Ruth C. Duck, *Gender and the Name of God: The Trinitarian Baptismal Formula* (New York: Pilgrim, 1991), 145, 174–175.

11 "The Apostles' Creed (Ecumenical)," in *The Presbyterian Hymnal* (Louisville, KY: Westminster John Knox, 1990), 14

12 "The Nicene Creed (Ecumenical)," in *The Presbyterian Hymnal* (Louisville, KY: Westminster John Knox, 1990), 15.

13 Duck, *Gender and the Name of God*, 76, citing Bernhard Lohse, *A Short History of Christian Doctrine* (Philadelphia, PA: Fortress, 1966), 65.

14 Stanley J. Grenz, *Rediscovering the Triune God: The Trinity in Contemporary Theology* (Minneapolis, MN: Fortress, 2004), 7–8; Leonardo Boff, *Trinity and Society* (Eugene, OR: Wipf and Stock, 1988), 60; Presbyterian Church USA, *The Book of Confessions* (Louisville, KY: Office of the General Assembly, 1996), 2–3; Henry Bettenson, ed., *Documents of the Christian Church*, 2nd ed. (New York: Oxford University Press, 1977), 24–26.

Johnson, *She Who Is*, quoting Basil of Caesarea, *De Spiritu Sancto* 9 (ET: *On the Holy Spirit* [Crestwood, NY: St. Vladimir's Seminary Press, 1980], 43).

16 Leonardo Boff, *Trinity and Society* (Eugene, OR: Wipf and Stock, 1988), 172.

17 John Baldovin, "History of the Latin Text and Rite," in *A Commentary on the Order of Mass of The Roman Missal: A New English Translation: Developed Under the Auspices of the Catholic Academy of Liturgy*, edited by Ed Foley (Collegeville, MN: Liturgical Press, 2011), 401–406: 405.

18 "Alexandrian Anaphora of Saint Basil," translated by John Baldovin (including parenthetical note), in ibid., 403–405.

19 Baldovin, "History of the Latin Text and Rite," 406; see "Great Thanksgiving 6: A Common Eucharistic Prayer," in *At the Lord's Table: A Communion Service Book for Use by the Minister*, Supplemental Resources 9 (Nashville, TN: Abingdon, 1981), 22–23; "Great Thanksgiving F" in *Book of Common Worship* (Louisville, KY: Westminster John Knox, 1993), 146–149; "Eucharistic Prayer D," in *The Book of Common Prayer* (New York: The Church Hymnal Corporation and The Seabury Press, 1979), 372–376.

20 *The Book of Common Prayer*, 373.

21 Ibid.

22 Ibid., 374.

23 Ibid., 373.

24 World Council of Churches, *Baptism, Eucharist and Ministry*, Faith and Order Paper 111 (Geneva: WCC, 1982), 10–11.

25 *Celebrating Communion: A Handbook for Elders Authorized to Lead Communion Services within the Presbyterian Church of Aotearoa New Zealand*, 2nd ed. (Wellington: The Special Committee on Lay Administration of the Sacraments, Presbyterian Church of Aotearoa New Zealand, 1994), 63, quoting PCUSA, *Book of Common Worship*, "Great Thanksgiving J" (Louisville, KY: Westminster John Knox, 1993), 156; see also PCUSA, *Book of Common Worship*, 2018 ed. (Louisville, KY: Westminster John Knox, 2018), 121–123.

26 Robert J. Daly, SJ, "Ecological Euchology," *Worship*, 89, no. 2 (March 2015): 166–172, 171; a revised copy of this prayer may be found at https://www.scribd.com/document/336413490/Jesuit-Fr-Robert-Daly-s-Eucharistic-Prayer-for-21st-century (accessed November 27, 2020) and discussed by Thomas Reese, "Eucharistic Prayer in the 21st Century," *National Catholic Reporter* (January 12, 2017), https://www.ncronline.org/blogs/faith-and-justice/Eucharistic-prayer-21st-century (accessed November 27, 2020); the exact wording here is from the revision.

27 Ibid., https://www.scribd.com/document/336413490/Jesuit-Fr-Robert-Daly-s-Eucharistic-Prayer-for-21st-century, p. 17.

28 Daly, *Worship*, p. 170.

29 Ibid., 169.

30 Ibid., 170, but the exact wording here is taken from the revision: https://www.scribd.com/document/336413490/Jesuit-Fr-Robert-Daly-s-Eucharistic-Prayer-for-21st-century.

31 Robert J. Daly, SJ, https://www.scribd.com/document/336413490/Jesuit-Fr-Robert-Daly-s-Eucharistic-Prayer-for-21st-century, 14–15 (accessed November 27, 2020), quoted by Thomas Reese, "Eucharistic Prayer in the 21st Century," *National Catholic Reporter* (January 12, 2017), https://www.ncronline.org/blogs/faith-and-justice/Eucharistic-prayer-21st-century (accessed November 27, 2020).

32 Olivia Warren, Mount Vernon Place United Methodist Church, April 10, 2019; this is also a form of address used by others on pastoral staff in this congregation, Lee Scriber and Donna Claycomb Sokol.

33 Norman Pittenger, *The Holy Spirit* (Philadelphia, PA: United Church Press, 1974), 124.

34 Norman Pittenger, *The Divine Triunity* (Philadelphia, PA: United Church Press, 1977), 109.
35 Ibid., 42, 64, citing Augustine, *De Trinitate*.
36 Pittenger, *The Holy Spirit*, 124.
37 Pittenger, *The Divine Triunity*, 116.
38 Pittenger, *The Holy Spirit*, 124.
39 Alfred N. Whitehead, *Process and Reality* (New York: Macmillan, 1967); Charles Hartshorne, *A Natural Theology for Our Time* (La Salle, IL: Open Court, 1973).
40 Sallie McFague, *Models of God: Theology for an Ecological Nuclear Age* (London: SCM, 1987), 91–92.
41 Ibid., 101.
42 Ibid., 130, citing Pittenger, *The Divine Triunity*, 109, also citing Norman Pittenger, *Love Looks Deep* (London: A. R. Mowbray, 1969).
43 McFague, *Models of God*, 135.
44 Ibid., 169.
45 Distinguishing her view from pantheism, McFague clarifies, "The model is monist and perhaps most precisely designated as panentheistic." Ibid., 72.
46 Sallie McFague, *Super, Natural Christians: How We Should Love Nature* (Minneapolis, MN: Augsburg Fortress, 1997).
47 Jürgen Moltmann, *The Trinity and the Kingdom* (Minneapolis: Fortress, 1993 [1981]), 106, citing John of Damascus, *De Fide Orthodoxa*, MPG 94, 789–1228. New critical edition: *Die Schriften des Johannes Damaskenos*, PTSt 12, vol. 2, ed. B. Kotter (Berlin and New York, 1993).
48 Ibid., 174–175.
49 Ibid., 103; Jürgen Moltmann, *God in Creation: An Ecological Doctrine of Creation*, The Gifford Lectures 1984–1985 (London: SCM, 1985), 95.
50 Ibid., 97–98.
51 Boff, *Trinity and Society*, 235.
52 Ibid., 221.
53 Ibid., 235.
54 Ibid., 222.
55 Leonardo Boff, *Cry of the Earth, Cry of the Poor* (Maryknoll, NY: Orbis, 1997), 167.
56 Ibid., 157.
57 Loida I. Martell-Otero, "From Foreign Bodies in Teacher Space to Embodied Spirit in *Personas Educadas* or, How to Prevent 'Tourists of Diversity' in Education," chapter 3 in *Teaching for a Culturally Diverse and Racially Just World*, edited by Eleazar S. Fernandez (Eugene, OR: Cascade, 2014), 64.
58 Martell-Otero, "From Foreign Bodies in Teacher Space to Embodied Spirit in *Personas Educadas*," 57, citing Boff, *Trinity and Society*, also citing John Zizioulas, "Communion and Otherness," *St. Vladimir's Theological Quarterly*, 38 (1994): 347–361, also citing Catherine Mowry LaCugna, *God for Us*.
59 Matthew Fox, *Original Blessing: A Primer in Creation Spirituality* (Santa Fe, NM: Bear & Co., 1983), 213.

60 Mathew Fox, *Illuminations of Hildegard of Bingen: Text by Hildegard of Bingen with Commentary by Matthew Fox* (Santa Fe, NM: Bear & Co., 1985), 23, citing Hildegard, *Brief*, 68–70, quoted by Johnson, *She Who Is*, 211.

61 Matthew Fox, *Sins of the Spirit, Blessings of the Flesh* (New York: Harmony Books, 1999), 95, quoting Hildegard of Bingen, *Book of Divine Works* (Santa Fe, NM: Bear & Co., 1987), 10.

62 Matthew Fox, *Creation Spirituality: Liberating Gifts for the People of the Earth* (New York: HarperCollins, 1991), 56.

63 Ibid., 58–59.

64 Ibid., 62.

65 Ibid., 64.

66 Johnson, *She Who Is*, 91.

67 Ibid., 213–214; I've presented this in the traditional order of First, Second, and Third Persons of the Trinity, though Johnson presents them in reverse order in accordance with a more intuitive revelatory experience of God in intimate relationship with us.

68 Ibid., 210–211.

69 Ibid., 210, 220, crediting John Damascene.

70 Ibid., 220.

71 Ibid., 99, translating Augustine, *De Trinitate* 4.20.27, see http://www.logicmuseum.com/wiki/Authors/Augustine/On_the_Trinity/On_the_Trinity_Book_IV#4_20_27 (accessed November 5, 2020).

72 Ibid., 165–166.

73 Elizabeth A. Johnson, *Creation and the Cross: The Mercy of God for a Planet in Peril* (Maryknoll, NY: Orbis, 2019), 186, citing Niels Henrik Gregersen, ed., *Incarnation: On the Scope and Depth of Christology* (Minneapolis, MN: Fortress Press, 2015), 18.

74 Ibid., 188, 192.

75 Ibid., 192–193, quoting Francis, *Laudato Si'*, paragraphs 96–100, 243; see http://www.vatican.va/content/francesco/en/encyclicals/documents/papa-francesco_20150524_enciclica-laudato-si.html (accessed November 12, 2020).

76 Pope Francis, "A Christian Prayer in Union with Creation," paragraph 246, in *Laudato si'* Copyright © Libreria Editrice Vaticana.

CHAPTER 9

1 This is a literal translation of verse 3. Many translations following the Masoretic interpretation prefer to read this as God "made us and we are his."

2 Bruce C. Birch, Jacqueline E. Lapsley, Cynthia Moe-Lobeda, and Larry L. Rasmussen remark that Martin Luther was inspired by this "psalm of tumult" in composing the hymn, "A Mighty Fortress is Our God" which acclaims Christ's sovereignty above all earthly powers raging and a "flood of ills prevailing." They note that the verse 10, "Be still and know that I am God," occurs in Psalm 46 (and often in our own lives) after "war, desolation, and conflict, as well as peacemaking." [*Bible and Ethics in the Christian Life: A New Conversation* (Minneapolis, MN: Fortress Press, 2018), 263–264].

3 Psalms 97:1a NIV.

4 Brian Wren, "Christ Is Alive" Words: Brian Wren © 1975, rev. 1995 Hope Publishing Company, Carol Stream, IL 60188. All rights reserved. Used by permission. Hymn 108 in *The Presbyterian Hymnal* (Louisville, KY: Westminster John Knox, 1990).

CHAPTER 10

1 Laurence Hull Stookey, *Calendar: Christ's Time for the Church* (Nashville, TN: Abingdon, 1996), 128.

2 "Light of the Stable," by Elizabeth Rhymer and Steven Rhymer is the title cut of Emmylou Harris's "Christmas Album" (Warner Brothers Records, 1980) and is appropriately sung during later Advent, Christmas, and Epiphany, https://www.youtube.com/watch?v=vjH7UavLq7U (accessed September 11, 2019).

3 Stookey, *Calendar*, 126–127.

4 Ibid., 128.

5 Ibid.

6 Kathryn D. Blanchard and Kevin J. O'Brien, *An Introduction to Christian Environmentalism: Ecology, Virtue, and Ethics* (Waco, TX: Baylor University Press, 2014). These quotations would probably not be read as part of the liturgy but might be reproduced in the bulletin with attribution.

7 This passage is considered by many biblical scholars to be part of Third Isaiah expressing the disillusionment of returning exiles, though others consider it earlier and exilic. For a review of the debate, see Blaženka Scheuer, "'Why Do You Let Us Wander, O Lord, From Your Ways?' (Isa. 63:17). Clarification of Culpability in the Last Part of the Book of Isaiah," in *Continuity and Discontinuity: Chronological and Thematic Development in Isaiah 40–66*, edited by Lena-Sofia Tiemeyer and Hans M. Barstad (Bristol, CT: Vandenhoeck & Ruprecht, 2014), 159–173.

8 The Roman Catholic Lectionary stops at verse 7 before the potter and clay metaphor and includes other verses preceding: Isaiah 63:16b–17, 19b; 64:2–7.

9 Blanchard and O'Brien, *An Introduction to Christian Environmentalism: Ecology, Virtue, and Ethics*, 120. This quotation would probably not be read as part of the liturgy but might be reproduced in the bulletin with attribution.

10 "Jesus is Coming Again," by John W. Peterson, © 1957 John W. Peterson Music Company. All rights reserved. Used by permission. Hymn 307 in *The New National Baptist Hymnal* (Nashville, TN: National Baptist Publishing Board, 1981), also Hymn 239 in *The Hymnal for Worship and Celebration* (Waco, TX: Word Music, 1986), also Hymn 190 in *Worship: Hymns of the Christian Life* (Camp Hill, PA: Christian Publications, 2003).

11 "The King Shall Come" by John Brownlie, Hymn 260 in *Evangelical Lutheran Worship* (Minneapolis, MN: Augsburg Fortress, 2006), also Hymn 73 in *The Hymnal 1982* (New York: The Church Hymnal Corporation, 1985), also Hymn 189 in *Worship: Hymns of the Christian Life* (Camp Hill, PA: Christian Publications, 2003).

12 Duncan Reid, "Enfleshing the Human: An Earth-Revealing, Earth-Healing Christology," chapter 4 in *Earth Revealing—Earth Healing: Ecology and Christian Theology*, edited by Denis Edwards (Collegeville, MN: Liturgical Press, 2001), 69–83, 70.

13 The Revised Common Lectionary also recommends Baruch 5:1–9 for year C but suggests as an alternate Malachi 3:1–4, the beginning of which seems to be quoted in Mark 1:2, "See, I am sending my messenger to prepare the way before me" (Mal 3:1a).

14 John W. Olley, "'The Wolf, the Lamb, and a Little Child': Transforming the Diverse Earth Community in Isaiah," in *The Earth Story in the Psalms and the Prophets*, Earth Bible vol. 4, edited by Norman C. Habeʻl (Cleveland, OH: Pilgrim, 2001), 219–229, 224 note 12. The Hebrew terms are *naar qaton, yoneq,* and *gamul*.

15 Ibid., 219 note 1, citing *A New Classified Concordance of the Bible: A Hebrew-English Thesaurus of the Bible*, edited by E. Katz (Jerusalem: Kiryat Sefer, 1992).

16 Olley, "'The Wolf, the Lamb, and a Little Child,'" 227.

17 The New Revised Common Lectionary gives this as the psalm for the third Sunday in Advent.

18 In personal correspondence [December 12, 2018], Benjamin Stewart describes Advent as having an interesting "hope and end-of-the-world dichotomy," which certainly describes this passage.

19 *The Oxford Annotated Bible* (New York: Oxford University Press, 1962), note on 2 Peter 3:13–14.

20 Douglas Harink, *1 & 2 Peter*, Brazos Theological Commentary on the Bible (Grand Rapids, MI: Brazos, 2009), 112.

21 Ibid., 184–185, citing Sergius Bulgakov, *The Bride of the Lamb*, translated by Boris Jakim (Grand Rapids, MI: Eerdmans, 2002), 379–526.

22 The Roman Catholic Lectionary has as the Epistle reading Romans 15:4–9 but stops short of the quotation from Isaiah 11:10 in verse 12 and the closing benediction.

23 Blanchard and O'Brien, *An Introduction to Christian Environmentalism: Ecology, Virtue, and Ethics*, 130. This quotation would probably not be read as part of the liturgy but might be reproduced in the bulletin with attribution.

24 "All Hail to God's Anointed," by James Montgomery (altered for inclusive language; first line originally "Hail to the Lord's Anointed"), Hymn 149, verse 3 in *Glory to God: The Presbyterian Hymnal* (Louisville, KY: Westminster John Knox, 2013).

CHAPTER 11

1 International Commission on English in the Liturgy, Entrance Antiphon A in Mass Formulary 2 for "The Blessed Virgin Mary and the Annunciation of the Lord," in *Collection of Masses of the Blessed Virgin Mary*, vol. 1 *Missal* (Collegeville, MN: Liturgical Press, 2012), 6, citing and paraphrasing Isaiah 45:8, recommended for use in Advent. Excerpts from the English translation of *Collection of Masses of the Blessed Virgin Mary* © 1989, 2012, International Commission on English in the Liturgy Corporation. All rights reserved.

2 Walter Brueggemann, *Isaiah 1–39* (Louisville, KY: Westminster John Knox, 1998), 275.

3 Ibid., 277.

4 David G. Horrell, Cherryl Hunt, and Christopher Southgate, *Greening Paul: Rereading the Apostle in a Time of Ecological Crisis* (Waco, TX: Baylor University Press, 2010), 195.

5 Joseph A. Fitzmyer, "The Letter to the Philippians," chapter 50 in *The Jerome Biblical Commentary*, The New Testament and Topical Articles (Englewood Cliffs, NJ: Prentice-Hall, 1968), 253; Elsa Tamez, "Philippians," in *Philippians, Colossians, Philemon*, Wisdom Commentary, vol. 51 (Collegeville, MN: Liturgical Press, 2017), 108–109.

6 Kathryn D. Blanchard and Kevin J. O'Brien, *An Introduction to Christian Environmentalism: Ecology, Virtue, and Ethics* (Waco, TX: Baylor University Press, 2014), 149, 152. These quotations would probably not be read as part of the liturgy but might be reproduced in the bulletin with attribution.

7 From Charles Coffin, "The Baptist Shouts on Jordan's Shore," transl. Hymn 115 in *The New Century Hymnal* (Cleveland: The Pilgrim Press, 1995).

8 "People Look East" by Eleanor Farjeon, #105 in *Glory to God: The Presbyterian Hymnal* (Louisville, KY: Westminster John Knox, 2013), from *The Oxford Book of Carols* (Oxford University Press).

9 Bruce K. Waltke, *A Commentary on Micah* (Grand Rapids, MI: William B. Eerdmans, 2007), 272–274.

10 Michael Goulder, *Isaiah as Liturgy* (Burlington, VT: Ashgate, 2004), 35.

11 Ibid., 33–36.

12 Frederick L. Moriarty, "Isaiah 1–39," chapter 16 in *The Jerome Biblical Commentary* (Englewood Cliffs, NJ: Prentice-Hall, 1968), 265–282, 270.

13 The first line has proved a suggestive title for works in global stewardship, environmental ethics, and ecology and liturgy, for example, *The Earth is the LORD's: Essays on Stewardship*, edited by Mary Evelyn Jegen and Bruno V. Manno (New York: Paulist Press, 1978); Dianne Bergant, *The Earth is the LORD's: The Bible, Ecology, and Worship* (Collegeville, MN: Liturgical Press, 1998); and Christopher J. H. Wright, "'The Earth is the LORD's': Biblical Foundations for Global Ecological Ethics and Mission," chapter 9 in *Keeping God's Earth: The Global Environment in Biblical Perspective*, edited by. Noah J. Toly and Daniel I. Block (Downers Grove, IL: IVP, 2010), 216–241.

14 Ibid., 217–224.

15 Hilary Marlow, *Biblical Prophets and Contemporary Environmental Ethics: Re-Reading Amos, Hosea, and First Isaiah* (New York: Oxford University Press, 2009), 237 note 139.

16 Wright, "'The Earth is the LORD's,'" 224.

17 David Gushee, "Environmental Ethics: Bringing Creation Care Down to Earth," chapter 10 in *Keeping God's Earth: The Global Environment in Biblical Perspective*, edited by Noah J. Toly and Daniel I. Block (Downers Grove, IL: IVP, 2010), 245–265, 247.

18 Bruce C. Birch and Larry L Rasmussen, *The Predicament of the Prosperous* (Philadelphia, PA: Westminster Press, 1978), 119.

19 Allen P. Ross, *A Commentary on the Psalms*, vol. 1 (1–41) (Grand Rapids, MI: Kregel, 2011), 575.

20 Ibid., 578.

21 Michael S. Northcott, "The Spirit of Environmentalism," chapter 19 in *The Care of Creation: Focusing Concern and Action* (Downers Grove, IL: IVP, 2000), 167–174, 169–170.

22 Curiously and unfortunately, the lectionaries omit from the suggested verses for each of these psalms those that are the most replete with images of creation (Ps

89:9–18) and of nature (Ps 80:8–14) discussed later; ecologically concerned liturgists might want to include them nonetheless.

23 Arthur Walker-Jones, *The Green Psalter: Resources for an Ecological Spirituality* (Minneapolis, MN: Fortress, 2009), 57.

24 Bruce C. Birch, *Let Justice Roll Down: The Old Testament, Ethics, and Christian Life* (Louisville, KY: Westminster/John Knox, 1991), 75–76.

25 Denise Dombkowski Hopkins, *Psalms: Books 2–3*, Wisdom Commentary vol. 21 (Collegeville, MN: Liturgical Press, 2016), 294.

26 Ibid.

27 Walker-Jones, *The Green Psalter*, 62.

28 Ibid., 63.

29 J. Clinton McCann, Jr., "The Book of Psalms," in *The New Interpreter's Bible: A Commentary in Twelve Volumes*, vol. 4 (Nashville, TN: Abingdon, 1996), 998–999.

30 Hopkins, *Psalms*, 296, quoting Jacqueline E. Lapsley, "'Look! The Children and I Are as Signs and Portents in Israel': Children in Isaiah," in *The Child in the Bible*, edited by Marcia J. Bunge, et al. (Grand Rapids, MI: Eerdmans, 2008), 82–102, 102.

31 From "O Loving Founder of the Stars," transl. Hymn 111 in *The New Century Hymnal* (Cleveland: The Pilgrim Press, 1995).

32 Alberto Taulé, "*Toda la Tierra*," Hymn 121 in ibid.

CHAPTER 12

1 World Commission on Environment and Development, Chairman: Gro Harlem Brundtland, *Our Common Future* (New York: Oxford University Press, 1987); see http://www.un-documents.net/wced-ocf.htm (accessed April 24, 2019).

2 Arthur J. Dyck in analyzing the population debate of the 1970s offers this summary of these more draconian proposals:

"Some of the policies mentioned in this literature include economic incentives, both positive and negative (Pohlman, 'Incentives'), compulsory abortion in certain cases (Davis; Ehrlich and Ehrlich), triage in matters of food policy (Green, 'Triage'; Hardin; Paddock and Paddock), and antifertility chemicals in water supplies (Ketchel, 'Fertility Control Agents')."

Arthur J. Dyck, "Alternative Views of Priorities in Population Policy" in *Population Perils*, edited by George W. Forell and William H. Lazareth (Philadelphia, PA: Fortress, 1979), 32–47: 34–35, citing Edward Pohlman, "Incentives: Not Ideal, but Necessary," in *The Population Crisis and Moral Responsibility*, edited by J. Philip Wogaman (Washington, DC: Public Affairs Press, 1973), 225–232; Kingley Davis, "Population Policy: Will Current Programs Succeed?" *Science* 158 (1969): 730–739, Paul Ehrlich and Anne Ehrlich, *Population, Resources, and Environment: Issues in Human Ecology* (San Francisco, CA: W. H. Freeman, 1970); Wade Green, "Triage: Who Shall Be Fed? Who Shall Starve?" *New York Times Magazine* (January 9, 1975); Garrett Hardin, "The Tragedy of the Commons," *Science* 162 (1969): 1243–1248; W. Paddock and P. Paddock, *Famine 197* (Little Brown & Co., 1967); Melvin M. Ketchel, "Fertility Control Agents as a Possible Solution to the World Population

Problem," *Perspect. Biol. Med.* 11 (1968): 687–703; also in Arthur J. Dyck, *On Human Care: An Introduction to Ethics* (Nashville, TN: Abingdon, 1980), 36. Dyck's comparative analysis of "crises environmentalists," "family planners," and "developmental distributivists" in the debate about population is percipient and is still relevant.

3 Mei Fong, *One Child: The Story of China's Most Radical Experiment* (New York: Houghton Mifflin Harcourt, 2016), x–xii, 65–84.

4 Robert Engelman, *More: Population, Nature, and What Women Want* (Washington, DC: Island Press, 2008), 6.

5 Dyck, "Alternative Views," 37; see also Dyck, *On Human Care*, 42.

6 Denise Dombkowski Hopkins, "Bridging the Divide between Bible and Pastoral Theology in 2 Kings 5," presented at a meeting of the faculty of Wesley Theological Seminary, April 22, 2019, *Practical Matters: A Journal of Religious Practices and Practical Theology* (forthcoming), citing "New Statistics: The Government Is Separating 65 Children a Day from Parents at the Border," https://www.vox.com/2018/6/19/17479138/how-many-families-separated-border-immigration (accessed September 8, 2018).

7 Only later after the flood, when the blessing of fertility is reiterated to Noah's family, are people given permission to eat animal flesh (Gen 9:1–3).

8 Christopher Ingraham, "Wealth Concentration Returning to 'Levels Last Seen During the Roaring Twenties,' According To New Research," *Washington Post* (February 8, 2019), https://www.washingtonpost.com/us-policy/2019/02/08/wealth-concentration-returning-levels-last-seen-during-roaring-twenties-according-new-research/?utm_term=.f6790eb05474 (accessed April 26, 2019), citing Gabriel Zucman, "World Inequality Database," https://wid.world/country/usa/.

9 Chloe Taylor, "Richest 26 People Now Own Same Wealth As Poorest Half of the World, Oxfam Claims," *CNBC* (January 20, 2019, updated January 21, 2019), https://www.cnbc.com/2019/01/21/oxfam-calls-for-global-tax-hikes-for-the-worlds-richest.html (accessed April 26, 2019); see Oxfam International, "Billionaire Fortunes Grew by $2.5 Billion a Day Last Year as Poorest Saw Their Wealth Fall" (January 21, 2019), https://www.oxfam.org/en/pressroom/pressreleases/2019-01-18/billionaire-fortunes-grew-25-billion-day-last-year-poorest-saw (accessed April 26, 2019).

10 Eileen M. Schuller, "Malachi," in *The New Interprete's Bible: A Commentary in Twelve Volumes*, vol. 7 (Nashville, TN: Abingdon, 1996), 876.

11 S. D. (Fanie) Snyman, *Malachi*, Historical Commentary on the Old Testament (Bristol, CT: Peeters, 2015), 1–6; Robert C. Dentan, "Malachi" in *The Interpreter's Bible*, vol. 6 (Nashville, TN: Abingdon, 1956), 1118.

12 Snyman, *Malachi*, 16–17, 181.

13 Ibid., 5–6.

14 Schuller, "Malachi," 876; Dentan, "Malachi," 1144.

15 Thomas H. Weber, "Sirach," chapter 33 in *The Jerome Biblical Commentary*, edited by Raymond E. Brown, Joseph A. Fitzmyer, and Roland E. Murphy (Englewood Cliffs, NJ: Prentice-Hall, 1968), 541; Edward Lee Beavin, "Ecclesiasticus or The Wisdom of Jesus the Son of Sirach," in *The Interpreter's One-Volume Commentary on the Bible*, edited by Charles M. Laymon (Nashville, TN: Abingdon, 1971), 550;

James L. Crenshaw, "Sirach," in *The New Interpreter's Bible: A Commentary in Twelve Volumes*, vol. 5 (Nashville, TN: Abingdon, 1996), 610–613.

16 The RSV is used here rather than the NRSV which inexplicably adds a possessive pronoun to verse 17 so as to read, "turn the hearts of the parents to *their* children." As argued earlier, our challenge and our promise is that we deepen and extend care to all children and not just our own—the children at the border and not just the ones in the living room.

17 First verse is verse 1 from UMH 196, "Come, Thou Long-Expected Jesus," by Charles Wesley and the second verse is verse 3 from UMH 577 "God of Grace and God of Glory" by Harry Emerson Fosdick.

CHAPTER 13

1 The Roman Catholic Lectionary for the Mass also provides for the first chapter of Matthew to be read on Christmas Eve.

2 Jonathan Magonet, "On Reading Psalms as Liturgy: Psalms 96–99," in *The Shape and Shaping of the Book of Psalms: The Current State of Scholarship*, edited by Nancy L. deClaissé-Walford (Atlanta, GA: SBL Press, 2014), 161–177, 174.

3 Ellen F. Davis, "Becoming Human: Biblical Interpretation and Ecological Responsibility," Kreitler Lecture, April 22, 2008, Virginia Theological Seminary, p. 9, https://bbk12e1-cdn.myschoolcdn.com/ftpimages/95/misc/misc_53462.pdf [downloaded November 13, 2019].

4 Patricia K. Tull, "Persistent Vegetative States: People as Plants and Plants as People in Isaiah," in *The Desert Will Bloom: Poetic Visions in Isaiah*, edited by A. Joseph Everson and Hyun Chul Paul Kim (Atlanta, GA: Society of Biblical Literature, 2009), 17–34, 26–27, quoting ibid.

5 Hilary Marlow, *Biblical Prophets and Contemporary Environmental Ethics* (New York: Oxford University Press, 2009), 196.

6 Claus Westermann, *Isaiah 40–66: A Commentary*, The Old Testament Library (Philadelphia, PA: Westminster, 1969), 250.

7 Arthur Walker-Jones, *The Green Psalter: Resources for an Ecological Spirituality* (Minneapolis, MN: Fortress, 2009), 134–138.

8 Ibid., 165–166.

9 Dianne Bergant, *Psalms 73–150*, New Collegeville Bible Commentary (Collegeville, MN: Liturgical Press, 2013), 64.

10 Magonet, "On Reading Psalms as Liturgy: Psalms 96–99," 161–177, 170.

11 *The New Century Hymnal Companion* (Cleveland, OH: Pilgrim, 1998), 277.

12 David Haas and Marty Haugen, *All the Ends of the Earth* (Chicago, IL: GIA Publications, 1983), https://www.giamusic.com/store/resource/all-the-ends-of-the-earth-psalm-98-print-g2703 (accessed January 17, 2020).

13 Bob Dufford, S.J., "All the Ends of the Earth" (Portland: Oregon Catholic Press, 2012), https://www.ocp.org/en-us/songs/6557/all-the-ends-of-the-earth (accessed January 17, 2020). "All the Ends of the Earth" ©1981, Robert J. Dufford, SJ and OCP. All rights reserved. Used with permission.

14 Wesley Granberg-Michaelson, *A Worldly Spirituality: The Call to Take Care of the Earth* (San Francisco, CA: Harper & Row, 1984), 74.

15 See, for example, this suggestion for an Episcopalian service: https://www.lectionarypage.net/YearABC/SpecServ/ChristmasLessonsAndCarols.html (accessed January 17, 2020).

16 John Lawson, ed., *The Wesley Hymns* (Grand Rapids, MI: Zondervan, 1987), 52.

17 Bracketed comments should be omitted from the spoken liturgy, and they may be omitted from the written order of service as well; they are given here to indicate particular earthward or ecologically relevant images in the Scripture or hymns.

18 John Browning, actually based on Isaiah 21:11–12; for a gender-inclusive translation, see "Watcher, Tell Us of the Night," *New Century Hymnal* (Cleveland, OH: Pilgrim, 1995), #103.

19 Joy F. Patterson, #77 in *Glory to God: The Presbyterian Hymnal* (Louisville, KY: Westminster John Knox, 2013).

20 Lawson, *The Wesley Hymns*, 52.

21 *The New Century Hymnal Companion*, 277.

22 *New Century Hymnal* (Cleveland, OH: Pilgrim, 1995), #132.

23 Ibid., #138.

24 *Come to Christmas: The Customs of the Christmas and Advent Season* (Nashville, TN: Abingdon, 1998), 20.

25 Bonaventure, "Life of Saint Francis," in *The Little Flowers of St. Francis, The Mirror of Perfection, The Life of St. Francis* (New York: E. P. Dutton & Co., 1941), 303–397, 368, reproduced at https://www.ecatholic2000.com/bonaventure/assisi/francis.shtml (accessed January 16, 2020).

26 Ibid., 353.

27 John S. Dwight, #148 in *The Hymnal for Worship and Celebration* (Waco, TX: Word Music, 1986).

28 Aurelius Clemens Prudentius, translated by John Mason Neale, #108 in *Glory to God: The Presbyterian Hymnal* (Louisville, KY: Westminster John Knox, 2013); a gender-inclusive rendering is available in *New Century Hymnal*, #118.

29 John L. Bell and Graham Maule, "Who Would Think that What was Needed," Copyright © 1987 WGRG c/o Iona Community, GIA Publications, Inc., agent.#138 in *Glory to God*.

30 A more gender inclusive version of this hymn titled as "To You, O God, All Creatures Sing," adapted by Miriam Therese Winter, is given as #17 in *The New Century Hymnal*; *The New Century Hymnal Companion* (Cleveland, OH: Pilgrim, 1998), 220, indicates that Saint Francis was actually inspired by the *Benedicite*, discussed previously in the chapters on the Easter vigil and Trinity Sunday.

31 Marion L. Soards and Darrell J. Pursiful, *Galations* (Macon, GA: Smyth & Helwys, 2015), 191, citing Walter Bauer, William F. Arndt, F. Wilbur Gingrich, and Frederick W. Danker, *A Greek-English Lexicon of the New Testament and Other Early Christian Literature*, 2nd ed. (Chicago, IL: University of Chicago Press, 1979), 768–769.

32 Mary Ann Beavis and HyeRan Kim-Cragg, *Hebrews*, Wisdom Commentary vol. 54 (Collegeville, MN: Liturgical Press, 2015), 22.

33 Elizabeth A. Johnson, *Creation and the Cross: The Mercy of God for a Planet in Peril* (Maryknoll, NY: Orbis, 2019), 174–178.

34 Ibid., 185–186, citing Niels Henrik Gregersen, ed., *Incarnation: On the Scope and Depth of Christology* (Minneapolis, MN: Fortress, 2015), 18.

35 Walker-Jones, *The Green Psalter: Resources for an Ecological Spirituality*, 142.

36 Ibid., 146–147.

37 Brenton Brown, Keith Getty, and Stuart Townend, "How Good It Is to Sing [Psalm 147]," (Capitol CMG Genesis/Brenton Brown Publishing Designee and Getty Music, 2018), https://www.stuarttownend.co.uk/song/psalm-147/ (accessed January 18, 2020).

38 Joel Payne, "In the Beginning," CCL# 7026971, RESOUNDworship.org and Jubilate Hymns Ltd, https://resoundworship.org/song/in_the_beginning (accessed January 19, 2020).

CHAPTER 14

1 James E. White, *Introduction to Christian Worship*, 3rd. ed. (Nashville, TN: Abingdon, 2000), 61–62.

2 Philo, *Every Good Man is Free*, 74, cited by S. V. McCasland in *The Interpreter's Dictionary of the Bible*, vol. 3, "magi," p. 222; see http://www.early-christianwritings.com/yonge/book33.html.

3 Referring to use of Psalm 72 in worship, Michael S. Northcott writes: "The connection between right worship and the right and ethical use of nature in the Old Testament is allied with another equally important connection between right worship, the practice of justice of God (*sedeq*), and the fertility and harmony of nature itself." "The Spirit of Environmentalism," chapter 19 in *The Care of Creation: Focusing Concern and Action*, edited by R. J. Berry (Downers Grove, IL: IVP, 2000), 170.

4 Anna Gardner, "Ecojustice or Anthropological Justice? A Study of the New Heavens and the New Earth in Isaiah 65:17," in *The Earth Story in the Psalms and the Prophets*, edited by Norman C. Habel (Cleveland, OH: Pilgrim Press, 2001), 213.

5 W. Stewart McCullough notes that this emphasis on the king's duty toward the poor is strongest in Psalm 72 of all those commonly categorized as Royal Psalms. "The Psalms," *The Interpreter's Bible*, vol. 4, *Psalms Proverbs* (Nashville, TN: Abingdon, 1955), 379, following Fleming James, *Thirty Psalmists* (New York: G. P. Putnam's Sons, 1938), 220.

6 Lawrence E. Toombs, "The Psalms," *The Interpreter's One-Volume Commentary on the Bible* (Nashville, TN: Abingdon, 1971), 282.

7 Arthur Walker-Jones, *The Green Psalter: Resources for an Ecological Spirituality* (Minneapolis: Fortress Press, 2009), 7.

8 Norman K. Gottwald, *All the Kingdoms of the Earth: Israelite Prophecy and International Relations in the Ancient Near East* (New York: Harper & Row, 1964), 197.

9 The NRSV notes that "foes" is more literally translated as "those who live in the wilderness," and McCullough [p. 382] suggests it might refer to "wild beasts."

10 Marvin Tate, *Word Biblical Commentary, Vol 20, Psalms 51–100* (Waco, TX: Word Books, 1990), 225, quoted by Brian Brock, *Singing the Ethos of God : On the Place of Christian Ethics in Scripture* (Grand Rapids, MI: Eerdmans, 2007), 190 note 52; Walter Brueggemann, *The Land: Place as Gift, Promise, and Challenge in Biblical Faith* (Minneapolis, MN: Fortress Press, 2002), 74 note 18, similarly notes three petitions in this psalm, being fertility, political triumphalism, and care for the powerless; Brock is aware of the problem of supersessionism when interpreting these passages in ways proclaiming Jesus Christ as embodying the just king in the Davidic line, and he appeals to the rabbinic tradition interpreting David as having "done everything that Moses did" without superseding Moses to argue that Jesus can be confessed to embody this tradition without superseding the tradition or the Jewish prophets and kings before him (p. 235, quoting *The Midrash on the* (sic) *Psalms*, vol. 1, translated by William Braude [New Haven, CT: Yale University Press, 1959], 5).

11 Norman C. Habel, *The Land is Mine: Six Biblical Land Ideologies, Overtures to Biblical Theology* (Minneapolis, MN: Fortress Press, 1995), 26.

12 "The Great Blessing of the Waters by St. Sophronius of Jerusalem (AD 634–8)," posted by Frederica Mathewes-Green, January 20, 2014, frederica.com/writings/the-great-blessing-of-the-waters-by-st-sophronius-of-jerusal.html (downloaded January 22, 2018), quoting Melkite Greek Catholic Church Information Center, "Great Feast of the Holy Theophany of Holy God the Son within the Holy Trinity / Our Lord, God and Savior, Jesus Christ—Celebration Great Blessing of Water Prayer," http://www.mliles.com/melkite/holytheophanywaterblessprayer.shtml (downloaded January 22, 2018); quoting Byzantine Melkite Euchologion (*Eparchy of Newton [Our Lady of the Annunciation Al Bisharah]*, Roslindale, Massachusetts, MA: Sophia Press); see also "The Theophany of Our Lord and Savior Jesus Christ: The Service for the Great Sanctification of the Water," posted by the Antiochian Orthodox Christian Diocese of Los Angeles and the West, http://www.antiochian.org/sites/default/files/liturgical_guides/5-theophany-waters_0.pdf (downloaded January 22, 2018).

13 Ibid.

14 Many of these prayers of thanksgiving over the water make use of Luther's "flood prayer." H. Paul Santmire, *Ritualizing Nature: Renewing Christian Liturgy in a Time of Crisis* (Minneapolis, MN: Fortress, 2008), 134–135, citing Benjamin M. Stewart, "Flooding the Landscape: Luther's Flood Prayer and Baptismal Theology," *CrossAccent*, 13, no. 1 (January 2005): 4–14; see also Gordon W. Lathrop, *Holy Ground: A Liturgical Cosmology* (Minneapolis, MN: Fortress Press, 2009), 109.

An ancient source for baptismal prayer remembering water's role in both sacred story and life on earth is the *Gelesian Sacramentary* named for Pope Gelasius from the fifth century but probably dating from the seventh or eighth century, quoted in Linda Gibler, *From The Beginning to Baptism: Scientific and Sacred Stories of Water, Oil, and Fire* (Collegeville, MN: Liturgical Press, 2010), 25–27, citing *Sacraments and Worship: Liturgy and Doctrinal Development of Baptism, Confirmation, and the Eucharist*, edited by Paul F. Palmer, Sources of Christian Theology 1 (Westminster, MD: Newman Press, 1955), 35–37.

15 Lathrop, *Holy Ground*, 113.
16 Ibid.
17 Ibid., 34.
18 Ibid., 37.
19 Ibid., 44.
20 Norman C. Habel and Geraldine Avent, "Rescuing Earth from a Storm God: Psalms 29 and 96–97," in *The Earth Story in the Psalms and the Prophets*, 42, citing Theodore Hiebert, "Theophany in the Old Testament," in *The Anchor Bible Dictionary*, vol. 6 (New York: Doubleday, 1992): 505–511, 505.
21 Habel and Avent, "Rescuing Earth from a Storm God," 43, citing William L. Holladay, *The Psalms Through Three Thousand Years: Prayerbook of a Cloud of Witnesses* (Minneapolis, MN: Augsburg, 1993), 20, also citing Othmar Keel, *The Symbolism of the Biblical World: An Ancient Near Eastern Iconography and the Book of Psalms* (London: SPCK, 1978), 212.
22 Lathrop, *Holy Ground*, 42 note 34.
23 Ibid., 114; citing Gail Ramshaw, "In the Name: Toward Alternate Baptismal Idioms," *Ecumenical Review* 54 (2002), 343–352; see also Ruth C. Duck, *Gender and the Name of God* (Cleveland, OH: Pilgrim Press, 1991), and Duck, *Worship for the Whole People of God* (Louisville, KY: Westminster John Knox, 2013), 176.
24 Linda Gibler, *From the Beginning to Baptism: Scientific and Sacred Stories of Water, Oil, and Fire* (Collegeville, MN: Liturgical Press, 2010), 1–2, 36. © 2010 by Order of Saint Benedict. Published by Liturgical Press, Collegeville, Minnesota.
25 The Revised Common Lectionary has Ephesians 3:1–12 as the reading for all three years; the Roman Catholic Lectionary for Mass also has a reading from the third chapter of Ephesians for this time (Eph 3:2–3a, 5–6), but it stops short of these verses; see http://catholic-resources.org/Lectionary/1998USL-Christmas.htm.
26 Scripture quotations taken from the (NASB®) New American Standard Bible®, Copyright © 1995 by The Lockman Foundation. Used by permission. All rights reserved. www.lockman.org
27 The Riverside Church augmentation of the traditional baptismal formula is used here; see Ramshaw, "In the Name: Toward Alternate Baptismal Idioms," 350, and Duck, *Gender and the Name of God*, 163–166, for a discussion of the pros and cons of this approach.

POSTLUDE: CONCLUSION

1 *From Ashes to Fire* (Nashville, TN: Abingdon, 1979), 188–194; and Catholic Culture, https://www.catholicculture.org/culture/liturgicalyear/prayers/view.cfm?id=1227 (accessed April 30, 2021).
2 *Dextera Dei ubique est*. Martin Luther, "That These Words, 'This is my Body,' Etc. Still Stand against the Fanatics," *Luther's Works*, edited by Robert H. Fischer (Philadelphia, PA: Muhlenberg, 1961), 37:62, quoted by H. Paul Santmire, *Ritualizing Nature: Renewing Christian Liturgy in a Time of Crisis* (Minneapolis, MN: Fortress, 2008), 115–116.

Biblical Citations

Genesis
1	27-30, 128
1:1–2:4a	87, 144-45
1:1–2	125, 136
1:1–3a	87
1:2	263
1:7	145
1:22	28, 212-13
1:26–27	252
1:27	113
1:28	29-30
1:29–30	27, 213
1:30	129
2	17, 22-23, 234
2:6–9	22
2:7	30
2:15	22, 28, 30, 150
2:24	113
3	17, 19-22, 31, 234-35
3:1–7	22
3:1-19	32
3:14–19	31
3:17-20	20-21
3:19	16
6-9	28
6:17	129
7–9	87-88
7:11b	88
7:14–16	88
7:15	129
7:18–24	88
8:11–13	88
8:17	29
8:17–9:17	88
8:19–22	88
9	16-17
9:1–4	28
9:1–7	88
9:2	29
9:8	27
9:12	28
9:13-15	27
9:15	180-1
11:1–9	126

Exodus
14	87, 280n15
19:5–6	131
20:4	145
23	46-47
23:15	46
23:16	46-47, 130
34:6	115
34:10, 18, 22, 25	46

Leviticus
16:10	70
23:10–11	46
23:15–17	46, 130
23:17	131

23:34	47	8:6–8	29
23:40	55, 275n25	19	270n6
23:40–43	47	19:1-4	8
		24	201-2, 206
Numbers		24:1	207
11:24–30	131-32	24:1–2	201-2
20:5	275n12	24: 3-4, 7, 10	202
		29	260
Deuteronomy		33:5b–9	143
4:32–34, 39–40	144	33:8	146
4:39	144	46:1-10	165-6
8:7–8	47	47	115-16
16:1	46	72	185, 189, 250-4
16:9	46, 130	72: 7. 16, 19	185
16:12	46, 131	80	201-5
16:13	47	80:3	179, 203
16:14	53	80:7, 14	203
18:10–14	70	80:8–18	204
26	26	80:17b	205
26:2	46, 130	85:10–11	184
26:8–9	46-47, 131	89	201-3
26:8–11	26	89:9–12a, 14	203
32:11	264	89:44–45	203
32:17	70	90–106	116
		91:1, 16	33-34
2 Samuel		91:11–13	33
7:1–17	197	93–99	231
7:8b–14a, 16	197-98	93	115-16, 164
7:12	198	95–99	116
7:16	199	95:3–6	165
		96–98	228, 231
Ezra		96	236
3:11b–13	217	96:1	231
		96:3, 7–8	231
Nehemiah		96:10–13	231
8:8	217	96:12	232
		96:13	228
Job		97	236
34:15	135	97:1a	169, 232
38:25–27	18-19	97:2	228
42:3	19	97:4–6	232
42:6	18-19, 272n6	98	236
		98:4	232
Psalms		98:7–9	232
8	29, 144-45, 157	98:10	228
8:6	68	100:1, 3	164-65

Biblical Citations

103:8–14	22-23	**Isaiah**	
103:13–14	36	1–39	230
103:14	16	2:1–4	174
103:15-17a	23	2:4–5	178
104	18, 125, 128-30	6:1–8	144
104:1, 10–18, 20–26	36-39	6:3	44, 53, 74, 144
104:30	125, 135-36	7	197-99
107–150	246	7:3	200
113–118	49pr	7:4	199
118	49-50, 266	7:9	199
118: [19–20] 24–27	54	7:10–14	236
118:25	49	7:14	201, 229
118:25-26	43-44, 50, 53, 275-76nn26-28	7:16–17	199
		7:23–25	200
118:25-27	275n20	9:1–7	228-29
126	184-85	9:6	183
126:6	185	11:1	229
139	112	11:1–5	182
139:13–15	18	11:1–9	235
146:5–6a	193	11:1–10	182-84
146:9b-10	193	11:6	171
147	245-46	11:6–9	32-33, 72, 182-83, 235
148	239-40, 246	11:9	171, 183-84, 267
150	129-30		
		11:10	187
Proverbs		12:2–6	194
3:19	157, 159	13:20–22	70
8	154, 157, 234, 243	20	230
		21:11-12	235, 295n18
8:1, 3b–4	90	25:6–9	98
8: [1–4], 22–31	146	34:13–15	70
8:1–8, 19–21; 9:4b–6	89	35:1–10	192-93
8:22–31	90	39	230
8:23–24, 27–29a	263	40:1	181
9	146, 157	40:1–11	180-2
		40:3–5	180
Sirach		40:5	180-1
1:1–10	218	40:6–7	181
24:1–6	248	40:12	181
24:1–17	242-44, 247	40:17	181
24:19–22	247	40:21–23	181
42:15–50:29	218	44:2–4	136
42:15-43:33	218-19	44:3–4	128
48:10–11	218-19	45:8	191, 290n1

52	228-31	**Hosea**	
52:7	230-31	10:8	75
52:7–10	235		
52:10	230, 232	**Joel**	
54:5–14	89	2:21–22, 28-32	126
55:1	128		
58:1–12	24-25	**Micah**	
60:1–6	250	4:1–4	174
61	193-94	4:3–4	207
61:1–2b	193-94	5:2–5a	198, 206
61:10–62:3	245		
61:11	194, 245	**Zephaniah**	
62	228-31	3:17–20b	194
62: [1–5] 6–12	235		
62:7	231	**Zechariah**	
62:11	230-1	9:9	274n1
63	230	12:10–14	75
63:7–64:12	175	14:8–9	128
64:1-3	175		
64:1–9	175-76	**Malachi**	
64:6b-8	175-76	1:1-2a	216
65:17	186	1:7–13	215
65:17–25	98	1:11	216
65:25	32-33	2:7–15	215-16
66:22	186	3:1a	214
		3:5	215
Jeremiah		3:10–11	215
4:23–26	72	4:2	221
31:1–6	98	4:4	217
31:7–14	244-45	4:5–6	214-17
33:9-16, 25	174-75		
		Matthew	
Baruch		1:18–24	227
3:9–15	89	1:18–25	236
3:29–34	89-90	1:20b–21	200-1
3:32-4:4	89	1:21, 25	201
5:1–9	182	1:23	198-99, 201, 267
5:7-8	182	2:1–12	249-51
5:8–9	188	2:2	254
		2:6	198
Ezekiel		3:17	6
3:1–29	90	4:6	33
3:52–90	90-1, 145-46	11:10	214
7:13b–14	168	12:39	113
34:11-24	169	16:4	113

16:28	5	15:33	74
17:5	6	15:38	74
17:12	5	15:39	259
21:2–5	274n1	16:8	92, 114
21:9	43	16:9–20	112
24:19	76	16:15	113
24:37	177	16:15–20	111-15
24:40–41	177		
24:42	177	**Luke**	
25:14–30	177	1:14–17	221
26:29	61	1:15	220
27:45	74	1:15b–17	209-10
27:45–54	81	1:17	214, 217
27:51	99	1:20	209
27: 51–52	73-74	1:26–38	222
27:54	74	1:28b–33	222-3
27:55-66	82	1:35	220
28	93	1:35, 37-38a	223
28:2	92, 99	1:39–45	223-4
28:16–20	111, 144	1:41–42	220
28:18	112	1:46–55	193, 224
28:19	261	1:67	220
28:20	112	1:68	239
		1:68–79	184, 225
Mark		1:75	184
1:1	259	1:76	214-5
1:2	214, 290n13	1:79	184, 220, 224, 267
1:9–11	259	1:80	184
1:10	259	2:1–7	236
1:11	250	2:8–20	233
1:12	16	2:8–21	237
1:12-15	32	2:10b–11a	191
1:13	32-33, 265	2:14	239-40, 249
8:11–13	113	2:17	219
8:38	113-14	2:19, 21b	278n47
9:7	6	2:29–32	238-39
9:9	5	3:4–6	180
10:6	113	3:6	180, 182, 188
11:2	274n1	3:16b–18a	191
11:9	43	4:10–11	33
13:4	114	4:16–19	193-94
13:17	76	7:27	214
13:19	113	9:31	4
13:24–25	113	9:35	6
13:33-37	177	11:27-28	76

11:29	113	2:21	51
13:29	64	3:5	128
17:11–37	177	3:13–14	112
19:12–27	177	3:16–17	127-28, 144
19:30	274n1	5:1	50
19:38,	43	6:58a	112
19:40	54	6:61b–62	112
21:20	76	7	50
21:20–24	76	7:30	51
21:23	76	7:37–38	51
21:25–27	176	7:37b–39a	128, 136
21:28	177	10:18	127
22:14–19	81	10:22–39	50
22:19	81	12:12-16	55
22:39–48	81	12:12–19	50
22:54–23:1	81	12:13	43
23:24–31	81	12:14-15	274n1
23:27-31	74	12:23	51
23:28–31	76	12:27	51
23:29	76	13:1	51
23:35	75	14:16, 26	127
23:36–38, 42	163-64	14:30	127
23:44-5	74	15:26	127
23:48	75	16:7	127
24:6–7, 9b	92	17:1	51
24:13–43	99	17:1–5	81
24:39	99	17:2	81, 127
24:46–53	111	17:5	112
24:47b	77	18:1–19:42	80
24:49	106	18:33–37	164
24:51	111	18:37–38a	81
		19:30	51, 104, 128
John		19:37	75
1	146, 227, 233, 238, 242-3	20:1	92
		20:17	111
1:1–3	247-48, 263	20:19–23	127
1:1–4	233	20:24–29	99
1:1–5, 14	237	21:1–14	99
1:3-5	247		
1:6–9	196	**Acts**	
1:9–10	247	1:1–11	111, 117
1:14	233, 247-48, 263	1:3–5	103
2:4	51	1:6–11a	117
2:11	250	1:8	126
2:13–25	50	2	130

2:1	103	15:19–26	98
2:1–2	125	15:20–26, 28	133, 166-68
2:1–21	126	15:24–26	104
2:4	114	15:24–27a	68
2:11	126		
2:16–18	126	**2 Corinthians**	
10:34–43	98	5:17-20	19
20:7, 11	83	13:11–13	160
28:3–6	114		

Galatians

3:27–29	240
4:3–7	240
4:3–9	186-87
4:8–9	240
5:22	138

Romans

1:7b	205-6
5	32
5:11–19	31
6:3–11	87, 91-92
6:3–6	16
6:7	71
6:12	92
6:14	92
8:12–17	143-44
8:15	146
8:19–23	104-5, 117
8:20–21	31
8:21–24a	139
8:22–23	131, 144
8:22–27	104
8:33b–35, 37–39	104
11:16–27	131
13:12	179
15:4–13	187-88
16:25-27	206

Ephesians

1:3–6	242
1:8b–10	242, 248, 262
1:15-18	242
1:15–23	166-67
1:20–23	105, 168
3	250
4:10	105, 120

Philippians

1:6	185
1:10b–11	185
2:5–11	54
2:6–11	41-42, 66-67
2:7–11	71-72
4:4–7	195

1 Corinthians

2:1–16	68
10:16	9, 58
11	132-33
11:23b	64
11:24–25	59, 132-33
11:25b–26	62
12	132-33
12:7	133
12:12–13	138
12:13	132-3
13-14	133
15	98
15:1–11	98

Colossians

1:11–20	166
1:13	167
1:15–20	67, 166-67, 243
1:16	67
1:20	166
2:10b	67
2:15	67, 71, 103-4

1 Thessalonians

5:16–20	195
5:23	195-96

Hebrews
1:1–4	238
1:2	241
1:2–3	243
1:2–4	233
2:10–11a	241
2:10–18	241
2:14	242

James
5:7–10	195
5:8b	196

1 Peter
3:18-22	27
3:21b–22	105

2 Peter
1:4	9
1:16b–19	6
1:17	7
3:5-7	186
3:8–15a	185-7

Revelation
1:4–6	164
1:10	83
5:13	97
6:12–17	75
22:17	127, 136-37

Index

AAP (American Academy of Pediatrics), 212
Abraham, 65, 78, 119, 175, 218, 224–25, 240
Adam, 20–21, 28, 30–32, 129, 234–35
adamah, 22
agriculture, xii, 26, 30, 43, 45–48, 58–59, 103, 121, 131, 185, 200, 210, 212, 229
air, 20, 27–29, 35–36, 49, 66, 91, 96, 108, 129–30, 132, 142, 145, 157, 207, 210, 212–13, 227, 241, 244, 257, 265
akathist, 11
Alexandrian Basil, 149
alien(s), 26, 193, 215
AME (African Methodist Episcopal Church), 61, 93
AME Zion (African Methodist Episcopal Zion Church), 61
anaphora, 9, 111, 150
angel(s), 3, 33–34, 83, 91, 93–94, 100, 104–5, 114, 149, 172, 191, 200, 209, 214, 216–17, 220, 222–23, 234, 236, 239, 249, 278n47
Anglican, 60–1
animal(s), 3, 12, 18–19, 27–30, 32–34, 36–37, 49, 55, 61, 69–70, 86–88, 91, 95, 98, 118, 121, 126, 129–30, 174, 177, 180–84, 196, 200, 204, 215, 236–37, 239, 245–46, 261, 267, 293n7
Anna the prophet, 238, 249, 278n47
Anselm of Canterbury, 142
Antarctic, 121
apocalyptic, apocalypse, 6, 76, 113–14, 128, 171, 177–78, 185–86, 270n4, 270n8
Apostles' Creed, 147–48
aravah, aravot, 47–48
archē, 67–68, 104–5
Armenian Apostolic, 254
ascension, xi, 4, 34, 42, 83, 103, 105–17, 126, 131, 133, 163–64, 166–68, 231, 242, 270, 282n21
asceticism, 20
ashes, 16–20, 23–25, 35, 39, 245
Ash Wednesday, 15–22, 24–26, 57, 135, 265
Assyria, 198–9, 205, 230
Athanasius, 7
Augustine, 25, 152, 158, 271n3, 287n35, 288n71
Avent, Geraldine, 260

Babel, 126
Babylon, 70–89, 214–17, 230, 244
Babylonian exile, 169, 175, 181, 202, 216, 231

307

Index

bacteria, 23
Baldovin, John, 149
baptism, 16, 25–27, 84, 87, 91–98, 105, 132–39, 144, 147–49, 250, 254–64, 297n14, 298n27
Baptism of Christ, xi, 6, 32, 176, 250, 254–55, 258–61, 265
Baptist, 4–5, 269–70n4. *See also* John the Baptist
Bartholomew, Patriarch, 20, 60
Baruch, 89, 182, 243
basar (flesh), 180
Basil (the Great) of Caesarea, 148–50
beast(s), 16, 27, 29, 32–33, 85, 213, 236–37, 265–66, 297n9
Beavis, Mary Ann, 241
Benedicite omnia opera, 90, 145, 295n30
Berdyaev, Nicolas, 7
Bergant, Dianne, 232, 291n13
Berry, Wendell, 135
Best, Ernest, 32
Bethlehem, 172, 198, 206, 236, 251, 254
Bikurim, 130
biosphere, 172
Birch, Bruce C., 202–3, 288n2
bird(s), 27–28, 85, 88, 197, 213
birth, childbirth, x–xi, 20, 85, 121, 157, 163, 171–72, 177, 184, 189, 191–92, 197–98, 209, 220–21, 224, 227, 239–40, 249–51, 254, 258, 261–64, 267, 278n47
Blanchard, Kathryn D., 173, 178, 187, 195
blessing of the waters, 250, 254
Bloch, Abraham P., 46–48, 131
blood, 9, 13, 21, 28–29, 57–61, 67, 133, 166–67, 229, 242, 253, 261, 265
bodies, 11, 17–18, 21, 23, 25, 73, 76–77, 91–95, 98–99, 104–5, 123, 131, 139, 144, 243, 261
bodily, 18–19, 62, 77, 99, 131, 135, 144, 151, 187, 243, 278n47
Boff, Leonardo, 148, 152, 155–56, 287n58
Bonaventure, Saint, 4, 237
Book of Common Prayer, xiii, 18, 22, 61, 65, 279n6, 280n15, 286n19

Book of Common Worship, xiii, 269n2, 278n51, 286n19, 286n25
Book of Worship, xiii, 80, 269n2, 278n51, 279n6, 280n15, 280n17
breath(e), 21–22, 27, 30, 35–39, 49, 66, 85–88, 91, 95–96, 99, 125, 127–30, 132, 134–37, 143, 150–51, 156, 181, 213, 227, 237, 243, 257, 265, 267, 272n13
Brown, Brenton, 246
Brueggemann, Walter, 192–93, 297n10
Bucharest 1974 A.D., 210

Caird, G. B., 69–72
Cana, 51, 64, 250, 261–62, 267
candle(s), 79–82, 84–87, 172, 178, 187–88, 195–96, 206, 220–25, 234
canticle, 90–91, 146, 173, 194, 209, 239
Cappadocian Fathers, 148
carrying capacity, 200, 210–11, 213
chai, 22
chaos, 66, 88, 95–96, 115, 145, 151, 164, 176, 193, 203, 232, 239
Chava, 22
chaya, 22
child, children, xiii, 23, 31, 36, 74–75, 77, 101, 104–5, 122, 139, 143, 157, 171, 173, 176, 183–84, 195–201, 205, 209–25, 228–29, 233, 235–41, 250–51, 254, 263–64, 267, 278n47, 280n16, 290n14, 292n30, 293n3, 293n6, 294n16
chochma, 146, 262
Christmas, ix–xii, 3, 5–6, 80, 106, 163, 166, 171–73, 176, 191, 198, 227–28, 230–46, 249–50, 289n2, 294n1
Chryssavgis, John, 5, 8, 60, 270n16, 276n3
citron, 47–49
climate, climate change, 20, 69, 116, 121, 245, 265, 273n14
communion, Communion, 3, 8–9, 16, 20, 41, 43–44, 53, 57–65, 90, 96–97, 107, 148, 155–56, 160, 266, 269n1, 286n19, 287n58
conception, 192, 209
conflict, 28–29, 70, 234, 288n2
consumption, 20, 29, 183, 211, 265

conversion, 19–20, 178
cosmos, cosmic, 5, 19, 32, 35, 60, 66, 72–73, 91–92, 133, 150, 152–58, 219, 234, 240, 242, 258–61, 267, 276n3
Council of Constantinople in 381 A.D., 148
Council of Nicea in 325 A.D., 148
covenant, 12–13, 16–17, 26–28, 46, 63, 65, 78, 88–89, 133, 135, 151, 175–77, 180, 198, 201, 215–17, 225, 273n17, 278n51
Cranmer, Thomas, 18, 61
creational justice, 246
Creator, 7–8, 18, 20, 39, 60, 63, 70–71, 91, 115–16, 129, 135, 145, 147, 149–50, 154–57, 166, 175–76, 188, 193, 200, 203, 207, 215, 231, 233, 238, 241–42, 244, 256, 261–62, 267
crucified, crucifixion, ix, 4, 10, 13, 41–42, 50–52, 57, 64, 68, 71–78, 83, 91–92, 97, 99, 104–5, 109–11, 127, 159, 163–64, 166, 243, 259–60
curse, 20–21, 30–32, 34, 76, 214, 216, 234
cycles (agricultural and ecological), 17, 35, 48, 58, 93–95, 103, 158, 172, 227, 243, 257, 265

Daly, Robert J., SJ, 150
darkness, 11–12, 24, 37, 74, 79–80, 83, 86–87, 91, 93, 100, 125, 130, 136, 157, 167, 179, 188, 220, 224–25, 228, 247, 256
date palm, 47
David, King, 75, 169, 174–75, 182, 197–205, 223, 225, 228–29, 253, 297n10
Davis, Ellen F., 229
death, 5, 10–11, 17–19, 31, 43, 57–58, 71, 76–77, 85–95, 98, 100, 110, 120–22, 130, 151, 153, 156, 220, 224–25, 242, 257, 259, 265
death, Christ's, xi, 4, 16, 41–42, 54, 57, 61–64, 67–68, 71–74, 78–81, 84, 87–88, 91–92, 94, 99, 104–5, 110, 113, 120, 133, 149, 159, 167–68, 242, 259, 266

deification, 7–8, 10, 59, 110, 270n4
deliverance, xi, 33, 46, 130–31, 199, 252
demon(ic), 70–71, 73, 113, 168
desert, 3, 11, 16, 18, 32, 48, 122, 192
Deuterocanonical, 89–90, 145, 148, 157, 210, 218, 242–43, 246
Deutero-Isaiah, 128, 181
devash (honey), 46, 131
devil, 32–33, 242
disobedience, 21, 31, 210, 214, 217, 219, 221
divinization, xii, 5–7, 10, 59–60
docetism, 99
Dombkowski Hopkins, Denise, 203, 205, 212
dominion, 17, 28–31, 34, 67, 71, 91–92, 105, 110, 115, 145, 149–50, 163–68, 251–52
dominium terrae, 29
dove, 176, 255–59, 263
doxology, 148, 206, 253
Dufford, Bob, 233
dunamis, 68, 104–5, 113
dust, 16–17, 18–25, 30, 35–39, 60, 73, 122, 130, 181, 252
Dyck, Arthur, 212, 292–93n2

earthling, ix, 109–10, 122, 265
Easter, ix–xii, 3, 5, 16–17, 25, 34, 41–42, 50, 57, 80, 83–106, 111, 117, 127, 131, 133, 135, 142, 145–46, 163, 167–68, 173, 242, 266
economic, economy, 24, 26, 29, 34, 68–69, 73, 147, 169, 174, 205–6, 211–16, 219, 229, 266, 292n2
ecosphere, ix, 266
ecotheological, 211
Eden, 17, 22, 28, 30, 32
ELCA. *See* Evangelical Lutheran Church in America
Eliezer, Rabbi, 48
Elijah, 4, 6, 13, 210, 214, 217–19, 221
Elizabeth (mother of John the Baptist), 192, 209, 219–20, 223–24
Elvey, Anne F., 76, 278n47
embodied, embody, ix, 19, 76–77, 87,

91–92, 99, 105, 122, 172, 176, 227, 233, 297n10
Emmanuel, 200–1, 225, 236. *See also* Immanuel
Engelman, Robert, 293n4
enthronement psalms, 115–16, 164, 228, 231–32
environment, 18, 20, 30, 35, 60, 63–64, 69, 72, 86, 104, 120, 169, 171, 187, 200, 210–11, 213, 227, 251–53, 266, 291n13, 293n2, 296n3
environmental degradation, 171, 187, 195
epiclesis, 95, 149–50, 263
Epiphany, ix–xii, 4–6, 106, 176, 185, 198, 227, 238, 249–51, 254, 258, 262–63, 267, 285n6, 289n2
Episcopal, xiii, 22, 61, 65, 91, 93, 109, 149, 282n21
eretz, 174, 184
eschatology, eschatological, 59–60, 62, 64, 107, 150, 172
etrog, 47–49
euangelion, 191
Eucharist, eucharistic, 3, 9–12, 42, 58–65, 78, 84, 96–97, 107, 109–10, 133, 148–51, 265
evangelica theology, 156
Evangelical Lutheran Church in America (ELCA), xiii, 87, 149, 277n26
Evangelical Lutheran Worship, xiii, 16, 21–23, 65–66, 95–96, 272n5, 280n20
Eve, 20–21, 30, 234
evolution, 73, 153
exile, 169, 175, 181, 202–3, 214, 216, 230–31
exodus, 46–47, 61, 65, 79, 87, 92–93, 95, 131, 144, 203, 258, 261
exousia, 67–68, 104–5, 168, 177
Exsultet, 84, 86, 266, 279n4, 279n6
extinction, 69, 77, 118, 121, 151, 153, 265

Fall, the, 31, 72, 234
Fall (autumn), 15, 47, 53

farmers, 47, 195, 229
fauna, 153
feminist xiii, 76, 153
fertile, fertility, 25, 28–29, 31, 85, 152, 204, 212, 214, 253–54, 292n2, 293n7, 296n3, 297n10
field(s), 11, 21, 23, 29, 47, 49, 55, 69, 90, 112, 126, 129, 159, 177, 181, 200–1, 204, 215, 231–33, 236, 253
Fiji, Fijian, 23, 96, 145, 272n13
Finlan, Stephen, 7–8
fire, 12, 49, 66, 84, 86, 91, 96, 120, 129, 134, 156, 165, 172, 175, 186–87, 191, 204, 229, 239, 241, 256, 260–61
first fruits, 26, 46, 98, 103–4, 122–23, 130–31, 133, 139, 144, 166–67
flesh, ix, 5, 10, 21, 26–28, 49, 59, 61, 67, 71, 81, 88–89, 91, 99, 112, 122, 126–27, 135, 146, 154, 157–59, 172, 177, 180–82, 188, 215, 227–28, 233, 238, 240, 242–43, 247–49, 256, 258, 265–67
flood(s), 12, 16–17, 27–29, 65, 69, 88–89, 95–96, 115, 129, 164, 177, 232, 236, 258–59, 261, 288n2, 293n7, 297n14
flora, 48, 153
font, 95, 136, 138–39, 261–62
food, 20–24, 27–28, 30–31, 37–38, 52, 54–55, 58, 129, 132, 137, 193, 200, 213–15, 245–46, 266, 273n13, 292n2
forest(s), 20, 35, 37, 100, 129–30, 157, 179, 182, 204, 231–32
Fosdick, Harry Emerson, 222
Fox, Matthew, 7, 134, 152, 156–57
Francis, Pope, 19–20, 60, 159
fruit, 17, 20–21, 25–27, 36, 46–47, 50, 54–55, 61, 77, 98, 126, 130–31, 138–39, 154, 204, 213, 220, 224, 239, 244–45, 253, 275n12
fruitful, 28–30, 88, 188–89, 212
fungi, 23

gamul, 290n14
garden, 21–22, 24–25, 30, 35, 102, 139, 150, 194, 196, 234, 238, 244–45

Gardner, Anne, 251
Garrett, Susan R., 32–33
gender(ed), 21, 126, 130, 142, 147, 152, 159, 239, 261, 263, 272n13, 295n18, 295n28, 295n30
generous, generosity, 20, 138, 148, 207, 213
genocide, 119
George, K. M., 7, 9–10
gestation, 76–77, 192, 197, 209, 278n47
Getty, Keith, 246
Gibler, Linda, 261, 297n14
Gillette, Carolyn Winfrey, 281n30
global, 20, 45, 120, 130, 174–75, 195, 211, 230–31, 265, 291n13
Gloria, 240
glorify, glorified, glorification, xi, xiv, 5, 7–8, 13, 43, 51–52, 65, 110, 112, 129, 144, 148–49, 187, 231, 257
Good Friday, xi, 41–43, 57–58, 68, 78, 80, 84, 92, 99, 103, 167, 242, 266
Gottwald, Norman, 252
grain, 46, 49, 130, 185, 244, 253
Granberg-Michaelson, Wesley, 234
greed, 20, 63, 73
Greek Orthodox, 135, 254, 271n24
greenhouse effect, 120–21
Gregersen, Niels, 288n73
Gregorios, Paulos, Metropolitan, 110
Gregory of Nazianzus, 7
Gregory of Nyssa, 148, 282n22
ground, 15, 18, 20–30, 36–39, 46, 48–49, 54, 91, 116, 125, 128, 130, 132, 136, 182, 184, 202–4, 234, 246, 258
Gushee, David, 201

Haas, David, 232
Habel, Norman, 30, 99, 253, 260
habitat(s), habitation, 19, 28, 36, 69, 129, 165, 200, 210, 265
hadar, hadas, hadassim, 47–48
Hagar's Well, 95
haggadah, 87
Hallel, 43, 49
Hanukkah, 50

Harakas, Stanley S., 10, 270n16
Harink, Douglas, 5, 186–87
Hartshorne, Charles, 153
harvest, 26, 44, 46–49, 130–31, 185, 229, 244, 266
Haugen, Marty, 109, 137, 232
health, healing, xii, 13
healthy, x, 19, 23–24, 33, 174, 179, 187, 210, 229
heaven, 5–6, 13, 34, 39, 42, 49, 53–54, 60–64, 67, 72, 84–85, 89, 93–94, 97, 99, 105–6, 109–13, 117, 120, 125, 141, 144–47, 149, 167–68, 175, 177, 180, 193, 203–4, 215, 218, 233, 236–39, 242–43, 248, 251, 255–56, 259, 266
herbicide, 86, 121
hermeneutic(al), xii, 3, 52–53, 252
Herod, 251, 254
Hickman, Hoyt, 63
Hildegard of Bingen, 134, 156, 284n4, 288nn60–61
holocaust, 119
Holy Spirit, xi, 9, 13, 21, 35, 83, 95, 98, 103–4, 107–8, 110–12, 117, 125–36, 142–51, 153–56, 160, 187–88, 191, 200, 210, 220–21, 223–24, 234, 240, 255–56, 259–60, 262–64, 267, 272n5
Holy Week, xi, 16, 41–42, 45, 52, 57, 67, 80, 103, 163
hope, 12, 25, 27, 33–34, 48, 55, 59, 63–64, 72–73, 101, 104–5, 109, 111, 120–22, 132, 134, 137, 139, 159, 163, 166, 169–74, 176, 183–89, 191, 193, 199–200, 202, 214, 216, 219–20, 222–24, 230, 246, 253–54, 267
Horrell, David G., 19
hosanna, 42–44, 49–55, 58, 266
Hoshana Rabba, 49, 51
Hoshanot, 49–50, 52
hubris, 21
humanity, 3, 8, 10, 20–21, 28–31, 55, 59, 71–73, 110–11, 150, 153, 157, 165, 180, 195, 204–5, 207, 212–13, 234, 242, 246, 249, 258, 260, 266

Hunt, Cherryl, 19
hypostaseis, 148

Immanuel, 107, 198–200, 205, 229, 236. *See also* Emmanuel
immigrant, immigration, 212, 216
incarnate, incarnation, ix, xi, 5, 10, 59–60, 78, 99, 106, 110, 112, 146, 153, 158–59, 164, 166, 176, 186, 227–28, 233–34, 238, 242–43, 246, 249, 263, 267, 270
Ingathering, 47
insect(s), 23, 85–86, 118
instrumental value, 211
intrinsic value, 202, 211, 246
Ioudaioi, 45
irony, 17, 27, 29, 31, 34, 273n22

Jeremias, Joachim, 32
Jerusalem, 4, 41–44, 49–55, 57, 64, 74–77, 117, 125–6, 128, 174–75, 178, 199–200, 205, 214, 217, 230–31, 238, 245, 266, 274n1, 278n47
Jewish Festivals, xii, 43–53, 103, 130–31
Johnson, Elizabeth A., 134, 142, 148, 152, 157–59, 243, 288n67
John the Baptist, 172, 180, 184, 188, 191, 193, 196, 209, 214, 267
Jordan River, 26, 95, 196, 250, 255–59, 261, 263, 265, 267
just, participatory, and sustainable society, 211
justice, 7, 12, 24–25, 34, 55, 60, 65, 68, 97, 99, 115–16, 136, 138, 157, 160, 169–71, 173–74, 176, 178–79, 1 84–85, 191, 193, 201–3, 210, 213–16, 219–22, 228–29, 232–33, 236, 246, 251–55, 266
justification, 30–31, 240

kabash, 30
Kadosh, kadosh, kadosh, 53
Keck, Leander, 31
kenosis, 10
Kharlamov, Vladimir, 7–8
Kim-Cragg, HyeRan, 241

KINGAFAP, 107–8
kingdom of God, 5, 60–61, 63–64, 68, 109, 128, 133, 154, 160, 164, 167, 198–99, 222–23, 228, 256
koinōnia, 9, 58, 158
Kraft, Colleen, 212
ktisis, 113–14
kurios, 177
kuriotētes, 67, 105

LaCugna, Catherine Mowry, 142
land, 13, 18, 20–21, 26–30, 34–35, 44, 46–48, 50, 55, 59, 74–77, 87, 98, 128, 131, 136–37, 165–66, 169, 174–75, 185, 192, 199–200, 202, 204, 207, 210, 214–16, 219, 228–29, 231, 234, 251, 253–54, 256
Lapsley, Jacqueline E., 205
Lathrop, Gordan, 258–61
Laudato si, 19, 60, 159
Lent, Lenten, ix, xi–xii, 4–5, 16–17, 22–23, 25–27, 31–34, 39, 52, 57, 59, 88, 96, 135, 145, 163, 173, 265–66, 271n3
Leontius of Cyprus, 8
lessons and carols, 233–35
liberation, 20, 24, 26, 43, 46, 55, 64, 71, 92, 108, 111, 138, 154–57, 193, 229–30, 240–42, 252
liturgical calendar, 43, 103, 106, 130
liturgical year, x, xii, 5, 7, 41, 58, 78
logos, 156–57, 242–43, 246, 260, 263
love, loving, xi–xii, 3, 16, 20–23, 35, 57, 59–60, 63–65, 72, 89, 99, 102, 104, 128, 133–34, 137–38, 141, 143–44, 150–56, 158–60, 170, 172–73, 175, 179, 184, 189, 194–97, 202–3, 207, 210, 216, 218, 220–21, 235, 237, 246, 264, 266
lulav, 44, 47–50
Luther, Martin, 106–7, 114, 267, 288n2
Lutheran, 79, 87, 91, 258. *See also* Evangelical Lutheran Church in America; *Evangelical Lutheran Worship*

magi, xi, 6, 172, 198, 227, 249–51, 254, 267
Magnificat, 192–93, 209, 223

Magonet, Jonathon, 232
Malachi, 210, 214–21, 290n13
Mali, 212
manifest, manifestation, xi, 6–7, 61, 65, 68, 113–14, 132–33, 135, 249–51, 259
Marlow, Hilary, 230
Martell-Otero, Loida I., 156
Mary, 77, 85, 92–93, 111, 151, 159, 172, 193, 205, 219–20, 222–24, 238, 249, 278n47
Maundy Thursday, 41–42, 57–58, 61, 64–65, 78, 80, 266
McFague, Sallie, 108, 110, 152–54
Medley, Mark S., 269n4
mercy, 16, 21–22, 35, 65–66, 79, 115, 175, 207, 224–25, 236, 260–61, 272n5
messenger(s), 83, 93, 129, 214, 220, 230, 290n13
messiah, messianic, 32–34, 77, 113–14, 163, 166, 168, 171, 173, 176–79, 182, 184–85, 191, 197–98, 233, 251, 267
metanoia, 5
Methodist, xii–xiii, 23, 60–64, 79–80, 87, 93, 96, 149, 167, 277n17, 282n21, 286n32
Mexican border, 212
Milky Way, 117
miracle, 126, 133, 210, 250
Moltmann, Jürgen, 152, 154
moon, 8, 11, 17, 66, 91, 96, 100, 141–42, 145, 176, 185, 219, 239, 252, 255, 257
morning star, 6, 86, 267
mortal(s), mortality, xi, 7, 10, 15–18, 21, 23, 25, 35, 39, 42, 57, 66–67, 71, 78, 92, 99, 115, 135, 145, 181, 212, 242, 265–66
Moses, 4, 6, 12–13, 34, 65, 78, 112, 131–32, 217, 255, 262, 297n10
mother, 3, 18, 21, 76, 92, 108, 122, 151–54, 157, 159, 210, 221, 224, 264, 267, 278n47
Mother Earth, 30, 105, 122, 151
mountain(s), 5–6, 13, 36–37, 66, 74–75, 89–91, 94, 98, 112, 120, 129, 137, 165, 171, 174–76, 179–85, 189, 204, 230, 232, 235, 239, 251–53, 256, 258, 260

myrtle, 47–48
mystic, mystical, mysticism, 3, 7, 60, 157, 235, 255

Naaman, 95
Nahar (river), 202
Nairobi 1975 A.D., 211
naked(ness), 21, 24, 104
National Council of Churches, 116
nativity, 164, 171, 198, 227, 231, 234–35, 238, 250, 254
nematodes, 23
nephesh, 129
new creation, xi, 19, 27, 42, 59, 61–63, 65, 78, 87, 91, 110, 122, 127, 131, 135, 143, 163, 235
New Zealand, 77, 116, 119, 150, 286n25
Neyrey, Jerome, 112
Nicea, 17, 148
Nicene-Constantinopolitan Creed, 148
Nicene Creed, 147–48
Noah, 12, 16, 26–28, 88–89, 95, 129, 177, 186, 258, 262, 273n17, 293n7
nocturnal life, 130
nonrenewable resources, 210, 213
Northcott, Michael S., 202, 296n3
Nunc Dimittis, 238

O'Brien, Kevin J., 173, 178, 187, 195
offering, 8–10, 12–13, 26, 46, 60, 70, 86, 110–11, 130–31, 150, 195, 197, 215–16
Olley, John W., 183
oppress, oppression, 24, 26, 30, 55, 64, 101, 111, 128, 138, 155, 169, 193–94, 215, 229, 237, 246, 252–53
ordinary time, xi, 4, 53, 142, 163
Orthodox, xi, xii, 4–8, 10–11, 58–59, 110, 135, 254–55, 258
ousia, 148
Oxfam, 213
ozone, 69, 101, 220

Palm/Passion Sunday, xii, 17, 41–44, 50, 52–53, 57–58, 67, 80
palm(s), 42–44, 47–55, 244
panentheism, 154, 287n45

panta, 241–42
pantheism, 7, 107, 154, 287n45
Pantocrator, 242
parousia, 73, 187
pasa sarx, 180
Pasch, 83, 87, 103. *See also* Passover
Passover, xii, 17, 43–46, 48–52, 59, 61, 64, 83–84, 87, 103, 130, 217
patriarchy, patriarchal, 106–8, 147–48, 153–54, 218, 220, 261
Patrick, Saint, 142
Payne, Joel, 247
penitential, 16, 18, 21, 173
Pentecost, ix, xi–xiii, 46, 90, 97, 103–6, 125–27, 130–36, 142, 157–58, 187, 267, 281n2
perichoresis, 154–56, 158
persecution, 11, 75, 104, 127, 278n51
Pesach, 45–46, 59. *See also* Passover
pesticide, 86, 121
Pfatteicher, Philip H., 91
Philip, Bijesh, 110
Philo, 251
Pittenger, Norman, 152–53
planet(ary), ix, 20, 60, 64–65, 94, 130, 154, 156, 158, 179, 188, 207, 210–11, 219, 243, 258, 260, 262
plant(s), 3, 12, 21–23, 25, 27–29, 37, 48, 50, 52, 54–55, 69, 85–87, 95, 98, 117, 121, 129–31, 172, 174, 181, 183, 196–97, 200, 204, 207, 213, 216, 229, 238, 244, 247, 261, 265, 267
pneuma, 130
pnoē, 130
poieo, 8
political, 25–26, 34, 68–71, 73, 75, 106, 116, 169, 175, 200, 212–13, 219, 229, 252, 297n10
pollution, 64, 69, 121, 210–11, 266
poor, 24, 73, 155, 157, 160, 182, 213, 251–53, 266, 296n5
population, 119, 131, 200, 210–13, 292n2, 293n2
Population Action International, 211
poverty, 179, 207, 211–12, 219–20

powers, 42–43, 57, 67–73, 83–84, 87, 91–92, 103–5, 111, 113–14, 163, 166–69, 176, 238, 240, 257, 266, 288n2
Presbyterian, xiii, 79, 109, 116, 149–50
priest(s), priestly, 3, 8–9, 26–27, 34, 58–60, 131, 209–10, 215, 217, 242
principalities, 67, 69–71, 92, 103–5, 266
process theology, 152–53
productivity, 26, 34, 43, 48, 52, 55, 58, 69–70, 131, 174, 192, 219, 251, 274n12
punishment, 6

radah, 30
rainbow, 27, 151, 219
rain forest, 157
rain(s), 8, 13, 18, 25, 43–44, 48, 50, 52, 55, 91, 94–95, 191, 195, 207, 216, 218–19, 246, 252, 258, 266
Rasmussen, Larry L., 116, 202, 288n2
Rattenbury, J. Ernest, 62
reconcile, reconciliation, 19–20, 31, 67, 72, 167, 236, 266
recycle, 93–94
redeem, reedemer, redemption, xii, 89, 121, 134, 144, 147, 154, 158, 167, 207, 225, 253
Reed, Sue, 23–24
refugees, 121, 216
regeneration, 5, 59, 62, 121, 213
remnant, 200, 205, 230
renewable, 210, 213
repent, repentance, 5, 16–21, 77, 172–73, 178, 180, 184, 186, 188, 196, 203, 215, 224, 265, 267, 272n6
respiration, 130, 267
resurrection, ix, xi, 4–6, 11, 16, 39, 41–42, 59, 68, 72, 80, 83–88, 91–95, 98–101, 103–5, 109–10, 112–13, 120–21, 127, 133, 158–59, 163, 166–68, 259–60, 266
revive, revival, 5, 74
Ringe, Sharon H., 32–33
Ross, Allen P., 202
royal psalms, 116, 253

ruach, 128–30, 132, 145, 263
Russian Orthodox, 11, 254

sacral(ity), 107
sacrament(al), 9, 20, 59–64, 91–92, 107, 110
sacrifice, 20, 63, 70, 86, 88, 111
saints, 54, 64, 73, 75, 78, 221
Salmon, Marilyn, 44–45, 275n23
sanctification, 5, 9, 59, 149, 242
Sanctifier, 147, 241
Sanctus, 13, 43–44, 53, 78, 149
Santmire, H. Paul, 106–7, 110
Satan, 32, 73
Schaffer, Arthur, 48, 274–75n12
sea, 12, 18, 28–29, 38, 62, 66, 87, 89–90, 95–97, 99, 116, 120, 129, 132, 141–43, 149, 164–66, 171, 176–77, 183, 188, 193, 197, 202–4, 218–19, 231–33, 239, 244, 248, 252, 256–57, 265, 267
season of creation, x
security, ix, 35, 121, 174, 206, 212
semeia, 113
serpent, 20, 112
shalom, 134, 206, 253
Shavuot (feast of Weeks), 46, 103, 130–31
Sherrard, Philip, 135
shofar, 45, 115
Simeon, 238–39, 249
sin, 5, 17–18, 20–21, 25, 31, 34, 70–73, 75, 91–92, 160, 172, 175, 200, 215, 234, 257
Sirach, 210, 218–20, 242–43, 246–47
sky, 6, 12, 15, 18, 27–28, 54, 74, 100, 106, 143, 170, 179, 184, 193, 197, 236, 251, 258–59, 263, 267
snake, 20, 235
soil, 23–24, 30, 39, 47–48, 55, 90, 100, 108, 122, 126, 131, 135, 157, 192, 204, 215, 229, 266, 273n13
solar systems, 258
Song of Zechariah, 184, 192, 209, 224
Sophia, xiii, 134, 146, 148, 154, 156–59, 242, 248, 262–63
Sophronius, Saint, 255, 297n12
Southgate, Christopher, 19

sovereign(ity), xi, 54, 66–68, 70–71, 105–6, 108, 110–12, 115, 144–45, 163–67, 169, 175–76, 181, 193, 199–200, 202–3, 205, 216, 219–20, 228–29, 231, 251, 254, 288n2
species, ix, 27, 31, 47–49, 69, 77, 86, 101, 118, 120–21, 153, 183, 187, 210, 212–13, 258, 265–66, 274n12
spirit, spiritual(izes), x–xi, 11, 20, 36–39, 49, 51, 55, 59, 61–62, 67–69, 71–72, 75, 87, 98–99, 106, 110, 113, 125, 128–36, 138, 143–44, 146, 157, 168, 182–84, 188, 193, 195–96, 210, 215, 219, 221, 224–25, 240–41, 255
spirituality, ix, 127, 130, 133–35, 267
star, 6, 86, 141, 151, 197, 246, 249, 254, 261, 267
Steck, Odil Hannes, 28
stewardship, 30, 64
Stibolt, Ginny, 23–24
stoicheia, 186, 240–42
Stookey, Laurence Hull, 63–64, 172
storm(s), 69, 101, 239, 260
stranger(s), 26, 53, 141
subdue, 29–30
Sudan, 212
sukkah, 47, 49
Sukkot, 43–53, 59, 217, 266, 274n12. *See also* Tabernacles
sun, 13, 38, 62, 66, 74, 91, 96, 100, 108, 117, 130, 142, 172, 176, 216, 219, 221, 237, 239, 246, 252, 255, 257
sunrise service, 93
supersessionism, supersessionist, 44–45, 52, 275n23, 297n10
supper (last), 13, 42, 58–59, 61, 64–65, 78, 81, 112, 133, 266
supper (Lord's), 61–62, 64, 78
Sursum corda, 12, 107
survival, 213
sustainability, 210–11, 266

Tabernacles (Booths), xii, 43–44, 46–47, 50, 52, 217. *See also* Sukkot
Tate, Marvin, 253, 297n10

technology, 20, 119, 266
Teilhard de Chardin, Pierre, 3–4, 11
temptation(s), 16, 26, 31–34, 71, 179
thanksgiving, 13, 47–48, 54, 65–66, 84,
    95–96, 136, 138–39, 150, 195, 245,
    247, 258, 263, 297n14
theophany, Theophany, 6, 250, 254, 260.
    See also Epiphany
theopoiesis, 8
theosis, 5, 7, 10, 58–59, 110
theosphere, 156
throne, 83, 97, 108, 115, 197–98, 203,
    218, 223, 228, 243
thronoi, 67
tomb, 4, 13, 41, 73, 83, 87–88, 91–94,
    100, 114, 120, 259, 266
Torvend, Samuel, 95
Townend, Stuart, 246
transfiguration, xi–xii, 3–13, 58–60, 110,
    163, 187, 265, 269–70n4
tree(s), 15, 22, 27, 37, 47, 49–50, 54–55,
    59, 94, 118, 126, 129, 174, 182, 188,
    207, 213, 231–32, 239, 244, 260, 266,
    275n12, 278n15
Trinity Sunday, xi, xiii, 90, 134,
    142–44, 146, 148, 159, 267, 285n6,
    295n30
Trinity, Trinitarian, 66, 96, 108, 134,
    141–60, 227, 260–61, 267, 297n12
Trump, President, 212
Tryphon (Turkestanov), Metropolitan, 11
tsedeq, 184
Tugaue, Ame, 23, 273n13
Tull, Patricia K., 229

uncreated light, 7
United Methodist, xii–xiii, 63–64,
    79–81, 96, 149, 169, 286n32
United States, 119–20, 212–13
universe, universal, 3–5, 9–10, 19, 27,
    31, 54, 60, 65–66, 72, 78, 87, 89, 96,
    112, 115–17, 120, 122, 125, 133–34,
    150–51, 153, 155–58, 160, 168–69,
    175–76, 186, 202, 206, 212–13, 216,
    219, 227–28, 233, 236–38, 240,
    242–43, 246, 250, 254–55, 257–58,
    261–62, 265

vegetarian, 28, 88, 213
vigil, Easter, 80, 83–87, 90–95, 97,
    145–46, 266, 295n30
vine, 59, 61, 126, 174, 200, 203–4, 207,
    215, 244, 275n12
violence, 29, 77, 119, 121, 134, 166,
    169, 171, 179, 183, 207, 212, 253

Wainwright, Geoffrey, 60, 143
Walker-Jones, Arthur, 115–16, 204, 246, 252
war, 74–76, 121, 170, 174, 178–79,
    200, 206–7, 219, 229, 246, 266,
    288n2
Ware, Kallistos, 8
Warren, Olivia, 152
wasteful, 20, 207
Watts, Isaac, 232, 236
wealth, wealthy, 73, 169–70, 213, 220,
    253–54
Wedderburn, A. J. M., 31
Wesleyan, 62
Wesley, Charles, xiii, 62, 234, 236
Wesley, John, 61–62
Westermann, Claus, 231
wetlands, 20
Whitehead, Alfred North, 153
wholeness, 25, 183, 185, 206
wilderness, 16, 26, 31–34, 55, 70, 95,
    112, 126, 180, 184–85, 192, 260, 265,
    275n12, 297n9
willow(s), 47–49, 54–55, 128, 136
Wilson, Gerald, 116
wind, 23, 87–88, 125, 127–30, 132, 135,
    137, 175, 219, 239, 245, 267
wisdom, 12, 38, 68, 89–90, 133–34,
    146–47, 154–55, 157–59, 182, 210,
    214, 217–19, 221–22, 234, 242–44,
    246–48, 251, 262–63
womankind, 21
womb, 18, 74, 76–77, 120, 122, 136,
    150–51, 159, 197, 210, 220–21,
    223–24, 258, 264, 278n47

Word, 80, 87, 90–91, 93, 107, 128, 142–43, 145–47, 150–51, 153–54, 158, 227, 233–34, 237–38, 242–43, 247–48, 250, 259, 263, 267
World Council of Churches, x, 149, 210–11
Worldwatch Institute, 211
worm(s), 15, 23, 118
Wren, Brian, 57, 107–8, 110, 169
Wright, Christopher J. H., 112, 201

xenophobia, 216

Yam (sea), 202
yeled (child), 183
Yugoslavia, 212

Zechariah, 75, 128, 184, 192, 205, 209, 214, 216–17, 220–21, 223–24, 239, 249, 274n1
Zizioulas, John, 8–9

About the Author

Joseph E. Bush, Jr. brings international experience as a preacher and teacher to this book on Christian worship. He takes an ecological perspective on the liturgical seasons celebrating Christ's presence on Earth. Ordained a United Methodist minister, he has served in pastoral ministry in New Jersey, New Zealand, and on two preaching circuits in the Republic of Fiji. He is currently pastor at Sparta Hill United Methodist Church and First United Methodist Church in Evergreen, Alabama. He has taught in the areas of ethics, worship, and practice of ministry in a variety of denominational and cultural contexts: New Brunswick Theological Seminary in New Jersey, the ecumenical Pacific Theological College in Fiji, the Presbyterian School of Ministry in New Zealand, United Theological Seminary of the Twin Cities, and currently as Professor at Wesley Theological Seminary in Washington, DC. Ecology and ecological health have been of ongoing concern to him in his approach to worship and ministry, and he served as Coordinator for the Washington Theological Consortium's Certificate in Ecology and Theology. He is active in the Society of Christian Ethics, the Ecology and Liturgy Seminar of the North American Academy of Liturgy, and is a former Chairperson of the Association for Theological Field Education. He is the author of two other books: *Practical Theology in Church and Society* and *Gentle Shepherding: Pastoral Ethics and Leadership*. He has also enjoyed playing 5-string banjo in the band, Little Falls, an acoustic praise band for Westmoreland United Church of Christ and the "house band" for the Little Falls Watershed Alliance.

www.ingramcontent.com/pod-product-compliance
Lightning Source LLC
Chambersburg PA
CBHW071828230426
43672CB00013B/2785